Name That Baby!

Name That Baby!

EVERY PARENT'S GUIDE TO NAMES

by Jane Bradshaw

©1998
by Jane Bradshaw
All rights reserved
Printed in the United States of America

0-8054-1271-9

Published by Broadman & Holman Publishers, Nashville, Tennessee
Page Design: Anderson Thomas Design, Nashville, Tennessee
Page Compositor: Desktop Miracles, Dallas, Texas
Editorial Team: Vicki Crumpton, Janis Whipple, Kim Overcash

Dewey Decimal Classification: 929.4
Subject Heading: NAMES, PERSONAL—
DICTIONARIES/BIBLE—QUOTATIONS
Library of Congress Card Catalog Number: 98-16140

Unless otherwise stated all Scripture citation
is from the Holy Bible, King James Version.

Library of Congress Cataloging-in-Publication Data

Bradshaw, Jane, 1936—
    Name that baby : every parents guide to names / Jane Bradshaw.
        p.   cm.
    ISBN 0-8054-1271-9 (pbk.)
    1. Names, Personal—Dictionaries.   2. Bible—Quotations.   I. Title.
CS2377.B7   1998
929.4'4—dc21   98-16140
                                                                  CIP

8 9 10 05 04 03

Table of Contents

Did you know your name has a meaning?

Since 1980, I have researched the meanings of well over 300,000 names to find as near the literal meaning as possible. I begin with the Bible, but most names are not there. Next I research the Aramaic, Greek, Hebrew, French, German, Italian, Spanish, Swedish, African, Polynesian, Asian, or whatever language source contains the name.

After finding the meaning, I look that meaning up in the Bible with the use of concordances. I find a verse that holds that meaning, thought, or connotation. This process is done carefully and prayerfully as this verse becomes the "life verse" for this name. The following examples show the selection of verse correlation with the meanings:

NICCOLE
Victorious Heart

> *But thanks be to God, which giveth us the <u>victory</u> through our Lord Jesus Christ.*
> I CORINTHIANS 15:57

JOINER
Creative Builder

> *According to the grace of God, which is given unto me, as a <u>wise master builder</u>, I have laid the foundation . . . For other foundation can no man lay than . . . Jesus Christ.*
> I CORINTHIANS 3:10

CLAYTON
In God's Mold

> Behold, as <u>the clay</u> is in the potter's hand, so are ye in mine hand.
> JEREMIAH 18:6

ABIGAEL
Source of Joy

> Thou wilt show me the path of life: in thy presence is <u>*fullness*</u> <u>*of joy*</u>; at thy right hand there are pleasures forevermore.
> PSALM 16:11

Double names are frequently used, and in this book, a limited number are provided. Both meanings for these double names are given if space permits; however, some of the names have the meaning to one or the other name. Examples which have the double names and both meanings include the following:

NANCY ANN
One of Grace

> . . . the Lord will give grace and glory: no good thing will he withhold from them that walk uprightly.
> PSALM 84:11

(Nancy and Ann both mean *Grace*)

SARAANNE
Princess of Grace

> . . . the Lord will give grace and glory: no good thing will he withhold from them that walk uprightly.
> PSALM 84:11

INTRODUCTION

SHEKEITHA
Unseen Faith and Secure

> *Now faith is the substance of
> things hoped for, the evidence of
> things not seen.*
> HEBREWS 11:1

SARABETH
Consecrated Princess

> *I will bless the Lord, who hath
> given me counsel . . . I have set
> the Lord always before me . . .
> he is at my right hand, I shall
> not be moved.*
> PSALM 16:7, 8

Since the beginning of time, parents have tried to give their children distinctive names. Naming children after important, famous, or respected people is frequently noted. Some names have an extra syllable such as La, Da or Di added to the beginning of the name. Examples are Lakeisha, Lashawn, Latanya, Latonya, Latasha and Latoya. "Created" names are taken apart syllable by syllable to find a meaning. Putting two or more names together requires special handling to combine meanings. Some names have derogatory meanings so I have used a little poetic license—one woman's name means "A girdle," for that I used "Of Firm Foundation"; one man's name means "Bald Headed Man"; for that I used "Shining Example."

Names are sometimes attributable to a particular source but could also be linked to various other languages through different spellings or pronunciations. Sema is a Kiswahili word meaning "to speak"; however, the Greek version is "sprout" and the Turkish meaning is "heavens."

Ethnic and cultural groups have unique naming traditions and research reveals that names can be traced several generations.

Names may be related to day of the week on which the child was born, a firstborn of twins, or a child delivered during a storm. Some examples follow:

Akosua   African name for a girl born on Sunday
Kwasi   African name for a boy born on Sunday

These names continue for each day of the week with a male and female version.

Odion   Nigerian male name for the first born of twins
Othieno   Kenya boy born at night
Sekai   Zimbabwe female name meaning laughter

The Latin sources may embrace Italian, Rumanian, and Spanish. The Slavic group will contain names and mixtures of names from (former) Czechoslovakia, Poland, and Russia. Perhaps the largest umbrella of names is referred to as Teutonic and will contain, but is not limited to: Old Anglo Saxon, Turkish, Scottish, German, Scandanavian, Norwegian, Sanskrit, and Lithuanian names. This book also contains names which are common in the Greek, Polynesian, Hindu, African, Arabic, North American Indian, and Asian cultures; including Vietnamese, Korean, Chinese, and Japanese.

Nicknames in America have been given to children and have become the official name of that person. Bubba, Skeeter, Squirrel, Scooter, Skip, and Sissy are a few examples.

The content of the book is a sample representation of my research. The names in this book account for less than two percent of the completed list. To give every name and the variations of names would require volumes. For instance, the name Susan has 134 spelling variations. The important emphasis is placed on the premise that each person who sees his or her name will also read the scripture reference and be encouraged by its meaning.

INTRODUCTION

Following are two examples of the layout for names included in this book. The name is followed by the meaning, researched as indicated above, and then the scripture verse and reference. Where other names have similar spellings or meanings, these are cross-referenced. Where names are highly unusual, the root language is sometimes noted.

ABBAS
Son of the Father

> *Unto us a child is born, . . . a*
> *son is given: . . . his name shall*
> *be called . . . everlasting Father.*
> ISAIAH 9:6
>
> Hebrew

ABBEY-GAIL *also* ABIGAIL
Source of Joy

> *In thy presence is fulness of joy;*
> *at thy right hand . . . pleasures*
> *for evermore.*
> PSALM 16:11
>
> Hebrew

—JANE BRADSHAW

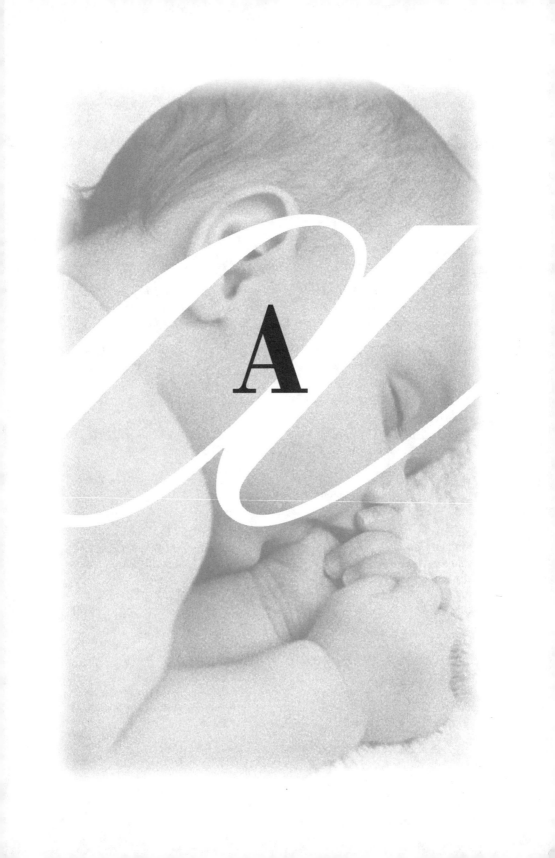

'AHULANI
A Heavenly Shrine
> I will lift up mine eyes unto the
> hills, from whence cometh my
> help . . . from the Lord.
> PSALM 121:1–2
>
> Polynesian

A'ALONA
One of Light
> Let your light so shine . . . that
> they may see your good works,
> and glorify your Father . . . in
> heaven.
> MATTHEW 5:16
>
> Polynesian

A'DELLA
Of Noble Rank
> I will go in the strength of the
> Lord God: . . . make mention of
> thy righteousness.
> PSALM 71:16
>
> Teutonic

AAGE
The Kind and Good
> And be ye kind one to another,
> tenderhearted, forgiving one
> another.
> EPHESIANS 4:32
>
> Teutonic

AAMY *also AMY*
Beloved One
> Beloved, let us love one another:
> for love is of God; . . . every one
> that loveth is born of God.
> 1 JOHN 4:7
>
> Latin

AANIKA
One of Grace
> For the Lord . . . will give grace
> and glory: no good thing will he
> withhold.
> PSALM 84:11
>
> Teutonic

AARESS
The Best
> O Lord our Lord, how excellent
> is thy name . . . who hast set thy
> glory above the heavens.
> PSALM 8:1
>
> Greek

AARIKA
Noble and Strong
> In God is my salvation . . . glory
> . . . strength, and my refuge, is
> in God.
> PSALM 62:7
>
> Teutonic

AARIS
Mighty in the Faith
> Fight the good fight of faith, lay
> hold on eternal life, whereunto
> thou art also called.
> 1 TIMOTHY 6:12
>
> Greek

AARON *also EAARON*
One of Light
> The Lord is my light . . .
> salvation . . . the strength of my
> life; of whom shall I be afraid?
> PSALM 27:1
>
> Hebrew

AARTJE
One of High Nobility
> *Ye have not chosen me, but I have chosen you, and ordained you, that ye should go and bring forth fruit.*
> JOHN 15:16
>
> Celtic

AARY
Best Leader
> *Thou hast . . . given me the shield of thy salvation: . . . thy gentleness hath made me great.*
> PSALM 18:35
>
> Greek

AASE
One Who Perseveres
> *I can do all things through Christ which strengtheneth me.*
> PHILIPPIANS 4:13
>
> Teutonic

AASHA
Blessed and Happy
> *Blessed are they that keep his testimonies, . . . that seek him with the whole heart.*
> PSALM 119:2
>
> Hebrew

ABAEISAIA
Salvation of the Lord
> *I will trust, and not be afraid: . . . the Lord JEHOVAH is my strength and . . . salvation.*
> ISAIAH 12:2
>
> Greek

ABALEAN
Of Resolute Firmness
> *I have set the Lord . . . before me: . . . he is at my right hand, I shall not be moved.*
> PSALM 16:8
>
> Hebrew

ABBA
Father
> *For unto us a child is born, . . . a son is given: . . . his name shall be called . . . The everlasting Father.*
> ISAIAH 9:6
>
> Hebrew

ABBAS
Son of the Father
> *For unto us a child is born, . . . a son is given: . . . his name shall be called . . . The everlasting Father.*
> ISAIAH 9:6
>
> Hebrew

ABBEY-GAIL   *also* ABIGAIL
Source of Joy
> *In thy presence is fulness of joy; at thy right hand . . . pleasures for evermore.*
> PSALM 16:11
>
> Hebrew

ABBOTT
Father
> *For the Son of man shall come in the glory of his Father with his angels.*
> MATTHEW 16:27
>
> Hebrew

ABBRA
The Exalted One

> God is my salvation; . . . the
> Lord JEHOVAH is my strength
> . . . he . . . is become my
> salvation.
> ISAIAH 12:2

Hebrew

ABBY
Source of Joy

> Restore unto me the joy of thy
> salvation; and uphold me with
> thy free Spirit.
> PSALM 51:12

Hebrew

ABDALLAH
Servant of God

> I will bless the Lord at all times:
> his praise shall continually be
> in my mouth.
> PSALM 34:1

Arabic

ABDUL
Son of . . .

> Thou art no more a servant, but
> a son; . . . an heir of God
> through Christ.
> GALATIANS 4:7

Arabic

ABE
Exalted Father

> It is a good thing to give thanks
> unto the Lord, and to sing
> praises unto thy name, O most
> High.
> PSALM 92:1

Hebrew

ABEDNEGO
Worship of God

> I will praise thee, O Lord, with
> my whole heart; . . . I will be
> glad and rejoice in thee.
> PSALM 9:1–2

Hebrew

ABEL
Breath

> Praise ye the Lord. . . . Let every
> thing that hath breath praise
> the Lord. Praise ye the Lord.
> PSALM 150:1, 6

Hebrew

ABELARDO
Noble and Firm

> I have set the Lord . . . before
> me: . . . he is at my right hand, I
> shall not be moved.
> PSALM 16:8

Teutonic

ABELINO
Breath of Life

> Let every thing that hath breath
> praise the Lord. Praise ye the
> Lord.
> PSALM 150:6

Teutonic

ABENA
Born on Tuesday

> Thy hands have made me and
> fashioned me: give me
> understanding . . . [to] learn thy
> commandments.
> PSALM 119:73

African

10

ABERHART
Resolute Father

> It is God that girdeth me with
> strength, and maketh my way
> perfect.
> PSALM 18:32
>
> Teutonic

ABIEZER
My Father Is Help

> I will praise thee: for thou hast
> heard me, and art become my
> salvation.
> PSALM 118:21
>
> Hebrew

ABIGAIL   also ABBEY-GAIL
Source of Joy

> Restore unto me the joy of thy
> salvation; and uphold me with
> thy free spirit.
> PSALM 51:12
>
> Hebrew

ABIJAH
Jehovah Is My Father

> God is my salvation; . . . the
> Lord JEHOVAH is my strength
> and my song.
> ISAIAH 12:2
>
> Hebrew

ABLE
Noble and Resolute

> I have set the Lord always
> before me: . . . he is at my right
> hand, I shall not be moved.
> PSALM 16:8
>
> Teutonic

ABNER
Of Light

> Let your light so shine before
> men, that they may see your
> good works, and glorify your
> Father . . . in heaven.
> MATTHEW 5:16
>
> Hebrew

ABNIS
One of Light

> Let your light so shine before
> men, that they may see your
> good works, and glorify your
> Father . . . in heaven.
> MATTHEW 5:16
>
> Hebrew

ABRA
Mother of Multitudes

> I would seek unto God, . . .
> Which doeth great . . . and . . .
> marvellous things without
> number.
> JOB 5:8–9
>
> Hebrew

ABRAHAM
Friend of God

> Abraham believed God, . . . and
> he was called the Friend of God.
> JAMES 2:23
>
> Hebrew

ABRANA
My Father Is Exalted

> The Lord JEHOVAH is my
> strength and my song; he also is
> become my salvation.
> ISAIAH 12:2
>
> Hebrew

ABREE
Radiant Light

> They that be wise shall shine as
> the brightness of the firmament;
> . . . as the stars for ever and ever.
> DANIEL 12:3

ABRIELLE
My Father Is Exalted

> That men may know that thou,
> whose name . . . is JEHOVAH,
> art the most high over all the
> earth.
> PSALM 83:18

ABU
Royal and Noble One

> Thou hast also given me the
> shield of thy salvation: . . . and
> thy gentleness hath made me
> great.
> PSALM 18:35

ACACIA
Heavenly Messenger

> How beautiful are the feet of
> them that preach the gospel . . .
> and bring glad tidings of good
> things.
> ROMANS 10:15

ACARA
A Friend

> Ye are my friends, if ye do
> whatsoever I command you.
> JOHN 15:14

ACE
One of Unity

> Till we all come in the unity of
> the faith, . . . of the knowledge
> of the Son of God.
> EPHESIANS 4:13

ACEA
Noble One

> Thou hast . . . given me the
> shield of thy salvation: . . . thy
> gentleness hath made me great.
> 2 SAMUEL 22:36

ACELA
Noble One

> Thy right hand hath holden me
> up, and thy gentleness hath
> made me great.
> PSALM 18:35

ACEY   *also* ACY
One Who Excels

> I can do all things through
> Christ which strengtheneth me.
> PHILIPPIANS 4:13

ACHAN
Nobly Bold

> I will declare thy name unto my
> brethren: in the midst of the
> congregation will I praise thee.
> PSALM 22:22

ACHELLE
Quiet One

> Let the words of my mouth, and
> the meditation of my heart, be
> acceptable in thy sight, O Lord.
> PSALM 19:14

ACHER
Nobly Bold

> I will bless the Lord at all times:
> his praise shall continually be
> in my mouth.
> PSALM 34:1

ACHILLE
Silent One

> Let the words of my mouth, and
> the meditation of my heart, be
> acceptable in thy sight, O Lord.
> PSALM 19:14

ACHIM
The Lord Will Judge

> But God is the judge: . . . [he]
> doest wonders: thou hast
> declared thy strength among
> the people.
> PSALM 75:7; 77:14
>
> Hebrew

ACHOD
Silent One

> Let the . . . meditation of my
> heart, be acceptable in thy sight,
> O Lord, my strength.
> PSALM 19:14

ACHSA
Joyful Spirit

> In thy presence is fulness of joy;
> at thy right hand . . . are
> pleasures for evermore.
> PSALM 16:11

ACHSAH
An Ornament

> I will praise thee; for I am
> fearfully and wonderfully
> made: marvelous are thy works.
> PSALM 139:14

ACHUES
Fervent Spirit

> Whatsoever ye do, do it heartily,
> as to the Lord, . . . for ye serve
> the Lord Christ.
> COLOSSIANS 3:23–24
>
> Greek

ACKLEY
Peaceful One of Strength

> In God is my salvation and my
> glory: the rock of my strength,
> . . . my refuge, is in God.
> PSALM 62:7

ACQUANETTA
One of Purity

> Blessed are the pure in heart:
> for they shall see God.
> MATTHEW 5:8

ACY   *also* ACEY
One Who Excels

> I can do all things through
> Christ which strengtheneth me.
> PHILIPPIANS 4:13

ADA
Happy Spirit

> Let all those that put their trust
> in thee rejoice: . . . shout for joy,
> . . . be joyful in thee.
> PSALM 5:11

ADABELLE
Happy and Beautiful One

> *In thy presence is fulness of joy;*
> *at thy right hand there are*
> *pleasures for evermore.*
> PSALM 16:11

ADABO
Noble One

> *Thou hast . . . given me the*
> *shield of thy salvation: . . . thy*
> *gentleness hath made me great.*
> 2 SAMUEL 22:36

ADAH
Beautiful Spirit

> *Let all those that put their trust*
> *in thee rejoice: let them ever*
> *shout for joy.*
> PSALM 5:11

ADAIAH
Jehovah Hath Adorned

> *Thou wilt show me the path of*
> *life: in thy presence is fulness of*
> *joy.*
> PSALM 16:11

ADAIR
Peaceful Dweller

> *The Lord is my shepherd; I shall*
> *not want. He maketh me to lie*
> *down in green pastures.*
> PSALM 23:1–2

ADALAYANNE *also* ADELINE
Of Noble Rank

> *Thou hast . . . given me the*
> *shield of thy salvation: . . . thy*
> *gentleness hath made me great.*
> PSALM 18:35

ADALBERTO
Illustrious Through Nobility

> *Ye are a chosen generation . . .*
> *ye should show forth the praises*
> *of him who hath called you.*
> 1 PETER 2:9

ADALEEN
Noble and of Good Cheer

> *I will praise thee, . . . be glad*
> *and rejoice in thee: I will sing*
> *praise to thy name.*
> PSALM 9:1–2

ADALGISA
Noble and Brave

> *God is my strength and power:*
> *and he maketh my way perfect.*
> 2 SAMUEL 22:33

ADALINE *also* ADELINE
One of Noble Rank

> *Ye are a chosen generation, . . . ye*
> *should show forth the praises of*
> *him who hath called you.*
> 1 PETER 2:9

ADALLA
Illustrious Through Nobility

> *Now the God of peace, . . . make*
> *you perfect in every good work*
> *to do his will.*
> HEBREWS 13:20–21

ADALU
Happy and Victorious

> *Let all those that put their trust*
> *in thee rejoice: . . . let them . . .*
> *that love thy name be joyful in*
> *thee.*
> PSALM 5:11

ADAM
God's Creation

> For we are his workmanship,
> created in Christ Jesus unto
> good works.
> EPHESIANS 2:10

ADARA
Noble One of Virtue

> Thy right hand hath holden me
> up, and thy gentleness hath
> made me great.
> PSALM 18:35

ADARIAN
Noble One

> The Lord is my light . . .
> salvation . . . the strength of my
> life; of whom shall I be afraid?
> PSALM 27:1

ADAYNA
Of Noble Birth

> I have chosen you, and ordained
> you, that ye should go and bring
> forth fruit.
> JOHN 15:16

ADCOCK
God's Creation

> For we are his workmanship,
> created in Christ Jesus unto
> good works.
> EPHESIANS 2:10

ADDEANNA
Noble and Radiant One

> They that be wise shall shine as
> the brightness of the firmament.
> DANIEL 12:3

ADDELINE   *also* ADELINE
Noble and of Good Cheer

> Thou wilt show me the path of
> life: in thy presence is fulness of
> joy.
> PSALM 16:11

ADDIE
Of Noble Manner

> I will go in the strength of the
> Lord God: . . . thou hast taught
> me from my youth.
> PSALM 71:16–17

ADDIS
Of Noble Rank

> I have chosen you, and ordained
> you, that ye should go and bring
> forth fruit.
> JOHN 15:16

ADDISON
Descendant of Adam

> For we are his workmanship,
> created in Christ Jesus unto
> good works.
> EPHESIANS 2:10

ADDRINNE
Noble and Brave

> The Lord is my light . . .
> salvation . . . the strength of my
> life; of whom shall I be afraid?
> PSALM 27:1

ADDY
Of Noble Manner

> I will go in the strength of the
> Lord God: . . . thou hast taught
> me from my youth.
> PSALM 71:16–17

ADEAN
A Quiet Spirit

> *The Lord is my strength and my*
> *shield; my heart trusted in him.*
> PSALM 28:7

ADEDOYIN
The Crown Has Become Sweet

> *When the chief Shepherd shall*
> *appear, ye shall receive a crown*
> *of glory that fadeth not away.*
> 1 PETER 5:4
>
> African

ADEEB
Loyal Messenger of Truth

> *I will bless the Lord at all times:*
> *his praise shall continually be*
> *in my mouth.*
> PSALM 34:1

ADEENA   *also* ADINA
Abounding Grace

> *By grace are ye saved through*
> *faith; . . . it is the gift of God.*
> EPHESIANS 2:8

ADEL
Noble and of Good Cheer

> *Surely goodness and mercy shall*
> *follow me all the days of my life.*
> PSALM 23:6

ADELA
Noble and Good Cheer

> *Surely goodness and mercy shall*
> *follow me all the days of my life.*
> PSALM 23:6

ADELAIDA
The Noble Rank

> *I will go in the strength of the*
> *Lord God: . . . thou hast taught*
> *me from my youth.*
> PSALM 71:16–17

ADELAIDE
Noble and of Good Cheer

> *I will be glad and rejoice in*
> *thee: I will sing praise to thy*
> *name.*
> PSALM 9:2

ADELAIPE
Of Noble Rank

> *Thou hast also given me the*
> *shield of thy salvation: . . . and*
> *thy gentleness hath made me*
> *great.*
> PSALM 18:35

ADELARD
Of Noble Rank

> *I will go in the strength of the*
> *Lord God: I will make mention*
> *of thy righteousness.*
> PSALM 71:16

ADELBERT
Of Noble Radiance

> *Let your light so shine . . . that*
> *they may see your good works,*
> *and glorify your Father which is*
> *in heaven.*
> MATTHEW 5:16

ADELCIER
Of Noble Rank

> *I will go in the strength of the*
> *Lord God: I will make mention*
> *of thy righteousness.*
> PSALM 71:16

ADELE
Woman of Esteem

> *Turn thou to thy God: keep*
> *mercy and judgment, and wait*
> *on thy God continually.*
> HOSEA 12:6

ADELEEN
Of Noble Rank

> *I have chosen you, and ordained*
> *you, that ye should go and bring*
> *forth fruit.*
> JOHN 15:16

ADELHEID
Noble and of Good Cheer

> *I will show forth all thy*
> *marvellous works. I will be glad*
> *and rejoice in thee.*
> PSALM 9:1–2

ADELIA
Noble and of a Good Cheer

> *Surely goodness and mercy shall*
> *follow me all the days of my life.*
> PSALM 23:6

ADELINE   *also* ADALINE
Noble and of Good Cheer

> *Let all those that put their trust*
> *in thee rejoice: let them ever*
> *shout for joy.*
> PSALM 5:11

ADELITA
Of Noble Rank

> *I will go in the strength of the*
> *Lord God: I will make mention*
> *of thy righteousness.*
> PSALM 71:16

ADELLE
Woman of Esteem

> *Turn thou to thy God: keep*
> *mercy and judgment, and wait*
> *on thy God continually.*
> HOSEA 12:6

ADELYN
Of Noble Rank

> *I will go in the strength of the*
> *Lord God: I will make mention*
> *of thy righteousness.*
> PSALM 71:16

ADEN
Abounding Grace

> *For by grace are ye saved*
> *through faith; . . . it is the gift of*
> *God.*
> EPHESIANS 2:8

ADER
Flock

> *He shall feed his flock like a*
> *shepherd: he shall gather the*
> *lambs with his arm.*
> ISAIAH 40:11

ADEYEMI
Prosperous One

> *I will sing unto the Lord,*
> *because he hath dealt*
> *bountifully with me.*
> PSALM 13:6

ADGER
One of Great Strength

> *The Lord is my rock, . . . my*
> *fortress, and my deliverer; . . .*
> *my strength, in whom I will*
> *trust.*
> PSALM 18:2

ADIA
Gift of God

> *Every good gift and every*
> *perfect gift is from above, and*
> *cometh down from the Father.*
> JAMES 1:17

ADIAN
Noble One

> *I have chosen you, and ordained*
> *you, that ye should go and bring*
> *forth fruit.*
> JOHN 15:16

ADIANI
Gift of God

> *Every good gift and every*
> *perfect gift is from above, and*
> *cometh down from the Father.*
> JAMES 1:17

ADIEL
Ornament of God

> *I will praise thee; for I am*
> *fearfully . . . wonderfully made:*
> *marvellous are thy works.*
> PSALM 139:14

ADIENNE
Abounding Grace

> *For by grace are ye saved through*
> *faith; . . . it is the gift of God.*
> EPHESIANS 2:8

ADIN
Given to Pleasure

> *In thy presence is fulness of joy;*
> *at thy right hand . . . are*
> *pleasures for evermore.*
> PSALM 16:11

ADINA
Abounding Grace

> *For by grace are ye saved through*
> *faith; . . . it is the gift of God.*
> EPHESIANS 2:8

ADISON
Noble Cheer

> *Thou wilt show me the path of*
> *life: in thy presence is fulness of*
> *joy.*
> PSALM 16:11

ADJI
One of Purpose

> *He only is my rock and my*
> *salvation; he is my defence; I*
> *shall not be greatly moved.*
> PSALM 62:2

ADJUTA
Leader of Strength

> *Thou hast . . . given me the*
> *shield of thy salvation: and thy*
> *right hand hath holden me up.*
> PSALM 18:35

ADJUTOR
Leader of Strength

> *God is my strength and power:*
> *and he maketh my way perfect.*
> 2 SAMUEL 22:33
>
> Teutonic German

ADLEE
Of Noble Rank

> *I will go in the strength of the*
> *Lord God: . . . thou hast taught*
> *me from my youth.*
> PSALM 71:16–17

ADLENE
Of Noble Rank

> *Ye are a chosen generation, . . .*
> *that ye should show forth the*
> *praises of him who hath called*
> *you.*
> 1 PETER 2:9

ADLOPHA
One of Nobility

> *Ye are a chosen generation, . . .*
> *that ye should show forth the*
> *praises of him who hath called*
> *you.*
> 1 PETER 2:9

ADNA
also EDNA

Delightful One

> *Delight thyself . . . in the Lord;*
> *and he shall give thee the*
> *desires of thine heart.*
> PSALM 37:4

ADOLA
Noble One

> *Thou hast . . . given me the*
> *shield of thy salvation: and thy*
> *right hand hath holden me up.*
> PSALM 18:35

ADOLF
One of Nobility

> *Ye are a chosen generation, . . . that*
> *ye should show forth the praises*
> *of him who hath called you.*
> 1 PETER 2:9
>
> German

ADON
Sovereign Nobility

> *Thou hast . . . given me the*
> *shield of thy salvation: and thy*
> *right hand hath holden me up.*
> PSALM 18:35

ADONELIA
Sovereign Nobility

> *Thou hast . . . given me the*
> *shield of thy salvation: and thy*
> *right hand hath holden me up.*
> PSALM 18:35

ADONIA
Beautiful Lady

> *Strength and honour are her*
> *clothing; and she shall rejoice in*
> *time to come.*
> PROVERBS 31:25

ADONIS
Sovereign Nobility

> *I will praise thee: for thou hast heard me, and art become my salvation.*
> PSALM 118:21

ADONTA
Sovereign Nobility

> *The right hand of the Lord is exalted: the right hand of the Lord doeth valiantly.*
> PSALM 118:16

ADONYA
Sovereign Nobility

> *Thou hast . . . given me the shield of thy salvation: and thy right hand hath holden me up.*
> PSALM 18:35

ADORA
A Gift

> *Every good gift and every perfect gift is from above, and cometh down from the Father.*
> JAMES 1:17

ADORATION
The Adored One

> *I will praise thee; for I am fearfully and wonderfully made: marvellous are thy works.*
> PSALM 139:14

ADORIA
A Gift

> *Every good gift and every perfect gift is from above, and cometh down from the Father.*
> JAMES 1:17

ADORN
Cherished Gift

> *Every good gift and every perfect gift is from above, and cometh down from the Father.*
> JAMES 1:17

ADORRIEANETT
Gracious Gift of Love

> *For God so loved the world, that he gave his only begotten Son.*
> JOHN 3:16

ADRA
One of Life

> *The Lord is my light and my salvation; . . . is the strength of my life; of whom shall I be afraid?*
> PSALM 27:1

ADRAIN
Brave and Noble

> *As for God, his way is perfect; . . . God is my strength and power: and he maketh my way perfect.*
> 2 SAMUEL 22:31, 33

ADREA
Noble Strength

> *The Lord is my light and my salvation; . . . is the strength of my life; of whom shall I be afraid?*
> PSALM 27:1

ADREANN
Creative Spirit

> *Create in me a clean heart, O God; and renew a right spirit within me.*
> PSALM 51:10

ADRIA
Noble Strength

> *The Lord is my light and my salvation; . . . the strength of my life; of whom shall I be afraid?*
> PSALM 27:1

ADRIAAN
Creative

> *Give her of the fruit of her hands; and let her own works praise her in the gates.*
> PROVERBS 31:31

ADRIAN
Creative

> *Create in me a clean heart, O God; and renew a right spirit within me.*
> PSALM 51:10

ADRIANA
One Who is Noble

> *The Lord is my light and my salvation; . . . the strength of my life, of whom shall I be afraid?*
> PSALM 27:1

ADRIANE
One Who is Brave

> *The Lord is my light and my salvation; . . . the strength of my life; of whom shall I be afraid?*
> PSALM 27:1

ADRIANNA
Creative

> *Give her of the fruit of her hands; and let her own works praise her in the gates.*
> PROVERBS 31:31

ADRIANUS
Noble and Brave

> *The Lord is my light and my salvation; . . . the strength of my life; of whom shall I be afraid?*
> PSALM 27:1

ADRIEANA
Noble and Brave

> *The Lord is my light and my salvation; . . . the strength of my life; of whom shall I be afraid?*
> PSALM 27:1

ADRIEL
Of God's Flock

> *If any man will come after me let him deny himself and take up his cross daily, and follow me.*
> LUKE 9:23

ADRIELLE
Of God's Flock

> *If any man will come after me, let him deny himself, and take up his cross daily, and follow me.*
> LUKE 9:23

ADRIEN
Noble and Brave

> *The Lord is my light and my salvation; . . . the strength of my life; of whom shall I be afraid?*
> PSALM 27:1

ADRIENNE
Noble and Brave

> *The Lord is my light and my salvation; . . . the strength of my life; of whom shall I be afraid?*
> PSALM 27:1

ADRINA
Courageous Heart

> *Be strong and of a good courage; . . . for the Lord thy God is with thee whithersoever thou goest.*
> JOSHUA 1:9

ADRIONNA
Noble and Brave

> *Be strong and of a good courage; . . . for the Lord thy God is with thee whithersoever thou goest.*
> JOSHUA 1:9

ADYNE
Abounding Grace

> *For by grace are ye saved through faith; . . . it is the gift of God.*
> EPHESIANS 2:8

AE'TRIC
Bringer of Joy

> *In thy presence is fulness of joy; at thy right hand there are pleasures for evermore.*
> PSALM 16:11

AEDEEN
Noble Beauty

> *I will praise thee; for I am fearfully and wonderfully made: marvellous are thy works.*
> PSALM 139:14

AELRED
One of Brightness

> *They that be wise shall shine as the brightness of the firmament; . . . as the stars for ever and ever.*
> DANIEL 12:3

AEMON
Faithful Protector

> *He that dwelleth in the secret place of the most High shall abide under the . . . Almighty.*
> PSALM 91:1

AENEA
Worthy of Praise

> *For the Lord is great, and greatly to be praised: . . . Honour and majesty are before him.*
> PSALM 96:4, 6

AENEAS
Hero with Courage

> *Be strong and of a good courage; . . . for the Lord thy God is with thee whithersoever thou goest.*
> JOSHUA 1:9
>
> Greek

AEREAL
Strength and Courage

> *The Lord is my light and my salvation; . . . the strength of my life; of whom shall I be afraid?*
> PSALM 27:1

AERIK
Kingly Nobility

> *Thy right hand hath holden me up, and thy gentleness hath made me great.*
> PSALM 18:35

AERIN
Queen of Brightness

> *They that be wise shall shine as the brightness of the firmament; ... as the stars for ever and ever.*
> DANIEL 12:3

AERYK
Powerful and Regal

> *God hath not given us the spirit ... of power, and of love, and of a sound mind.*
> 2 TIMOTHY 1:7

AFELLE
Of Noble Fame

> *Ye have not chosen me, but I have chosen you, and ordained you, that ye should go and bring forth fruit.*
> JOHN 15:16

AFFIE
Of Noble Fame

> *Ye have not chosen me, but I have chosen you, and ordained you, that ye should go and bring forth fruit.*
> JOHN 15:16

AFRA
One of Peace

> *The Lord will give strength unto his people; the Lord will bless his people with peace.*
> PSALM 29:11

AFRAZIER
One of Peace

> *The Lord will give strength unto his people; the Lord will bless his people with peace.*
> PSALM 29:11

AFRIKA
Pleasant One of Strength

> *It is God that girdeth me with strength, and maketh my way perfect.*
> PSALM 18:32

Celtic

AFSHIN
Of Noble Fame

> *Thou hast ... given me the shield of thy salvation; ... Thy gentleness hath made me great.*
> PSALM 18:35

AFTEN
Firm of Purpose

> *I have set the Lord ... before me: ... he is at my right hand, I shall not be moved.*
> PSALM 16:8

AFTYN
Firm of Purpose

> *I have set the Lord ... before me: ... he is at my right hand, I shall not be moved.*
> PSALM 16:8

AGANETHA
One of Purity

> *Blessed are the pure in heart: for they shall see God.*
> MATTHEW 5:8

AGAPE
Love

> Let us love one another: for love
> is of God; and every one that
> loveth is born of God, and
> knoweth God.
> 1 JOHN 4:7
>
> Greek

AGAR
Gladness and Joy

> I will praise thee, O Lord, with
> my whole heart; . . . I will be
> glad and rejoice in thee.
> PSALM 9:1–2

AGATHA
Kind and Good

> Be ye kind one to another:
> tenderhearted, forgiving one
> another.
> EPHESIANS 4:32

AGGE
The Kind and Good

> Be ye kind one to another,
> tenderhearted, forgiving one
> another.
> EPHESIANS 4:32

AGGNETHA
One of Purity

> Blessed are the pure in heart:
> for they shall see God.
> MATTHEW 5:8

AGNELLA
One of Purity

> Blessed are the pure in heart:
> for they shall see God.
> MATTHEW 5:8

AGNES
Lady of Meekness

> For the Lord taketh pleasure in
> his people: he will beautify the
> meek with salvation.
> PSALM 149:4

AGNETTE
One of Purity

> Blessed are the pure in heart:
> for they shall see God.
> MATTHEW 5:8

AGNITA
One of Meekness

> For the Lord taketh pleasure in
> his people: he will beautify the
> meek with salvation.
> PSALM 149:4

AGNUS
The Lamb of Purity

> Blessed are the pure in heart:
> for they shall see God.
> MATTHEW 5:8

AGOSTINA
Worthy of Honor

> The Lord is great, and greatly to
> be praised: . . . Honour and
> majesty are before him.
> PSALM 96:4, 6
>
> Latin

AGURANN
One of Shining Light

> Let your light so shine . . . that
> they may see your good works,
> and glorify your Father which is
> in heaven.
> MATTHEW 5:16

AH SENG
Victorious

> Thanks be to God, which giveth
> us the victory through our Lord
> Jesus Christ.
> 1 CORINTHIANS 15:57
>
> Asian

AHARON
Exalted One of Light

> The Lord is great, and greatly to
> be praised: . . . Honour and
> majesty are before him.
> PSALM 96:4, 6

AHLEA
One of Truth

> Make me to understand the way
> of thy precepts: . . . I have
> chosen the way of truth.
> PSALM 119:27, 30

AHLERT
Noble and Illustrious

> Thou hast also given me the
> shield of thy salvation: . . . and
> thy gentleness hath made me
> great.
> PSALM 18:35

AHMED
The Most Praised

> The Lord is great, and greatly to
> be praised: . . . Honour and
> majesty are before him.
> PSALM 96:4, 6

AHNA
also ANNA

One of Grace

> The Lord will give grace and
> glory; no good thing will he
> withhold from them that walk
> uprightly.
> PSALM 84:11

AHNWAR
Light and Grace

> The Lord will give grace and
> glory: no good thing will he
> withhold from them that walk
> uprightly.
> PSALM 84:11
>
> Arabic

AHRESE
One of Strength

> In God is my salvation and my
> glory: the rock of my strength,
> and my refuge, is in God.
> PSALM 62:7

AHREY
Of Power and Strength

> The Lord is my rock, . . . my
> fortress, and my deliverer; . . .
> my strength, in whom I will
> trust.
> PSALM 18:2

AHUDA
One of Praise

> I will bless the Lord at all times;
> his praise shall continually be
> in my mouth.
> PSALM 34:1

AI HIONG
From a Strong Heritage

*Thy testimonies have I taken as
an heritage for ever: for they
are the rejoicing of my heart.*
PSALM 119:111

Chinese

AICHA
Divine One

*[There] are given unto us . . .
great and precious promises:
that by these ye might be
partakers of the divine nature.*
2 PETER 1:4

AIDA
Happy

*In thy presence is fulness of joy;
at thy right hand . . . are
pleasures for evermore.*
PSALM 16:11

AIDAN
The Fiery One

*Let us have grace, whereby we
may serve God . . . For our God
is a consuming fire.*
HEBREWS 12:28–29

AIDEN
Strong Spirit

*I press toward the mark for the
prize of the high calling of God
in Christ Jesus.*
PHILIPPIANS 3:14

AIDET
Prosperous One

*I will sing unto the Lord,
because he hath dealt
bountifully with me.*
PSALM 13:6

AIESHIA
Blessed and Happy

*I will praise thee, O Lord, with
my whole heart; I will show
forth all thy marvellous works.*
PSALM 9:1

AIJA
Fame of the Land

*Wait on the Lord, and keep his
way, and he shall exalt thee to
inherit the land.*
PSALM 37:34

AIKA
The Happy One

*In thy presence is fulness of joy;
at thy right hand . . . are
pleasures for evermore.*
PSALM 16:11

AIKAKA
United in Spirit

*Let the words of my mouth, and
the meditation of my heart, be
acceptable in thy sight, O Lord.*
PSALM 19:14

AIKEN
One of Strength

*In God is my salvation and my
glory: the rock of my strength,
and my refuge, is in God.*
PSALM 62:7

AIKO
Little Beloved One

> Let us love one another: for love
> is of God; and every one that
> loveth is born of God, and
> knoweth God.
> 1 JOHN 4:7

AIKUE
Blessed Protector

> In God is my salvation and my
> glory: the rock of my strength,
> and my refuge, is in God.
> PSALM 62:7

AILDA
Strong in the Faith

> Fight the good fight of faith, lay
> hold on eternal life, . . . thou art
> also called.
> 1 TIMOTHY 6:12

AILECIA
Noble One of Truth

> I am thy servant; give me
> understanding, that I may know
> thy testimonies.
> PSALM 119:125

AILEEN
Lady of Light

> Let your light so shine . . . that
> they may see your good works,
> and glorify your Father which is
> in heaven.
> MATTHEW 5:16

AILENE
Light Bearer

> They that be wise shall shine as
> the brightness of the firmament.
> DANIEL 12:3

AILINA
One of Peace

> The Lord will give strength unto
> his people; the Lord will bless
> his people with peace.
> PSALM 29:11

AILINE
One of Peace

> The Lord will give strength unto
> his people; the Lord will bless
> his people with peace.
> PSALM 29:11

AILSA
Noble and of Good Cheer

> In thy presence is fulness of joy;
> at thy right hand . . . are
> pleasures for evermore.
> PSALM 16:11

AILUENE
Blessed Protector

> In God is my salvation and my
> glory: the rock of my strength,
> and my refuge, is in God.
> PSALM 62:7

AILUKUNI
Blessed Protector

> In God is my salvation and my
> glory: the rock of my strength,
> and my refuge, is in God.
> PSALM 62:7

AIMA
Beloved

> *Beloved, let us love one another: for love is of God; and every one that loveth is born of God, and knoweth God.*
> 1 JOHN 4:7

AIMEERENEE
Beloved One Born Anew

> *Let us love one another: for love is of God; and every one that loveth is born of God, and knoweth God.*
> 1 JOHN 4:7

AINA
Pure Heart

> *Blessed are the pure in heart: for they shall see God.*
> MATTHEW 5:8

AIND
One of Joy

> *In thy presence is fulness of joy; at thy right hand . . . are pleasures for evermore.*
> PSALM 16:11

AINEKI
Pure Heart

> *Blessed are the pure in heart: for they shall see God.*
> MATTHEW 5:8

AINO
One of Joy

> *I will be glad and rejoice in thee: I will sing praise to thy name, O thou most High.*
> PSALM 9:2

AINONIOK
One of Understanding and Peace

> *My mouth shall speak of wisdom; and the meditation of my heart shall be of understanding.*
> PSALM 49:3
>
> Greek

AINSLEY
Peaceful One of Grace

> *For by grace are ye saved through faith; . . . it is the gift of God.*
> EPHESIANS 2:8

AINSLI
One's Own Meadow

> *The Lord is my Shepherd; . . . He maketh me to lie down in green pastures.*
> PSALM 23:1–2

AIREABELLA
Beautiful Altar

> *Let them bring me unto thy holy hill, . . . Then will I go unto the altar of God, . . . my . . . joy.*
> PSALM 43:3–4

AIREN
One of Light

> *Let your light so shine . . . that they may see your good works, and glorify your Father which is in heaven.*
> MATTHEW 5:16

AISHA
One of Truth

> *Lead me in thy truth, and teach me: for thou art the God of my salvation; on thee do I wait.*
> PSALM 25:5

AISLINN
Heavenly Guidance

> I will instruct thee and teach
> thee in the way which thou shalt
> go: I will guide thee.
> PSALM 32:8

AIVARS
Refuge in Battle

> The Lord is my defence; and my
> God is the rock of my refuge.
> PSALM 94:22

Teutonic

AIXA
Noble

> Ye are a chosen generation, . . .
> ye should show forth the praises
> of him who hath called you.
> 1 PETER 2:9

AIYONIA
Eternal Life

> God so loved the world, that he
> gave his . . . Son, that whosoever
> believeth [would] . . . have
> everlasting life.
> JOHN 3:16

North American Indian

AIZA
Precious and Noble

> Thou art my God, and I will
> praise thee: thou art my God, I
> will exalt thee.
> PSALM 118:28

Hebrew

AJA
Noble One

> Blessed is the man that feareth
> the Lord, that delighteth . . . in
> his commandments.
> PSALM 112:1

AJALON
Ennobled by God

> Thou hast . . . given me the
> shield of thy salvation: . . . thy
> gentleness hath made me great.
> PSALM 18:35

AJUA
Born on Monday

> This is the day which the Lord
> hath made; we will rejoice and
> be glad in it.
> PSALM 118:24

African

AKA
The Happy One

> In thy presence is fulness of joy;
> at thy right hand there are
> pleasures for evermore.
> PSALM 16:11

AKAELA
God Is Exalted

> The Lord is great, and greatly to
> be praised: Honour and majesty
> are before him.
> PSALM 96:4, 6

AKAKA
The Good and Kind

> Be ye kind one to another,
> tenderhearted, forgiving one
> another.
> EPHESIANS 4:32

AKALINA
Of Noble Rank

> *I have chosen you, and ordained you, that ye should go and bring forth fruit.*
> JOHN 15:16
>
> Polynesian

AKAMU
God's Creation

> *We are his workmanship, created in Christ Jesus unto good works.*
> EPHESIANS 2:10
>
> Polynesian

AKE
Bold and Powerful

> *Thou hast . . . given me the shield of thy salvation: thy right hand hath holden one up, and thy gentleness hath made me great.*
> PSALM 18:35

AKEEM
God Will Establish

> *Thou hast . . . given me the shield of thy salvation: . . . thy gentleness hath made me great.*
> PSALM 18:35

AKELAIKA
Of Noble Rank

> *I have chosen you, and ordained you, that ye should go and bring forth fruit.*
> JOHN 15:16
>
> Polynesian

AKELINA
Of Noble Rank

> *I have chosen you, and ordained you, that ye should go and bring forth fruit.*
> JOHN 15:16

AKEMI
God Will Establish

> *Thou hast . . . given me the shield of thy salvation: and thy gentleness hath made me great.*
> 2 SAMUEL 22:36

AKENA
Belonging to God

> *Thou art my rock and my fortress; . . . for thy name's sake lead me, and guide me.*
> PSALM 31:3

AKENAKA
Belonging to God

> *Thou art my rock and my fortress; . . . for thy name's sake lead me, and guide me.*
> PSALM 31:3
>
> Polynesian

AKENEKI
Pure Heart

> *Blessed are the pure in heart: for they shall see God.*
> MATTHEW 5:8

AKESHA
Safe and Secure

> *I will say of the Lord, He is my refuge and my fortress: my God; in him will I trust.*
> PSALM 91:2

AKIKO
One of Knowledge

> *For the Lord giveth wisdom: out of his mouth cometh knowledge and understanding.*
> PROVERBS 2:6
>
> Japanese

AKIL
One of Knowledge

> *My mouth shall speak of wisdom; and the meditation of my heart shall be of understanding.*
> PSALM 49:3

AKILAH
Intelligent One Who Reasons

> *For the Lord giveth wisdom: out of his mouth cometh knowledge and understanding.*
> PROVERBS 2:6
>
> Arabic

AKIO
One of Radiant Light

> *Let your light so shine . . . that they may see your good works, and glorify your Father which is in heaven.*
> MATTHEW 5:16

AKISHA
Safe and Secure

> *I will say of the Lord, He is my refuge and my fortress: my God; in him will I trust.*
> PSALM 91:2

AKRE
Peaceful Dweller

> *The Lord will give strength unto his people; the Lord will bless his people with peace.*
> PSALM 29:11

AKRISA
A Christian

> *Ye are washed, . . . sanctified, . . . justified in the name of the Lord Jesus.*
> 1 CORINTHIANS 6:11

AL
Noble and Brilliant

> *My mouth shall speak of wisdom; and the meditation of my heart shall be of understanding.*
> PSALM 49:3

ALACIA
Noble One of Truth

> *Thou art near, O Lord; and all thy commandments are truth.*
> PSALM 119:151

ALADRAINE
Height of Faith

> *Faith is the substance of things hoped for, the evidence of things not seen.*
> HEBREWS 11:1

ALAH
Glorious and One of Greatness

> *I will praise thee, O Lord, with my whole heart, . . . I will sing praise to thy name.*
> PSALM 9:1–2

ALAIN
One of Light

> *Let your light so shine . . . that*
> *they may see your good works,*
> *and glorify your Father.*
> MATTHEW 5:16

ALAINA
One of Harmony

> *Let the words of my mouth, and*
> *the meditation of my heart be*
> *acceptable in thy sight, O Lord.*
> PSALM 19:14

ALAINE
Harmony and Light

> *Let the words of my mouth, and*
> *the meditation of my heart be*
> *acceptable in thy sight, O Lord.*
> PSALM 19:14

ALAIR
One of Cheer and Joy

> *In thy presence is fulness of joy;*
> *at thy right hand . . . are*
> *pleasures for evermore.*
> PSALM 16:11

ALALIA
A Quiet Spirit

> *Let the words of my mouth, and*
> *the meditation of my heart be*
> *acceptable in thy sight, O Lord.*
> PSALM 19:14

ALAN
Friendly One

> *Ye are my friends, if ye do*
> *whatsoever I command you.*
> JOHN 15:14

ALAPAKI
Illustrious Through Nobility

> *Now the God of peace, . . . Make*
> *you perfect in every good work*
> *to do his will.*
> HEBREWS 13:20–21

ALAPELA
Beautiful Consecrated One

> *I have set the Lord . . . before*
> *me: . . . he is at my right hand, I*
> *shall not be moved.*
> PSALM 16:8

ALARIC
Noble and Powerful

> *Thou hast also given me the*
> *shield of thy salvation: . . . thy*
> *gentleness hath made me great.*
> PSALM 18:35

ALASKA
Great Land

> *In thy presence is fulness of joy;*
> *at thy right hand . . . are*
> *pleasures for evermore.*
> PSALM 16:11

ALASTAIR
Helper of Mankind

> *The Lord is my helper, and I*
> *will not fear what man shall do*
> *unto me.*
> HEBREWS 13:6

ALAUETTE
One of Truth

> *Lead me in thy truth, and teach*
> *me: for thou art the God of my*
> *salvation.*
> PSALM 25:5

ALAUNA
One of Truth

> Lead me in thy truth and teach me: for thou art the God of my salvation.
> PSALM 25:5

ALAWINA
Beloved Friend

> Beloved, let us love one another: for love is of God.
> 1 JOHN 4:7

ALAYNA
One of Harmony

> Her ways are ways of pleasantness, and all her paths are peace.
> PROVERBS 3:17

ALBA
One of Purity

> The commandment of the Lord is pure, enlightening the eyes.
> PSALM 19:8

ALBANY
Pure Heart

> Blessed are the pure in heart: for they shall see God.
> MATTHEW 5:8

ALBENNER
Wise and Powerful Ruler

> Thou hast . . . given me the shield of thy salvation: and thy gentleness hath made me great.
> 2 SAMUEL 22:36

ALBERDINA
One of Radiant Light

> They that be wise shall shine as the brightness of the firmament.
> DANIEL 12:3

ALBERIC
Noble One

> Thou hast also given me the shield of thy salvation: . . . thy gentleness hath made me great.
> PSALM 18:35

ALBERT
Noble and Brilliant

> Thy righteousness is like the great mountains; thy judgments are a great deep.
> PSALM 36:6

ALBERTA
One of Noble Character

> Holding forth the word of life; that I may rejoice in the day of Christ.
> PHILIPPIANS 2:16

ALBERTINA
Illustrious Through Nobility

> Make you perfect in every good work to do . . . that which is wellpleasing in his sight.
> HEBREWS 13:21

ALBIN
One of Virtue

> Whatsoever things are true, . . . honest, . . . just, . . . if . . . any virtue, . . . think on these things.
> PHILIPPIANS 4:8

ALBRECHT
Noble and Brilliant

> I will give thee thanks in the
> great congregation: . . . my
> tongue shall speak of thy
> righteousness.
> PSALM 35:18, 28

ALCENIO
Brave Warrior

> Fight the good fight of faith, lay
> hold on eternal life, . . . thou art
> also called.
> 1 TIMOTHY 6:12

ALCO
Sound Mind and Understanding

> My mouth shall speak of wisdom;
> and the meditation of my heart
> shall be of understanding.
> PSALM 49:3

ALDA
Prosperous One

> I will sing unto the Lord,
> because he hath dealt
> bountifully with me.
> PSALM 13:6

ALDEAN
Wise Protector

> I will bless the Lord, who hath
> given me counsel: . . . I have set
> the Lord always before me.
> PSALM 16:7–8

ALDORA
Noble Gift

> By grace are ye saved through
> faith; and that not of
> yourselves: it is the gift of God.
> EPHESIANS 2:8

ALDRIC
Wise

> The Lord giveth wisdom: out of
> his mouth cometh knowledge
> and understanding.
> PROVERBS 2:6

ALDWIN
Old Friend

> Ye are my friends, if ye do
> whatsoever I command you.
> JOHN 15:14

ALEASE
Devoted One

> I will bless the Lord at all times:
> his praise shall continually be
> in my mouth.
> PSALM 34:1

ALEDA
Rich Raiment

> Bless the Lord, . . . thou art very
> great; thou art clothed with
> honour and majesty.
> PSALM 104:1

ALEESE
Noble One of Truth

> My mouth shall speak of
> wisdom; and the meditation of
> my heart shall be of
> understanding.
> PSALM 49:3

ALEGRA
One of Happiness

In thy presence is fulness of joy;
at thy right hand . . . are
pleasures for evermore.
PSALM 16:11

ALEJANDRO
Helper of Mankind

Let us . . . come . . . unto the
throne of grace, . . . obtain
mercy, and find grace to help in
time of need.
HEBREWS 4:16

ALENA
One of Light

Let your light . . . shine . . . that
they may see your good works,
and glorify your Father . . . in
heaven.
MATTHEW 5:16

ALENE
Noble One of Truth

My mouth shall speak of
wisdom; and the meditation of
my heart shall be of
understanding.
PSALM 49:3

ALEXANDER
Helper of Mankind

Now the God of peace, . . . Make
you perfect in every good work
to do his will.
HEBREWS 13:20–21

ALEXANDRA
Helper of Mankind

Let us . . . come . . . unto the
throne of grace, . . . obtain
mercy, and find grace to help in
time of need.
HEBREWS 4:16

ALF
Wise and Good Counsel

As for God, his way is perfect:
the word of the Lord is tried.
PSALM 18:30

ALFERD
Extremely Wise

The Lord giveth wisdom: out of
his mouth cometh knowledge
and understanding.
PROVERBS 2:6

ALFREDO
Extremely Wise

The Lord giveth wisdom: out of
his mouth cometh knowledge
and understanding.
PROVERBS 2:6

ALI-RAE
Greatest and Highest

For the Lord is great, and greatly
to be praised: . . . Honour and
majesty are before him.
PSALM 96:4, 6

ALICE
Noble One of Truth

> *Then said Jesus . . . If ye*
> *continue in my word, then are*
> *ye my disciples indeed; And ye*
> *shall know the truth, and the*
> *truth shall make you free.*
> JOHN 8:31–32

ALICEA
Noble One of Truth

> *Then said Jesus . . . If ye*
> *continue in my word, then are*
> *ye my disciples indeed; And ye*
> *shall know the truth, and the*
> *truth shall make you free.*
> JOHN 8:31–32

ALICHIA
Noble One of Truth

> *I will meditate in thy precepts,*
> *. . . I will delight myself in thy*
> *statutes: I will not forget thy*
> *word.*
> PSALM 119:15–16

ALICIA
Noble Lady

> *Strength and honour are her*
> *clothing; . . . a woman that*
> *feareth the Lord, she shall be*
> *praised.*
> PROVERBS 31:25, 30

ALIDA
Prosperous One

> *I will sing unto the Lord,*
> *because he hath dealt*
> *bountifully with me.*
> PSALM 13:6

ALIESJE
Noble One of Truth

> *My mouth shall speak of*
> *wisdom; and the meditation of*
> *my heart shall be of*
> *understanding.*
> PSALM 49:3

ALIETA
One of Truth

> *Thy testimonies have I taken as*
> *an heritage for ever: for they*
> *are the rejoicing of my heart.*
> PSALM 119:111

ALIS
One of Truth

> *The entrance of thy words*
> *giveth light; it giveth*
> *understanding unto the simple.*
> PSALM 119:130

ALISA
One of Great Joy

> *Behold, God is my salvation; I*
> *will trust, and not be afraid: . . .*
> *Therefore with joy shall ye draw*
> *water out of the wells of*
> *salvation.*
> ISAIAH 12:2–3

ALISABETH
Consecrated to God

> *I have set the Lord always*
> *before me: because he is at my*
> *right hand, I shall not be*
> *moved.*
> PSALM 16:8

ALISAL
One of Truth

I have chosen the way of truth: thy judgments have I laid before me.
PSALM 119:30

ALKINI
Noble and Pure One

Blessed are the pure in heart: for they shall see God.
MATTHEW 5:8

ALLAIRE
One of Cheer and Joy

Thou wilt show me the path of life: in thy presence is fulness of joy; at thy right hand there are pleasures for evermore.
PSALM 16:11

ALLANETTE
Beloved Friend

Ye are my friends, if ye do whatsoever I command you.
JOHN 15:14

ALLBRITTEN
Illustrious Through Nobility

Ye have not chosen me, but I have chosen you, and ordained you, that ye should go and bring forth fruit.
JOHN 15:16

ALLDA
Rich in Wisdom

For the Lord giveth wisdom: out of his mouth cometh knowledge and understanding.
PROVERBS 2:6

ALLELUIA
Praise Ye the Lord

I will praise thee, O Lord, with my whole heart; . . . I will be glad and rejoice in thee: I will sing praise to thy name.
PSALM 9:1–2

ALLEYNE
My Child

For thou art my hope, O Lord God: thou art my trust from my youth.
PSALM 71:5

ALLISON
Of Sacred Fame

At the name of Jesus every knee should bow, . . . every tongue should confess that Jesus . . . is Lord.
PHILIPPIANS 2:10–11

ALVARO
Noble Ruler

He that ruleth over men must be just, ruling in the fear of God.
2 SAMUEL 23:3

AMANDA
Worthy of Love

Blessed are they that keep his testimonies, and that seek him with the whole heart.
PSALM 119:2

AMBER
Jewel of Purity

The word is very pure; therefore thy servant loveth it.
PSALM 119:140

AMELIA
Industrious One

> Whatsoever ye do, do it heartily,
> as to the Lord, . . . for ye serve
> the Lord Christ.
> COLOSSIANS 3:23–24

AMPARO
Compassionate Spirit

> I will praise thee: for thou hast
> heard me, and art become my
> salvation.
> PSALM 118:21

AMY   *also* AAMY
Cherished One

> The Lord hath appeared of old
> unto me, . . . I have loved thee
> with an everlasting love.
> JEREMIAH 31:3

ANA   *also* ANNA
Grace

> Grow in grace, and in the
> knowledge of our Lord and
> Saviour Jesus Christ.
> 2 PETER 3:18

ANAIS
One of Grace

> The Lord will give grace and
> glory: no good thing will he
> withhold from them that walk
> uprightly.
> PSALM 84:11

ANDEE
Woman of the Lord

> I will bless the Lord at all times:
> his praise shall continually be
> in my mouth.
> PSALM 34:1

ANDREA
Woman of the Lord

> I have set the Lord . . . before
> me: . . . he is at my right hand, I
> shall not be moved.
> PSALM 16:8

ANDREW
Strong and Manly

> Be strong and of a good courage;
> . . . the Lord thy God is with thee
> whithersoever thou goest.
> JOSHUA 1:9

ANDY
A Man of God

> A wise man is strong; yea, a
> man of knowledge increaseth
> strength.
> PROVERBS 24:5

ANGEL
Heavenly Messenger

> For unto you is born this day in
> the city of David a Saviour,
> which is Christ the Lord.
> LUKE 2:11

ANGELA
Heavenly Messenger

> For unto you is born this day in
> the city of David a Saviour,
> which is Christ the Lord.
> LUKE 2:11

ANGIE
Heavenly Messenger

> How beautiful are the feet of
> them that preach the gospel of
> peace.
> ROMANS 10:15

ANITA
One of Grace

> The Lord will give grace and
> glory: no good thing will he
> withhold from them that walk
> uprightly.
> PSALM 84:11

ANN
One of Grace

> The Lord will give grace and
> glory: no good thing will he
> withhold from them that walk
> uprightly.
> PSALM 84:11

ANNA   *also* AHNA
One of Grace

> Grow in grace, and in the
> knowledge of our Lord and
> Saviour Jesus Christ.
> 2 PETER 3:18

ANNE
One of Grace

> The Lord will give grace and
> glory: no good thing will he
> withhold from them that walk
> uprightly.
> PSALM 84:11

ANNEMARIE
One of Grace

> Grow in grace and in the
> knowledge of our Lord and
> Saviour, Jesus Christ.
> 2 PETER 3:18

ANNETTE
One of Grace

> Grow in grace and in the
> knowledge of our Lord and
> Saviour, Jesus Christ.
> 2 PETER 3:18

ANSELITA
Divine Protectress

> I will lift up mine eyes unto the
> hills, from whence cometh my
> help.
> PSALM 121:1

ANTHEA
Lady of the Flowers

> I will praise thee; for I am
> fearfully and wonderfully
> made: marvellous are thy
> works.
> PSALM 139:14

ANTHONY
Beyond Praise

> For the Lord is great, and greatly
> to be praised: . . . Honour and
> majesty are before him.
> PSALM 96:4, 6

ANTOINETTE
Beyond Praise

> For the Lord is great, and greatly
> to be praised: . . . Honour and
> majesty are before him.
> PSALM 96:4, 6

ANTON
Beyond Praise

> For the Lord is great, and
> greatly to be praised: . . .
> Honour and majesty are
> before him.
> PSALM 96:4, 6

ANTONIO
Beyond Praise

> For the Lord is great, and
> greatly to be praised: . . .
> Honour and majesty are before
> him.
> PSALM 96:4, 6

AREC
Powerful and Regal

> As for God, his way is perfect;
> . . . God is my strength and
> power: and he maketh my way
> perfect.
> 2 SAMUEL 22:31, 33

AREMINA
Noble One of High Degree

> It is God that girdeth me with
> strength, and maketh my way
> perfect.
> PSALM 18:32

ARESTEA
Excellent Valor and Virtue

> The Lord is my rock, and my
> fortress, and my deliverer;
> . . . my strength, in whom I
> will trust.
> PSALM 18:2

ARIANA
The Holy One

> Give unto the Lord the glory due
> unto his name; worship the Lord
> in the beauty of holiness.
> PSALM 29:2

ARIANN
The Holy One

> Give unto the Lord the glory due
> unto his name; worship the Lord
> in the beauty of holiness.
> PSALM 29:2

ARIZONA
Place of the Small Spring

> He maketh me to lie down in
> green pastures; he leadeth me
> beside the still waters.
> PSALM 23:2

ARLENE
A Pledge

> I will bless the Lord at all times:
> his praise shall continually be
> in my mouth.
> PSALM 34:1

ARMANDO
One of Nobility

> Ye have not chosen me, but I
> have chosen you, and ordained
> you, . . . go and bring forth fruit.
> JOHN 15:16

ARNEDA
One of Strength

> Trust ye in the Lord for ever: for
> in the Lord JEHOVAH is
> everlasting strength.
> ISAIAH 26:4

ARNI
Mighty as the Eagle

> They that wait upon the Lord
> . . . renew their strength; they
> shall mount up with wings as
> eagles.
> ISAIAH 40:31

ARNOLD
Mighty as the Eagle

> They that wait upon the Lord
> . . . renew their strength; they
> shall mount up with wings as
> eagles.
> ISAIAH 40:31

ARTHUR
One of Strength and Valor

> The angel of the Lord . . . said
> unto him, The Lord is with thee,
> thou mighty man of valor.
> JUDGES 6:12

ARTURO
One of Strength and Valor

> The angel of the Lord . . . said
> unto him, The Lord is with thee,
> thou mighty man of valor.
> JUDGES 6:12

ASA
A Physician

> The Spirit of the Lord is upon
> me, . . . he hath anointed me to
> preach the gospel [and] to heal
> the brokenhearted.
> LUKE 4:18

ASHA
Blessed and Happy

> I will praise thee, O Lord, . . . I
> will be glad and rejoice in thee:
> I will sing praise to thy name.
> PSALM 9:1–2

ASHLEE
Peaceful Dweller

> He maketh me to lie down in
> green pastures: he leadeth me
> beside the still waters.
> PSALM 23:2

ASHLEY
A Peaceful Heart

> The peace of God, which passeth
> all understanding, shall keep
> your hearts and minds through
> Christ Jesus.
> PHILIPPIANS 4:7

AUBREY
Rich and Powerful Strength

> The Lord is my rock, . . . my
> fortress, and my deliverer; my
> God, my strength, in whom I
> will trust.
> PSALM 18:2

AUDREY
Noble Strength

> The Lord is my light and my
> salvation; . . . the strength of my
> life; of whom shall I be afraid?
> PSALM 27:1

AUGUSTINA
Worthy of Honor

> *The Lord is great, and greatly to be praised: . . . Honour and majesty are before him.*
> PSALM 96:4, 6

AUSTIN
Worthy of Honor

> *The Lord is great, and greatly to be praised: . . . Honour and majesty are before him.*
> PSALM 96:4, 6

AUTUMN
Harvest

> *Lift up your eyes, and look on the fields; for they are white already to harvest.*
> JOHN 4:35

AVA
Life

> *The Lord is my light and my salvation; . . . the strength of my life; of whom shall I be afraid?*
> PSALM 27:1

AVA MARIE
Life

> *The Lord is my light and my salvation; . . . the strength of my life; of whom shall I be afraid?*
> PSALM 27:1

AVERY
A Good Counselor

> *I will bless the Lord, who hath given me counsel: . . . he is at my right hand.*
> PSALM 16:7–8

AVIS
One of Comfort

> *Be of good comfort, . . . live in peace; and the God of love and peace shall be with you.*
> 2 CORINTHIANS 13:11

AVRAM
My Father Is Exalted

> *The Lord is great, and greatly to be praised: . . . Honour and majesty are before him.*
> PSALM 96:4, 6

Hebrew

AZALEE
Ennobled by God

> *I will praise thee; for I am fearfully and wonderfully made; marvellous are thy works.*
> PSALM 139:14

AZEMA
Defender

> *The Lord is my rock, and my fortress, and my deliverer; my God, my strength, in whom I will trust.*
> PSALM 18:2

AZER
God Hath Helped

> *I will praise thee; for thou hast heard me, and art become my salvation.*
> PSALM 118:21

AZIA
Of Noble Rank

> Ye are a chosen generation, . . .
> Ye should show forth the praises
> of him who . . . called you.
> 1 PETER 2:9

AZIM
Defender

> Fight the good fight of faith, lay
> hold on eternal life, whereunto
> thou art . . . called.
> 1 TIMOTHY 6:12

AZIR
God Hath Helped

> I will bless the Lord, who hath
> given me counsel: . . . he is at my
> right hand.
> PSALM 16:7–8

AZIZ
Precious and One of Strength

> The Lord is my rock, . . . my
> fortress and my deliverer; . . .
> my strength, in whom I will
> trust.
> PSALM 18:2

AZLYNN
Peaceful Spirit

> The Lord will give strength unto
> his people; the Lord will bless
> his people with peace.
> PSALM 29:11

AZUCENA
To Ascend

> Thou hast ascended on high, . . .
> Blessed be the Lord, who daily
> loadeth us with benefits.
> PSALM 68:18–19

AZUREE
A Precious Jewel

> I will praise thee; for I am
> fearfully and wonderfully
> made; marvellous are thy
> works.
> PSALM 139:14

AZZIE
Having Power from God

> Thou hast . . . given me the
> shield of thy salvation: and thy
> right hand hath holden me up.
> PSALM 18:35

AZZIELEAS
Ennobled by God

> Thou hast . . . given me the
> shield of thy salvation: . . . thy
> gentleness hath made me great.
> PSALM 18:35

Hebrew

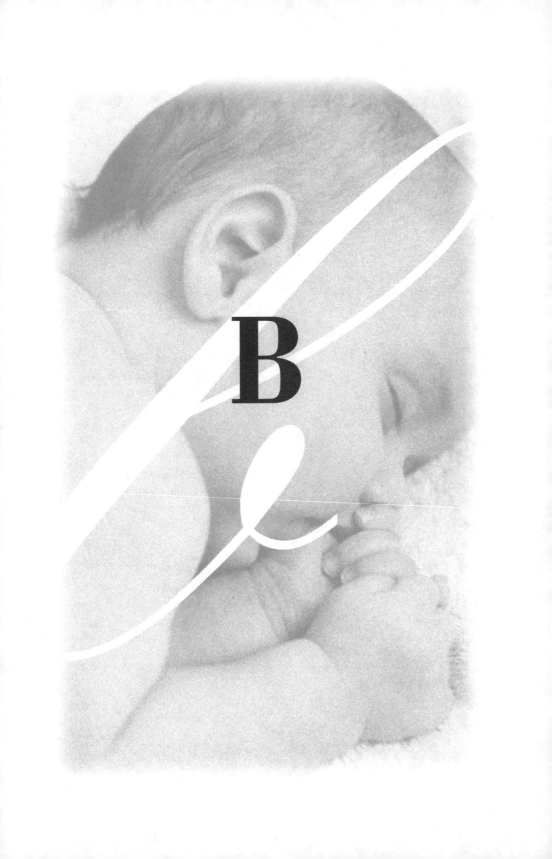

BABE
Consecration

> *I will bless the Lord at all times:*
> *his praise shall continually be*
> *in my mouth.*
> PSALM 34:1

BABI
Grandmother

> *The aged women likewise . . . be*
> *in behaviour as becometh*
> *holiness, . . . teachers of good*
> *things.*
> TITUS 2:3

BACILIO
Bold Protector

> *In whom we have boldness and*
> *access with confidence by the*
> *faith of him.*
> EPHESIANS 3:12

BADAK
One of Nobility

> *Thou hast . . . given me the*
> *shield of thy salvation; and thy*
> *right hand hath holden me up.*
> PSALM 18:35

BADEN
Honor and Courage

> *Be strong and of a good*
> *courage; . . . for the Lord thy*
> *God is with thee whithersoever*
> *thou goest.*
> JOSHUA 1:9

BAILEY
Leader of Strength

> *Thou hast . . . given me the*
> *shield of thy salvation; . . . thy*
> *gentleness hath made me great.*
> PSALM 18:35

BAIR
A Traveler

> *Thy word is a lamp unto my*
> *feet, and a light unto my path.*
> PSALM 119:105

BAIRL
Devoted Service

> *I will bless the Lord at all times:*
> *his praise shall continually be*
> *in my mouth.*
> PSALM 34:1

BAIRN
One of Strength and Courage

> *In God is my salvation and my*
> *glory: . . . my strength, and my*
> *refuge, is in God.*
> PSALM 62:7

BAKARI
Blessed

> *Blessed are they that keep his*
> *testimonies, and that seek him*
> *with the whole heart.*
> PSALM 119:2

> African

BAKER
One Who Made Bread

> *Whatsoever ye do, do it heartily,*
> *as to the Lord, . . . for ye serve*
> *the Lord Christ.*
> COLOSSIANS 3:23–24

B

BAKHSHINDRA
Longlife and Virtue

> *Whatsoever things are true, . . .*
> *honest, . . . just, . . . of good*
> *report. . . any virtue [or] . . .*
> *praise, think on these things.*
> PHILIPPIANS 4:8
>
> Hinov

BALDEMAR
Of Princely Fame

> *Ye have not chosen me, but I*
> *have chosen you, . . . that ye*
> *should go and bring forth fruit.*
> JOHN 15:16

BALDWIN
One of Victory

> *Whatsoever is born of God*
> *overcometh the world: . . . this is*
> *the victory . . . even our faith.*
> 1 JOHN 5:4

BALEEN
Mighty Soldier

> *Fight the good fight of faith, lay*
> *hold on eternal life, . . . to which*
> *thou art called.*
> 1 TIMOTHY 6:12

BALERIA
One of Courage

> *The Lord is my light and my*
> *salvation; . . . the strength of my*
> *life; of whom shall I be afraid?*
> PSALM 27:1

BALINBIN
To Be Strong and Valiant

> *The Lord is my strength . . . and*
> *shield; my heart trusteth in him.*
> PSALM 28:7
>
> Polynesian

BALLARD
Joy and Singing

> *In thy presence is fulness of joy;*
> *at thy right hand there are*
> *pleasures for evermore.*
> PSALM 16:11

BALTAZAR
Royal Protection

> *I will say of the Lord, He is my*
> *refuge and my fortress: my God;*
> *in him will I trust.*
> PSALM 91:2
>
> Slavic

BAMA
Child

> *O Lord my God, thou hast made*
> *thy servant . . . and I am but a*
> *little child.*
> 1 KINGS 3:7
>
> Latin

BAMBI
Little Baby

> *I will praise thee; for I am*
> *fearfully and wonderfully made:*
> *marvellous are thy works.*
> PSALM 139:14

NAME *That* BABY!

BANNISTER
Industrious and Courageous

> Whatsoever ye do, do it heartily,
> as to the Lord, . . . for ye serve
> the Lord Christ.
> COLOSSIANS 3:23–24

BAO
Strong Leader

> Thou hast . . . given me the shield
> of thy salvation: and thy
> gentleness hath made me great.
> 2 SAMUEL 22:36
>
> Teutonic

BAPTIST
The Baptized

> And Jesus, when he was
> baptized, went up straightway
> out of the water.
> MATTHEW 3:16

BARAKA
Divine Blessings

> Every good gift and every perfect
> gift is from above and cometh
> down from the Father of lights.
> JAMES 1:17
>
> Muslim

BARBARA
A Stranger

> Nevertheless the foundation of
> God standeth sure, . . . The Lord
> knoweth them that are his.
> 2 TIMOTHY 2:19

BARCLAY
Peaceful Dweller

> The Lord is my shepherd; I shall
> not want. . . . he leadeth me
> beside the still waters.
> PSALM 23:1–2

BARDO
Son of the Earth

> For we are his workmanship,
> created in Christ Jesus unto
> good works.
> EPHESIANS 2:10

BARENGER
Noble Warrior

> The Lord is my light and my
> salvation: . . . the strength of my
> life; of whom shall I be afraid?
> PSALM 27:1

BARIS
Noble and Firm of Purpose

> I will bless the Lord, who hath
> given me counsel: . . . I have set
> the Lord . . . before me.
> PSALM 16:7–8

BARNARD
Brave and Strong

> The Lord is my rock, and my
> fortress, . . . my strength, in
> whom I will trust.
> PSALM 18:2

BARON   *also* BARRON
A Noble Warrior

> Fight the good fight of faith, lay
> hold on eternal life, whereunto
> thou art also called.
> 1 TIMOTHY 6:12

B

BARR
Wise and Learned One

> *The Lord giveth wisdom: out of*
> *his mouth cometh knowledge*
> *and understanding.*
> PROVERBS 2:6

BARRINGTON
Noble and Firm of Purpose

> *I will bless the Lord, who hath*
> *given me counsel: . . . because he*
> *is at my right hand, I shall not*
> *be moved.*
> PSALM 16:7–8

BARRON   *also* BARON
Noble Warrior

> *Fight the good fight of faith, lay*
> *hold on eternal life, whereunto*
> *thou art also called.*
> 1 TIMOTHY 6:12

BARRY
One of Courage

> *Be strong and of a good*
> *courage, . . . the Lord thy God,*
> *he it is that doth go with thee.*
> DEUTERONOMY 31:6

BART
Firm of Purpose

> *I have set the Lord . . . before*
> *me: . . . he is at my right hand, I*
> *shall not be moved.*
> PSALM 16:8

BARTEL
Firm of Purpose

> *I have set the Lord . . . before*
> *me: . . . he is at my right hand, I*
> *shall not be moved.*
> PSALM 16:8

BARTHOLEMEW
Firm of Purpose

> *I have set the Lord . . . before*
> *me: . . . he is at my right hand, I*
> *shall not be moved.*
> PSALM 16:8

BASCOM
One of Virtue

> *Whatsoever things are true, . . .*
> *honest, . . . just, . . . of good*
> *report . . . any virtue, [or]*
> *praise, think on these things.*
> PHILIPPIANS 4:8

BASHA
One of Virtue

> *Whatsoever things are true, . . .*
> *honest, . . . just, . . . of good*
> *report . . . any virtue, [or]*
> *praise, think on these things.*
> PHILIPPIANS 4:8

BASHIR
Foreteller

> *Let the words of my mouth and*
> *the meditation of my heart, be*
> *acceptable in thy sight.*
> PSALM 19:14

Arabic

BASIL
Bold Protector

> *In whom we have boldness and*
> *access with confidence by the*
> *faith of him.*
> EPHESIANS 3:12

BATTAGLIA
Honor and Truth

> Thou art near, O Lord; and all
> thy commandments are truth.
> PSALM 119:151
>
> Teutonic

BATYA
The Happy and Blessed One

> Blessed are they that keep his
> testimonies, and that seek him
> with the whole heart.
> PSALM 119:2

BAWANA
Friend

> Ye are my friends, if ye do
> whatsoever I command you.
> JOHN 15:14
>
> African

BAXTER
A Baker

> Oh magnify the Lord with me,
> and let us exalt his name
> together.
> PSALM 34:3

BAYLOR
Leader of Strength

> Thou hast . . . given me the
> shield of thy salvation: . . . thy
> gentleness hath made me great.
> PSALM 18:35

BEA
Bringer of Joy

> In thy presence is fulness of joy;
> at thy right hand . . . are
> pleasures for evermore.
> PSALM 16:11

BEATRICE
Bringer of Joy

> In thy presence is fulness of joy;
> at thy right hand . . . are
> pleasures for evermore.
> PSALM 16:11

BEATRIZ
Bringer of Joy

> This is the day which the Lord
> hath made; we will rejoice and
> be glad in it.
> PSALM 118:24

BEAU
Beautiful Thoughts

> Whatsoever things are true, . . .
> honest, . . . just, . . . of good
> report . . . any virtue, [or]
> praise, think on these things.
> PHILIPPIANS 4:8

BEAUMONT
From the Beautiful Mountain

> They that trust in the Lord shall
> be as mount Zion, which cannot
> be removed, but abideth for
> ever.
> PSALM 125:1

BEAUREGARD
Beautiful Thoughts

> Whatsoever things are true, . . .
> honest, . . . just, . . . of good
> report . . . any virtue, [or]
> praise, think on these things.
> PHILIPPIANS 4:8

BEAUTON
One Who is Blessed

> Blessed are they that keep his testimonies, and that seek him with the whole heart.
> PSALM 119:2

BEAVER
Industrious One

> Whatsoever ye do, do it heartily, as to the Lord, . . . for ye serve the Lord Christ.
> COLOSSIANS 3:23–24

BECCA
Faithfully Steadfast

> Be ye steadfast, unmovable, always abounding in the work of the Lord.
> 1 CORINTHIANS 15:58

BECKY
Faithfully Steadfast

> Be ye steadfast, unmovable, always abounding in the work of the Lord.
> 1 CORINTHIANS 15:58

BEDA
A Prayer

> I love the Lord, . . . he hath heard my voice and my supplications. . . . God is merciful.
> PSALM 116:1, 5

BEDAR
Peaceful Leader

> The Lord will give strength unto his people; the Lord will bless his people with peace.
> PSALM 29:11

BEDE
A Prayer

> I love the Lord, . . . he hath heard my voice and my supplications. Gracious is the Lord.
> PSALM 116:1, 5

BEDELLA
Messenger

> How beautiful are the feet of them that preach the gospel of peace.
> ROMANS 10:15

BEDRI
Peaceful Leader

> The Lord will give strength unto his people; the Lord will bless his people with peace.
> PSALM 29:11

BELA
God's Oath

> The Lord shall endure for ever: he hath prepared his throne for judgment. . . . he shall judge in righteousness.
> PSALM 9:7, 8

BELDEANA
From the Beautiful Valley

> The Lord is my shepherd; . . . He maketh me to lie down in green pastures . . . beside the still waters.
> PSALM 23:1–2

Celtic

BELEN
An Arrow

> The Lord . . . and his arrow
> shall go forth as the lightening:
> . . . great is his goodness.
> ZECHARIAH 9:14, 17

BELENDA
Wise One

> The Lord giveth wisdom: out of
> his mouth cometh knowledge
> and understanding.
> PROVERBS 2:6

BELGIE
Fame of the Land

> Wait on the Lord, and keep his
> way, and he shall exalt thee to
> inherit the land.
> PSALM 37:34

BELGIUM
Fame of the Land

> Wait on the Lord, and keep his
> way, and he shall exalt thee to
> inherit the land.
> PSALM 37:34

BELINDA
Wise One

> The Lord giveth wisdom: and
> out of his mouth cometh wisdom
> and understanding.
> PROVERBS 2:6

BELLE
Beautiful

> I will praise thee; for I am
> fearfully and wonderfully made:
> marvellous are thy works.
> PSALM 139:14

BELMA
Chosen Protection

> Ye have not chosen me, but I
> have . . . ordained you, that ye
> should go and bring forth fruit.
> JOHN 15:16

BELPA
Beautiful Retreat

> He that dwelleth in the secret
> place of the most High shall
> abide under the . . . Almighty.
> PSALM 91:1

BELTON
Beautiful Town

> He . . . showed me . . . the holy
> Jerusalem, . . . the glory of God
> did lighten it.
> REVELATION 21:10, 23

BELVA
Fair One

> I will praise thee; for I am
> fearfully and wonderfully made:
> marvellous are thy works.
> PSALM 139:14

BELVIA
Fair One

> I will praise thee; for I am
> fearfully and wonderfully made;
> marvellous are thy works.
> PSALM 139:14

BEMERY
Fair in Speech

> Let the words of my mouth, and
> the meditation of my heart, be
> acceptable in thy sight.
> PSALM 19:14

Greek

B

BEN
Son of My Right Hand

> *Withhold not thou thy . . .*
> *mercies from me: let thy*
> *lovingkindness and . . . truth . . .*
> *preserve me.*
> PSALM 40:11

BENAIAH
The Blessed

> *Blessed are they that keep his*
> *testimonies, and that seek him*
> *with the whole heart.*
> PSALM 119:2

Latin

BENEDICT
The Blessed

> *Blessed are they that keep his*
> *testimonies, and that seek him*
> *with the whole heart.*
> PSALM 119:2

BENETA
The Blessed

> *Blessed are they that keep his*
> *testimonies, and that seek him*
> *with the whole heart.*
> PSALM 119:2

BENETH
One of my Strength

> *The Lord is my light and my*
> *salvation; . . . the strength of my*
> *life; of whom shall I be afraid?*
> PSALM 27:1

BENITA
The Blessed

> *Blessed are they that keep his*
> *testimonies, and that seek him*
> *with the whole heart.*
> PSALM 119:2

BENJAMIN
Son of my Right Hand

> *Withhold not thou thy tender*
> *mercies from me . . . Let thy*
> *lovingkindness and your truth*
> *. . . continually preserve me.*
> PSALM 40:11

BENNETT
Blessed by God

> *Blessed are thou that keep his*
> *testimonies, and that seek him*
> *with the whole heart.*
> PSALM 119:2

BENNIE
Beloved Son

> *Herein is love, not that we loved*
> *God, but that he loved us, and*
> *sent his Son.*
> 1 JOHN 4:10

BENNION
Blessed and Beloved One

> *Blessed are they that keep his*
> *testimonies, and that seek him*
> *with the whole heart.*
> PSALM 119:2

BENSER
Blessed

> *Blessed are they that keep his*
> *testimonies, and that seek him*
> *with the whole heart.*
> PSALM 119:2

BENTLEY
From the Peaceful Meadow

> The Lord is my Shepherd; . . .
> He maketh me to lie down in
> green pastures . . . beside the
> still waters.
> PSALM 23:1–2

BENTON
Favorite Son

> The Lord is the portion of mine
> inheritance . . . yea, I have a
> goodly heritage.
> PSALM 16:5, 6

BENWAR
Son, Strong in Battle

> Fight the good fight of faith, lay
> hold on eternal life, whereunto
> thou art also called.
> 1 TIMOTHY 6:12

BERBAGE
Brave and Strong

> The Lord is my rock, . . . my
> fortress, and my deliverer; . . . my
> strength, in whom I will trust.
> PSALM 18:2

BERDELLA
One of Radiant Light

> Let your light so shine . . . that
> they may see your good works,
> and glorify your Father . . . in
> heaven.
> MATTHEW 5:16

BERESFORD
From the Barley Ford

> Thy word is a lamp unto my
> feet, and a light unto my path.
> PSALM 119:105

BERIAH
God's Creature

> For we are his workmanship,
> created in Christ Jesus unto
> good works.
> EPHESIANS 2:10

BERLINDA
One of Great Strength

> The Lord is my rock, . . . my
> fortress, and my deliverer; . . . my
> strength, in whom I will trust.
> PSALM 18:2

BERNADETTE
Woman of God

> It is God that girdeth me with
> strength, and maketh my way
> perfect.
> PSALM 18:32

BERNADINE
Brave and Strong

> The Lord is my rock, . . . my
> fortress, and my deliverer; . . . my
> strength, in whom I will trust.
> PSALM 18:2

BERNALDA
Bringer of Victory

> Whatsoever is born of God
> overcometh the world: and this
> is the victory . . . even our faith.
> 1 JOHN 5:4

BERNARD
Brave and Strong

> The Lord is my rock, . . . my
> fortress, and my deliverer; . . . my
> strength, in whom I will trust.
> PSALM 18:2

BERNHARD
Brave and Strong

> The Lord is my rock, . . . my
> fortress, and my deliverer; . . .
> my strength, in whom I will
> trust.
> PSALM 18:2

BERNIE
Brave and Strong

> The Lord is my rock, . . . my
> fortress, and my deliverer; . . . my
> strength, in whom I will trust.
> PSALM 18:2

BERNIECE
Bringer of Victory

> Whatsoever is born of God
> overcometh the world: and this
> is the victory . . . even our faith.
> 1 JOHN 5:4

BERSABE
Victory and Courage

> Be strong and of a good courage;
> . . . the Lord thy God is with thee.
> JOSHUA 1:9

BERT
One of Brightness

> They that be wise shall shine as
> the brightness of the firmament;
> . . . as the stars for ever and ever.
> DANIEL 12:3

BERTHA
Bright One

> Light is sown for the righteous,
> and gladness for the upright in
> heart.
> PSALM 97:11

BERTOLI
Ruling in Splendor

> Thy right hand hath holden me
> up, and thy gentleness hath
> made me great.
> PSALM 18:35

BERTRAM
Of Bright Fame

> Now thanks be unto God, which
> always causeth us to triumph in
> Christ.
> 2 CORINTHIANS 2:14

BERURIA
Chosen by God

> Ye have not chosen me, but I
> have chosen you, and ordained
> you, that ye should go and bring
> forth fruit.
> JOHN 15:16

BERYL
Crystal Clear

> The commandment of the Lord
> is pure, enlightening the eyes.
> PSALM 19:8

BERYLE
Crystal Pure

> The commandment of the Lord
> is pure, enlightening the eyes.
> PSALM 19:8

BESS
Devoted One

> I delight to do thy will, O my
> God: . . . thy law is within my
> heart.
> PSALM 40:8

BETH
Devoted One

> *I delight to do thy will, O my God: . . . thy law is within my heart.*
> PSALM 40:8

BETHANY
Abiding Place of God

> *I have set the Lord . . . before me: . . . he is at my right hand, I shall not be moved.*
> PSALM 16:8

BETHEL
House of God

> *Goodness and mercy shall follow me . . . and I will dwell in the house of the Lord forever.*
> PSALM 23:6

BETSY
Consecrated to God

> *Give me understanding, . . . I shall keep thy law; I shall observe it with my whole heart.*
> PSALM 119:34

BETTIE
Devoted One

> *I delight to do thy will, O my God: yea, thy law is within my heart.*
> PSALM 40:8

BETTY
Devoted One

> *I delight to do thy will, O my God: . . . thy law is within my heart.*
> PSALM 40:8

BETTYJANE
Consecrated Gift of God

> *Every good gift and every perfect gift is from above, and cometh down from the Father.*
> JAMES 1:17

BEULAH
Bethrothed

> *Who can find a virtuous woman? . . . for her price is far above rubies. . . . a woman that feareth the Lord, she shall be praised.*
> PROVERBS 31:10, 30

BEVERLEY
Industrious One

> *Whatsoever ye do, do it heartily, as to the Lord, . . . for ye serve the Lord Christ.*
> COLOSSIANS 3:23–24

BEVERLY
Industrious One

> *Whatsoever ye do, do it heartily, as to the Lord, . . . for ye serve the Lord Christ.*
> COLOSSIANS 3:23–24

BEZA
In the Protection of God

> *He that dwelleth in the secret place of the most High shall abide under . . . the Almighty.*
> PSALM 91:1

B

BHADURI
Constant of Purpose

> *I have set the Lord . . . before*
> *me: . . . I shall not be moved.*
> PSALM 16:8
>
> Pakistan

BHEKI
Humble Believer

> *But he giveth more grace. . . .*
> *God . . . giveth grace unto the*
> *humble.*
> JAMES 4:6
>
> Hebrew

BHUPENDRA
Famous Commander

> *Thy right hand hath holden me*
> *up, and thy gentleness hath*
> *made me great.*
> PSALM 18:35

BHUVANESHWARI
Famous Counselor

> *Thou hast . . . given me the*
> *shield of thy salvation: . . . thy*
> *gentleness hath made me*
> *great.*
> PSALM 18:35
>
> Hindu

BIA
Shining and Blessed One

> *Blessed are they that keep his*
> *testimonies, and that seek him*
> *with the whole heart.*
> PSALM 119:2

BIANCA
Very Fair

> *Rejoice in the Lord, O ye*
> *righteous: for praise is comely*
> *for the upright.*
> PSALM 33:1

BIFF
Of Brotherly Love

> *Beloved, let us love one another:*
> *for love is of God; . . . every one*
> *that loveth is born of God, and*
> *knoweth God.*
> 1 JOHN 4:7

BILL
Bold Protector

> *Be strong in the Lord, and in the*
> *power of his might. Put on the*
> *whole armour of God.*
> EPHESIANS 6:10–11

BILLIE
Great Protector

> *The Lord is my light and my*
> *salvation; . . . the strength of my*
> *life; of whom shall I be afraid?*
> PSALM 27:1

BINA
The Blessed

> *Blessed are they that keep his*
> *testimonies, and that seek him*
> *with the whole heart.*
> PSALM 119:2

BINITHA
The Blessed

> *Blessed are they that keep his*
> *testimonies, and that seek him*
> *with the whole heart.*
> PSALM 119:2

BINTANG
Wise One

> The Lord giveth wisdom: out of
> his mouth cometh knowledge
> and understanding.
> PROVERBS 2:6

> > Hebrew

BINYON
Wisdom and Understanding

> My mouth shall speak of
> wisdom; . . . the meditation of
> my heart shall be of
> understanding.
> PSALM 49:3

BIONKA
One of Life

> The Lord is my light and my
> salvation; . . . the strength of my
> life; of whom shall I be afraid?
> PSALM 27:1

BIRDIE
Peaceful One

> Great peace have they which
> love thy law: . . . all my ways
> are before thee.
> PSALM 119:165, 168

BISHOP
A Bishop

> If a man desire the office of a
> bishop, he desireth a good work.
> 1 TIMOTHY 3:1

BITHIAH
Worshiper of Jehovah

> The Lord is great, and greatly to
> be praised: . . . Honour and
> majesty are before him.
> PSALM 96:4, 6

BJORN
The One of Courage

> Be strong and of a good
> courage; . . . the Lord thy God is
> with thee whithersoever thou
> goest.
> JOSHUA 1:9

> > Teutonic

BLAIR
Child of the Fields

> I love the Lord, because he hath
> heard my voice . . . I will walk
> before the Lord in the land of
> the living.
> PSALM 116:1, 9

BLAKE
To Make White and Pure

> Purge me with hyssop, and I
> shall be clean: wash me, and I
> shall be whiter than snow.
> PSALM 51:7

BLAKELEY
Pure and Compassionate

> Thy hands have made me and
> fashioned me: give me
> understanding that I may learn
> thy commandments.
> PSALM 119:73

BLANCA
Radiant One

> Let your light so shine . . . that
> they may see your good works,
> and glorify your Father which is
> in heaven.
> MATTHEW 5:16

BLANCHARD
One of Radiant Light

> *Let your light so shine . . . that*
> *they may see your good works,*
> *and glorify your Father which is*
> *in heaven.*
> MATTHEW 5:16

BLESSED
The Blessed

> *Blessed are they that keep his*
> *testimonies, and that seek him*
> *with the whole heart.*
> PSALM 119:2

BLESSING
A Blessing

> *The blessing of the Lord, it*
> *maketh rich, and he addeth no*
> *sorrow with it.*
> PROVERBS 10:22

BLEWITTE
Faithful

> *I have set the Lord . . . before*
> *me: . . . he is at my right hand, I*
> *shall not be moved.*
> PSALM 16:8

BLISS
Perfect Joy

> *In thy presence is fulness of joy;*
> *at thy right hand there are*
> *pleasures for evermore.*
> PSALM 16:11

BLONDIE
Fair One

> *I will praise thee; for I am*
> *fearfully and wonderfully made;*
> *marvellous are thy works.*
> PSALM 139:14

BLOSSOM
Refreshing Perfect Flower

> *I will praise thee; for I am*
> *fearfully and wonderfully made;*
> *marvellous are thy works.*
> PSALM 139:14

BLYTHE
One of Joy

> *In thy presence is fulness of joy;*
> *at thy right hand there are*
> *pleasures for evermore.*
> PSALM 16:11

BO
Precious

> *I will praise thee; for I am*
> *fearfully and wonderfully made:*
> *marvellous are thy works.*
> PSALM 139:14

BOAZ
In Him There Is Strength

> *The Lord is my light and my*
> *salvation; . . . the strength of my*
> *life; of whom shall I be afraid?*
> PSALM 27:1

BOB
Illustrious One

> *The God of peace . . . make you*
> *perfect in every good work to do*
> *his will, working in that which*
> *is well pleasing in his sight.*
> HEBREWS 13:20–21

BOBBY
Illustrious One

> *The God of peace . . . make you*
> *perfect in every good work to do*
> *his will, working in that which*
> *is well pleasing in his sight.*
> HEBREWS 13:20–21

BODIE
One of Consecration

> Let the words of my mouth, and
> the meditation of my heart, be
> acceptable in thy sight.
> PSALM 19:14

BOGART
Strong as a Bow

> In God is my salvation and . . .
> glory: the rock of my strength,
> . . . my refuge, is in God.
> PSALM 62:7

BOGUSLAW
Glory and Victory

> Whatsoever is born of God
> overcometh the world: and this
> is the victory, . . . even our faith.
> 1 JOHN 5:4
>
> Slavic

BONANZA
Prosperous Find

> Seek ye first the kingdom of
> God, and his righteousness; and
> all these things shall be added
> unto you.
> MATTHEW 6:33

BONAVENTURE
Adventurous Builder

> For other foundation can no
> man lay than that is laid, which
> is Jesus Christ.
> 1 CORINTHIANS 3:11
>
> Latin

BOND
A Strong Alliance

> Let all those who seek thee
> rejoice and be glad in thee: . . .
> such as love thy salvation say
> . . . The Lord be magnified.
> PSALM 40:16

BONITA
Pretty

> Deck thyself now with majesty
> . . . and excellency . . . array
> thyself with glory and beauty.
> JOB 40:10

BONNIE
The Good and Blessed

> Blessed are they that keep his
> testimonies, and that seek him
> with the whole heart.
> PSALM 119:2

BOOKER
Literary One

> I will instruct thee and teach thee
> in the way which thou shalt go: I
> will guide thee with mine eye.
> PSALM 32:8

BORIS
Warrior for the Faith

> Fight the good fight of faith, lay
> hold on eternal life, . . .
> whereunto thou art also called.
> 1 TIMOTHY 6:12

BOSWORTH
Rich Heritage

> I have set the Lord . . . before
> me: . . . he is at my right hand, I
> shall not be moved.
> PSALM 16:8

BOWMAN
Warrior Archer

> *Fight the good fight of faith, lay hold on eternal life, whereunto thou art also called.*
> 1 TIMOTHY 6:12

BRACKAN
Abundant Life

> *I am come that they might have life, and . . . have it more abundantly.*
> JOHN 10:10

BRAD
Abundant Provider

> *The Lord is my shepherd; I shall not want.*
> PSALM 23:1

BRADLEY
Abundant Provider

> *The Lord is my shepherd; I shall not want.*
> PSALM 23:1

BRANDI
One of Authority

> *When the righteous are in authority, the people rejoice.*
> PROVERBS 29:2

BRANDIE
One of Authority

> *When the righteous are in authority, the people rejoice.*
> PROVERBS 29:2

BRANDON
One of Authority

> *When the righteous are in authority, the people rejoice.*
> PROVERBS 29:2

BRANDY
One of Authority

> *When the righteous are in authority, the people rejoice.*
> PROVERBS 29:2

BRANFORD
Raven on the Meadow

> *Consider the ravens: for they neither sow nor reap; . . . God feedeth them.*
> LUKE 12:24

BRANITA
Sword of the Spirit

> *Take unto you the whole armour of God, . . . the helmet of salvation, and the sword of the Spirit.*
> EPHESIANS 6:13, 17

BRANNAN
A Flaming Sword

> *Take unto you the whole armour of God, . . . the helmet of salvation, and the sword of the Spirit.*
> EPHESIANS 6:13, 17

BRANNON
A Flaming Sword

> *Take unto you the whole armour of God, . . . the helmet of salvation, and the sword of the Spirit.*
> EPHESIANS 6:13, 17

BRANTLEY
Shining and Peaceful

> Thy word is a lamp unto my
> feet, and a light unto my path.
> PSALM 119:105

BRATTON
Strong in Spirit

> Thou art my rock and my
> fortress; . . . for thy name's sake
> lead me, and guide me.
> PSALM 31:3

BREEZIE
Strong Spirit

> I press toward the mark for the
> prize of the high calling of God
> in Christ Jesus.
> PHILIPPIANS 3:14

BRENDA
Sword of the Spirit

> Take unto you the whole armour
> of God, . . . the helmet of
> salvation, and . . . sword of the
> spirit.
> EPHESIANS 6:13, 17

BRENDAN
Strong in Victory

> Thanks be unto God, which
> always causeth us to triumph in
> Christ.
> 2 CORINTHIANS 2:14

BRENNA
One of Power and Strength

> God is my salvation and my
> glory: the rock of my strength,
> . . . my refuge, is in God.
> PSALM 62:7

BRENT
Upright

> He layeth up sound wisdom for
> the righteous: he is a buckler to
> them that walk uprightly.
> PROVERBS 2:7

BRENTLEY
Upright

> He layeth up sound wisdom for
> the righteous: he is a buckler to
> them that walk uprightly.
> PROVERBS 2:7

BRET
Strength

> A wise man is strong; yea, a
> man of knowledge increaseth
> strength.
> PROVERBS 24:5

BRETAGNE
One of Strength

> I will love thee, O Lord,
> my strength. . . . my rock, . . .
> my fortress, . . . my deliverer;
> . . . in whom I will trust.
> PSALM 18:1–2

BRETT
One of Strength

> The Lord is my rock, . . . my
> fortress, and my deliverer; . . .
> my strength, in whom I will
> trust.
> PSALM 18:2

B

BREWSTER
A Brewer

> *Whatsoever ye do, do it heartily,
> as to the Lord, . . . for ye serve
> the Lord Christ.*
> COLOSSIANS 3:23–24

BRIAN
One of Strength

> *The Lord stood with me, and
> strengthened me; . . . the Lord
> shall deliver me . . . and will
> preserve me.*
> 2 TIMOTHY 4:17–18

BRIANNA
Strength and Courage

> *Wait on the Lord: be of good
> courage, and he shall strengthen
> thine heart.*
> PSALM 27:14

BRIANNE
Strong in the Lord

> *The Lord is my rock, . . . my
> fortress, and my deliverer; . . .
> my strength, in whom I will
> trust.*
> PSALM 18:2

BRIAR
Of God's Strength

> *Thy right hand hath holden me
> up, and thy gentleness hath
> made me great.*
> PSALM 18:35

BRIC
One Who Excels

> *I press toward the mark for the
> prize of the high calling of God
> in Christ Jesus.*
> PHILIPPIANS 3:14

BRICE
One Who Excels

> *I press toward the mark for the
> prize of the high calling of God
> in Christ Jesus.*
> PHILIPPIANS 3:14

BRIDGER
Builder of Bridges

> *According to the grace of God
> which is given unto me, as a
> wise masterbuilder, I have laid
> the foundation.*
> 1 CORINTHIANS 3:10

BRIDGETTE
Lady of Strength

> *Trust ye in the Lord for ever: for
> in the Lord JEHOVAH is
> everlasting strength.*
> ISAIAH 26:4

BRIDGITTE
Lady of Strength

> *Trust ye in the Lord for ever; for
> in the Lord JEHOVAH is
> everlasting strength.*
> ISAIAH 26:4

BRIGETTE
Lady of Strength

> *Trust ye in the Lord for ever: for
> in the Lord JEHOVAH is
> everlasting strength.*
> ISAIAH 26:4

BRITAIN
The Strong One

> *In God is my salvation and . . . glory: the rock of my strength, . . . my refuge, is in God.*
> PSALM 62:7

BRITTANY
The Strong

> *Finally, my brethren, be strong in the Lord, and in the power of his might.*
> EPHESIANS 6:10

BRITTNEY
Strength

> *Strength and honour are her clothing; and she shall rejoice in time to come.*
> PROVERBS 31:25

BROADUS
Rich in Fame

> *Whatsoever ye do . . . do all in the name of the Lord Jesus, . . . for ye serve the Lord Christ.*
> COLOSSIANS 3:17, 24

BROC
Strong Champion

> *They shall fight against thee, but . . . shall not prevail . . . for I am with thee to save thee and to deliver thee, saith the Lord.*
> JEREMIAH 15:20

BROCK
Strong Champion

> *They shall fight against thee, but . . . shall not prevail . . . for I am with thee to save thee and to deliver thee, saith the Lord.*
> JEREMIAH 15:20

BRODERICK
Rich in Fame

> *Wait on the Lord, and keep his way, and he shall exalt thee to inherit the land.*
> PSALM 37:34

BRONISLAVA
Weapon of Glory

> *Fight the good fight of faith, lay hold on eternal life, whereunto thou art also called.*
> 1 TIMOTHY 6:12

Slavic

BRONSON
Strong Follower

> *We are his workmanship, created in Christ Jesus unto good works, which God hath . . . ordained that we should walk in them.*
> EPHESIANS 2:10

BROOKE
Peaceful Dweller

> *The Lord will give strength unto his people; the Lord will bless his people with peace.*
> PSALM 29:11

B

BROOKLYN
From the Peaceful Brook

> The Lord is my shepherd; . . . he
> maketh me to lie down in green
> pastures . . . beside the still
> waters.
> PSALM 23:1–2

BROSHA
Crowned with Victory

> Whatsoever is born of God
> overcometh the world: . . . even
> our faith.
> 1 JOHN 5:4

BROSISLAUS
Glory and Honor

> I will praise thee, . . . with all
> my heart: and I will glorify thy
> name for evermore.
> PSALM 86:12

BROXTON
Of Determined Purpose

> I press toward the mark for the
> prize of the high calling of God
> in Christ Jesus.
> PHILIPPIANS 3:14

BRUCE
Safe and Secure

> Thou shalt be secure, because
> there is hope; . . . and thou shalt
> take thy rest in safety.
> JOB 11:18

BRUCHILLICA
Safe and Secure

> I have set the Lord always
> before me. . . . I shall not be
> moved.
> PSALM 16:8

Teutonic

BRUNETTA
Little Brunette

> I will praise thee; for I am
> fearfully and wonderfully
> made; marvellous are thy
> works.
> PSALM 139:14

BRUNETTE
Little Brunette

> I will praise thee; for I am
> fearfully and wonderfully
> made; marvellous are thy
> works.
> PSALM 139:14

BRUNO
Firm of Purpose

> I will bless the Lord, who hath
> given me counsel: . . . I have set
> the Lord always before me.
> PSALM 16:7, 8

BRYAN
One of Strength

> The Lord stood with me, and
> strengthened me; . . . and will
> preserve me unto his heavenly
> kingdom.
> 2 TIMOTHY 4:17–18

BRYANT
Strong in Spirit

Thou art my rock and my fortress; therefore for thy name's sake lead me, and guide me.
PSALM 31:3

BRYNGLESON
Victory and Strength

Thanks be to God, which giveth us the victory through our Lord Jesus Christ.
1 CORINTHIANS 15:57

BUBBA
Brother

There is a friend that sticketh closer than a brother.
PROVERBS 18:24

BUBBLES
Cherished and Beloved

Beloved, let us love one another: for love is of God; . . . every one that loveth is born of God.
1 JOHN 4:7

BUCK
Strong and Courageous

I can do all things through Christ which strengtheneth me.
PHILIPPIANS 4:13

BUCKY
Strong and Courageous

I can do all things through Christ which strengtheneth me.
PHILIPPIANS 4:13

BUD
Victorious One

But thanks be to God, which giveth us the victory through our Lord Jesus Christ.
1 CORINTHIANS 15:57

BUELL
One of Praise

Praise the Lord, call upon his name, . . . make mention that his name is exalted.
ISAIAH 12:4

BUFFIE
One of Hope

My mouth shall show forth thy righteousness and . . . I will go in the strength of the Lord God.
PSALM 71:15–16

BUFORD
Peaceful Dweller

The Lord is my Shepherd; . . . He maketh me to lie down in green pastures: he leadeth me beside the still waters.
PSALM 23:1–2

BUNNY
Forerunner of Victory

Whatsoever is born of God overcometh the world: and this is the victory . . . even our faith.
1 JOHN 5:4

BUNSAVAGE
Foundation

Fight the good fight of faith, lay hold on eternal life, . . . thou art also called.
1 TIMOTHY 6:12

BURCHARD
Firm of Purpose
> *I have set the Lord always before me: . . . I shall not be moved.*
> PSALM 16:8

BUSTER
Steadfast
> *He only is my rock and my salvation: he is my defence; I shall not be moved.*
> PSALM 62:6

BUTLER
Servant of the Lord
> *I will meditate in thy precepts, . . . I will delight myself in thy statutes: I will not forget thy word.*
> PSALM 119:15–16

BUTTERSCOTCH
Sweetness
> *How sweet are thy words unto my taste! yea, sweeter than honey to my mouth.*
> PSALM 119:103

BWANA
God Is Gracious
> *But thou . . . art a God full of compassion, . . . gracious, . . . longsuffering, . . . mercy and truth.*
> PSALM 86:15
> Swahili

BYRON
Full of Strength
> *Because of his strength will I wait upon thee: for God is my defence.*
> PSALM 59:9

BYTHIA
One of Light
> *Let your light so shine . . . that they may see your good works, and glorify your Father.*
> MATTHEW 5:16

BYUNG-OCK
Protected One
> *He that dwelleth in the secret place of the most High shall abide under the . . . Almighty.*
> PSALM 91:1
> Vietnamese

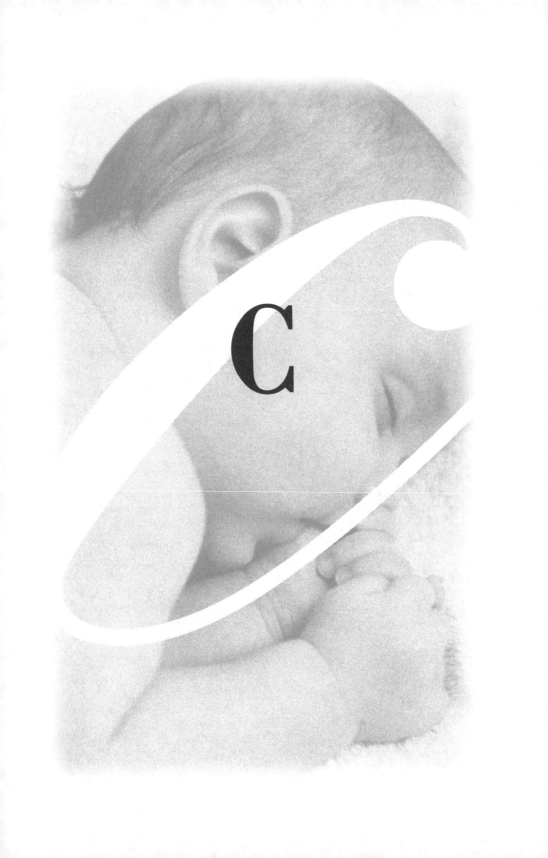

CABLE
Warrior for the Faith

> *Fight the good fight of faith, lay hold on eternal life.*
> 1 TIMOTHY 6:12

CABOT
Peaceful Dweller

> *The Lord will give strength unto his people; the Lord will bless his people with peace.*
> PSALM 29:11

CABRINI
One of Purity and Strength

> *Every word of God is pure: he is a shield unto them that put their trust in him.*
> PROVERBS 30:5

CADE
Strong Defense

> *He only is my rock and my salvation; he is my defence; I shall not be moved.*
> PSALM 62:2

CADEN
One of Joy

> *In thy presence is fulness of joy; at thy right hand are pleasures for evermore.*
> PSALM 16:11

CADMUS
One who Adorns

> *I have chosen you, and ordained you, that ye should go and bring forth fruit.*
> JOHN 15:16

CADOW
Strong in Battle

> *Fight the good fight of faith, lay hold on eternal life, whereunto thou art also called.*
> 1 TIMOTHY 6:12

CAELAN
Pure Heart

> *Blessed are the pure in heart: for they shall see God.*
> MATTHEW 5:8

CAESAR
Kingly Authority

> *Mercy and truth preserve the king: and his throne is upholden by mercy.*
> PROVERBS 20:28

CAILAN
Ardent Spirit

> *I can do all things through Christ which strengtheneth me.*
> PHILIPPIANS 4:13

CAIO
Rejoicing

> *I will praise thee, O Lord, with my whole heart; . . . I will sing praise to thy name.*
> PSALM 9:1–2

CAIRINE
Pure Heart

> *Blessed are the pure in heart: for they shall see God.*
> MATTHEW 5:8

C

CAITLEN
The Pure

> Blessed are the pure in heart:
> for they shall see God.
> MATTHEW 5:8

CAITLIN
Pure One

> The statutes of the Lord are
> right, . . . the commandment of
> the Lord is pure.
> PSALM 19:8

CALANDRA
A Lark

> Thy hands have made me and
> fashioned me: give me
> understanding.
> PSALM 119:73

CALDEIRA
Beautiful Gift

> Every good gift and . . . perfect
> gift is from above, and cometh
> down from the Father.
> JAMES 1:17

CALDER
Rock of Strength

> In God is my salvation and . . .
> glory: . . . my strength, and my
> refuge, is in God.
> PSALM 62:7

CALEB
Faithfulness

> I have set the Lord . . . before
> me: . . . he is at my right hand, I
> shall not be moved.
> PSALM 16:8

CALEIGH
Ardent Love

> Beloved, let us love one another:
> for love is of God; . . . every one
> that loveth . . . knoweth God.
> 1 JOHN 4:7

CALHOUN
Warrior for the Faith

> Fight the good fight of faith, lay
> hold on eternal life, whereunto
> thou art also called.
> 1 TIMOTHY 6:12

CALISTE
The Most Beautiful

> I will praise thee; for I am
> fearfully and wonderfully
> made: marvellous are thy
> works.
> PSALM 139:14

CALLEEN
Mighty in Battle

> I will say of the Lord, He is my
> refuge and my fortress: my God;
> in him will I trust.
> PSALM 91:2

CALLIE
Most Beautiful

> For the Lord taketh pleasure in
> his people: he will beautify the
> meek with salvation.
> PSALM 149:4

CALVERT
One Who Leads

> Thou art my rock and my
> fortress; . . . for thy name's sake
> lead me, and guide me.
> PSALM 31:3

CAMALIA
Noble Messenger of Truth

> How beautiful are the feet of
> them that preach the gospel of
> peace.
> ROMANS 10:15

CAMBRAY
One of Honor

> The Lord is great, and greatly to
> be praised: . . . Honour and
> majesty are before him.
> PSALM 96:4, 6

CAMERON
One of Prominence

> I will praise the Lord according
> to his righteousness: and . . .
> sing praise to the . . . Lord.
> PSALM 7:17

CAMILLE
Noble Messenger of Truth

> How beautiful are the feet of
> them that preach the gospel of
> peace.
> ROMANS 10:15

CAMMY
Self-Sacrificing

> I press toward the mark for the
> prize of the high calling of God
> in Christ Jesus.
> PHILIPPIANS 3:14

CAMP
Peaceful Dweller

> The Lord is my Shepherd; . . .
> He maketh me to lie down in
> green pastures: he leadeth me
> beside the still waters.
> PSALM 23:1–2

CANAAN
From the Lowlands

> Thy word is a lamp unto my
> feet, and a light unto my path.
> PSALM 119:105

CANDACE
Glowing Queen

> Strength and honour are her
> clothing; and she shall rejoice in
> time to come.
> PROVERBS 31:25

CANDLE
Provider of Light

> Let your light so shine . . . that
> they may see your good works,
> and glorify your Father which
> is in heaven.
> MATTHEW 5:16

CANDLER
Provider of Light

> Let your light so shine . . . that
> they may see your good works,
> and glorify your Father which
> is in heaven.
> MATTHEW 5:16

CANDY
Woman of Honor

> Strength and honour are her
> clothing; and she shall rejoice in
> time to come.
> PROVERBS 31:25

C

CANYON
Narrow Valley

> The Lord is my shepherd; . . . He
> maketh me to lie down in green
> pastures: he leadeth me beside
> still waters.
> PSALM 23:1–2

CAPEZZUTO
Prosperous One

> I will sing unto the Lord,
> because he hath dealt
> bountifully with me.
> PSALM 13:6
>   Teutonic, English Gypsy

CAPITOLA
One of Authority

> As for God, his way is perfect,
> . . . God is my strength and
> power: and he maketh my way
> perfect.
> 2 SAMUEL 22:31, 33

CARA
Friend

> Ye are my friends, if ye do
> whatsoever I command you.
> JOHN 15:14

CARA-LEIGH
Dear Friend

> Ye are my friends, if ye do
> whatsoever I command you.
> JOHN 15:14

CAREY
Beloved

> Beloved, let us love one another:
> for love is of God.
> 1 JOHN 4:7

CARIE
A Woman of the Lord

> I will bless the Lord at all times:
> his praise shall continually be
> in my mouth.
> PSALM 34:1

CARL
Strong and Manly

> I take pleasure . . . in
> persecutions, in distresses for
> Christ's sake: for when I am
> weak, then am I strong.
> 2 CORINTHIANS 12:10

CARLA
Woman of the Lord

> Thou art my rock and . . .
> fortress; . . . for thy name's sake
> lead me, and guide me.
> PSALM 31:3

CARLENE
A Woman of God

> Be not dismayed; for I am thy
> God: I will strengthen thee; . . .
> [and] uphold thee.
> ISAIAH 41:10

CARLISLE
One of Strength

> In God is my salvation and my
> glory: the rock of my strength,
> . . . my refuge, is in God.
> PSALM 62:7

CARLOS
Man of God

> Be strong in the Lord, and in the
> power of his might.
> EPHESIANS 6:10

CARMELA
Fruitful Vineyard

> *Herein is my Father glorified, that ye bear much fruit; so shall ye be my disciples.*
> JOHN 15:8

CARMELLIA
God's Vineyard

> *I have chosen you, and ordained you, that ye should go and bring forth fruit.*
> JOHN 15:16

CARMEN
Song of Praise

> *Sing unto the Lord, bless his name; show forth his salvation, from day to day.*
> PSALM 96:2

CARMENE
Song of Praise

> *Sing unto the Lord, bless his name; show forth his salvation from day to day.*
> PSALM 96:2

CAROL
A Woman of the Lord

> *Thou art my rock and . . . fortress; . . . for thy name's sake lead me, and guide me.*
> PSALM 31:3

CAROLENA
A Woman of the Lord

> *Thou art my rock and . . . fortress; . . . for thy name's sake lead me, and guide me.*
> PSALM 31:3

CAROLINA
A Woman of the Lord

> *Thou art my rock and . . . fortress; . . . for thy name's sake lead me, and guide me.*
> PSALM 31:3

CAROLINE
A Woman of the Lord

> *Thou art my rock and . . . fortress; . . . for thy name's sake lead me, and guide me.*
> PSALM 31:3

CAROLYN
A Woman of the Lord

> *Thou art my rock and . . . fortress; . . . for thy name's sake lead me, and guide me.*
> PSALM 31:3

CARPENTER
Master Builder

> *As a wise masterbuilder, I have laid the foundation, and another buildeth thereon.*
> 1 CORINTHIANS 3:10

CARRIE *also* CARIE
A Woman of the Lord

> *Thou art my rock and . . . fortress; . . . for thy name's sake lead me, and guide me.*
> PSALM 31:3

CARRIGAN
From the Fortress

> *The Lord is my rock, . . . my fortress, and my deliverer; . . . my strength, in whom I will trust.*
> PSALM 18:2

74

CARRIN
also KAREN
Pure Heart

> Blessed are the pure in heart:
> for they shall see God.
> MATTHEW 5:8

CARRINGTON
Guardian Protector

> He that dwelleth in the secret
> place of the most High shall
> abide under the . . . Almighty.
> PSALM 91:1

CARSTELLA
Strong and Radiant

> They that be wise shall shine as
> the brightness of the firmament.
> DANIEL 12:3

CARTER
A Peaceful Guide

> Thou wilt keep him in perfect
> peace, whose mind is stayed on
> thee.
> ISAIAH 26:3

CARTWRIGHT
Creative Builder

> According to the grace of God
> . . . as a wise masterbuilder, I
> have laid the foundation and
> another buildeth thereon.
> 1 CORINTHIANS 3:10

CARVEL
Spear Ruler of Strength

> Take unto you the whole armour
> of God, . . . the sword of the
> Spirit, which is the word of God.
> EPHESIANS 6:13, 17
>
> Old French

CARVER
Skilled Wood Sculptor

> Whatsoever ye do, do it heartily,
> as to the Lord, . . . for ye serve
> the Lord Christ.
> COLOSSIANS 3:23–24

CARY
One of the Lord

> For thou art my rock and . . .
> fortress; . . . for thy name's sake
> lead me, and guide me.
> PSALM 31:3

CASEY
Mighty One of Valor

> Be strong and of a good
> courage; . . . the Lord thy God is
> with thee whithersoever thou
> goest.
> JOSHUA 1:9

CASMIR
Command for Peace

> The Lord will give strength unto
> his people; the Lord will bless
> his people with peace.
> PSALM 29:11
>
> Slavic

CASSIE
One of Truth

> Thou art near, O Lord; . . . all
> thy commandments are truth.
> PSALM 119:151

CATHARINE *also* KATHERINE
Pure One

> Blessed are the pure in heart:
> for they shall see God.
> MATTHEW 5:8

CATHERINE *also* KATHERINE
Pure One

> *Blessed are the pure in heart:*
> *for they shall see God.*
> MATTHEW 5:8

CATHY *also* KATHY
Pure One

> *Blessed are the pure in heart:*
> *for they shall see God.*
> MATTHEW 5:8

CAVIN
Gentle and Kind

> *Be ye kind one to another,*
> *tenderhearted, forgiving one*
> *another.*
> EPHESIANS 4:32

CECILA
Unseen Faith

> *Faith is the substance of things*
> *hoped for, the evidence of things*
> *not seen.*
> HEBREWS 11:1

CECILIA
Unseen Faith

> *Faith is the substance of things*
> *hoped for, the evidence of things*
> *not seen.*
> HEBREWS 11:1

CEDRIC
Battle Chief

> *Fight the good fight of faith, lay*
> *hold on eternal life, whereunto*
> *thou art also called.*
> 1 TIMOTHY 6:12

CELESTE
Heavenly

> *He hath made his wonderful*
> *works to be remembered: the*
> *Lord is gracious and full of*
> *compassion.*
> PSALM 111:4

CELESTIAL
The Heavenly

> *The works of the Lord are great,*
> *. . . honourable and glorious: . . .*
> *wonderful works to be*
> *remembered.*
> PSALM 111:2, 3, 4

CEONIA
One of Knowledge

> *My mouth shall speak of*
> *wisdom; and the meditation of*
> *my heart shall be of*
> *understanding.*
> PSALM 49:3

CEPHUS
Strong as a Rock

> *God is my salvation and my*
> *glory: the rock of my strength,*
> *. . . my refuge, is in God.*
> PSALM 62:7

CERENA
Serene and Peaceful

> *I have set the Lord . . . before*
> *me: . . . he is at my right hand, I*
> *shall not be moved.*
> PSALM 16:8

CESARE
Kingly Royalty

I have chosen you, and ordained you, that ye should go and bring forth fruit.
JOHN 15:16

CEYLON
Lion Courage and Strength

God is my salvation and my glory: the rock of my strength, . . . my refuge, is in God.
PSALM 62:7

CHAD
God's Warrior

Fight the good fight of faith, lay hold on eternal life, whereunto thou art also called.
1 TIMOTHY 6:12

CHADALIN
God's Warrior

Fight the good fight of faith, lay hold on eternal life, whereunto thou art also called.
1 TIMOTHY 6:12

CHAFRENA
Shining Example

Study to show thyself approved unto God, . . . rightly dividing the word of truth.
2 TIMOTHY 2:15

CHALANDA
Woman of the Lord

Strength and honour are her clothing; and she shall rejoice in time to come.
PROVERBS 31:25

CHALICE
From the Royal Household

I was glad when they said unto me, Let us go into the house of the Lord.
PSALM 122:1

CHALLEY
Strong and of Noble Spirit

Whatsoever ye do, do it heartily, as to the Lord, . . . for ye serve the Lord Christ.
COLOSSIANS 3:23–24

CHAMBRAI
Of a Noble Family

Ye are a chosen generation, . . . an holy nation, . . . that ye should show forth the praises of him.
1 PETER 2:9

English

CHAMICA
Rock of Strength

God is my salvation and my glory: the rock of my strength, . . . my refuge, is in God.
PSALM 62:7

Eskimo

CHAN KEI
Establishing a Foundation

For other foundation can no man lay than that is laid, which is Jesus Christ.
1 CORINTHIANS 3:11

Chinese

CHANC
Authority and Understanding

> My mouth shall speak of wisdom,
> . . . the meditation of my heart
> shall be of understanding.
> PSALM 49:3

CHANCE
Precious

> I will praise thee; for I am
> fearfully and wonderfully made:
> marvellous are thy works.
> PSALM 139:14

CHANCEY
Learned One of Authority

> The Lord giveth wisdom: out of
> his mouth cometh knowledge
> and understanding.
> PROVERBS 2:6

CHANCIE
A Wise Scholar

> For the Lord giveth wisdom: out
> of his mouth cometh knowledge
> and understanding.
> PROVERBS 2:6

CHANDONETTE
Illustrious and Radiant

> Let your light so shine before
> men, . . . and glorify your Father
> which is in heaven.
> MATTHEW 5:16

Hindu

CHANDRA
The Illustrious One

> Whatsoever ye do, do it heartily,
> as to the Lord, . . . for ye serve
> the Lord Christ.
> COLOSSIANS 3:23–24

CHANG-HO
Constantly Good

> The steps of a good man are
> ordered by the Lord: . . . he
> delighteth in his way.
> PSALM 37:23

Chinese

CHANNING
One of Knowledge

> The Lord giveth wisdom: out of
> his mouth cometh knowledge
> and understanding.
> PROVERBS 2:6

CHANOOK
Learned One

> My mouth shall speak of
> wisdom; . . . the meditation of
> my heart shall be of
> understanding.
> PSALM 49:3

CHANTAE
One of Rejoicing

> In thy presence is fulness of joy;
> at thy right hand . . . are
> pleasures for evermore.
> PSALM 16:11

CHANTELLA
One of Rejoicing

> In thy presence is fulness of joy;
> at thy right hand . . . are
> pleasures for evermore.
> PSALM 16:11

CHANTHY
One of Rejoicing

> *I will praise thee, O Lord, with my whole heart; . . . I will be glad and rejoice in thee: I will sing praise.*
> PSALM 9:1–2

CHAP
Skillful One

> *Whatsoever ye do, do it heartily, as to the Lord, . . . for ye serve the Lord Christ.*
> COLOSSIANS 3:23–24

CHAPMAN
A Tradesman

> *Whatsoever ye do, do it heartily, as to the Lord, . . . for ye serve the Lord Christ.*
> COLOSSIANS 3:23–24

CHARAMAINE
A Song

> *I will praise thee, O Lord, with my whole heart; . . . I will be glad and rejoice [and] sing praise to thy name.*
> PSALM 9:1–2

CHARESE
Grace, Love, Kindness

> *The Lord will give grace and glory: no good thing will he withhold from them that walk uprightly.*
> PSALM 84:11

CHARIANNA
One of Joy and Grace

> *I will praise the Lord according to his righteousness: and will sing praise to the name of the Lord most high.*
> PSALM 7:17

CHARITY
Love

> *Beloved, let us love one another: for love is of God.*
> 1 JOHN 4:7

CHARLA
Belonging to the Lord

> *As ye have therefore received Christ Jesus the Lord, so walk ye in him.*
> COLOSSIANS 2:6

CHARLENE
A Woman of the Lord

> *Thou art my rock and . . . fortress; . . . for thy name's sake lead me, and guide me.*
> PSALM 31:3

CHARLES
Man of God

> *I have put my trust in the Lord God, that I may declare all thy works.*
> PSALM 73:28

CHARLETTE
One of Strength

> *In God is my salvation and my glory: the rock of my strength, and my refuge, is in God.*
> PSALM 62:7

CHARLIE
Strong in the Lord

> *I will say of the Lord, He is my refuge and my fortress: . . . in him will I trust.*
> PSALM 91:2

CHARLOTTE
A Woman of the Lord

> *For thou art my rock and . . . fortress; . . . for thy name's sake lead me, and guide me.*
> PSALM 31:3

CHARLSIE
Woman of God

> *Fear thou not; for I am with thee: be not dismayed; for I am thy God.*
> ISAIAH 41:10

CHARMAINE
A Song

> *I will praise thee, O Lord, with my whole heart; . . . I will be glad and rejoice . . . [and] sing praise to thy name.*
> PSALM 9:1, 2

CHARMICA
Rock of Strength

> *In God is my salvation and my glory: the rock of my strength, and my refuge, is in God.*
> PSALM 62:7

CHASE
A Hunter

> *Sing praises to his name: extol him that rideth upon the heavens by his name.*
> PSALM 68:4

CHASTAIN
One of Purity

> *The commandment of the Lord is pure, enlightening the eyes.*
> PSALM 19:8

CHASTITY
One of Purity

> *Blessed are the pure in heart: for they shall see God.*
> MATTHEW 5:8

CHELSIE
One of Courage

> *The Lord is my light and my salvation; whom shall I fear? The Lord is the strength of my life; of whom shall I be afraid?*
> PSALM 27:1

CHEO
The Famed

> *Wait on the Lord, and keep his way, and he shall exalt thee to inherit the land.*
> PSALM 37:34

CHER
My Sweetheart

> *My . . . beloved and longed for, my joy and crown, . . . stand fast in the Lord, my dearly beloved.*
> PHILIPPIANS 4:1

CHERE
Cherished and Beloved

*Beloved, let us love one another:
for love is of God; and every one
that loveth is born of God, and
knoweth God.*
1 JOHN 4:7

CHERILIN
Cherished and Beloved

*Beloved, let us love one another:
for love is of God; . . . every one
that loveth is born of God, and
knoweth God.*
1 JOHN 4:7

CHEROKEE
Great Warrior

*Fight the good fight of faith, lay
hold on eternal life, whereunto
thou art also called.*
1 TIMOTHY 6:12

CHERYL
A Woman of the Lord

*For thou art my rock and . . .
fortress; . . . for thy name's sake
lead me, and guide me.*
PSALM 31:3

CHESLEY
One of Courage

*The Lord is my light and my
salvation; . . . of whom shall I be
afraid?*
PSALM 27:1

CHESNEE
From Strong Protection

*Be strong and of a good
courage; . . . the Lord thy God is
with thee.*
JOSHUA 1:9

CHEVAL
Fighter for the Faith

*Fight the good fight of faith, lay
hold on eternal life, whereunto
thou art also called.*
1 TIMOTHY 6:12

CHEYLA
Unseen Faith

*Faith is the substance of things
hoped for, the evidence of things
not seen.*
HEBREWS 11:1

CHI
Great Protection

*He that dwelleth in the secret
place of the most High shall
abide under the . . . Almighty.*
PSALM 91:1

Nigerian

CHIA
Jehovah Is Strength

*The Lord is my strength and
song, and is become my
salvation.*
PSALM 118:14

CHIANTE
Song of Joy

*I will praise thee, O Lord, with
my whole heart; I will show
forth all thy marvellous works.*
PSALM 9:1

CHIBUZO
God Comes First

> *I will praise thee: . . . thou hast heard me, and art become my salvation.*
> PSALM 118:21
>
> African

CHIBWE
Stone of Hope

> *God is my salvation and . . . glory: the rock of my strength, and my refuge, is in God.*
> PSALM 62:7
>
> African

CHICKY
Little Girl

> *Thy hands have made me and fashioned me: give me understanding.*
> PSALM 119:73

CHICORY
Learned One

> *For the Lord giveth wisdom: out of his mouth cometh knowledge and understanding.*
> PROVERBS 2:6

CHIDEL
The Defender

> *In God is my salvation and my glory: the rock of my strength, and my refuge, is in God.*
> PSALM 62:7

CHIN
Gift of God

> *By grace are ye saved through faith; and that not of yourselves: it is the gift of God.*
> EPHESIANS 2:8
>
> Korean

CHINA
Royal Dynasty

> *Being justified by his grace, we should be made heirs according to the hope of eternal life.*
> TITUS 3:7

CHING
One of Victory

> *But thanks be to God, which giveth us the victory through our Lord Jesus Christ.*
> 1 CORINTHIANS 15:57

CHING-HOYNG
One of Greatness

> *Thou hast . . . given me the shield of thy salvation: . . . and thy gentleness hath made me great.*
> PSALM 18:35
>
> Chinese

CHIP
Son Who Is Steadfast

> *Be ye stedfast, unmovable, always abounding in the work of the Lord.*
> 1 CORINTHIANS 15:58

C

CHIPPER
Son Who is Steadfast

> *Be ye stedfast, unmovable,*
> *always abounding in the work*
> *of the Lord.*
> 1 CORINTHIANS 15:58

CHIQUIS
Little Precious One

> *I will praise thee; for I am*
> *fearfully and wonderfully*
> *made: marvellous are thy*
> *works.*
> PSALM 139:14
>
> Spanish

CHIQUITEA
Little Girl

> *I will praise thee; for I am*
> *fearfully and wonderfuly made:*
> *marvellous are thy works.*
> PSALM 139:14, 17
>
> Spanish

CHITO
Cherished One

> *The Lord hath appeared of old*
> *unto me, saying, . . . I have loved*
> *thee with an everlasting love.*
> JEREMIAH 31:3

CHLOE
Young in Spirit

> *I will go in the strength of the*
> *Lord God: . . . thou hast taught*
> *me from my youth: and . . . I*
> *declared thy wondrous works.*
> PSALM 71:16, 17

CHLORIS
A Pale Flower

> *I will praise thee; for I am*
> *fearfully and wonderfully*
> *made: marvellous are thy*
> *works.*
> PSALM 139:14

CHRIS
Steadfast for Christ

> *Be ye stedfast, unmovable,*
> *always abounding in the work*
> *of the Lord.*
> 1 CORINTHIANS 15:58

CHRISTA
A Christian

> *Ye are washed, . . . sanctified,*
> *. . . justified in the name of the*
> *Lord Jesus.*
> 1 CORINTHIANS 6:11

CHRISTI
Follower of Christ

> *Ye are washed, . . . sanctified,*
> *. . . justified in the name of the*
> *Lord Jesus.*
> 1 CORINTHIANS 6:11

CHRISTIE
A Christian

> *Ye are washed, . . . sanctified,*
> *. . . justified in the name of the*
> *Lord Jesus.*
> 1 CORINTHIANS 6:11

NAME *That* BABY!

CHRISTIN   *also* KRISTIN
A Christian

> *Ye are washed, . . . sanctified,*
> *. . . justified in the name of the*
> *Lord Jesus.*
> 1 CORINTHIANS 6:11

CHRISTINA   *also* KRISTINA
A Christian

> *Ye are washed, . . . sanctified,*
> *. . . justified in the name of the*
> *Lord Jesus.*
> 1 CORINTHIANS 6:11

CHRISTINE   *also* KRISTINE
A Christian

> *Ye are washed, . . . sanctified,*
> *. . . justified in the name of the*
> *Lord Jesus.*
> 1 CORINTHIANS 6:11

CHRISTINIA
A Christian

> *Ye are washed, . . . sanctified,*
> *. . . justified in the name of the*
> *Lord Jesus.*
> 1 CORINTHIANS 6:11

CHRISTMAS
Yuletide

> *For unto you is born this day in*
> *the city of David a Saviour,*
> *which is Christ the Lord.*
> LUKE 2:11

CHRISTOFER
Follower of Christ

> *Be ye stedfast, unmovable,*
> *always abounding in the work*
> *of the Lord.*
> 1 CORINTHIANS 15:58

CHRISTOFEROS
Steadfast for Christ

> *Be ye stedfast, unmovable,*
> *always abounding in the work*
> *of the Lord.*
> 1 CORINTHIANS 15:58

CHRISTOPHER
Steadfast for Christ

> *Be ye stedfast, unmovable,*
> *always abounding in the work*
> *of the Lord.*
> 1 CORINTHIANS 15:58

CHRISTY
A Christian

> *Ye are washed, . . . sanctified,*
> *. . . justified in the name of the*
> *Lord Jesus.*
> 1 CORINTHIANS 6:11

CHUCK
A Man of God

> *Trust ye in the Lord for ever: for*
> *in the Lord JEHOVAH is*
> *everlasting strength.*
> ISAIAH 26:4

CHUCKY
A Man of God

> *In God is my salvation and . . .*
> *glory: the rock of my strength,*
> *. . . my refuge, is in God.*
> PSALM 62:7

CHULITA
Strong in the Lord

> The Lord is my light and my
> salvation; . . . the strength of my
> life; of whom shall I be afraid?
> PSALM 27:1

CHUN HUI
Abundant in Wisdom

> The Lord giveth wisdom; out of
> his mouth cometh knowledge
> and understanding.
> PROVERBS 2:6
>
> Chinese

CHUN-YIP
Spring

> I will praise thee; for I am
> fearfully and wonderfully made;
> marvellous are thy works.
> PSALM 139:14

CHUY
Strong Man of the Lord

> In God is my salvation and . . .
> glory: the rock of my strength,
> . . . my refuge, is in God.
> PSALM 62:7

CIARA
One of Light

> They that be wise shall shine as
> the brightness of the firmament;
> . . . as the stars for ever and ever.
> DANIEL 12:3

CINDERELLA
Little One of the Ashes

> I will praise thee; for I am
> fearfully and wonderfully made;
> marvellous are thy works.
> PSALM 139:14

CINDI
Radiant One

> They that be wise shall shine as
> the brightness of the firmament;
> . . . as the stars for ever and ever.
> DANIEL 12:3

CINDY
Radiant One

> They that be wise shall shine as
> the brightness of the firmament;
> . . . as the stars for ever and ever.
> DANIEL 12:3

CINNAMON *also* CYNNAMON
Spice of Life

> Let the words of my mouth, and
> . . . meditation of my heart, be
> acceptable in thy sight, O Lord,
> my strength, and my redeemer.
> PSALM 19:14

CIPRIANO
From the Island of Cyprus

> I will praise thee; for I am
> fearfully and wonderfully
> made: . . . How precious also are
> thy thoughts unto me.
> PSALM 139:14, 17

CLAIRE
Giver of Light

> I will not rest, until the
> righteousness thereof go forth
> as brightness.
> ISAIAH 62:1

CLAIRENE
Giver of Light

> They that be wise shall shine as
> the brightness of the firmament;
> . . . as the stars for ever and ever.
> DANIEL 12:3

CLARK
Learned Man

> In the lips of him that hath
> understanding wisdom is found:
> . . . Wise men lay up knowledge.
> PROVERBS 10:13–14

CLARKE
Learned One

> My mouth shall speak of
> wisdom; and the meditation of
> my heart shall be of
> understanding.
> PSALM 49:3

CLAUDE
Submission to God

> Gladly . . . will I . . . glory in my
> infirmities, that the power of
> Christ may rest upon me.
> 2 CORINTHIANS 12:9

CLAUDIA
Submission to God

> Gladly . . . will I . . . glory in my
> infirmities, that the power of
> Christ may rest upon me.
> 2 CORINTHIANS 12:9

CLAUDINE
Submission to God

> And he said unto me, my grace
> is sufficient for thee: for my
> strength is made perfect in
> weakness.
> 2 CORINTHIANS 12:9

CLAVERON
Strong and Good Value

> With him is wisdom and
> strength, he hath counsel and
> understanding.
> JOB 12:13

Latin

CLAYTON
In God's Mold

> Behold, as the clay is in the
> potter's hand, so are ye in mine
> hand.
> JEREMIAH 18:6

CLEATA
Chosen and Called

> I have chosen you, and ordained
> you, that ye should go and bring
> forth fruit.
> JOHN 15:16

CLEDELL
Chosen and Called

> Ye have not chosen me, but I
> have chosen you, and ordained
> you, that ye should go and bring
> forth fruit.
> JOHN 15:16

CLEIDE
Heard from Afar

> *I will praise thee: for thou hast heard me, and art become my salvation.*
> PSALM 118:21

CLELLA
Of Great Fame

> *Wait on the Lord, and keep his way, and he shall exalt thee to inherit the land.*
> PSALM 37:34

CLEMENT
Mercy and Kindness

> *The Lord is good; his mercy is everlasting; and his truth endureth to all generations.*
> PSALM 100:5

CLEMENTE
Mercy and Kindness

> *The Lord is good; his mercy is everlasting; and his truth endureth to all generations.*
> PSALM 100:5

CLEMENTINE
One of Mercy

> *The Lord is good; his mercy is everlasting; and his truth endureth to all generations.*
> PSALM 100:5

CLENTON
Peaceful One

> *The Lord will give strength unto his people, the Lord will bless his people with peace.*
> PSALM 29:11

CLEO
Strong in Character

> *Be ye stedfast, unmoveable, always abounding in the work of the Lord, . . . your labour is not in vain in the Lord.*
> 1 CORINTHIANS 15:58

CLIF
One of Great Prominence

> *For promotion cometh neither from the east, . . . west, nor . . . south. But God is the judge: he putteth down one, and setteth up another.*
> PSALM 75:6–7

CLINT
Great in Forgiveness

> *Let judgment run down as waters, and righteousness as a mighty stream.*
> AMOS 5:24

CLOVER
The Sweet

> *How sweet are thy words unto my taste! yea, sweeter than honey to my mouth!*
> PSALM 119:103

CLUSTER
To Gather as a Flock

> *He shall feed his flock like a shepherd: he shall gather the lambs with his arm.*
> ISAIAH 40:11

CLYDA
Heard from Afar

> I will praise thee: for thou hast heard me, and art become my salvation.
> PSALM 118:21

CODY
Virtuous Spirit

> I will bless the Lord who hath given me counsel: . . . I have set the Lord always before me.
> PSALM 16:7–8

COLBY
Of Rich Earth

> How manifold are thy works! . . . the earth is full of thy riches.
> PSALM 104:24

CONCHETA
Little Shell

> I will praise thee; for I am fearfully and wonderfully made; marvellous are thy works.
> PSALM 139:14

CONNIE
Loyal One

> I will bless the Lord at all times: his praise shall continually be in my mouth.
> PSALM 34:1

CONSTANTINE
Loyal and Firm of Purpose

> I have set the Lord . . . before me: . . . he is at my right hand, I shall not be moved.
> PSALM 16:8

CONSUELO
Compassionate Spirit

> I will praise thee: for thou hast heard me, and art become my salvation.
> PSALM 118:21

CONSWELLO
Compassionate Spirit

> I will praise thee; for thou hast heard me, and art become my salvation.
> PSALM 118:21

CONWAY
Wise and Royal Way

> So teach us to number our days, that we may apply our hearts unto wisdom.
> PSALM 90:12

COOKIE
One of Grace

> The Lord will give grace and glory: no good thing will he withhold from them that walk uprightly.
> PSALM 84:11

CORA
Young at Heart

> Thou shalt love the Lord thy God with all thine heart, . . . thy soul, and with all thy might.
> DEUTERONOMY 6:5

C

CORBAN
One of Valor

> My brethren, be strong in the Lord, and in the power of his might.
>
> EPHESIANS 6:10

CORDY
Creative and Industrious Spirit

> Whatsoever ye do, do it heartily, as to the Lord, and not unto men; . . . for ye serve the Lord Christ.
>
> COLOSSIANS 3:23–24

CORENE
Maiden

> I will praise thee; for I am fearfully and wonderfully made: marvellous are thy works.
>
> PSALM 139:14

COREY   also CORY
Prosperous One

> I will sing unto the Lord, because he hath dealt bountifully with me.
>
> PSALM 13:6

CORINTHIAN
One from Corinth

> Thy word is a lamp unto my feet, and a light unto my path.
>
> PSALM 119:105

CORKY
Joyful Spirit

> In thy presence is fulness of joy; at thy right hand . . . are pleasures for evermore.
>
> PSALM 16:11

CORLETTE
Strong in the Lord

> Fight the good fight of faith, lay hold on eternal life, whereunto thou art also called.
>
> 1 TIMOTHY 6:12

CORLYNE
Warrior of Strength

> Every word of God is pure: he is a shield unto them that put their trust in him.
>
> PROVERBS 30:5

CORMA
Gift of Jehovah

> Every good gift and every perfect gift is from above, and cometh down from the Father of lights.
>
> JAMES 1:17

CORMAC
Heavenly Vessel

> I will bless the Lord, who hath given me counsel: . . . I have set the Lord always before me: . . . I shall not be moved.
>
> PSALM 16:7, 8

CORNACE
Warrior Strength

> Fight the good fight of faith, lay hold on eternal life, whereunto thou art also called.
>
> 1 TIMOTHY 6:12

CORNELIA
One of Nobility

> Ye are a chosen generation, a
> royal priesthood, . . . that ye
> should show forth the praises of
> him who hath called you.
> 1 PETER 2:9

CORRIN
Young at Heart

> For thou art my hope, O Lord
> God: thou art my trust from my
> youth.
> PSALM 71:5

CORTEZ
One of Courage

> The Lord is my light and my
> salvation; . . . the strength of my
> life; of whom shall I be afraid?
> PSALM 27:1

CORY   *also* COREY
Prosperous One

> I will sing unto the Lord,
> because he hath dealt
> bountifully with me.
> PSALM 13:6

COURTNEY
The Protector

> Be strong in the Lord, and in the
> power of his might. Put on the
> whole armour of God.
> EPHESIANS 6:10–11

COWEESTA
Guardian Protector

> He that dwelleth in the secret
> place of the most High shall
> abide under the shadow of the
> Almighty.
> PSALM 91:1

CRAIG
At the Crest

> Thou shalt increase my
> greatness, and comfort me on
> every side.
> PSALM 71:21

CRANDALL
Dwelling in Quiet and Peace

> The Lord will give strength unto
> his people; the Lord will bless
> his people with peace.
> PSALM 29:11

CRISTA
A Christian

> Ye are washed, . . . sanctified,
> . . . justified in the name of the
> Lord Jesus.
> 1 CORINTHIANS 6:11

CRISTINA
A Christian

> Ye are washed, . . . sanctified,
> . . . justified in the name of the
> Lord Jesus.
> 1 CORINTHIANS 6:11

CRYSTAL
Brilliantly Pure

> Blessed are the pure in heart:
> for they shall see God.
> MATTHEW 5:8

CULBERT
Bright and Shining Radiance

> *They that be wise shall shine as*
> *the brightness of the firmament;*
> *. . . as the stars for ever and ever.*
> DANIEL 12:3

CULEN
One of Victory

> *For whatsoever is born of God*
> *overcometh the world: and this*
> *is the victory that overcometh*
> *the world, even our faith.*
> 1 JOHN 5:4

CUMI
Heroic Strength

> *The Lord is my light and my*
> *salvation; whom shall I fear?*
> *the Lord is the strength of my*
> *life; of whom shall I be afraid?*
> PSALM 27:1

CUPID
Symbol of Love

> *God so loved the world, that he*
> *gave his only . . . Son, that*
> *whosoever believeth in him . . .*
> *should have everlasting life.*
> JOHN 3:16

CURTIS
Courteous

> *Be ye all of one mind, having*
> *compassion one of another, love*
> *as brethren, . . . be courteous.*
> 1 PETER 3:8

CYBILL
One of Wisdom

> *My mouth shall speak of wisdom;*
> *and the meditation of my heart*
> *shall be of understanding.*
> PSALM 49:3

CYMRI
With Royal Might

> *Thou hast also given me the*
> *shield of thy salvation: . . . thy*
> *gentleness hath made me great.*
> PSALM 18:35

CYNNAMON *also* CINNAMON
One of Strength

> *In God is my salvation and . . .*
> *glory: . . . the rock of my strength,*
> *. . . my refuge, is in God.*
> PSALM 62:7

CYNTHIA
Radiant One

> *They that be wise shall shine as*
> *the brightness of the firmament;*
> *. . . as the stars for ever and ever.*
> DANIEL 12:3

CYRENE
Noble One

> *Thou hast also given me the*
> *shield of thy salvation: . . . thy*
> *gentleness hath made me great.*
> PSALM 18:35

CZARINA
Of High Nobility

> *Ye are a chosen generation, a*
> *royal priesthood, . . . show forth*
> *the praises of him who hath*
> *called you.*
> 1 PETER 2:9

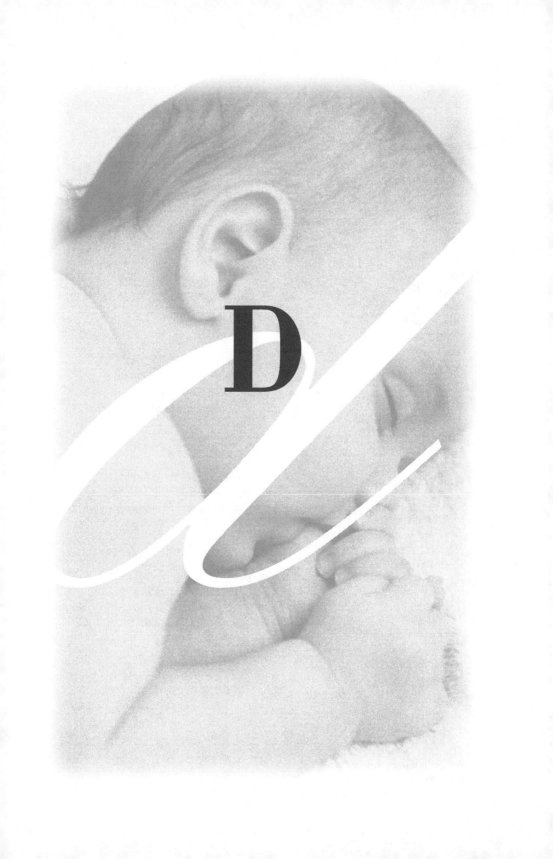

D

DAAGYE
Glorious Day

> This is the day which the Lord
> hath made; we will rejoice and
> be glad in it.
> PSALM 118:24
>
> Norwegian

DABEIBA
Beloved

> Beloved, let us love one another:
> for love is of God; and every one
> that loveth is born of God.
> 1 JOHN 4:7
>
> Hebrew

DABELYNN
A Refreshing Spirit

> The times of refreshing shall
> come from the presence of the
> Lord.
> ACTS 3:19

DABNEY
From the Small Town

> Thy word is a lamp unto my
> feet, and a light unto my path.
> PSALM 119:105

DAC
One of Honor

> The Lord is great, and greatly to
> be praised: Honour and majesty
> are before him.
> PSALM 96:4, 6

DACEY
From the Southern Province

> Thy word is a lamp unto my
> feet, and a light unto my path.
> PSALM 119:105

DACHELLE
Like Unto the Lord

> The Lord is my strength and
> song, and he is become my
> salvation: . . . I will exalt him.
> EXODUS 15:2

DACHIA
One of Peace

> The Lord will give strength unto
> his people; the Lord will bless
> his people with peace.
> PSALM 29:11

DACI
From the Roman Province

> Thy word is a lamp unto my
> feet, and a light to my path.
> PSALM 119:105

DACIA
From the Roman Province

> Thy word is a lamp unto my
> feet, and a light unto my path.
> PSALM 119:105

DACILE
Life

> The Lord is my light and my
> salvation; . . . the strength of my
> life; of whom shall I be afraid?
> PSALM 27:1

DACOREY
The Chosen

> I have chosen you, and ordained
> you, that ye should go and bring
> forth fruit.
> JOHN 15:16

DADE
Strong Workman

> *Study to show thyself approved unto God, a workman that needeth not to be ashamed, rightly dividing the word of truth.*
> 2 TIMOTHY 2:15

DADIE
Strong Worker

> *Study to show thyself approved unto God, a workman that needeth not to be ashamed, rightly dividing the word of truth.*
> 2 TIMOTHY 2:15

DADRE
One in Control

> *I can do all things through Christ which strengtheneth me.*
> PHILIPPIANS 4:13

DAEHLER
Peaceful from the Valley

> *The Lord is my shepherd; . . . He maketh me to lie down in green peastures.*
> PSALM 23:1–2

DAEL   *also* DALE
One of Serenity

> *I have set the Lord . . . before me: . . . he is at my right hand, I shall not be moved.*
> PSALM 16:8

DAELYN
One of Serenity

> *I have set the Lord . . . before me: . . . he is at my right hand, I shall not be moved.*
> PSALM 16:8

DAEMION   *also* DAMION
Loyal Friendship

> *Ye are my friends, if ye do whatsoever I command you.*
> JOHN 15:14

DAESOO
A Refreshing Spirit

> *The times of refreshing shall come from the presence of the Lord.*
> ACTS 3:19

DAGAN
Earth and Ceremonial Grain

> *I will praise thee, O Lord, with my whole heart; I will show forth all thy marvellous works.*
> PSALM 9:1

DAGIAN
Of Shining Brightness

> *Let your light so shine . . . that they may see your good works, and glorify your Father . . . in heaven.*
> MATTHEW 5:16

DAGMAR
Famous Thinker

> *Whatsoever things are true, . . . honest, . . . just, . . . pure, . . . of good report; . . . [or] praise, . . . think on these things.*
> PHILIPPIANS 4:8

DAGMARA
Famous Meditation

> *Whatsoever things are true, . . . honest, . . . pure, . . . if any virtue, [or] . . . praise, think on these things.*
> PHILIPPIANS 4:8

DAGMAWE
One of Brightness

> *They that be wise shall shine as the brightness of the firmament.*
> DANIEL 12:3

DAGNA
Bright as Day

> *Let your light so shine . . . that they may see your good works, and glorify your Father . . . in heaven.*
> MATTHEW 5:16

DAGNALL
Radiant as Day

> *Let your light so shine . . . that they may see your good works, and glorify your Father . . . in heaven.*
> MATTHEW 5:16

DAGNY
Radiant as Day

> *Let your light so shine . . . that they may see your good works, and glorify your Father . . . in heaven.*
> MATTHEW 5:16

DAHIA
From the Peaceful Valley

> *The Lord is my shepherd; . . . He maketh me to lie down in green pastures.*
> PSALM 23:1–2

DAHLIA
From the Peaceful Valley

> *The Lord is my shepherd; . . . He maketh me to lie down in green pastures.*
> PSALM 23:1–2

DAHNA
Industrious Spirit

> *Whatsoever ye do, do it heartily, as to the Lord, . . . for ye serve the Lord Christ.*
> COLOSSIANS 3:23–24

DAIBHIBH
Ardent and Zealous Spirit

> *Whatsoever ye do in word or deed, do all in the name of the Lord Jesus, . . . ye serve the Lord Christ.*
> COLOSSIANS 3:17, 24

Gaelic

DAIBIDH
Ardent and Zealous Spirit

> *Whatsoever ye do in word or deed, do all in the name of the Lord Jesus.*
> COLOSSIANS 3:17

D

DAIDRE
Ardent Spirit

> I press toward the mark for the
> prize of the high calling of God
> in Christ Jesus.
> PHILIPPIANS 3:14

DAIDREAN
Ardent Spirit

> I press toward the mark for the
> prize of the high calling of God
> in Christ Jesus.
> PHILIPPIANS 3:14

DAIGLE
Of the Day

> This is the day which the Lord
> hath made; we will rejoice and
> be glad in it.
> PSALM 118:24

DAILYN
Molded by God

> Behold, as the clay is in the
> potter's hand, so are ye in mine
> hand.
> JEREMIAH 18:6

DAIMYSEI
Precious Gem

> I will praise thee; for I am
> fearfully and wonderfully
> made; marvellous are thy
> works.
> PSALM 139:14

Latin

DAIN
also DANE

God Is My Judge

> The Lord shall endure forver:
> . . . he shall judge the world in
> righteousness.
> PSALM 9:7–8

DAIR
Wisdom and Compassion

> My mouth shall speak of
> wisdom; and the meditation of
> my heart shall be of
> understanding.
> PSALM 49:3

DAIRL
also DARRELL

Beloved One

> Beloved, let us love one another:
> for love is of God; and every one
> that loveth is born of God.
> 1 JOHN 4:7

DAISAN
Leader of Strength

> It is God that girdeth me with
> strength, and maketh my way
> perfect.
> PSALM 18:32

DAISEY
also DAZIE

A Precious Pearl

> I will praise thee; for I am
> fearfully and wonderfully
> made: marvellous are thy
> works.
> PSALM 139:14

DAISHA
Gift of God

> For by grace are ye saved through
> faith; . . . it is the gift of God.
> EPHESIANS 2:8

DAISYMAE
A Pearl

> *I will praise thee; for I am
> fearfully and wonderfully
> made; marvellous are thy
> works.*
> PSALM 139:14

DAIYANNA
Divine One of Grace

> *The Lord will give grace and
> glory: no good thing will he
> withhold from them that walk
> uprightly.*
> PSALM 84:11

DA'JUAN
God Is Gracious

> *Thou, . . . art a God full of
> compassion, . . . gracious,
> longsuffering, and plenteous in
> mercy.*
> PSALM 86:15
>
> Spanish

DAK
Messenger of Truth

> *I will meditate in thy precepts,
> . . . I will not forget thy word.*
> PSALM 119:15–16

DAKESHA
Friendly One

> *I will praise thee, O Lord,
> among the people: I will sing
> unto thee among the nations.*
> PSALM 57:9

DA-KORIA
Strong in Counsel

> *I will bless the Lord, who hath
> given me counsel: . . . he is at my
> right hand.*
> PSALM 16:7–8
>
> German

DAKOTA
Friendly One

> *Ye are my friends, if ye do
> whatsoever I command you.*
> JOHN 15:14
>
> American Indian

DAKOTAH
Friendly One

> *Ye are my friends, if ye do
> whatsoever I command you.*
> JOHN 15:14

DALAINA
One of Light

> *They that be wise shall shine as
> the brightness of the firmament.*
> DANIEL 12:3

DALANA
True and Faithful

> *Let us draw near with a true
> heart in full assurance of faith.*
> HEBREWS 10:22

DALAREE
Noble One

> *Ye have not chosen me, but I
> have chosen you, . . . that ye
> should go and bring forth fruit.*
> JOHN 15:16

D

DALAUNA
True and Faithful

Let us draw near with a true heart in full assurance of faith.
HEBREWS 10:22

DALBERT
Illustrious through Nobility

The God of peace, . . . Make you perfect in every good work to do his will.
HEBREWS 13:20–21

DALBY
From the Bright Vale

Let your light so shine before men, that they may see your good works, and glorify your Father . . . in heaven.
MATTHEW 5:16

DALBYS
From the Bright Vale

Let your light so shine . . . that they may see your good works.
MATTHEW 5:16

DALE   *also* DAEL
One of Serenity

I have set the Lord . . . before me: . . . he is at my right hand, I shall not be moved.
PSALM 16:8

DALENE
Watch-Tower

The Lord is my rock, and . . . fortress, . . . my strength, . . . the horn of my salvation, . . . my high tower.
PSALM 18:2

DALETHA
One of Serenity

The Lord will give strength . . . the Lord will bless his people with peace.
PSALM 29:11

DALIA
One of Tenderness

Be ye kind one to another, tenderhearted, forgiving one another, as God . . . hath forgiven you.
EPHESIANS 4:32

DALILA
One of Tenderness

Be ye kind one to another, tenderhearted, forgiving one another.
EPHESIANS 4:32

DALIN
Molded by God

Behold, as the clay is in the potter's hand, so are ye in mine hand.
JEREMIAH 18:6

DALINA
One of Radiance

They that be wise shall shine as the brightness of the firmament.
DANIEL 12:3

DALKEITH
Peaceful and Secure

The Lord will give strength unto his people; the Lord will bless his people with peace.
PSALM 29:11

DALLAS
Peaceful Dweller

> He maketh me to lie down in
> green pastures: he leadeth me
> beside the still waters.
> PSALM 23:2

DALLEN   *also* DALYN
Molded by God

> Behold, as the clay is in the
> potter's hand, so are ye in mine
> hand.
> JEREMIAH 18:6

DALLIN
Molded by God

> Behold, as the clay is in the
> potter's hand, so are ye in mine
> hand.
> JEREMIAH 18:6

DALLIS
One of Wisdom

> For the Lord giveth wisdom: out
> of his mouth cometh knowledge
> and understanding.
> PROVERBS 2:6

DALLON
Molded by God

> Behold, as the clay is in the
> potter's hand, so are ye in mine
> hand.
> JEREMIAH 18:6

DALONNA
Molded by God

> Behold, as the clay is in the
> potter's hand, so are ye in mine
> hand.
> JEREMIAH 18:6

DALSING
Beloved One

> The Lord hath appeared of old
> unto me, saying, . . . I have loved
> thee with an everlasting love.
> JEREMIAH 31:3

DALTON
One of Serenity

> The hidden man of the heart,
> . . . a meek and quiet spirit,
> which is in the sight of God of
> great price.
> 1 PETER 3:4

DALVAY
Beloved One

> Let us love one another: for love
> is of God; and every one that
> loveth is born of God.
> 1 JOHN 4:7

DALYCE
The Skilled One

> Whatsoever ye do, do it heartily,
> as to the Lord . . . for ye serve
> the Lord Christ.
> COLOSSIANS 3:23–24

DALYN   *also* DALLEN
Molded of God

> Behold, as the clay is in the
> potter's hand, so are ye in mine
> hand.
> JEREMIAH 18:6

DAMACIA
Noble Lady

> Strength and honour are her
> clothing; and she shall rejoice in
> time to come.
> PROVERBS 31:25

D

DAMAIN
Loyal Freindship

> *Ye are my friends, if ye do*
> *whatsoever I command you.*
> JOHN 15:14

DAMALA
Gentle and Noble Lady

> *Strength and honour are her*
> *clothing; and she shall rejoice in*
> *time to come.*
> PROVERBS 31:25

DAMANI
Loyal Friendship

> *Ye are my friends, if ye do*
> *whatsoever I command you.*
> JOHN 15:14

DAMARA
Gentle Lady

> *Be ye kind one to another, . . .*
> *forgiving one another, even as*
> *God . . . hath forgiven you.*
> EPHESIANS 4:32

DAMARIS
Gentle and Mild

> *Be ye kind one to another, . . .*
> *forgiving one another, even as*
> *God . . . hath forgiven you.*
> EPHESIANS 4:32

DAMARY
Gentle Spirit

> *Be ye kind one to another, . . .*
> *forgiving one another, even as*
> *God . . . hath forgiven you.*
> EPHESIANS 4:32

DAMASCUS
Silent Is the Sackcloth Weaver

> *Let the words of my mouth, and*
> *the meditation of my heart, be*
> *acceptable in thy sight, O Lord,*
> *my strength.*
> PSALM 19:14

DAMEN
Loyal Friendship

> *Ye are my friends, if ye do*
> *whatsoever I command you.*
> JOHN 15:14

DAMIEN
Loyal Friendship

> *Ye are my friends, if ye do*
> *whatsoever I command you.*
> JOHN 15:14

DAMION   *also* DAEMION
Loyal Friendship

> *Ye are my friends, if ye do*
> *whatsoever I command you.*
> JOHN 15:14

DAMITA
Consecrated to God

> *I will bless the Lord at all times:*
> *his praise shall continually be*
> *in my mouth.*
> PSALM 34:1

DAMYANTI
A Precious Pearl

> *I will praise thee; for I am*
> *fearfully and wonderfully*
> *made; . . . how precious also are*
> *thy thoughts.*
> PSALM 139:14, 17

Teutonic

101

DAN
God Is My Judge

> *God is the judge: . . . God that doest wonders; . . . hast declared thy strength among the people.*
> PSALM 75:7; 77:14

DANA
Industrious One

> *Whatsoever ye do, do it heartily, as to the Lord, . . . for ye serve the Lord Christ.*
> COLOSSIANS 3:23–24

DANALYNN
The Morning Star

> *They that be wise shall shine as the brightness of the firmament; . . . as the stars for ever and ever.*
> DANIEL 12:3

DANEA
The Morning Star

> *They that be wise shall shine as the brightness of the firmament; . . . as the stars for ever and ever.*
> DANIEL 12:3

DANEILLE
God Is My Judge

> *God is the judge: . . . God that doest wonders; . . . hast declared thy strength among the people.*
> PSALM 75:7; 77:14

DANFORD
From the Peaceful Valley

> *The Lord is my shepherd; . . . He maketh me to lie down in green pastures.*
> PSALM 23:1–2

DANGERFIELD
Of Power and Strength

> *The Lord is my light and my salvation; . . . [my] strength . . . of whom shall I be afraid?*
> PSALM 27:1

French

DANGUOLE
Strong and Secure

> *I love the Lord, . . . he hath heard my voice and my supplications.*
> PSALM 116:1

DANIEL
God Is My Judge

> *God is the judge: . . . God that doest wonders; . . . hast declared thy strength among the people.*
> PSALM 75:7; 77:14

DANIELITTA
God Is My Judge

> *God is the judge: . . . God that doest wonders; . . . hast declared thy strength among the people.*
> PSALM 75:7; 77:14

DANIELLE
God Is My Judge

> *God is the judge: . . . God that doest wonders; . . . hast declared thy strength among the people.*
> PSALMS 75:7; 77:14

DANIKA
The Morning Star

> *This is the day which the Lord hath made; we will rejoice and be glad in it.*
> PSALM 118:24

D

DANISHA
God Is My Judge

> *God is the judge: . . . God that doest wonders; . . . hast declared thy strength among the people.*
> PSALM 75:7; 77:14

DANTE
One of Strength and Endurance

> *Thou hast given me the shield of thy salvation: . . . thy gentleness hath made me great.*
> PSALM 18:35

DANJY
Given by God

> *Every good gift and every perfect gift is from above.*
> JAMES 1:17

DANYA
Given by God

> *Every good gift and every perfect gift is from above.*
> JAMES 1:17

DANKA
The Morning Star

> *Let your light so shine before men, that they may see your good works.*
> MATTHEW 5:16

DAPHENE
Lady of Victory

> *Thanks be to God, which giveth us the victory through our Lord Jesus Christ.*
> 1 CORINTHIANS 15:57

DANNETTE
God Is My Judge

> *God is the judge: . . . God that doest wonders; . . . hast declared thy strength among the people.*
> PSALM 75:7; 77:14

DAPHNE
Lady of Victory

> *Thanks be to God, which giveth us the victory through our Lord Jesus Christ.*
> 1 CORINTHIANS 15:57

DANNIE
God Is My Judge

> *God is the judge: . . . God that doest wonders; . . . hast declared thy strength among the people.*
> PSALM 75:7; 77:14

DAPHNEE
Lady of Victory

> *Thanks be to God, which giveth us the victory through our Lord Jesus Christ.*
> 1 CORINTHIANS 15:57

DANNY
God Is My Judge

> *God is the judge: . . . God that doest wonders; . . . hast declared thy strength among the people.*
> PSALM 75:7; 77:14

DAR
Bold and Courageous

> *Be strong and of a good courage; . . . for the Lord thy God is with thee.*
> JOSHUA 1:9

DARA
Heart of Wisdom

> For the Lord giveth wisdom: out
> of his mouth cometh knowledge
> and understanding.
> PROVERBS 2:6

DARAH
The Bold

> Be strong and of a good
> courage; . . . for the Lord thy
> God is with thee.
> JOSHUA 1:9

DARAKA
Heart of Wisdom

> The Lord giveth wisdom: out of
> his mouth cometh knowledge
> and understanding.
> PROVERBS 2:6

DARALD
Beloved

> The Lord hath appeared . . .
> saying, I have loved thee with
> an everlasting love.
> JEREMIAH 31:3

DARAN
Blessed with Bounty

> The blessing of the Lord, it
> maketh rich, and he addeth no
> sorrow with it.
> PROVERBS 10:22

DARBY
Faithful One

> I will meditate in thy precepts,
> . . . I will delight myself in thy
> statutes: I will not forget thy
> word.
> PSALM 119:15–16

DARCELLA
From the Stronghold

> The Lord is my rock, . . . my
> fortress, and my deliverer; . . . my
> strength, in whom I will trust.
> PSALM 18:2

DARCIE
also DARSIE
From the Stronghold

> The Lord is my rock, . . . my
> fortress, and my deliverer; . . . my
> strength, in whom I will trust.
> PSALM 18:2

DARCUS
Prosperous One

> I will sing unto the Lord,
> because he hath dealt
> bountifully with me.
> PSALM 13:6

DARE
Fearless One

> The Lord is my light and my
> salvation; . . . [my] strength . . .
> of whom shall I be afraid?
> PSALM 27:1

DARENDA
Great

> Thou hast given me . . . thy
> salvation: . . . thy gentleness
> hath made me great.
> PSALM 18:35

DARGAN
Pearl of Wisdom

> The Lord giveth wisdom: out of
> his mouth cometh knowledge
> and understanding.
> PROVERBS 2:6

D

DARIA
Prosperous One

> *I will sing unto the Lord,*
> *because he hath dealt*
> *bountifully with me.*
> PSALM 13:6

DARIAN
Possessing Wealth

> *I will sing unto the Lord,*
> *because he hath dealt*
> *bountifully with me.*
> PSALM 13:6

DARICK
One of Victory

> *For whatsoever is born of God*
> *overcometh the world, and this*
> *is the victory that overcometh*
> *the world, even our faith.*
> 1 JOHN 5:4

DARIEN
Possessing Wealth

> *I will sing unto the Lord,*
> *because he hath dealt*
> *bountifully with me.*
> PSALM 13:6

DARILYN
Tenderly Beloved

> *Love one another: for love is of*
> *God; and every one that loveth*
> *is born of God.*
> 1 JOHN 4:7

DARIN
Fearless One

> *The Lord is my light and my*
> *salvation; . . . [my] strength . . .*
> *of whom shall I be afraid?*
> PSALM 27:1

DARINA
One of Greatness

> *I will praise thee, O Lord, . . . I*
> *will sing praise to thy name, O*
> *thou most High.*
> PSALM 9:1–2

DARIS
Royal and Noble

> *I have chosen you, and ordained*
> *you, that ye should go and bring*
> *forth fruit.*
> JOHN 15:16

DARIUS
Possessing Wealth

> *I will sing unto the Lord,*
> *because he hath dealt*
> *bountifully with me.*
> PSALM 13:6

DARJEEL
Bold One of Courage

> *Be strong and of a good courage;*
> *. . . the Lord thy God is with thee.*
> JOSHUA 1:9

DARLEEN
Dearly Beloved

> *Let us love one another: for love*
> *is of God; and every one that*
> *loveth is born of God.*
> 1 JOHN 4:7

DARLENE
Dearly Beloved

> *Let us love one another: for love*
> *is of God; and every one that*
> *loveth is born of God.*
> 1 JOHN 4:7

DARLETTE
Dearly Beloved

> Love one another: for love is of
> God; and every one that loveth
> is born of God.
> 1 JOHN 4:7

DARMAND
Beloved Protector

> I love the Lord, . . . he hath
> heard my voice and my
> supplications.
> PSALM 116:1

DARNALL
Secure One

> My help cometh from the Lord,
> which made heaven and earth.
> PSALM 121:2

DARNEISHA
Secure One

> My help cometh from the Lord,
> which made heaven and earth.
> PSALM 121:2

DARNELL
Secure One

> I will lift up mine eyes unto the
> hills, from whence cometh my
> help.
> PSALM 121:1

DARNETT
Safe and Secure

> I will lift up mine eyes unto the
> hills. . . . My help cometh from
> the Lord.
> PSALM 121:1–2

DARNITA
Secure One

> I will lift up mine eyes unto the
> hills. . . . My help cometh from
> the Lord.
> PSALM 121:1–2

DARROW
Brave Heart

> I have fought a good fight, . . . I
> have kept the faith.
> 2 TIMOTHY 4:7

DARRAGH
One of Courage

> Be strong and of a good
> courage, . . . for the Lord thy
> God, . . . is . . . with thee.
> DEUTERONOMY 31:6

DARRANCE
Blessed with Bounty

> The Lord thy God shall bless
> thee . . . in all the works of thine
> hands.
> DEUTERONOMY 16:15

DARREK
Ruler of the People

> He that ruleth over men must be
> just, ruling in the fear of God.
> 2 SAMUEL 23:3

DARREL
Dearly Beloved

> What manner of love the Father
> hath bestowed upon us, that we
> should be called the sons of God.
> 1 JOHN 3:1

D

DARRELL
Dearly Beloved
> *What manner of love the Father hath bestowed upon us, that we should be called the sons of God.*
> 1 JOHN 3:1

DARRY
Brave
> *I have fought a good fight, . . . I have kept the faith.*
> 2 TIMOTHY 4:7

DARSIE   *also* DARCIE
From the Strong Fortress
> *The Lord is my rock, my fortress, and my deliverer; . . . my strength, in whom I will trust.*
> PSALM 18:2

DARWIN
A Strong Friend
> *Ye are my friends, if ye do whatsoever I command you.*
> JOHN 15:14

DARYEN
Great and Prosperous One
> *For the Lord is great, and greatly to be praised.*
> PSALM 96:4

DASCHA
God's Gift
> *For by grace are ye saved through faith; . . . it is the gift of God.*
> EPHESIANS 2:8

DASEA
A Pearl
> *I will praise thee; for I am fearfully and wonderfully made.*
> PSALM 139:14

DASHANDA
Gift of God
> *Every good . . . and every perfect gift . . . cometh down from the Father of lights.*
> JAMES 1:17
>
> Greek

DASHEAN
God's Gift
> *For by grace are ye saved through faith; . . . it is the gift of God.*
> EPHESIANS 2:8

DASHELDA
Gift of God
> *Every good . . . and every perfect gift . . . cometh down from the Father of lights.*
> JAMES 1:17

DASON
Rich Gift
> *For by grace are ye saved through faith; . . . it is the gift of God.*
> EPHESIANS 2:8

DATASKA
Word of God
> *Thy hands have made me and fashioned me: . . . that I may learn thy commandments.*
> PSALM 119:73

DATHAN
Gift of God

> For by grace are ye saved through faith; . . . it is the gift of God.
> EPHESIANS 2:8

DATIVA
Dearly Beloved

> Beloved, let us love one another: for love is of God.
> 1 JOHN 4:7

DAUCIE
From the Strong Fortress

> The Lord is my rock, . . . my fortress, . . . in whom I will trust.
> PSALM 18:2

DAULTON
One of Peace and Serenity

> Let it be the hidden man of the heart, . . . a meek and quiet spirit, which is in the sight of God of great price.
> 1 PETER 3:4

DAUNE   *also* DAWN
Break of Day

> This is the day which the Lord hath made; we will rejoice and be glad in it.
> PSALM 118:24

DAUNINE
Break of Day

> This is the day which the Lord hath made; we will rejoice and be glad in it.
> PSALM 118:24

DAVA
Beloved One

> Beloved, let us love one another: for love is of God.
> 1 JOHN 4:7

DAVAR
Beloved

> Beloved, let us love one another: for love is of God.
> 1 JOHN 4:7

DAVE
Beloved One

> The beloved of the Lord shall dwell in safety by him; . . . the Lord shall cover him.
> DEUTERONOMY 33:12

DAVEN
One of Wisdom

> For the Lord giveth wisdom: out of his mouth cometh knowledge.
> PROVERBS 2:6

DAVERLE
Beloved One of Nobility

> Beloved, let us love one another: for love is of God.
> 1 JOHN 4:7

DAVIANNE
Beloved One of Grace

> The Lord will give grace and glory: no good thing will he withhold.
> PSALM 84:11

D

DAVID
Beloved One

*The beloved of the Lord shall
dwell in safety by him; . . . the
Lord shall cover him all the day
long.*
DEUTERONOMY 33:12

DAVIDSON
Beloved Son

*Beloved, let us love one another:
for love is of God.*
1 JOHN 4:7

DAVON
One of Wisdom

*For the Lord giveth wisdom: out
of his mouth cometh knowledge.*
PROVERBS 2:6

DAW GYI
Beloved and Wonderful Child

*Every one that loveth is born of
God, and knoweth God.*
1 JOHN 4:7

Muslim

DAWANNA
Walking With the Lord

*Thy word is a lamp unto my
feet, and a light unto my path.*
PSALM 119:105

DAWANYA
Beloved

*Beloved, let us love one another:
for love is of God.*
1 JOHN 4:7

DAWE
The Day of the Lord

*This is the day which the Lord
hath made; we will rejoice and
be glad in it.*
PSALM 118:24

DAWN   *also* DAUNE
Break of Day

*This is the day which the Lord
hath made; we will rejoice and
be glad in it.*
PSALM 118:24

DAWNELLE
Dawn of Day

*This is the day which the Lord
hath made; we will rejoice and
be glad in it.*
PSALM 118:24

DAWSON
Beloved One

*Beloved, let us love one another:
for love is of God.*
1 JOHN 4:7

DAX
One of Excellent Skill

*It is God that girdeth me with
strength, and maketh my way
perfect.*
PSALM 18:32

DAXTON
One of Excellent Valor

*It is God that girdeth me with
strength, and maketh my way
perfect.*
PSALM 18:32

DAYAN
also DIANE
Divine One

> That by these ye might be
> partakers of the divine nature.
> 2 PETER 1:4

DAYDRAH
also DEIDRE
One in Control

> I can do all things through
> Christ which strengtheneth me.
> PHILIPPIANS 4:13

DAYLE
Courageous

> As for God, his way is perfect:
> . . . he is a buckler to all those
> that trust in him.
> PSALM 18:30

DAYLENE
Of the Day

> This is the day which the Lord
> hath made; we will rejoice and
> be glad in it.
> PSALM 118:24

DAZIE
also DAISY
A Precious Pearl

> I will praise thee; . . . How
> precious also are thy thoughts
> unto me, O God!
> PSALM 139:14, 17

DEACON
Appointed One

> I have chosen you, . . . that ye
> should go and bring forth fruit.
> JOHN 15:16

DEAMANTINA
Like a Diamond

> I will praise thee; for I am
> fearfully and wonderfully made.
> PSALM 139:14

DEAN
Peaceful Spirit

> Thou wilt keep him in perfect
> peace, whose mind is stayed on
> thee.
> ISAIAH 26:3

DEANA
God's Princess

> The Lord shall rise upon thee,
> and his glory shall be seen upon
> thee.
> ISAIAH 60:2

DEANIE
Peaceful Spirit

> The Lord will give strength unto
> his people; the Lord will bless
> his people with peace.
> PSALM 29:11

DEANN
One of Grace

> The Lord God is a sun and
> shield: the Lord will give grace
> and glory.
> PSALM 84:11

DEANNA
Divine Nature

> Given unto us [are] precious
> promises: that . . . ye might be
> partakers of the divine nature.
> 2 PETER 1:4

DEATHERAGE
Bringer of Joy

*Thou wilt show me the path of
life: in thy presence is fulness of
joy.*
PSALM 16:11

DEBBIE
Loyal Messenger of Truth

*Let the words of my mouth, . . .
be acceptable in thy sight, O
Lord, . . . my redeemer.*
PSALM 19:14

DEBI
Loyal Messenger of Truth

*Let the words of my mouth, . . .
be acceptable in thy sight, O
Lord, . . . my redeemer.*
PSALM 19:14

DEBORAH
Loyal Messenger of Truth

*Let the words of my mouth, . . .
be acceptable in thy sight, O
Lord, . . . my redeemer.*
PSALM 19:14

DECHANTAL
One of Rejoicing and Song

*I will be glad and rejoice in thee:
I will sing praise to thy name.*
PSALM 9:2

DECHERD
Creative Worker

*As a wise masterbuilder, I have
laid the foundation, . . . which is
Jesus Christ.*
1 CORINTHIANS 3:10–11

DECI
Brave and Strong

*Be strong and of a good
courage; be not afraid, neither
be thou dismayed.*
JOSHUA 1:9

DECIMA
The Tenth

*I would seek unto God, and unto
God would I commit my cause.*
JOB 5:8

DECLAN
One of Fame

*For the Lord is great, and
greatly to be praised.*
PSALM 96:4

DEDERICK
Gift of God

*For by grace are ye saved
through faith; . . . it is the gift of
God.*
EPHESIANS 2:8

DEDIE
Gift of God

*Every good gift and every
perfect gift is from above, and
cometh down from the Father of
lights.*
JAMES 1:17

DEDRA
One in Control

*I can do all things through
Christ which strengtheneth me.*
PHILIPPIANS 4:13

DEE
Radiant One

> They that be wise shall shine as
> the brightness of the firmament.
> DANIEL 12:3

DEE ANN
One of Grace

> The Lord will give grace and
> glory: no good thing will he
> withhold from them that walk
> uprightly.
> PSALM 84:11

DEETER
One of Joy and Gladness

> My lips shall greatly rejoice
> when I sing unto thee.
> PSALM 71:23

DEETRA
Gift of God

> For by grace are ye saved
> through faith; . . . it is the gift of
> God.
> EPHESIANS 2:8

DEHLIA
A Bright Jewel

> I will praise thee; for I am
> fearfully and wonderfully made.
> PSALM 139:14

DEITRICH
Divine Gift

> Every good . . . and every
> perfect gift . . . cometh down
> from the Father of lights.
> JAMES 1:17

DEJAN
Delightful Virtue

> If there be any virtue, and . . .
> praise, think on these things.
> PHILIPPIANS 4:8

DEJARLE
Spear Ruler of Strength

> Take unto you the whole armour
> of God, . . . and the sword of the
> Spirit, which is the word of God.
> EPHESIANS 6:13, 17

DELANCY
One Who Serves

> Serve the Lord with gladness:
> come before his presence with
> singing.
> PSALM 100:2

DELANEY
Man of Health

> Beloved, I wish above all things
> that thou mayest prosper and be
> in health.
> 3 JOHN 2

DELAPHINE
Serenity and Living Fragrance

> Marvellous are thy works; . . .
> How precious . . . are thy
> thoughts unto me.
> PSALM 139:14, 17

DELAVAN
Of Noble Heritage

> Ye have not chosen me, but I
> have chosen you . . . that you
> should go and bear fruit.
> JOHN 15:16

D

DELBERT
Nobly Bright

> *The voice of the Lord is*
> *powerful; the voice of the Lord*
> *is full of majesty.*
> PSALM 29:4

DELBRA
Illustrious Through Nobility

> *My God, thou art very great;*
> *thou art clothed with honour*
> *and majesty.*
> PSALM 104:1

DELCINA
Charming and Sweet One

> *I will praise thee; for I am*
> *fearfully and wonderfully made.*
> PSALM 139:14

DELDA
Noble

> *Thy right hand hath holden me*
> *up, and thy gentleness hath*
> *made me great.*
> PSALM 18:35

DELEISHA
Devoted One

> *I will bless the Lord at all times:*
> *his praise shall continually be*
> *in my mouth.*
> PSALM 34:1

DELESILYNN
Dedicated One

> *I will bless the Lord at all times:*
> *his praise shall continually be*
> *in my mouth.*
> PSALM 34:1

DELETTA
Radiant One

> *Let your light so shine before*
> *men, . . . and glorify your Father*
> *which is in heaven.*
> MATTHEW 5:16

DELFERD
Illustrious Through Bold Nobility

> *Now the God of peace, . . . Make*
> *you perfect in every good work*
> *to do his will.*
> HEBREWS 13:20–21

DELFINA
The Larkspur Flower

> *I will praise thee; for I am*
> *fearfully and wonderfully*
> *made: marvellous are thy*
> *works.*
> PSALM 139:14

DELIA
One of Nobility

> *These were more noble . . . in*
> *that they received the Word with*
> *all readiness of mind.*
> ACTS 17:11

DELICIA
One of Delight and Virtue

> *If there be any virtue, . . . any*
> *praise, think on these things.*
> PHILIPPIANS 4:8

DELIGHT
One of Joy and Delight

> *Delight thyself . . . in the Lord;*
> *and he shall give thee the*
> *desires of thine heart.*
> PSALM 37:4

DELILA
The Delicate One

> *Be of good courage, and he shall strengthen your heart.*
> PSALM 31:24

DELILAH
The Delicate and Tender

> *Be ye kind one to another, tenderhearted, forgiving one another.*
> EPHESIANS 4:32

Hebrew

DELL
Bright as Day

> *Let your light so shine before men, . . . and glorify your Father which is in heaven.*
> MATTHEW 5:16

DELLA
One of Nobility

> *These were more noble . . . in that they received the Word with all readiness of mind.*
> ACTS 17:11

DELMA
Of the Sea

> *Wherefore glorify ye the Lord in the fires, even . . . in the isles of the sea.*
> ISAIAH 24:15

DELONDA
Victorious one

> *Thanks be to God, which giveth us the victory through our Lord Jesus Christ.*
> 1 CORINTHIANS 15:57

DELORES
Compassionate Spirit

> *I will praise thee: for thou hast heard me, and art become my salvation.*
> PSALM 118:21

DELPHINA
One of Peace

> *The peace of God, . . . shall keep your hearts and minds through Christ Jesus.*
> PHILIPPIANS 4:7

DELPHINE
One of Peace

> *And the peace of God, . . . shall keep your hearts and minds through Jesus Christ.*
> PHILIPPIANS 4:7

DELROSE
Illustrious through Nobility

> *Now the God of peace, . . . Make you perfect in every good work to do his will.*
> HEBREWS 13:20–21

DELTHIA
One of Nobility and Truth

> *Ye are a chosen generation, a royal priesthood.*
> 1 PETER 2:9

DEMEATRICE
Productive One

> *The Lord thy God shall bless thee in all thine increase and in all the works of thine hands.*
> DEUTERONOMY 16:15

D

DEMETRA
Productive One

*The Lord thy God shall bless
thee in all thine increase, and in
all the works of thine hands.*
DEUTERONOMY 16:15

Greek

DEMETRESS
God will Increase

*The Lord thy God shall bless
thee in all thine increase, and in
all the works of thine hands.*
DEUTERONOMY 16:15

DEMETRIA
Productive One

*The Lord thy God shall bless
thee in all thine increase, and in
all the works of thine hands.*
DEUTERONOMY 16:15

Greek

DEMMER   *also* DIEMER
Builder of Dams

*As a wise master builder, I have
laid the foundation . . . Jesus
Christ.*
1 CORINTHIANS 3:10

DEMOND
Faith Protector

*The Lord is my rock, . . . my fortress,
and my deliverer; my God, my
strength, in whom I will trust.*
PSALM 18:2

DENARD
Brave and Strong

*The Lord is my rock, . . . my
strength, in whom I will trust.*
PSALM 18:2

DENISE
A Believer

*Ye are washed, . . . sanctified,
. . . justified in the name of the
Lord Jesus.*
1 CORINTHIANS 6:11

DENNELL
Peaceful Dweller

*The Lord is my shepherd; . . . He
maketh me to lie down in green
pastures.*
PSALM 23:1–2

DENNIS
A Believer

*Ye are washed, . . . sanctified,
. . . justified in the name of the
Lord Jesus.*
1 CORINTHIANS 6:11

DENVER
Peaceful Dweller

*The Lord is my shepherd; I shall
not want. . . . he leadeth me
beside the still waters.*
PSALM 23:1–2

DENWOOD
A Peaceful Spirit

*The Lord will give strength . . .
the Lord will bless his people
with peace.*
PSALM 29:11

DENYSE
A Believer

*Ye are washed, . . . sanctified,
. . . justified in the name of the
Lord Jesus.*
1 CORINTHIANS 6:11

DEOLA
Divine Nature

> That by these ye might be partakers of the divine nature.
> 2 PETER 1:4

DERMA
Ruler of the People

> He that ruleth over men must be just, ruling in the fear of God.
> 2 SAMUEL 23:3

DERONICA
Bringer of Victory

> This is the victory that overcometh the world, even our faith.
> 1 JOHN 5:4

DERWARD
Guardian Protector

> He . . . shall abide under the shadow of the Almighty.
> PSALM 91:1

DERWOOD
Doorkeeper

> Blessed are they . . . I had rather be a doorkeeper in the house of my God.
> PSALM 84:4, 10

DESDEMONA
True Spirit

> Let the words of my mouth, . . . be acceptable in thy sight, O Lord.
> PSALM 19:14

DESERIE
The Desired One

> One thing have I desired of the Lord, . . . that I may dwell in the house of the Lord all the days of my life.
> PSALM 27:4

DESIREE
The Desired One

> One thing have I desired of the Lord, . . . that I may dwell in the house of the Lord all the days of my life.
> PSALM 27:4

DESKIN
Powerful Ruler

> Thy gentleness hath made me great.
> 2 SAMUEL 22:36

DESMOND
Gracious Protector

> He shall cover thee with his feathers, and under his wings shalt . . . trust: his truth shall be thy shield and buckler.
> PSALM 91:4

DESPIN
Valiant One

> Thy right hand hath holden me up, . . . thy gentleness hath made me great.
> PSALM 18:35

DESRA
Helper

> The Lord is the strength of my life; of whom shall I be afraid?
> PSALM 27:1

D

DESTIN
Firm of Purpose

> I have set the Lord always before me: . . . he is at my right hand, I shall not be moved.
> PSALM 16:8

DESTINA
Firm of Purpose

> I have set the Lord always before me: . . . he is at my right hand, I shall not be moved.
> PSALM 16:8

DESTINI
Firm of Purpose

> I have set the Lord always before me: . . . he is at my right hand, I shall not be moved.
> PSALM 16:8

DESTINY
Firm of Purpose

> I have set the Lord always before me: . . . he is at my right hand, I shall not be moved.
> PSALM 16:8

DETLEF
A Descendant

> We are the children of God: . . . and joint-heirs with Christ.
> ROMANS 8:16–17

DEVA
Divine and Heavenly

> Given unto us . . . [are] precious promises: that . . . ye might be partakers of the divine nature.
> 2 PETER 1:4

DEVEN
Worthy of Praise

> For the Lord is great, and greatly to be praised: . . . Honour and majesty are before him.
> PSALM 96:4, 6

DEVERNE
Brave and One of Courage

> Be strong and of a good courage; . . . for the Lord thy God is with thee.
> JOSHUA 1:9

DEVIN
Poet

> As certain . . . of your own poets have said, For we are also his offspring.
> ACTS 17:28

DEVLIN
One of Courage and Valor

> Be strong and of a good courage, . . . the Lord thy God . . . doth go with thee.
> DEUTERONOMY 31:6

DEVRON
One of Greatness and Strength

> Thy right hand hath holden me up, . . . thy gentleness hath made me great.
> PSALM 18:35

DEWARD
Watchful One

> Watch ye, stand fast in the faith, quit you like men, be strong.
> 1 CORINTHIANS 16:13

DEXTER
One of Excellent Skill

> *God gave them knowledge and skill in all learning and wisdom.*
> DANIEL 1:17

DEXTON
One of Excellent Skill

> *God gave them knowledge and skill in all learning and wisdom.*
> DANIEL 1:17

DIALLO
Light of God

> *Let your light so shine before men, . . . and glorify your Father . . . in heaven.*
> MATTHEW 5:16

DIAMOND
The Radiant Protector

> *He that dwelleth in the secret place of the most High shall abide under . . . the Almighty.*
> PSALM 91:1

DIANA
Divine One

> *Given unto us . . . [are] precious promises: that by these ye might be partakers of the divine nature.*
> 2 PETER 1:4

DIANDRA
A Flower

> *Thy hands have made . . . and fashioned me: give me understanding, . . . [to] learn thy commandments.*
> PSALM 119:73

DIANE
Divine One

> *Given unto us . . . [are] precious promises: that by these ye might be partakers of the divine nature.*
> 2 PETER 1:4

DIANNA
In God's Glory

> *My kindness shall not depart from thee, neither . . . the covenant of my peace be removed.*
> ISAIAH 54:10

DIANNE
Divine One

> *Given unto us . . . [are] precious promises: that by these ye might be partakers of the divine nature.*
> 2 PETER 1:4

DIANTHA
Divine Flower

> *I will praise thee; for I am fearfully and wonderfully made.*
> PSALM 139:14

DIEGO
Following after the Lord

> *Be ye . . . followers of God, as dear children; And walk in love, as Christ also hath loved us.*
> EPHESIANS 5:1,2

DIEMER *also* DEMMER
Master Builder

> *As a wise masterbuilder, I have laid the foundation, . . . Jesus Christ.*
> 1 CORINTHIANS 3:10

DIETRICH
Divine Gift

> *Every good gift and every perfect gift is from above, and cometh down from the Father of lights.*
> JAMES 1:17

DILIP
Faithful

> *I will praise thee: for thou hast heard me, and art become my salvation.*
> PSALM 118:21

DILLARD
Faithful and True

> *Be thou faithful unto death, and I will give thee a crown of life.*
> REVELATION 2:10

DILLON
The Faithful

> *I will praise thee: . . . thou art my God, I will exalt thee.*
> PSALM 118:21, 28

DINAH
In God's Glory

> *Let all those that put their trust in thee rejoice: [and] . . . shout for joy.*
> PSALM 5:11

DIOMEDES
Warrior for the Faith

> *Fight the good fight of faith, lay hold on eternal life.*
> 1 TIMOTHY 6:12

Greek

DIONNA
One of Sovereign Nobility

> *Ye are a chosen generation, . . . ye should show forth the praises of him who . . . called you.*
> 1 PETER 2:9

DIONNE
Divine Queen

> *Given unto us [are] exceeding great and precious promises: that . . . ye might be partakers of the divine nature.*
> 2 PETER 1:4

DIRON
Radiant One of Strength

> *They that be wise shall shine as the brightness of the firmament.*
> DANIEL 12:3

DITZAH
Joy

> *Thou wilt show me the path of life: in thy presence is fulness of joy.*
> PSALM 16:11

DIVINE
Like God

> *Given unto us [are] exceeding great and precious promises: that . . . ye might be partakers of the divine nature.*
> 2 PETER 1:4

DIVINITY
Divine Nature

> That by these ye might be
> partakers of the divine nature.
> 2 PETER 1:4

DIXIANA
The Blessed

> Blessed are they that keep his
> testimonies, and that seek him.
> PSALM 119:2

DIXIE
The Blessed

> Blessed is he that cometh in the
> name of the Lord.
> PSALM 118:26

DIXON
The Blessed

> Blessed are they that keep his
> testimonies, . . . that seek him
> with the whole heart.
> PSALM 119:2

DMISHA
Consecrated to God

> I will bless the Lord at all times:
> his praise shall continually be
> in my mouth.
> PSALM 34:1

DOCIA   *also* DOSHIA
God's Gift

> Every good . . . and every
> perfect gift . . . cometh down
> from the Father of lights.
> JAMES 1:17

DODSON
Exalted One

> Thy right hand hath holden me
> up, . . . thy gentleness hath made
> me great.
> PSALM 18:35

DOLAN
Strong in Spirit

> It is good for me to draw near to
> God: I have put my trust in the
> Lord God, that I may declare all
> thy works.
> PSALM 73:28

DOLLIE
Sweet Gift

> My God shall supply all your
> need according to his riches in
> glory by Christ Jesus.
> PHILIPPIANS 4:19

DOLLY
Sweet Gift

> My God shall supply all your
> need according to his riches in
> glory by Christ Jesus.
> PHILIPPIANS 4:19

DOLLYANNA
Gift of Grace

> The Lord will give grace and
> glory: no good thing will he
> withhold.
> PSALM 84:11

DOLORES
God Is My Help

> I will praise thee: for thou hast
> heard me, and art become my
> salvation.
> PSALM 118:21

D

DOMINIQUE
Belonging to the Lord

> *The Lord is my rock, and my*
> *fortress, . . . my strength, in*
> *whom I will trust.*
> PSALM 18:2

DON
Gainer of Victory

> *Whatsoever is born of God*
> *overcometh the world: . . . this is*
> *the victory which overcometh*
> *the world, even our faith.*
> 1 JOHN 5:4

DONABELLE
One of Beauty and Honor

> *I will praise thee; for I am*
> *fearfully and wonderfully made.*
> PSALM 139:14

DONALD
Gainer of Victory

> *Whatsoever is born of God*
> *overcometh the world: . . . this is*
> *the victory which overcometh*
> *the world, even our faith.*
> 1 JOHN 5:4

DONATO
Gift

> *Every good . . . and every*
> *perfect gift . . . cometh down*
> *from the Father of lights.*
> JAMES 1:17

DONEANNE
Victory and Grace

> *The Lord will give grace and*
> *glory: no good thing will he*
> *withhold.*
> PSALM 84:11

DONNA
One of Honor

> *The Lord is great, and greatly to*
> *be praised: . . . Honour and*
> *majesty are before him.*
> PSALM 96:4, 6

DONNABETH
One of Honor and Grace

> *I have set the Lord always*
> *before me: . . . I shall not be*
> *moved.*
> PSALM 16:8

DONNAFAYE
Honour and Trust

> *Strength and honour are her*
> *clothing; and she shall rejoice in*
> *time to come.*
> PROVERBS 31:25

DONNIE
Gainer of Victory

> *Whatsoever is born of God*
> *overcometh the world: . . . this is*
> *the victory which overcometh*
> *the world, even our faith.*
> 1 JOHN 5:4

DONNIS
Gainer of Victory

> *Thanks be unto God, which*
> *always causeth us to triumph in*
> *Christ.*
> 2 CORINTHIANS 2:14

DONTE
Enduring and Firm of Purpose

> *I have set the Lord always*
> *before me: because he is at my*
> *right hand, I shall not be moved.*
> PSALM 16:8

DORA
A Gift

> The Gift of God is eternal life
> through Jesus Christ our Lord.
> ROMANS 6:23

DORCUS
Symbol of Beauty

> He will beautify the meek with
> salvation.
> PSALM 149:4

DORI
Gift of God

> For by grace are ye saved
> through faith; and that not of
> yourselves: it is the gift of God.
> EPHESIANS 2:8

DORINDA
Beautiful Gift

> For by grace are ye saved
> through faith; and that not of
> yourselves: it is the gift of God.
> EPHESIANS 2:8

DORIS
Bountiful

> I will sing unto the Lord,
> because he hath dealt
> bountifully with me.
> PSALM 13:6

DOROTHY
Gift of God

> For by grace are ye saved
> through faith; and . . . not of
> yourselves: it is the gift of God.
> EPHESIANS 2:8

DORWOOD
Guardian

> I will instruct thee and teach
> thee . . . I will guide thee with
> mine eye.
> PSALM 32:8

DOSHIA *also* DOCIA
God's Gift

> For by grace are you saved
> through faith; . . . it is the gift of
> God.
> EPHESIANS 2:8

DOTTIE
Gift of God

> For by grace are ye saved
> through faith; . . . it is the gift of
> God.
> EPHESIANS 2:8

DOUG
One of Mystery

> The Lord seeth not as man
> seeth; for man looketh on the
> outward appearance, but the
> Lord looketh on the heart.
> 1 SAMUEL 16:7

DOUGLAS
One of Mystery

> The Lord seeth not as man
> seeth; for man looketh on the
> outward appearance, but the
> Lord looketh on the heart.
> 1 SAMUEL 16:7

DOVE
One of Peace

> The Lord will give strength . . .
> [and] bless his people with peace.
> PSALM 29:11

DOYLE
A Stranger

> The foundation of God standeth
> sure, . . . The Lord knoweth
> them that are his.
> 2 TIMOTHY 2:19

DRAKE
Leader of Strength

> The Lord is my rock, and my
> fortress, . . . my strength, in
> whom I will trust.
> PSALM 18:2

DREAMA
Heavenly Guidance

> I will instruct thee and teach
> thee . . . I will guide thee with
> mine eye.
> PSALM 32:8

DREMA
Heavenly Guidance

> I will instruct thee and teach
> thee . . . I will guide thee with
> mine eye.
> PSALM 32:8

DREW
Skillful One

> I am now come forth to give thee
> skill and understanding.
> DANIEL 9:22

DRISCOLL
Interpreter

> I will make thy name to be
> remembered . . . therefore shall
> the people praise thee.
> PSALM 45:17

DUANE   *also* DWAYNE, DWAIN
Cheerful of Heart

> Yet I will rejoice in the Lord, I
> will joy in the God of my
> salvation.
> HABAKKUK 3:18

DUCHESS
Harmonious Spirit

> For thou, Lord, hast made me
> glad through thy work.
> PSALM 92:4

DUFFY
Strong Spirit

> Thou hast also given me the
> shield of thy salvation: . . . thy
> right hand hath holden me up.
> PSALM 18:35

DUFORT
From the Strong Fortress

> The Lord is my rock, and my
> fortress, and my deliverer; my
> God, my strength, in whom I
> will trust.
> PSALM 18:2

DUGAN
Rules with Strength

> The Lord is my rock, and my
> fortress, and my deliver, my
> God, my strength, in whom I
> will trust.
> PSALM 18:2

DUKE
Leader of Faith

> Lead me in thy truth, . . . for
> thou art the God of my
> salvation.
> PSALM 25:5

DULCIMER
Harmonious Spirit

> For thou, Lord, hast made me
> glad through thy work.
> PSALM 92:4

DUNCAN
One of Strength

> For the Lord is great, . . .
> strength and beauty are in his
> sanctuary.
> PSALM 96:4, 6

DUNDEE
Peaceful Dweller

> The Lord is my shepherd; . . . He
> maketh me to lie down in green
> pastures.
> PSALM 23:1–2

DURELLE
One of Endurance

> I have set the Lord always
> before me: because he is at my
> right hand, I shall not be
> moved.
> PSALM 16:8

DURHAM
Peaceful Spirit

> Thou wilt keep him in perfect
> peace, whose mind is stayed on
> thee.
> ISAIAH 26:3

DURWARD
Doorkeeper

> I had rather be a doorkeeper in
> the house of my God.
> PSALM 84:10

DUSTEN
Valiant Fighter

> I have fought a good fight, I
> have finished my course, I have
> kept the faith.
> 2 TIMOTHY 4:7

DUSTI
Valiant One

> I have fought a good fight, I
> have finished my course, I have
> kept the faith.
> 2 TIMOTHY 4:7

DUSTIN
Valiant One

> The Lord stood with me, and
> strengthened me.
> 2 TIMOTHY 4:17

DUSTON
Valiant Fighter

> I have fought a good fight, I
> have finished my course, I have
> kept the faith.
> 2 TIMOTHY 4:7

DUSTY
The Valiant One

> Thou hast also given me the
> shield of thy salvation.
> PSALM 18:35

DUTCH
One from Afar

> Blessed is the nation whose God
> is the Lord.
> PSALM 33:12

DUWANNA
Cheerful of Heart

> Yet I will rejoice in the Lord, I
> will joy in the God of my
> salvation.
> HABAKKUK 3:18

DWAIN   *also* DUANE
Cheerful of Heart

> Yet I will rejoice in the Lord, I
> will joy in the God of my
> salvation.
> HABAKKUK 3:18

DWAYNE   *also* DUANE
Cheerful of Heart

> Yet I will rejoice in the Lord, I
> will joy in the God of my
> salvation.
> HABAKKUK 3:18

DWIGHT
Dwelling in the Light

> Let your light so shine before
> men, that they may see your
> good works, glorify your Father
> . . . in heaven.
> MATTHEW 5:16

DYONSSALYNN
Divine and Refreshing Spirit

> The times of refreshing shall
> come from the presence of the
> Lord.
> ACTS 3:19

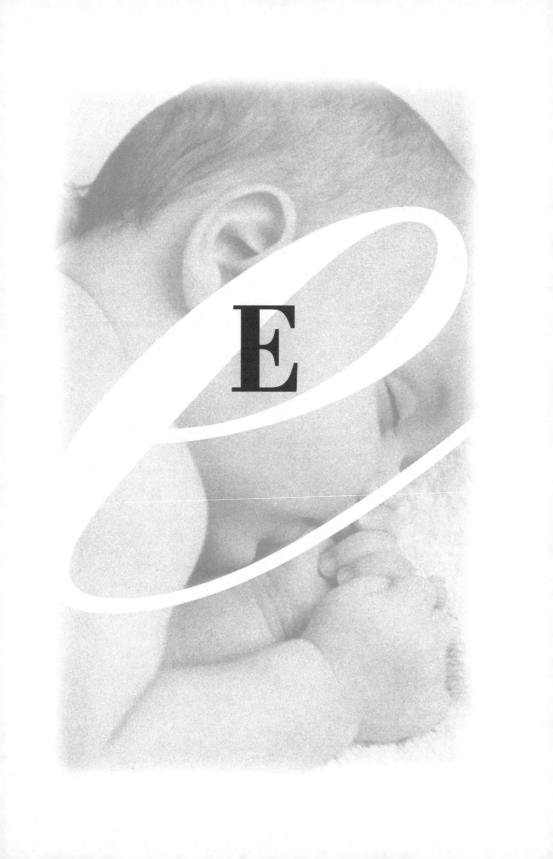

EAARON *also* AARON
One Of Light

> Let your light so shine before
> men, that they may see your
> good works, and glorify your
> Father which is in heaven.
> MATTHEW 5:16

EADY
Rich gift

> Whosoever believeth on him
> shall not be ashamed. . . . for the
> same Lord over all is rich unto
> all that call upon him.
> ROMANS 10:11–12

EAMMON
Rich Protection

> I have set the Lord always
> before me: because he is at my
> right hand, I shall not be
> moved.
> PSALM 16:8

EARLE
A Nobleman

> The steps of a good man are
> ordered by the Lord: and he
> delighteth in his way.
> PSALM 37:23

EARLENE
Of Noble Rank

> Ye are a chosen generation, a
> royal priesthood, . . . show forth
> the praises of him who hath
> called you.
> 1 PETER 2:9

EARLETTA
One of Nobility

> Ye are a chosen generation, a
> royal priesthood, . . . show forth
> the praises of him who hath
> called you.
> 1 PETER 2:9

EARLINE
One of Noble Rank

> Ye are a chosen generation, a
> royal priesthood, . . . show forth
> the praises of him who hath
> called you.
> 1 PETER 2:9

EARNEST
Strong Determination

> I will bless the Lord, . . . I have
> set the Lord always before me:
> . . . he is at my right hand, I
> shall not be moved.
> PSALM 16:7–8

EATON
Riverside Village

> He shall be like a tree . . . that
> bringeth forth his fruit in his
> season; . . . and whatsoever he
> doeth shall prosper.
> PSALM 1:3

EBB
Symbol of Strength

> Thy hands have made me and
> fashioned me: give me
> understanding, that I may learn
> thy commandments.
> PSALM 119:73

EBENEZER
Rock of Strength

> In God is my salvation and my glory: the rock of my strength, and my refuge, is in God.
> PSALM 62:7

EBONY
Symbol of Strength

> God is my salvation . . . glory: [and] my strength, . . . my refuge, is in God.
> PSALM 62:7

ECHELON
One of Authority

> When the righteous are in authority, the people rejoice.
> PROVERBS 29:2

ECHO
Repeated Voice

> I will praise thee: for thou hast heard me, and art become my salvation.
> PSALM 118:21

Greek

ECLOTHIA
Illustrious and Courageous

> For whatsoever is born of God overcometh the world: and this is the victory that overcometh the world, even our faith.
> 1 JOHN 5:4

ECOUIA
Regal and Upright One

> Surely the righteous shall give thanks unto thy name: the upright shall dwell in thy presence.
> PSALM 140:13

ED
A Witness

> A true witness delivereth souls.
> PROVERBS 14:25

EDA
Rich Gift

> Every good gift and every perfect gift is from above, and cometh down from the Father of lights.
> JAMES 1:17

EDAIN
A Strong Spirit

> Fight the good fight of faith, lay hold on eternal life, whereunto thou art also called.
> 1 TIMOTHY 6:12

EDDIE
A Witness

> I will not rest, until the righteousness thereof go forth as brightness, and the salvation thereof as a lamp that burneth.
> ISAIAH 62:1

EDDISSIA
Prosperous and Happy

> *Thou wilt show me the path of life: in thy presence is fulness of joy; at thy right hand there are pleasures for evermore.*
> PSALM 16:11

EDEEN
Prosperous and Pleasant One

> *I will sing unto the Lord, because he hath dealt bountifully with me.*
> PSALM 13:6

EDELTRAUD
Noble One

> *Thou hast also given me the shield of thy salvation: . . . thy gentleness hath made me great.*
> PSALM 18:35

EDEN
Delight

> *I delight to do thy will, O my God: yea, thy law is within my heart.*
> PSALM 40:8

EDER
A Flock

> *He shall feed his flock like a shepherd: . . . gather the lambs with his arm, and . . . gently lead those that are with young.*
> ISAIAH 40:11

EDERLAINE
Noble One

> *Ye are a chosen generation, a royal priesthood, . . . show forth the praises of him who hath called you.*
> 1 PETER 2:9

EDIE
God's Gift

> *For by grace are ye saved through faith; and that not of yourselves: it is the gift of God.*
> EPHESIANS 2:8

EDITHE
Rich Gift

> *Whosoever believeth on him shall not be ashamed. . . . for the same Lord over all is rich unto all that call upon him.*
> ROMANS 10:11–12

EDMONDO
Prosperous Protector

> *Let the Lord be magnified, which hath pleasure in the prosperity of his servant.*
> PSALM 35:27

EDMUND
Prosperous Protector

> *Let them shout for joy, . . . Let the Lord be magnified, which hath pleasure in the prosperity of his servant.*
> PSALM 35:27

EDNA
also ADNA
One of Delight

> *Delight thyself... in the Lord;*
> *and he shall give thee the*
> *desires of thine heart.*
> PSALM 37:4

EDOVAR
Blessed Protector

> *In God is my salvation and my*
> *glory: the rock of my strength,*
> *and my refuge, is in God.*
> PSALM 62:7
>
> French

EDRIE
The Mighty One

> *Thou hast also given me the*
> *shield of thy salvation: ... and*
> *thy gentleness hath made me*
> *great.*
> PSALM 18:35

EDUARDO
Blessed Protector

> *In God is my salvation and my*
> *glory: the rock of my strength,*
> *and my refuge, is in God.*
> PSALM 62:7

EDWARDANNE
Blessed Protector

> *In God is my salvation and my*
> *glory: the rock of my strength,*
> *and my refuge, is in God.*
> PSALM 62:7

EDWIN
Rich Friend

> *For such as are blessed by him*
> *shall inherit the earth.*
> PSALM 37:22

EDWINA
Blessed Protector

> *In God is my salvation and my*
> *glory: the rock of my strength,*
> *and my refuge, is in God.*
> PSALM 62:7

EERICA
also ERIKA, ERICKA
Mighty Heroine

> *Fight the good fight of faith, lay*
> *hold on eternal life, whereunto*
> *thou art also called.*
> 1 TIMOTHY 6:12

EFFIE
One of Nobility

> *Ye are a chosen generation, ...*
> *ye should show forth the praises*
> *of him who hath called you.*
> 1 PETER 2:9

EFI
Of Noble Fame

> *Wait on the Lord, and keep his*
> *way, and he shall exalt thee to*
> *inherit the land.*
> PSALM 37:34

EFIM
Of Good Report

> *Whatsoever things are true,*
> *honest, ... just, ... pure, ...*
> *lovely, ... of good report; if*
> *there be any virtue,... think on*
> *these things.*
> PHILIPPIANS 4:8

EFRAIN
Blessed

> Blessed be the Lord God, the
> God of Israel, who only doeth
> wondrous things. . . . And
> blessed be his glorious name.
> PSALM 72:18–19.

EFREM
Very Fruitful

> Ye have not chosen me, but I
> have chosen you, and ordained
> you, that ye should go and bring
> forth fruit.
> JOHN 15:16

EGAN
A Strong Spirit

> Fight the good fight of faith, lay
> hold on eternal life, whereunto
> thou art also called.
> 1 TIMOTHY 6:12

EHIN
The Honored

> For the Lord is great, and
> greatly to be praised: . . .
> Honour and majesty are
> before him.
> PSALM 96:4, 6

EICAPATOLA
One of Noble Rank

> Thou hast also given me the
> shield of thy salvation: . . . thy
> gentleness hath made me great.
> PSALM 18:35

EIDDWEN
Blessed and Happy

> Thou wilt show me the path of
> life: in thy presence is fulness of
> joy; at thy right hand . . . are
> pleasures for evermore.
> PSALM 16:11

EIJA
Strong Mountian

> They that trust in the Lord shall
> be as Mount Zion, which cannot
> be removed, but abideth forever.
> PSALM 125:1

EILEEN
Lady of Brightness

> I will not rest, until the
> righteousness thereof go forth as
> brightness.
> ISAIAH 62:1

EILLEEN
One of Light

> Let your light so shine before
> men, that they may see your
> good works, and glorify your
> Father which is in heaven.
> MATTHEW 5:16

EINAR
Strong Warrior

> Fight the good fight of faith, lay
> hold on eternal life, whereunto
> thou art also called.
> 1 TIMOTHY 6:12

E

EIRENE
One of Peace

> The Lord will give strength unto
> his people; the Lord will bless
> his people with peace.
> PSALM 29:11

ELAINA
A Shining Light

> Let your light so shine before
> men, that they may see your
> good works, and glorify your
> Father which is in heaven.
> MATTHEW 5:16

ELAINE
One of Light

> They that be wise shall shine as
> the brightness of the firmament;
> . . . as the stars for ever and ever.
> DANIEL 12:3

ELBERTA
Illustrious Through Nobility

> Now the God of peace, . . . Make
> you perfect in every good work
> to do his will . . . through Jesus
> Christ.
> HEBREWS 13:20–21

ELBYS
Illustrious Through Nobility

> Now the God of peace, . . . Make
> you perfect in every good work
> to do his will, . . . through Jesus
> Christ.
> HEBREWS 13:20–21

ELDEAN
One of Wisdom

> For the Lord giveth wisdom: out
> of his mouth cometh knowledge
> and understanding.
> PROVERBS 2:6

ELDEXTER
One of Excellent Skill

> God gave them knowledge and
> skill in all learning and wisdom.
> DANIEL 1:17

ELDIE
Trustworthy Elder

> Let the elders that rule well be
> counted worthy of double
> honour, especially they who
> labour in the word and doctrine.
> 1 TIMOTHY 5:17

ELDON
The Gift of Experience

> Every good gift and every
> perfect gift is from above, and
> cometh down from the Father of
> lights.
> JAMES 1:17

ELDOR
Gift of Wisdom

> Give instruction to a wise man,
> and he will be yet wiser: teach a
> just man, and he will increase in
> learning.
> PROVERBS 9:9

ELDRED
One Of Counsel

> *I will bless the Lord, who hath
> given me counsel: . . . I have set
> the Lord always before me: . . . I
> shall not be moved.*
> PSALM 16:7–8

ELDRIDGE
Wise Counselor

> *I will bless the Lord, who hath
> given me counsel: . . . I have set
> the Lord always before me: . . . I
> shall not be moved.*
> PSALM 16:7–8

ELDWIN
Old Friend

> *A man that hath friends must
> show himself friendly: and there
> is a friend that sticketh closer
> than a brother.*
> PROVERBS 18:24

ELEANORA
A Bright Spirit

> *A merry heart maketh a
> cheerful countenance.*
> PROVERBS 15:13

ELEASE
God Hath Helped

> *Many, O Lord . . . are thy
> wonderful works . . . if I would
> declare and speak of them, they
> are more than can be numbered.*
> PSALM 40:5

ELEFTHERIA
One of Great Strength

> *Blessed be the Lord . . . My
> goodness, . . . fortress, . . . high
> tower, . . . deliverer; my shield,
> and he in whom I trust.*
> PSALM 144:1–2

ELEMA
Noble and Famous

> *Wait on the Lord, and keep his
> way, and he shall exalt thee to
> inherit the land.*
> PSALM 37:34

ELENEKINA
Vigorous Determination

> *I have set the Lord always
> before me: because he is at my
> right hand, I shall not be
> moved.*
> PSALM 16:8

ELENIEDA
Shining with Light

> *And they that be wise shall
> shine as the brightness of the
> firmament.*
> DANIEL 12:3

ELER
The Lord Is My Light

> *The Lord is my light and my
> salvation; whom shall I fear?
> the Lord is the strength of my
> life; of whom shall I be afraid?*
> PSALM 27:1

E

ELERY
Of Noble Rank
> *Ye have not chosen me, but I have chosen you, and ordained you, that ye should go and bring forth fruit.*
> JOHN 15:16

ELESPERIO
One from Afar
> *Blessed is the nation whose God is the Lord; and the people whom he hath chosen for his own inheritance.*
> PSALM 33:12

ELETHA
One of Truth
> *For his merciful kindness is great toward us: and the truth of the Lord endureth for ever. Praise ye the Lord.*
> PSALM 117:2

ELEUTHERA
One Who Is Free
> *Stand fast therefore in the liberty wherewith Christ hath made us free.*
> GALATIANS 5:1

ELFRED
Wise and Good Counsel
> *I will instruct thee and teach thee in the way which thou shalt go: I will guide thee with mine eye.*
> PSALM 32:8

ELGENE
Royal and Noble
> *Ye have not chosen me, but I have chosen you, and ordained you, that ye should go and bring forth fruit.*
> JOHN 15:16

ELGIN
Jehovah Is My God
> *Behold, God is my salvation; I will trust, and not be afraid: for the Lord JEHOVAH is my strength and my song; . . . my salvation.*
> ISAIAH 12:2

ELGON
Noble and Pure
> *The statutes of the Lord are right, rejoicing the heart: the commandment of the Lord is pure, enlightening the eyes.*
> PSALM 19:8

ELIA   *also* ELIAH
Jehovah Is God
> *That men may know that thou, whose name alone is JEHOVAH, art the most high over all the earth.*
> PSALM 83:18

ELIADES
Gift of God
> *Every good gift and every perfect gift is from above, and cometh down from the Father of lights.*
> JAMES 1:17

ELIAH
Jehovah Is God

> That men may know that thou, whose name alone is JEHOVAH, art the most high over all the earth.
> PSALM 83:18

ELIANNA
God Has Answered Me

> I will praise thee; for thou hast heard me, and art become my salvation.
> PSALM 118:21

ELIANNE
Light and Grace

> The Lord will give grace and glory: no good thing will he withhold from them that walk uprightly.
> PSALM 84:11

ELIAS
Jehovah Is God

> That men may know that thou, whose name alone is JEHOVAH, art the most high over all the earth.
> PSALM 83:18

ELIDOMI
Warm and Radiant One

> And they that be wise shall shine as the brightness of the firmament.
> DANIEL 12:3

ELIGIA
Jehovah Is My God

> I will trust, and not be afraid: for the Lord JEHOVAH is my strength and my song: he also is . . . my salvation.
> ISAIAH 12:2
>
> Hebrew

ELIHU
Jehovah Is God

> Keep not thou silence, O God: . . . That men may know . . . thou, whose name alone is JEHOVAH.
> PSALM 83:1, 18
>
> Hebrew

ELIKAPEKA
Devoted One

> I will bless the Lord at all times: his praise shall continually be in my mouth.
> PSALM 34:1
>
> Hawaiian

ELIOTT
Jehovah Is God

> That men may know that thou, whose name alone is JEHOVAH, art the most high over all the earth.
> PSALM 83:18

ELISE
Consecrated to God

> Teach me, O Lord, the way of thy statutes; and I shall keep it unto the end.
> PSALM 119:33

E

ELISEBETH
Devoted One

I will bless the Lord at all times: his praise shall continually be in my mouth.
PSALM 34:1

ELISEO
Consecrated to God

Give me understanding, and I shall keep thy law; yea, I shall observe it with my whole heart.
PSALM 119:34

ELISEUS
God Is My Salvation

I will praise thee: for thou hast heard me, and art become my salvation.
PSALM 118:21

ELISHIA
My God Is Salvation

I will praise thee: for thou hast heard me, and art become my salvation.
PSALM 118:21

ELISIA
Consecrated to God

I will bless the Lord, who hath given me counsel: . . . I have set the Lord always before me: . . . I shall not be moved.
PSALM 16:7–8

ELITA
The Chosen One

Ye have not chosen me, but I have chosen you, and ordained you, that ye should go and bring forth fruit.
JOHN 15:16

ELIYA
God Is My Lord

I will trust, and not be afraid: . . . the Lord JEHOVAH is my strength and my song; . . . he also is . . . my salvation.
ISAIAH 12:2

ELIZABETH
Devoted One

I will bless the Lord at all times: his praise shall continually be in my mouth.
PSALM 34:1

ELIZABETH ANN
Devotion and Grace

The Lord will give grace and glory: no good thing will he withhold from them that walk uprightly.
PSALM 84:11

ELLANNE
One of Light and Grace

The Lord will give grace and glory: no good thing will he withhold from them that walk uprightly.
PSALM 84:11

ELLIE
Giver of Light

> *I will not rest, until the righteousness thereof go forth as brightness, and the salvation thereof as a lamp that burneth.*
> ISAIAH 62:1

ELLIS
God Is My Salvation

> *But God commendeth his love toward us, . . . while we were sinners, Christ died for us. . . . we shall be saved.*
> ROMANS 5:8–9

ELLISSA
God Is Salvation

> *God is my salvation; I will trust, and not be afraid: . . . the Lord JEHOVAH is my strength, . . . my song, . . . [and] my salvation.*
> ISAIAH 12:2

ELOIS
One of Victory

> *Whatsoever is born of God overcometh the world, this is the victory . . . even our faith.*
> 1 JOHN 5:4

ELOISE
Victorious

> *Thanks be unto God, which always causeth us to triumph in Christ.*
> 2 CORINTHIANS 2:14

ELONA
Great One of Strength

> *In God is my salvation and my glory: the rock of my strength, and my refuge, is in God.*
> PSALM 62:7

ELONZO
Noble One

> *Thou hast also given me the shield of thy salvation: . . . thy gentleness hath made me great.*
> PSALM 18:35

ELOUISE
Victorious

> *Now thanks be unto God, which always causeth us to triumph in Christ.*
> 2 CORINTHIANS 2:14

ELRICK
Noble and Powerful

> *But ye are a chosen generation, a royal priesthood . . . that ye should show forth the praises of him who hath called you.*
> 1 PETER 2:9

ELTON
Noble and Brilliant

> *I will give thee thanks in the great congregation: . . . my tongue shall speak of thy righteousness and of thy praise.*
> PSALM 35:18, 28

ELVIA
One of Wisdom

*With my whole heart have I
sought thee: . . . Thy word have
I hid in mine heart, . . . teach me
thy statutes.*
PSALM 119:10, 11, 12

ELVIN
Noble Friend

*A man that hath friends must
show himself friendly: and there
is a friend that sticketh closer
than a brother.*
PROVERBS 18:24

ELVIRA
One of Purity

*Blessed are the pure in heart:
for they shall see God.*
MATTHEW 5:8

ELVIS
One of Wisdom

*For the Lord giveth wisdom: . . .
knowledge and understanding.*
PROVERBS 2:6

ELYSHA
God Is Salvation

*Behold, God is my salvation; I
will trust, and not be afraid: for
the Lord JEHOVAH is my
strength . . . song.*
ISAIAH 12:2

ELYSIA
God Is Salvation

*Behold, God is my salvation; I
will trust, and not be afraid: for
the Lord JEHOVAH is my
strength and my song.*
ISAIAH 12:2

ELYSSE
Consecrated to God

*Give me understanding, and I
shall keep thy law; . . . [and]
observe it with my whole heart.*
PSALM 119:34

EMELEINE
One Who is Industrious

*And whatsoever ye do, do it
heartily, as to the Lord, . . . for
ye serve the Lord Christ.*
COLOSSIANS 3:23–24

EMERY
The Industrious Leader

*The Lord is my light and my
salvation; whom shall I fear?
the Lord is the strength of my
life; of whom shall I be afraid?*
PSALM 27:1

EMILIO
Industrious

*Whatsoever ye do, do it heartily,
as to the Lord, . . . for ye serve
the Lord Christ.*
COLOSSIANS 3:23–24

EMILY
Industrious

> Whatsoever ye do, do it heartily,
> as to the Lord, . . . for ye serve
> the Lord Christ.
> COLOSSIANS 3:23–24

EMMANUEL
God with Us

> Lo, I am with you always, even
> unto the end of the world. Amen.
> MATTHEW 28:20

EMMETTE
Industrious

> Whatsoever ye do, do it heartily,
> as to the Lord, . . . for ye serve
> the Lord Christ.
> COLOSSIANS 3:23–24

ENCARNATION
Divine One

> Given unto us [are] exceedingly
> great and precious promises:
> that by these ye might be
> partakers of the divine nature.
> 2 PETER 1:4

ENRIQUE
Ruler of the Home

> Through wisdom is an house
> builded; and by understanding
> it is established.
> PROVERBS 24:3
>
> Spanish

EPIPHANY
Manifestation of Christ

> For God . . . hath shined in our
> hearts, to give the light of the
> knowledge of the glory of God in
> the face of Jesus Christ.
> 2 CORINTHIANS 4:6

ERIC
Mighty One

> Thou hast . . . given me the
> shield of thy salvation: . . . thy
> gentleness hath made me great.
> PSALM 18:35

ERICA
Mighty Heroine

> Fight the good fight of faith, lay
> hold on eternal life, whereunto
> thou art also called.
> 1 TIMOTHY 6:12

ERICKA
Powerful and Regal

> God hath not given us the spirit
> of fear; but of power, . . . love,
> and of a sound mind.
> 2 TIMOTHY 1:7

ERIK
Ever Powerful

> God hath not given us the spirit
> of fear; but of power, . . . love,
> and of a sound mind.
> 2 TIMOTHY 1:7

ERIKA
Mighty Heroine

> Fight the good fight of faith, lay
> hold on eternal life, whereunto
> thou art also called.
> 1 TIMOTHY 6:12

ERIN
One of Peace

> The Lord will give strength unto
> his people; the Lord will bless
> his people with peace.
> PSALM 29:11

ERMA
Power

> God is my strength and power:
> and he maketh my way perfect.
> 2 SAMUEL 22:33

ERNESTINE
Vigorous Determination

> I have set the Lord always
> before me: . . . he is at my right
> hand, I shall not be moved.
> PSALM 16:8

ESME
The Emerald

> I will praise thee; for I am
> fearfully and wonderfully made.
> PSALM 139:14

ESTHER
Radiant One

> The path of the just is as the
> shining light, that shineth . . .
> unto the perfect day.
> PROVERBS 4:18

ESTRELLA
Child of the Stars

> They that be wise shall shine as
> the brightness of the firmament.
> DANIEL 12:3

ETHAN
Strong and Steadfast

> Be ye stedfast, unmovable,
> always abounding in the work
> of the Lord.
> 1 CORINTHIANS 15:58

ETHEL
Noble One

> I will praise thee, O Lord, among
> the people: and I will sing praises
> unto thee among the nations.
> PSALM 108:3

ETHELENE
Of Noble Rank

> Ye are a chosen generation, . . .
> show forth the praises of him
> who hath called you.
> 1 PETER 2:9

EUGENE
One of Nobility

> Lead a quiet and peaceable life
> . . . this is good and acceptable
> in the sight of God our Saviour.
> 1 TIMOTHY 2:2–3

EUGENIE
One of Nobility

> Lead a quiet and peaceable life
> . . . this is good and acceptable
> in the sight of God our Saviour.
> 1 TIMOTHY 2:2–3

EUREKA
I Have Found It

> I will praise thee: for thou hast
> heard me, and art become my
> salvation.
> PSALM 118:21

EVA
One of Life

> *The Lord is my light and my salvation; . . . the strength of my life; of whom shall I be afraid?*
> PSALM 27:1

EVALYN
One of Life

> *The Lord is my light and my salvation; . . . the strength of my life; of whom shall I be afraid?*
> PSALM 27:1

EVAN
God's Gift

> *The gift of God is eternal life through Jesus Christ our Lord.*
> ROMANS 6:23

EVANGELINA
Bearer of Glad Tidings

> *How beautiful are the feet of them that preach the gospel of peace, and bring glad tidings.*
> ROMANS 10:15

EVELYN
A Life Well-Pleasing

> *Make you perfect in every good work to do his will.*
> HEBREWS 13:21

EVERETT
Strong and Brave

> *Wait on the Lord; be of good courage, and he shall strengthen thine heart.*
> PSALM 27:14

EVONNE
also YVONNE, IVONNE

Grace of the Lord

> *By grace are ye saved through faith; . . . it is the gift of God.*
> EPHESIANS 2:8

EVY
One of Life

> *The Lord is my light and my salvation; . . . the strength of my life; of whom shall I be afraid?*
> PSALM 27:1

EZEKIEL
God Makes Strong

> *The Lord is my light and my salvation; . . . the strength of my life; of whom shall I be afraid?*
> PSALM 27:1

FABIAN
Tiller of the Soul

> *He that tilleth his land shall have plenty of bread: . . . A faithful man shall abound with blessings.*
> PROVERBS 28:19–20

FABIO
Tiller of the Soil

> *He that tilleth his land shall have plenty of bread: . . . A faithful man shall abound with blessings.*
> PROVERBS 28:19–20

FABRICIUS
Skilled One

> *Whatsoever ye do, do it heartily, as to the Lord, . . . for ye serve the Lord Christ.*
> COLOSSIANS 3:23–24

FABRINA
One of Wisdom

> *For the Lord giveth wisdom: out of his mouth cometh knowledge and understanding.*
> PROVERBS 2:6

FACON
A Strong Spirit

> *And whatsoever ye do, do it heartily, as to the Lord, . . . for ye serve the Lord Christ.*
> COLOSSIANS 3:23–24

FADEKE
One of Courage

> *Be strong and of a good courage, . . . for the Lord thy God is with thee whithersoever thou goest.*
> JOSHUA 1:9

Ukrainian

FADI
One of Faith and Trust

> *I will say of the Lord, He is my refuge and my fortress: my God; in him will I trust.*
> PSALM 91:2

FADRIENNE
One of Faith and Trust

> *I will say of the Lord, He is my refuge and my fortress: my God; in him will I trust.*
> PSALM 91:2

FAGALE
The Beautiful

> *For the Lord taketh pleasure in his people: he will beautify the meek with salvation.*
> PSALM 149:4

FAIR
Fair One

> *I will praise thee; for I am fearfully and wonderfully made: marvellous are thy works.*
> PSALM 139:14

F

FAIRABEA
The Fair and Blessed One
> Blessed are they that keep his
> testimonies, and that seek him
> with the whole heart.
> PSALM 119:2

FAIRFAX
Fair One and Blessed
> Thy hands have made me and
> fashioned me: give me
> understanding, that I may learn
> thy commandments.
> PSALM 119:73

FAIRLEY
Fair One
> I will praise thee; for I am
> fearfully and wonderfully
> made: marvellous are thy
> works.
> PSALM 139:14

FAIRY
Dearly Beloved
> Beloved, let us love one another:
> for love is of God; and every one
> that loveth is born of God, and
> knoweth God.
> 1 JOHN 4:7

FAITH
Completely Trusting
> Now faith is the substance of
> things hoped for, the evidence of
> things not seen.
> HEBREWS 11:1

FALICIA   *also* FELICIA
The Happy One
> I will be glad and rejoice in
> thee: I will sing praise to thy
> name, O thou most High.
> PSALM 9:2

FALIN
Ruler with Strength
> God is my strength and power:
> and he maketh my way perfect.
> 2 SAMUEL 22:33

FALLEN
Ruler with Strength
> God is my strength and power:
> and he maketh my way perfect.
> 2 SAMUEL 22:33

FAMANTHA
Established by God
> O Lord our Lord, how excellent
> is thy name in all the earth! who
> has set thy glory above the
> heavens.
> PSALM 8:1

FANCHEA
One of Freedom
> Stand fast therefore in the
> liberty wherewith Christ hath
> made us free.
> GALATIANS 5:1

FANNIE
One Who Is Free
> Stand fast therefore in the
> liberty wherewith Christ hath
> made us free.
> GALATIANS 5:1

FARAH
Pleasant and Beautiful

> Let the words of my mouth, and
> the meditation of my heart, be
> acceptable in thy sight.
> PSALM 19:14

FARAJI
One Who Is Pleasant

> Let the words of my mouth, and
> the meditation of my heart, be
> acceptable in thy sight, O Lord.
> PSALM 19:14

FARGO
Explorer

> Thy word is a lamp unto my
> feet, and a light unto my path.
> PSALM 119:105

FARLEY
From the Meadow

> The Lord is my shepherd; . . . He
> maketh me to lie down in green
> pastures.
> PSALM 23:1–2

FAROUK
Valor and Strength

> 'The Lord is my rock, . . . my
> fortress, and my deliverer; my
> God, my strength, in whom I
> will trust.
> PSALM 18:2
>
>   Arabic

FARRAH
Pleasant and Beautiful

> I will praise thee; for I am
> fearfully and wonderfully made.
> PSALM 139:14

FARREL
One of Valor

> My brethren, be strong in the
> Lord, and in the power of his
> might.
> EPHESIANS 6:10

FARRIS
One of Strength

> They that wait upon the Lord
> shall renew their strength; they
> shall mount up with wings as
> eagles.
> ISAIAH 40:31

FATE
Full of Trust and Hope

> But let all those that put their
> trust in thee rejoice: . . . let them
> also that love thy name be joyful
> in thee.
> PSALM 5:11

FAUN
Young and Graceful

> For thou art my hope, O Lord
> God: thou art my trust from my
> youth.
> PSALM 71:5

FAUSTINA
Talented One

> I press toward the mark for the
> prize of the high calling of God
> in Christ Jesus.
> PHILIPPIANS 3:14

F

FAVORILETTE
One of Virtue and Favor

> *Whatsoever things are true, . . .*
> *honest, . . . just, . . . of good*
> *report; if there be any virtue,*
> *and . . . praise, think on these*
> *things.*
> PHILIPPIANS 4:8

FAWN
Young and Graceful

> *The Lord will give grace and*
> *glory: no good thing will he*
> *withhold from them that walk*
> *uprightly.*
> PSALM 84:11

FAYE
Full of Trust

> *And they that know thy name*
> *will put their trust in thee: . . .*
> *thou, Lord, hast not forsaken*
> *them that seek thee.*
> PSALM 9:10

FEATHER
One of Victory

> *For whatsoever is born of God*
> *overcometh the world.*
> 1 JOHN 5:4

FEBRA
Strong and Prosperous One

> *I will love thee, O Lord, my*
> *strength. . . . my rock, . . . my*
> *fortress, and my deliverer: . . . in*
> *whom I will trust.*
> PSALM 18:1

FEHRA
Pleasant and Beautiful

> *I will praise thee; for I am*
> *fearfully and wonderfully made.*
> PSALM 139:14

FELDER
Of the Open Country

> *Thy word is a lamp unto my*
> *feet, and a light unto my path.*
> PSALM 119:105

FELICIA   *also* FALICIA
The Happy One

> *I will be glad and rejoice in*
> *thee: I will sing praise to thy*
> *name, O thou most High.*
> PSALM 9:2

FELIMON
Of Loving Mind

> *My mouth shall speak of*
> *wisdom; and the meditation of*
> *my heart shall be of*
> *understanding.*
> PSALM 49:3

FELIX
Happy and Prosperous

> *I will sing unto the Lord,*
> *because he hath dealt*
> *bountifully with me.*
> PSALM 13:6

FELTON
Dweller by the Meadow

> *The Lord is my shepherd; I shall*
> *not want. He maketh me to lie*
> *down in green pastures.*
> PSALM 23:1–2

FENTON
From the Town Near the Marsh

> *I will praise thee; for I am fearfully and wonderfully made: marvellous are thy works.*
> PSALM 139:14

FERDINAND
Abundant Life

> *I am come that they might have life, and that they might have it more abundantly.*
> JOHN 10:10

FERGUS
The Choice One

> *Ye have not chosen me, but I have chosen you, . . . that ye should go and bring forth fruit.*
> JOHN 15:16

FERN
Bold Peace

> *The Lord will give strength unto his people; the Lord will bless his people with peace.*
> PSALMS 29:11

FERNANDO
Abundant Life

> *I am come that they might have life, and that they might have it more abundantly.*
> JOHN 10:10

FERRIN
One of Valor

> *My brethren, be strong in the Lord, and in the power of his might.*
> EPHESIANS 6:10

FESTUS
The Joyful One

> *Thou wilt show me the path of life: in your presence is fulness of joy; at thy right hand there are pleasures for evermore.*
> PSALM 16:11

FIANALEA
One of Purity and Peace

> *Thou wilt keep him in perfect peace, whose mind is stayed on thee: . . . he trusteth in thee.*
> ISAIAH 26:3

FIDELIA
Faithful

> *I have set the Lord always before me: because he is at my right hand, I shall not be moved.*
> PSALM 16:8

FIELDING
Dwelling in Quiet Peace

> *The Lord will give strength unto his people; the Lord will bless his people with peace.*
> PSALM 29:11

FIFI
He Shall Add

> *The Lord thy God shall bless thee in all thine increase, . . . therefore thou shalt surely rejoice.*
> DEUTERONOMY 16:15

F

FINATA
Fair One and Sincere
> But it is good for me to draw
> near to God: I have put my trust
> in the Lord God.
> PSALM 73:28

FINDLAY
Fair Hero
> The Lord is my light and my
> salvation; whom shall I fear?
> the Lord is the strength of my
> life; of whom shall I be afraid?
> PSALM 27:1

FINEST
One Of Excellent Virtue
> Whatsoever things are true, . . .
> honest, . . . just, . . . of good
> report; if there be any virtue, . . .
> [or] praise, think on these things.
> PHILIPPIANS 4:8

FITU
Complete
> And ye are complete in him,
> which is the head of all
> principality and power.
> COLOSSIANS 2:10

Polynesian

FITZGERALD
Spear Ruler of Strength
> Take unto you the whole armour
> of God, . . . and the sword of the
> Spirit, which is the word of God.
> EPHESIANS 6:13, 17

FITZHUGH
Son of Wisdom
> My mouth shall speak of
> wisdom; and the meditation of
> my heart shall be of
> understanding.
> PSALM 49:3

FITZPATRICK
Son of Patrick, the Noble
> But ye are a chosen generation,
> a royal priesthood . . . show
> forth the praises of him who
> hath called you.
> 1 PETER 2:9

FLEMMING
Dutchman
> I will praise thee; for I am
> fearfully and wonderfully made:
> marvellous are thy works.
> PSALM 139:14

FLETCHER
Maker of Arrows
> The labour of the righteous
> tendeth to life.
> PROVERBS 10:16

FLEURETTE
Flourishing One
> Those that be planted in the
> house of the Lord shall flourish
> in the courts of our God.
> PSALM 92:13

FLINT
Living Water
> Whosoever drinketh of the
> water that I shall give him shall
> never thirst.
> JOHN 4:14

FLORA
Flourishing One

> *Those that be planted in the house of the Lord shall flourish in the courts of our God.*
> PSALM 92:13

FLORASTELLA
Flourishing Star

> *I will praise thee; for I am fearfully and wonderfully made: marvellous are thy works.*
> PSALM 139:14

FLORIANNE
Flourishing in Grace

> *The Lord will give grace and glory: no good thing will he withhold from them that walk uprightly.*
> PSALM 84:11

FLOSSIE
The Flourishing One

> *I will praise thee; for I am fearfully and wonderfully made.*
> PSALM 139:14

FLOYD
Wise One

> *The fear of the Lord is the beginning of wisdom: . . . his praise endureth forever.*
> PSALM 111:10

FLYNN
One of Courage

> *The Lord is my light and my salvation; whom shall I fear? the Lord is the strength of my life; of whom shall I be afraid?*
> PSALM 27:1

FONS
Of Noble Family

> *But ye are a chosen generation, a royal priesthood.*
> 1 PETER 2:9

FORBES
Rich Heritage

> *I will sing unto the Lord, because he hath dealt bountifully with me.*
> PSALM 13:6

FORD
One Who Is Steadfast

> *My beloved brethren, be ye stedfast, unmovable, always abounding in the work of the Lord.*
> 1 CORINTHIANS 15:58

FOREST
Of the Forest

> *Now I have prepared with all my might for the house of my God.*
> 1 CHRONICLES 29:2

F

FORTINO
Strong, Powerful Shield

> Take unto you the whole armour
> of God, . . . the shield of faith . . .
> the sword of the Spirit, which is
> the word of God.
> EPHESIANS 6:13–14, 17

FOSTER
One of Protection

> Be strong and of a good
> courage; . . . for the Lord thy
> God is with thee whithersoever
> thou goest.
> JOSHUA 1:9

FOWLER
Keeper of Birds

> And whatsoever ye do, do it
> heartily, as to the Lord, . . . for
> ye serve the Lord Christ.
> COLOSSIANS 3:23–24

FRAN
Free

> Stand fast therefore in the
> liberty wherewith Christ hath
> made us free.
> GALATIANS 5:1

FRANCENA
One of Freedom

> Stand fast therefore in the
> liberty wherewith Christ hath
> made us free.
> GALATIANS 5:1

FRANCES
One of Freedom

> Stand fast therefore in the
> liberty wherewith Christ hath
> made us free.
> GALATIANS 5:1

FRANCESCA
One of Freedom

> Stand fast therefore in the
> liberty wherewith Christ hath
> made us free.
> GALATIANS 5:1

FRANCISCO
One of Freedom

> Stand fast therefore in the
> liberty wherewith Christ hath
> made us free.
> GALATIANS 5:1

FRANK
One of Freedom

> Stand fast therefore in the
> liberty wherewith Christ hath
> made us free.
> GALATIANS 5:1

FRASHER
Peace Rule

> Thou wilt keep him in perfect
> peace, whose mind is stayed in
> thee: because he trusteth in thee.
> ISAIAH 26:3

FRAWNDA
Wise Thoughts

My mouth shall speak of wisdom; and the meditation of my heart shall be of understanding.
PSALM 49:3

Greek

FRAZIER
Peace Rule

Thou wilt keep him in perfect peace whose mind is stayed on thee: because he trusteth in thee.
ISAIAH 26:3

FRED
One of Peace

The peace of God, . . . shall keep your hearts and minds through Christ Jesus.
PHILIPPIANS 4:7

FREDA
Peaceful

The peace of God, . . . shall keep your hearts and minds through Christ Jesus.
PHILIPPIANS 4:7

FREDDIE
One of Power and Peace

The peace of God, which passeth all understanding, shall keep your hearts and minds through . . . Jesus.
PHILIPPIANS 4:7

FREDERICK
One of Peace

The Lord will give strength unto his people the Lord will bless his people with peace.
PSALM 29:11

FREMONT
Guardian of Freedom

Stand fast therefore in the liberty wherewith Christ hath made us free.
GALATIANS 5:1

FRITZ
One of Peace

The Lord will give strength unto his people; the Lord will bless his people with peace.
PSALM 29:11

FUCHSIA
Scarlet in Color

Thy hands have made me and fashioned me: give me understanding, that I may learn thy commandments.
PSALM 119:73

FURMAN
Firm and Constant of Purpose

I have set the Lord always before me: because he is at my right hand, I shall not be moved.
PSALM 16:8

G

GABRIEL
God Is my Strength

> The Lord is my light and my
> salvation; . . . the strength of my
> life; of whom shall I be afraid?
> PSALM 27:1

GABRIELA
God Is my Strength

> The Lord is my light and my
> salvation; . . . the strength of my
> life; of whom shall I be afraid?
> PSALM 27:1

GABRIELLE
God Is my Strength

> The Lord is my light and my
> salvation; . . . the strength of my
> life; of whom shall I be afraid?
> PSALM 27:1

GADBERRY
Happy Warrior

> Fight the good fight of faith, lay
> hold on eternal life, whereunto
> thou art also called.
> 1 TIMOTHY 6:12

GAGE
A Pledge of Security

> For God so loved the world, that
> he gave his only begotten Son,
> that whosoever believeth in him
> should not perish.
> JOHN 3:16

GAIL
Source of Joy

> Thou wilt show me the path of
> life: in thy presence is fulness of
> joy.
> PSALM 16:11

GAILYNNE
Source of Joy

> I will be glad and rejoice in thee:
> I will sing praise to thy name.
> PSALM 9:2

GAINES
Prosperous One

> I will sing unto the Lord,
> because he hath dealt
> bountifully with me.
> PSALM 13:6

GAITHER
The Rejoiced In

> I will praise thee, O Lord, with
> my whole heart; . . . I will sing
> praise to thy name.
> PSALM 9:1–2

GALEANN
Joy and Grace

> The Lord will give grace and
> glory: no good thing will he
> withhold from them that walk
> uprightly.
> PSALM 84:11

GALEN
Philosopher

> Beware lest any man spoil you
> through philosophy . . . For in
> him dwelleth all the fulness of
> the Godhead bodily.
> COLOSSIANS 2:8–9

G

GALINA
One of Light

> Let your light so shine . . . that
> they may see your good works,
> and glorify your Father . . . in
> heaven.
> MATTHEW 5:16

GALLOWAY
Fair One

> Thy hands have made me and
> fashioned me: give me
> understanding, that I may learn
> thy commandments.
> PSALM 119:73

GALYNNE
God Has Redeemed

> I will praise thee: for thou hast
> heard me, and art become my
> salvation.
> PSALM 118:21

GAMBYSS
God's Reward

> I will praise thee: for thou hast
> heard me, and art become my
> salvation.
> PSALM 118:21

GAMMAH
Brave and One of Valor

> Be strong and of a good
> courage; . . . for the Lord thy
> God is with thee whithersoever
> thou goest.
> JOSHUA 1:9

GANNELL
One of Virtue

> Whatsoever things are true, . . .
> honest, . . . just, . . . pure, . . . of
> good report; if there be any
> virtue, and . . . praise, think on
> these things.
> PHILIPPIANS 4:8

GARAN
Spear Ruler of Strength

> Take unto you the whole armour
> of God, . . . the sword of the
> Spirit, which is the word of God.
> EPHESIANS 6:13, 17

GARATH
Mighty with the Spear

> Give unto the Lord, O ye mighty,
> give unto the Lord glory and
> strength. . . . worship the Lord.
> PSALM 29:1–2

GARCIA
Warrior

> Take unto you the whole armour
> of God, . . . taking . . . faith, . . .
> salvation, and the . . . Spirit,
> which is the word of God.
> EPHESIANS 6:13, 16–17

GARDENIA
The Protected

> He that dwelleth in the secret
> place of the most High shall
> abide under the . . . Almighty.
> PSALM 91:1

GARDINER
Keeper of a Garden

> For as the earth bringeth forth
> her bud, . . . so . . . God will
> cause righteousness and praise
> to spring forth.
> ISAIAH 61:11

GARELD
Spear Ruler of Strength

> Take unto you the whole armour
> of God, . . . the helmet of
> salvation, and the sword of the
> Spirit, which is the word of God.
> EPHESIANS 6:13, 16–17

GARETT
Strong with the Spear

> Take unto you the whole armour
> of God, . . . the helmet of
> salvation, and the sword of the
> Spirit, which is the word of God.
> EPHESIANS 6:13, 16–17

GARFIELD
Spear Field

> Take unto you the whole armour
> of God, . . . the helmet of
> salvation, and the sword of the
> Spirit, which is the word of God.
> EPHESIANS 6:13, 16–17

GARITH
Spear Ruler of Strength

> Be strong in the Lord, and . . .
> take . . . the sword of the Spirit,
> which is the word of God.
> EPHESIANS 6:10, 17

GARLAND
Crowned for Victory

> There is laid up for me a crown
> of righteousness, which the
> Lord, the righteous judge, shall
> give me at that day.
> 2 TIMOTHY 4:8

GARNER
Strong Protection

> He that dwelleth in the secret
> place of the most High shall
> abide under the shadow of the
> Almighty.
> PSALM 91:1

GARNET
A Jewel

> And they shall be mine, saith the
> Lord of hosts, in that day when
> I make up my jewels.
> MALACHI 3:17

GARREN
Spear Ruler of Strength

> Take unto you the whole armour
> of God, . . . the helmet of
> salvation, and the sword of the
> Spirit, which is the word of God.
> EPHESIANS 6:13, 16–17

GARRISON
Spear Ruler of Strength

> Take unto you the whole armour
> of God, . . . the helmet of
> salvation, and the sword of the
> Spirit, which is the word of God.
> EPHESIANS 6:13, 16–17

GARY
Fighter for the Faith

Put on the whole armour of God, that ye may be able to stand . . . taking the shield of Faith.
EPHESIANS 6:11, 16

GASPER
Strong in Victory

Whatsoever is born of God overcometh the world, this is the victory . . . even our faith.
1 JOHN 5:4

GATES
Guardian Protector

He that dwelleth in the secret place of the most High shall abide under the . . . Almighty.
PSALM 91:1

GAVEN
Strong in Victory

Be ye stedfast, unmovable, always abounding in the work of the Lord.
1 CORINTHIANS 15:58

GAY
Source of Joy

Thou wilt show me the path of life: in thy presence is fulness of joy.
PSALM 16:11

GAYLA
Source of Joy

Thou wilt show me the path of life: in thy presence is fulness of joy.
PSALM 16:11

GAYLORD
Happy in the Lord

Whoso trusteth in the Lord, happy is he.
PROVERBS 16:20

GAYNELLE
Rejoicing in Life

I will praise thee, O Lord, with my whole heart; . . . I will be glad and rejoice in thee: I will sing praise to thy name.
PSALM 9:1–2

GAYNOR
Prosperous One

I will sing unto the Lord, because he hath dealt bountifully with me.
PSALM 13:6

GEARLDINE
Victorious One

Whatsoever is born of God overcometh the world, this is the victory . . . even our faith.
1 JOHN 5:4

GELETA
My Joy Is Eternal

Thou wilt show me the path of life: in thy presence is fulness of joy.
PSALM 16:11

GEM
A Precious Jewel

I will praise thee; for I an fearfully and wonderfully made: marvellous are thy works.
PSALM 139:14

GENA
One of Peace

> The meek shall inherit the earth;
> and . . . delight themselves in the
> abundance of peace.
> PSALM 37:11

GENE
Courteous Spirit

> Be ye kind one to another,
> tenderhearted, forgiving one
> another, even as God . . . hath
> forgiven you.
> EPHESIANS 4:32

GENESIS
In the Beginning

> In the beginning was the Word,
> and the Word was with God.
> JOHN 1:1

GENEVA
Of Peace

> The meek shall inherit the earth;
> and shall delight themselves in
> the abundance of peace.
> PSALM 37:11

GENEVIEVE
Courteous Spirit

> Be ye kind one to another,
> tenderhearted, forgiving one
> another, even as God . . . hath
> forgiven you.
> EPHESIANS 4:32

GENGHIS
Conquering One

> But thanks be to God, which
> giveth us the victory through
> our Lord Jesus Christ.
> 1 CORINTHIANS 15:57

GENISE
One of Nobility

> Ye are a chosen generation, a
> royal priesthood . . . that ye
> should show . . . the praises of
> him who hath called you.
> 1 PETER 2:9

GENO
One of Nobility

> Ye are a chosen generation, a
> royal priesthood, . . . show forth
> the praises of him who hath
> called you.
> 1 PETER 2:9

GENOA
Noble and Blessed of God

> Thou hast also given me the
> shield of thy salvation: . . . thy
> gentleness hath made me great.
> PSALM 18:35

GENTRY
One of Noble Birth

> Ye are a chosen generation, a
> royal priesthood, . . . show forth
> the praises of him who hath
> called you.
> 1 PETER 2:9

GEOFFERY   *also* JEFFREY
God's Peace

> The wisdom that is from above
> is first pure, then peaceable,
> gentle, . . . full of mercy and
> good fruits.
> JAMES 3:17

GEOFFREY   *also* JEFFREY
God's Peace

> *The wisdom that is from above is first pure, then peaceable, gentle, . . . full of mercy and good fruits.*
> JAMES 3:17

GEORGE
Tiller of the Soil

> *He that tilleth his land shall have plenty.*
> PROVERBS 28:19

GEORGI
Industrious One

> *Whatsoever ye do, do it heartily, as to the Lord, . . . for ye serve the Lord Christ.*
> COLOSSIANS 3:23–24

GEORGIA
Industrious One

> *Strength and honour are her clothing; and she shall rejoice in time to come.*
> PROVERBS 31:25

GEORGIANA
Industrious One of Grace

> *The Lord will give grace and glory.*
> PSALM 84:11

GEOSS
In God Secure

> *Thou wilt keep him in perfect peace, whose mind is stayed on thee: because he trusteth in thee.*
> ISAIAH 26:3

GERALD   *also* JERALD
Spear Ruler of Strength

> *Whatsoever ye do in word or deed, do all in the name of the Lord Jesus.*
> COLOSSIANS 3:17

GERALDINE
Victorious One

> *Holding forth the word of life, that I may rejoice in the day of Christ.*
> PHILIPPIANS 2:16

GERAMEY
Exalted of the Lord

> *Thou hast . . . given me the shield of thy salvation: . . . thy gentleness hath made me great.*
> PSALM 18:35

GERDA
The Protected

> *The Lord is my light and my salvation; whom shall I fear? the Lord is the strength of my life; of whom shall I be afraid?*
> PSALM 27:1

GERE
One of Victory and Courage

> *For whatsoever is born of God overcometh the world: and this is the victory that overcometh the world, even our faith.*
> 1 JOHN 5:4

GERHARDT
Strong

> Be strong and of a good courage;
> . . . for the Lord thy God is with
> thee withersoever thou goest.
> JOSHUA 1:9

GERMAN
One Who Proclaims

> As it is written, "How beautiful
> are the feet of them that preach
> the gospel of peace."
> ROMANS 10:15

GERONIMO
The Holy Name

> For our heart shall rejoice in
> him, because we have trusted in
> his holy name.
> PSALM 33:21

GERRY
Appointed by God

> My servant . . . shall be exalted
> and extolled, and be very high.
> ISAIAH 52:13

GERTHA
One of Strength

> The Lord is my rock, . . . my
> fortress, and my deliverer; my
> God, my strength, in whom I
> will trust.
> PSALM 18:2

GERTRUDE
Maiden of Strength

> God is my salvation; I will trust,
> . . . the Lord . . . is my strength
> and . . . song; . . . my salvation.
> ISAIAH 12:2

GERVAISE
Spear Sharp

> Take unto you the whole armour
> of God, . . . take . . . salvation,
> and the sword of the Spirit,
> which is the word of God.
> EPHESIANS 6:13, 17

GIAN
Gracious Gift of God

> Every good gift and every
> perfect gift is from above, . . .
> and cometh down from the
> Father.
> JAMES 1:17

GIBSTON
A Pledge

> As it is written, "How beautiful
> are the feet of them that preach
> the gospel of peace."
> ROMANS 10:15

GIDEON
A Mighty Hewer

> The crooked shall be made
> straight, . . . the rough . . .
> smooth; And all flesh shall see
> the salvation of God.
> LUKE 3:5–6

GIFFORD
A Splendid Gift

> For by grace are ye saved
> through faith; and that not of
> yourselves: it is the gift of God.
> EPHESIANS 2:8

GILADA
My Joy Is Eternal

> *Thou wilt show me the path of*
> *life: in thy presence is fulness of*
> *joy; at thy right hand there are*
> *pleasures for evermore.*
> PSALM 16:11

GILBERT
Of Great Promise

> *If that which ye have heard*
> *from the beginning shall remain*
> *in you, ye . . . shall continue in*
> *the Son.*
> 1 JOHN 2:24

GILLIAM
Servant of Christ

> *I am thy servant; give me*
> *understanding, that I may know*
> *thy testimonies.*
> PSALM 119:125

GILLIS
Shield Bearer

> *Take unto you the whole armour*
> *of God, . . . the shield of faith,*
> *. . . the helmet of salvation, and*
> *the sword of the Spirit.*
> EPHESIANS 6:13, 16–17

GILMER
Noble in Honor

> *He shall call upon me, and I*
> *will answer him: I will be with*
> *him in trouble; I will deliver*
> *him and honour him.*
> PSALM 91:15

GINA
Immortal One

> *I am the resurrection, and . . .*
> *life: . . . whosoever liveth and*
> *believeth in me shall never die.*
> JOHN 11:25–26

GINGER
Pure One

> *With the pure thou wilt show*
> *thyself pure; and with the*
> *forward thou wilt show thyself*
> *forward.*
> PSALM 18:26

GINI
One of Purity

> *Blessed are the pure in heart:*
> *for they shall see God.*
> MATTHEW 5:8

GINNY
Pure One

> *Blessed are the pure in heart:*
> *for they shall see God.*
> MATTHEW 5:8

GINO
One of Nobility

> *Lead a quiet and peaceable life*
> *. . . this is good and acceptable*
> *in the sight of God.*
> 1 TIMOTHY 2:2–3

GIOIA
Joyous Little Angel

> *I say unto you, there is joy in the*
> *presence of the angels of God*
> *over one sinner that repenteth.*
> LUKE 15:10

GIOVANNI
God Is Gracious

> The Lord God, merciful and
> gracious, longsuffering, and
> abundant in goodness.
> EXODUS 34:6
>
> Hebrew

GISELLE
One Who Is Secure

> I have set the Lord . . . before
> me: . . . he is at my right hand, I
> shall not be moved.
> PSALM 16:8

GIULIANO
Bold Protector

> He that dewlleth in the secret
> place of the most High shall
> abide under the shadow of the
> Almighty.
> PSALM 91:1

GLACIER
God's Handiwork

> For we are his workmanship,
> created in Christ Jesus unto
> good works.
> EPHESIANS 2:10

GLADWIN
Merry Friend

> Ye are my friends, if ye do
> whatsoever I command you.
> JOHN 15:14

GLADYS
Submissive Spirit

> I . . . glory in my infirmities,
> that the power of Christ may
> rest upon me. . . . for when I am
> weak, then am I strong.
> 2 CORINTHIANS 12:9–10

GLEASON
Abundant and Shining One

> O Lord our Lord, how excellent
> is thy name in all the earth! who
> hast set thy glory above the
> heavens.
> PSALM 8:1

GLEN
A Quiet Spirit

> He maketh me to lie down in
> green pastures: he leadeth me
> beside the still waters.
> PSALM 23:2

GLENDA
A Quiet Spirit

> He maketh me to lie down in
> green pastures: he leadeth me
> beside the still waters.
> PSALM 23:2

GLENN
A Quiet Spirit

> He maketh me to lie down in
> green pastures: he leadeth me
> beside the still waters.
> PSALM 23:2

G

GLENNA
A Quiet Spirit

He maketh me to lie down in green pastures: he leadeth me beside the still waters.
PSALM 23:2

GLESSNER
Crystal Pure

The statutes of the Lord are right, rejoicing the heart.
PSALM 19:8

GLIMERENA
A Shining Light

Let your light so shine before men, that they may see your good works, and glorify your Father . . . in heaven.
MATTHEW 5:16

GLO
Shining Example

Let your light so shine before men, that they may see your good works, and glorify your Father . . . in heaven.
MATTHEW 5:16

GLORIA
Glorious One

The King's daughter is all glorious within: her clothing is of wrought gold.
PSALM 45:13

GLORIANNA
One of Glorious Grace

The Lord will give grace and glory.
PSALM 84:11

GLORIETTA
Glorious One

The King's daughter is all glorious within: her clothing is of wrought gold.
PSALM 45:13

GLOVIA
In Praise of God

I will praise the Lord with my whole heart, . . . His work is honourable and glorious.
PSALM 111:1, 3

GODFRED
One of Peace

The Lord will give strenth unto his people; the Lord will bless his people with peace.
PSALM 29:11

GODWIN
Friend of God

Ye are my friends, if ye do whatsoever I command you.
JOHN 15:14

GOLDEN
One of Precious Quality

Thy hands have made me and fashioned me: give me understanding, that I may learn thy commandments.
PSALM 119:73

GOLDIE
One of Precious Quality

Thy hands have made me and fashioned me: give me understanding, that I may learn thy commandments.
PSALM 119:73

GOODFELLOW
Pleasant Companion

> *Ye are my friends, if ye do whatsoever I command you.*
> JOHN 15:14

GORDON
One of Inspiration

> *The Lord put forth his hand, and touched my mouth. And the Lord said unto me, . . . I have put my words in thy mouth.*
> JEREMIAH 1:9

GOTTLIEB
Love of God

> *God so loved the world, that he gave his . . . Son, that whosoever believeth . . . should . . . have everlasting life.*
> JOHN 3:16

GOVERNOR
Ruler with Strength

> *As for God, his way is perfect; . . . God is my strength and power.*
> 2 SAMUEL 22:31, 33

GRACE
Lady of Grace

> *The Lord will give grace and glory: no good thing will he withhold from them that walk uprightly.*
> PSALM 84:11

GRADY
Noble and Illustrious

> *The God of peace, . . . Make you perfect in every good work to do his will.*
> HEBREWS 13:20–21

GRAHAM
One of Power

> *God is my strength and power: and he maketh my way perfect.*
> 2 SAMUEL 22:33

GRANT
A Great Promise

> *For God so loved the world, that he gave his only begotten Son.*
> JOHN 3:16

GRAY
One of Dignity

> *It is God that girdeth me with strength, and maketh my way perfect.*
> PSALM 18:32

GREG
Watchful One

> *Watch thou in all things, endure afflictions, do the work of an evangelist, make full proof of thy ministry.*
> 2 TIMOTHY 4:5

GREGORY
Watchful One

> *Watch thou in all things, endure afflictions, do the work of an evangelist, make full proof of thy ministry.*
> 2 TIMOTHY 4:5

GRETCHEN
A Precious Pearl

*I will praise thee; for I am
fearfully and wonderfully
made: . . . marvelous are thy
works; . . . how precious are
thy thoughts.*
PSALM 139:14, 17

GREYLING
Noble and Wise One

*The Lord giveth wisdom: out of
his mouth cometh knowledge
and understanding.*
PROVERBS 2:6

GRIFFIN
Of Strong Faith

*Fight the good fight of faith, lay
hold on eternal life, whereunto
thou art also called.*
1 TIMOTHY 6:12

GRISELLE
Great Strength and Patience

*The Lord is my rock, and . . .
fortress, . . . my deliverer; my
God, my strength, in whom I
will trust.*
PSALM 18:2

GROVER
Peaceful Dweller

*For he is our peace, who hath
made both one.*
EPHESIANS 2:14

GUADA LUPE
Victorious Nobility

*Thanks be to God, which giveth
us the victory through our Lord
Jesus Christ.*
1 CORINTHIANS 15:57

GUENTER
Strong Warrior

*Fight the good fight of faith, lay
hold on eternal life, whereunto
thou art also called.*
1 TIMOTHY 6:12

GUILLAUME
Bold Protector

*The Lord is my light and my
salvation; whom shall I fear?
the Lord is the strength of my
life; of whom shall I be afraid?*
PSALM 27:1

GUILLERMO
Resolute Protector

*God is my salvation and my
glory: the rock of my strength.*
PSALM 62:7

GUSTAVE
One of Nobility

*But ye are a chosen generation,
a royal priesthood . . . show
forth the praise of him who hath
called you.*
1 PETER 2:9

GUTHRIDGE
Warrior for the Faith

> *Fight the good fight of faith, lay hold on eternal life, whereunto thou art also called.*
> 1 TIMOTHY 6:12

GUY
Wise Leadership

> *But there is a spirit in man: and the inspiration of the Almighty giveth them understanding.*
> JOB 32:8

GUYLAINE
Wise Leadership

> *But there is a spirit in man: and the inspiration of the Almighty giveth them understanding.*
> JOB 32:8

GWEN
Blessed of God

> *Thou hast . . . given me the shield of thy salvation: . . . thy gentleness hath made me great.*
> PSALM 18:35

GWENDOLYNN
Blessed of God

> *Thou hast . . . given me the shield of thy salvation: . . . thy gentleness hath made me great.*
> PSALM 18:35

GYPSY
The Wanderer

> *Thy word is a lamp unto my feet, and a light unto my path.*
> PSALM 119:105

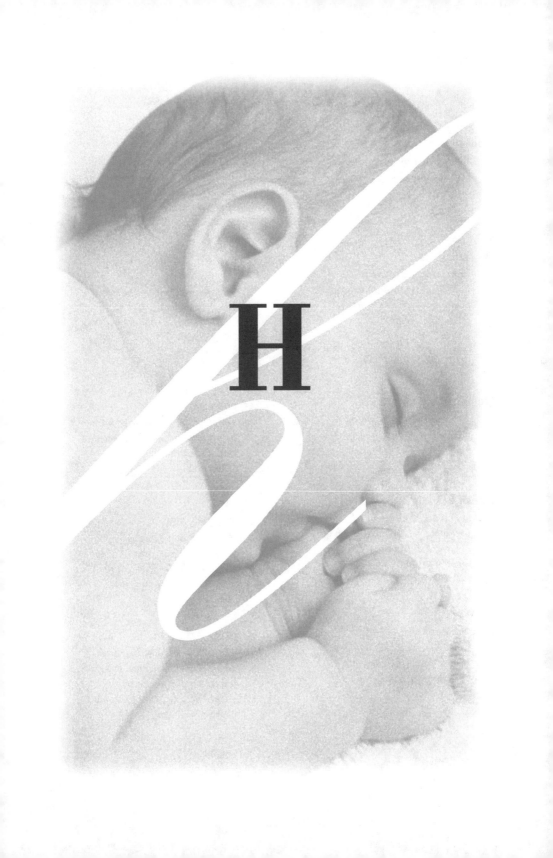

H

HABBAH
Beloved

> Beloved, let us love one another:
> for love is of God.
> 1 JOHN 4:7

> Arabic

HADASSAH
Flowering Vine

> I am the vine, ye are the
> branches: He that abideth in
> me, and I in him, . . . bringeth
> forth much fruit.
> JOHN 15:5

> Hebrew

HADDON
From the Heath Moor

> Thy word is a lamp unto my
> feet, and a light unto my path.
> PSALM 119:105

HADLEY
One of Wisdom

> My mouth shall speak of
> wisdom; and the meditation of
> my heart shall be of
> understanding.
> PSALM 49:3

HAHN
Diligent Worker

> For thou, Lord, hast made me
> glad through thy work: . . . O
> Lord, how great are thy works!
> PSALM 92:4–5

HAILEY
One of Wisdom

> My mouth shall speak of
> wisdom; and the meditation of
> my heart shall be of
> understanding.
> PSALM 49:3

HAINES
Protected One

> He that dwelleth in the secret
> place of the most High shall
> abide under the shadow of the
> Almighty.
> PSALM 91:1

HAKIMU
Learned One

> For the Lord giveth wisdom: out
> of his mouth cometh knowledge
> and understanding.
> PROVERBS 2:6

HAL
Leader of Strength

> Be strong and of a good
> courage; be not afraid, . . . for
> the Lord thy God is with thee
> whithersoever thou goest.
> JOSHUA 1:9

HALAVALU
Chosen One of Strength

> Ye have not chosen me, but I
> have chosen you, . . . that ye
> should go and bring forth fruit.
> JOHN 15:16

HALBERT
Radiant Home Ruler

> They that be wise shall shine as
> the brightness of the firmament.
> DANIEL 12:3

HALE
A Hero

> Thou hast also given me the
> shield of thy salvation: . . . thy
> gentleness hath made me great.
> PSALM 18:35

HALEY
One of Wisdom

> My mouth shall speak of
> wisdom; and the meditation
> of my heart shall be of
> understanding.
> PSALM 49:3

HALIMA
Patient and Kind

> Be ye kind one to another,
> tenderhearted, forgiving . . .
> even as God for Christ's sake
> hath forgiven you.
> EPHESIANS 4:32

HALLEY
One of Wisdom

> My mouth shall speak of
> wisdom; and the meditation of
> my heart shall be of
> understanding.
> PSALM 49:3

HALLMAN
A Servant

> Thy word is very pure: therefore
> thy servant loveth it.
> PSALM 119:140

HALWIN
Protective Guardian

> He that dwelleth in the secret
> place of the most High shall
> abide under the shadow of the
> Almighty.
> PSALM 91:1

HAMILTON
From the Mountain Hamlet

> Thy word is a lamp unto my
> feet, and a light unto my path.
> PSALM 119:105

HAMPTON
Peaceful Dweller

> The Lord will give strength . . .
> the Lord will bless his people
> with peace.
> PSALM 29:11

HANDEL
Artistic One

> I will praise thee; for I am
> fearfully and wonderfully
> made: marvellous are thy
> works.
> PSALM 139:14

HANNAH
Divine Grace

> The Lord will give grace and
> glory.
> PSALM 84:11

HANSFORD
God's Gracious Gift

> The Lord make his face shine
> upon thee, and be gracious unto
> thee.
> NUMBERS 6:25

HAPPY
One of Joy

> Thou wilt show me the path of
> life: in thy presence is fulness of
> joy; at thy right hand . . . are
> pleasures for evermore.
> PSALM 16:11

HARLOW
From the Hill Fort

> Thy word is a lamp unto my
> feet, and a light unto my path.
> PSALM 119:105

HARMONY
One of Harmony

> Let the words of my mouth, and
> the meditation of my heart, be
> acceptable in thy sight.
> PSALM 19:14

HAROLD
Leader of Strength

> Be strong and of a good
> courage; be not afraid, . . . the
> Lord thy God is with thee.
> JOSHUA 1:9

HARPER
One Who Plays the Harp

> And whatsoever ye do, do it
> heartily, as to the Lord, . . . for
> ye serve the Lord Christ.
> COLOSSIANS 3:23–24

HARRIETT
Full of Wisdom

> For the Lord giveth wisdom: out
> of his mouth cometh knowledge
> and understanding.
> PROVERBS 2:6

HARRIS
Strong Leader

> Have not I commanded thee? Be
> strong and of a good courage; be
> not afraid.
> JOSHUA 1:9

HARRY
Leader of Strength

> Be strong and of a good
> courage; . . . for the Lord thy
> God is with thee whithersoever
> thou goest.
> JOSHUA 1:9

HARVEY
Worthy of Battle

> For whatsoever is born of God
> overcometh the world . . . this is
> the victory . . . even our faith.
> 1 JOHN 5:4

HASKELL
Wisdom and Understanding

> For this cause we . . . desire that
> ye might be filled with the
> knowledge of his will . . .
> wisdom and spiritual
> understanding.
> COLOSSIANS 1:9

HAYDEE
Noble and Kind

> Be ye kind one to another,
> tenderhearted, forgiving one
> another.
> EPHESIANS 4:32

HAYYIM
Life
> He that hath the Son hath life;
> and he that hath not the Son of
> God hath not life.
> 1 JOHN 5:12
>
> Hebrew

HAZEL
Protected by God
> The Lord . . . will preserve me
> unto his heavenly kingdom.
> 2 TIMOTHY 4:18

HEATHER
One of Excellent Virture
> Many daughters have done
> virtuously, but thou excellest
> them all.
> PROVERBS 31:29

HEAVEN
Eternal Home
> I will say of the Lord, He is my
> refuge and my fortress: my God;
> in him will I trust.
> PSALM 91:2

HEBRON
Strength in Unity
> Every word of God is pure: he is
> a shield unto them that put
> their trust in him.
> PROVERBS 30:5

HEIDI
Cheerfully Noble
> I can do all things through
> Christ which strengtheneth me.
> PHILIPPIANS 4:13

HEINDRICH
Ruler of the Home
> Through wisdom is an house
> builded; and by understanding
> it is established.
> PROVERBS 24:3

HELEN
One of Light
> They that be wise shall shine as
> the brightness of the firmament.
> DANIEL 12:3

HELENA
One of Light
> Let your light so shine . . . that
> they may see your good works,
> and glorify your Father.
> MATTHEW 5:16

HELGA
The Holy
> I will praise thee, O Lord, . . . I
> will be glad and rejoice in thee:
> I will sing praise to thy name, O
> thou most High.
> PSALM 9:1–2

HELMER
With Strong Protection
> It is God that girdeth me with
> strength, and maketh my way
> perfect.
> PSALM 18:32

HELMUT
One of Strength and Courage
> Be strong and of a good
> courage; be not afraid . . . for
> the Lord thy God is with thee.
> JOSHUA 1:9
>
> German

HELOISE
One of Light

> Let your light so shine before men, that they may see your good works, and glorify your Father.
> MATTHEW 5:16

HENRY
Ruler of the Home

> Through wisdom is an house builded; and by understanding it is established.
> PROVERBS 24:3

HENZLER
Gracious Gift of Jehovah

> Every good gift and every perfect gift is from above, and cometh down from the Father of lights.
> JAMES 1:17

HERCULES
Of Lordly Fame

> Thou hast also given me the shield of thy salvation: . . . thy gentleness hath made me great.
> PSALM 18:35

HERMAN
Warrior

> Thou therefore endure hardness, as a good soldier of Jesus Christ.
> 2 TIMOTHY 2:3

HERMOINE
Noble Warrior of the Faith

> Fight the good fight of faith, lay hold on eternal life, whereunto thou art also called.
> 1 TIMOTHY 6:12

HERNANDO
Abundant Life

> I am come that they might have life, and that they might have it more abundantly.
> JOHN 10:10

HERSCHELL
One of Strength

> The Lord is my light and my salvation: whom shall I fear? the Lord is the strength of my life, of whom shall I be afraid?
> PSALM 27:1

HESLEP
Radiant Star

> They that be wise shall shine as the brightness of the firmament; . . . as the stars for ever and ever.
> DANIEL 12:3

HESTER
Radiant One

> But the path of the just is as the shining light, that shineth more and more unto the perfect day.
> PROVERBS 4:18

HILAH
He Hath Praised

> For the Lord is great, and greatly to be praised.
> PSALM 96:4

HILARY
One of Cheer and Joy

> Thou wilt show me the path of life: in thy presence is fulness of joy.
> PSALM 16:11

HILDA
Maiden of God

> Behold, . . . our eyes wait upon
> the Lord our God.
> PSALM 123:2

HILDEGARDE
Strong Protectress

> I will say of the Lord, He is my
> refuge and my fortress: my God;
> in him will I trust.
> PSALM 91:2

HILDRED
Battle Counsel

> I will bless the Lord, who hath
> given me counsel.
> PSALM 16:7

HILGA
The Holy

> I will praise thee, O Lord, with
> my whole heart; . . . I will sing
> praise to thy name, O thou most
> High.
> PSALM 9:1–2

HILLARD
Battle Guard

> Thus saith the Lord unto you,
> Be not afraid nor dismayed . . .
> for the battle is not yours, but
> God's.
> 2 CHRONICLES 20:15

HIRAM
One of Noble Lineage

> Ye have not chosen me, but I
> have chosen you, . . . that ye
> should go and bring forth fruit.
> JOHN 15:16

HO'ONANI
To Glorify

> For the Lord is great, and
> greatly to be praised: . . .
> Honour and majesty are before
> him.
> PSALM 96:4, 6

Polynesian

HOBART
One Of Wisdom

> My mouth shall speak of
> wisdom; and the meditation of
> my heart shall be of
> understanding.
> PSALM 49:3

HOLLI
Belonging to God

> We are labourers together with
> God: ye are God's husbandry,
> . . . God's building.
> 1 CORINTHIANS 3:9

HOMER
Pledge

> I delight to do thy will, O my
> God: yea, thy law is within my
> heart.
> PSALM 40:8

HONEY
Sweet

> I will sing unto the Lord as long
> as I live: . . . My meditation of
> him shall be sweet: I will be
> glad in the Lord.
> PSALM 104:33–34

HONG
Noble Lineage

> *Ye are a chosen generation, a royal priesthood.*
> 1 PETER 2:9
>
> Vietnamese

HONOR
Of Honor

> *Thou art my strong refuge. Let my mouth be filled with thy praise and with thy honour all the day.*
> PSALM 71:7–8

HOPE MARIE
One of Hope and Trust

> *Be of good courage, and he shall strengthen your heart, all ye that hope in the Lord.*
> PSALM 31:24

HORACE
Keeper of the Hours

> *The Lord God is a sun and shield: the Lord will give grace and glory: no good thing will he withhold from them that walk uprightly.*
> PSALM 84:11

HORATIO
Keeper of the Hours

> *The Lord God is a sun and shield: the Lord will give grace and glory: no good thing will he withhold from them that walk uprightly.*
> PSALM 84:11

HORST
One of Strength

> *In God is my salvation and my glory: the rock of my strength, and my refuge, is in God.*
> PSALM 62:7

HORTENSE
Of a Garden

> *As the garden causeth the things that are sown . . . to spring forth; so the Lord God will cause righteousness and praise.*
> ISAIAH 61:11

HOSANNA
Save, We Pray

> *Save me, O God, by thy name, and judge me by thy strength. Hear my prayer, O God.*
> PSALM 54:1–2

HOSEA
Salvation

> *Behold, God is my salvation; I will trust, and not be afraid.*
> ISAIAH 12:2

HOUSTON
Intellectual Mind

> *Let this mind be in you, which was also in Christ Jesus.*
> PHILIPPIANS 2:5

HOWARD
Watchful One

> *Thy watchmen shall lift up the voice; with the voice together shall they sing.*
> ISAIAH 52:8

HOYT
Cheerful Heart

> Yet I will rejoice in the Lord, I
> will joy in the God of my
> salvation.
> HABAKKUK 3:18

HUDSON
One of Strong Rule

> Thou hast also given me the
> shield of thy salvation: . . . thy
> gentleness hath made me great.
> PSALM 18:35

HUELANI
Opening Up to Heaven

> I will praise thee: for thou hast
> heard me, and art become my
> salvation.
> PSALM 118:21
>
> Polynesian

HUGH
Victorious Mind

> I will instruct thee and teach
> thee in the way which thou shalt
> go: I will guide thee with mine
> eye.
> PSALM 32:8

HULALIOKALANI
To Make Heavenly Music

> I will praise thee, O Lord, with
> my whole heart; . . . I will be
> glad and rejoice in thee: I will
> sing praise to thy name.
> PSALM 9:1–2
>
> Polynesian

HUMBERTO
Brightness of the Home

> They that be wise shall shine as
> the brightness of the firmament.
> DANIEL 12:3

HUNTER
Prosperous One

> He shall be like a tree planted
> by the rivers of water, . . .
> whatsoever he doeth shall
> prosper.
> PSALM 1:3

HYMAN
Life

> The Lord is my light and my
> salvation; whom shall I fear?
> the Lord is the strength of my
> life; of whom shall I be afraid?
> PSALM 27:1

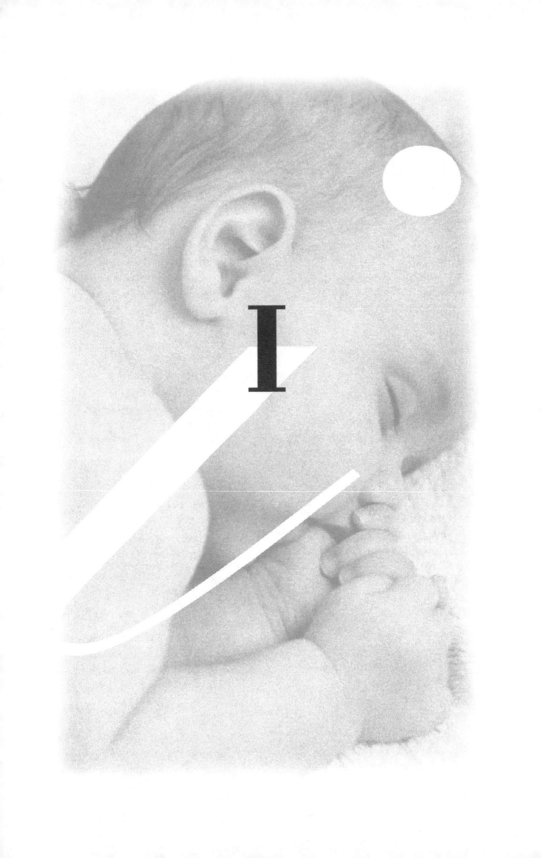

I

IAIN
Gracious Gift of God

> *Every good gift and every perfect gift is from above, and cometh down from the Father of lights.*
> JAMES 1:17

IAKONA
The Healing One

> *The Spirit of the Lord God is upon me; . . . the Lord hath anointed me to preach good tidings.*
> ISAIAH 61:1

Polynesian

IAO
One of Radiance

> *They that be wise shall shine as the brightness of the firmament; . . . as the stars for ever and ever.*
> DANIEL 12:3

IB
Consecrated to God

> *I will bless the Lord at all times: his praise shall continually be in my mouth.*
> PSALM 34:1

IDA
Like God

> *I will praise thee; for I am fearfully and wonderfully made.*
> PSALM 139:14

IGNACIO
One of Ardent Spirit

> *I press toward the mark for the prize of the high calling of God in Christ Jesus.*
> PHILIPPIANS 3:14

IKONA
Of the Light

> *They that be wise shall shine as the brightness of the firmament; . . . as the stars for ever and ever.*
> DANIEL 12:3

ILA
One of Strength

> *It is God that girdeth me with strength, and maketh my way perfect.*
> PSALM 18:32

ILENA
One of Light

> *Let your light so shine before men, that they may see your good works, and glorify your Father which is in heaven.*
> MATTHEW 5:16

ILISE
Consecrated to God

> *I will bless the Lord at all times: his praise shall continually be in my mouth.*
> PSALM 34:1

ILLIANNA
Of Light and Grace

> *They that be wise shall shine as the brightness of the firmament; . . . as the stars for ever and ever.*
> DANIEL 12:3

IMANI
Faith

> *For thou art my rock and my fortress; therefore for thy name's sake lead me, and guide me.*
> PSALM 31:3

I

IMELDA
An Image

> For whom he did foreknow, he
> also did predestinate to be
> conformed to the image of his
> Son.
> ROMANS 8:29

IMMANUEL
God with Us

> Teaching them to observe all
> things whatsoever I have
> commanded you: ... I am with
> you always.
> MATTHEW 28:20

INDRAWAHYUNI
God of Power

> For the Lord is great, and
> greatly to be praised: ...
> Honour and majesty are before
> him.
> PSALM 96:4, 6

Hindu

INES
One of Purity

> Blessed are the pure in heart:
> for they shall see God.
> MATTHEW 5:8

INEZ
Pure, Gentle, Meek

> Be ye kind one to another,
> tenderhearted, forgiving ...
> even as God for Christ's sake
> hath forgiven you.
> EPHESIANS 4:32

INGA
One of Virtue

> Whatever things are true, ...
> honest, ... just, ... lovely, ... of
> good report; if there be any
> virtue, and ... praise, think on
> these things.
> PHILIPPIANS 4:8

INGABERG
Tower of Protection

> The Lord is my rock, ... my
> fortress, ... my deliverer; my
> God, my strength, in whom I
> will trust.
> PSALM 18:2

INGRAM
Strength of a Warrior

> Fight the good fight of faith, lay
> hold on eternal life, whereunto
> thou art also called.
> 1 TIMOTHY 6:12

INGRID
Inner Beauty

> For the righteous Lord loveth
> righteousness; his countenance
> doth behold the upright.
> PSALM 11:7

INNOCENT
Pure One

> Blessed are the pure in heart:
> for they shall see God.
> MATTHEW 5:8

INOCENCIA
Pure of Heart

> Blessed are the pure in heart:
> for they shall see God.
> MATTHEW 5:8
>
> Spanish

IRA
Descendant

> There is laid up . . . a crown of
> righteousness . . . unto all them
> . . . that love his appearing.
> 2 TIMOTHY 4:8

IRELAND
One of Peace

> Thou wilt keep him in perfect
> peace, whose mind is stayed on
> thee: because he trusteth in thee.
> ISAIAH 26:3

IRENE
Messenger of Peace

> How beautiful . . . are the feet of
> him . . . that publisheth peace;
> [and] . . . salvation.
> ISAIAH 52:7

IRIS
The Rainbow

> Like the appearance of the bow
> . . . in the cloud in the day of
> rain, so was . . . the glory of the
> Lord.
> EZEKIEL 1:28

IRMA
Maid of High Degree

> He hath put down the mighty
> from their seats, and exalted
> them of low degree.
> LUKE 1:52

IRVIN
One of Virtue

> Whatever things are true, . . .
> honest, . . . just, . . . lovely . . .
> of good report; if there be any
> virtue, and . . . praise, think on
> these things.
> PHILIPPIANS 4:8

ISAAC
Cheerful Faith

> Thou wilt show me the path of
> life: in thy presence is fulness of
> joy.
> PSALM 16:11

ISABEL
Consecrated to God

> Commit thy works unto the
> Lord, and thy thoughts shall be
> established.
> PROVERBS 16:3

ISADORE
The Fruitful One

> Ye have not chosen me, but I
> have chosen you, . . . that ye
> should go and bring forth fruit.
> JOHN 15:16

ISAIAH
Salvation of the Lord

> For by grace are ye saved
> through faith; and that not of
> yourselves: it is the gift of God.
> EPHESIANS 2:8

I

ISANGIDIEN
Good Journey in the Lord

Thy word is a lamp unto my feet, and a light unto my path.
PSALM 119:105

African

ISHAMEL
God Heareth

I have called upon thee, for thou wilt hear me, O God: incline thine ear unto me, and hear my speech.
PSALM 17:6

ISIDRA
Diligent Harvester

Jesus saith . . . behold, I say unto you, Lift up your eyes, and look on the fields; for they are white already to harvest.
JOHN 4:34–35

ISMAEL
Heard of God

I will praise thee: for thou hast heard me and art become my salvation.
PSALM 118:21

ISRAEL
Soldier of God

Thou shalt also be a crown of glory in the hand of the Lord, and a royal diadem in the hand of thy God.
ISAIAH 62:3

IVAN
Gracious Gift of Jehovah

Every good gift and every perfect gift is from above and cometh down from the Father of lights.
JAMES 1:17

IVAR
Strong Warrior

Fight the good fight of faith, lay hold on eternal life, whereunto thou art also called.
1 TIMOTHY 6:12

IVONNE
also EVONNE, YVONNE
Grace of the Lord

By grace are ye saved through faith; . . . it is the gift of God.
EPHESIANS 2:8

IVORY
Noble

I will praise thee: for I am fearfully and wonderfully made: . . . How precious are thy thoughts unto me, O God!
PSALM 139:14, 17

IVY
Dedicated

It is good for me to draw near to God: I have put my trust in the Lord God, that I may declare all thy works.
PSALM 73:28

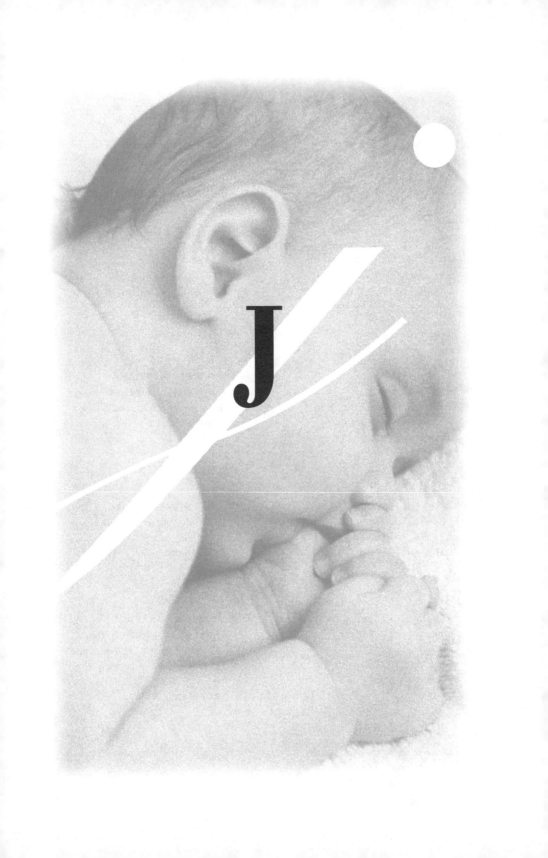

J

JAALAM
Protected One

> He that dwelleth in the secret
> place . . . shall abide under the
> shadow of the Almighty.
> PSALM 91:1

JAAMIYL
Following After the Lord

> Therefore be followers of God,
> . . . walk in love, as Christ also
> hath loved us, and hath given
> himself for us.
> EPHESIANS 5:2

JAASIEL
God Maketh

> Thy hands have made me and
> fashioned me: . . . that I may
> learn thy commandments.
> PSALM 119:73

JABARI
Rejoice

> In God we boast all the day long,
> and praise thy name for ever.
> PSALM 44:8

JABBAR
Rejoice

> I will praise thee, O Lord, . . . I
> will be glad and rejoice in thee:
> . . . [and] sing praise to thy
> name.
> PSALM 9:1–2

JABE
One of Wisdom

> The Lord giveth wisdom; out of
> his mouth cometh knowledge
> and understanding.
> PROVERBS 2:6

JABEL
Peaceful Dweller by the River

> And he shall be like a tree
> planted by the rivers of water,
> that bringeth forth his fruit.
> PSALM 1:3

JABEN
One of Wisdom

> The Lord giveth wisdom: out of
> his mouth cometh knowledge
> and understanding.
> PROVERBS 2:6

JABEZ
Of Sorrow and Honor

> I will bless the Lord at all times:
> his praise shall continually be
> in my mouth.
> PSALM 34:1

JABIR
Comforter

> I will praise thee for thou hast
> heard me, and art become my
> salvation.
> PSALM 118:21

Arabic

JACANDA
Following After the Lord

> Therefore be followers of God,
> . . . walk in love, as Christ also
> hath loved us, and hath given
> himself for us.
> EPHESIANS 5:2

J

JACCI
Following After the Lord

*Therefore be followers of God,
. . . walk in love, as Christ also
hath loved us, and hath given
himself for us.*
EPHESIANS 5:2

JACHIN
The Lord Will Judge

*There is . . . a crown of
righteousness, which the Lord,
the righteous judge, shall give
me.*
2 TIMOTHY 4:8

JACINDA
Most Beautiful One

*I will praise thee; for I am
fearfully and wonderfully
made: Marvellous are thy
works.*
PSALM 139:14

JACINTA
Royal Flower

*I will praise thee; for I am
fearfully and wonderfully made.*
PSALM 139:14

JACINTHA
Royal Flower

*I will praise thee; for I am
fearfully and wonderfully made.*
PSALM 139:14

JACK
Following After the Lord

*The Lord is my rock, . . . my
fortress, and my deliverer; my
God, my strength in whom I will
trust.*
PSALM 18:2

JACKIE
Following After the Lord

*The Lord is my rock, . . . my
fortress, . . . my deliverer; my
God, my strength, in whom I
will trust.*
PSALM 18:2

JACOB
God Will Increase

*The Lord thy God shall bless
thee in all thine increase, and
. . . the works of thine hands.*
DEUTERONOMY 16:15

JACQUELINE
Following After the Lord

*The Lord is my rock, and my
fortress, and my deliverer; my
God, my strength, in whom I
will trust.*
PSALM 18:2

JACQUI
Following After the Lord

*Be ye . . . followers of God, as
dear children; And walk in love,
as Christ . . . hath loved us.*
EPHESIANS 5:1–2

NAME *That* BABY!

JACY
The Supplanter

> *Walk in love, as Christ also hath loved us, and hath given himself for us.*
> EPHESIANS 5:2

JADA
Belonging to God

> *I will praise thee; for I am fearfully and wonderfully made: . . . How precious also are thy thoughts unto me.*
> PSALM 139:14, 17

JADE
Belonging to God

> *I will praise thee; for I am fearfully and wonderfully made: marvellous are thy works.*
> PSALM 139:14

JADEAL
Wise

> *The Lord giveth wisdom; out of his mouth cometh knowledge and understanding.*
> PROVERBS 2:6

JADEN
Ruling with Strength

> *Thou hast given me the shield of thy salvation: . . . thy gentleness hath made me great.*
> PSALM 18:35

JADEY
Known of God

> *I will bless the Lord, who hath given me counsel: . . . I have set the Lord always before me.*
> PSALM 16:7–8

JADIDIAH
Beloved of Jehovah

> *Let us love one another: for love is of God; and every one that loveth is born of God.*
> 1 JOHN 4:7

JADON
One Who Is Wise

> *The Lord giveth wisdom: out of his mouth cometh knowledge and understanding.*
> PROVERBS 2:6

JAEL
Giver of Light

> *Let your light so shine . . . that they may see your good works, and glorify your father in heaven.*
> MATTHEW 5:16

JAELEEN
Strong in Virtue

> *Whatsoever things are true, . . . honest, . . . just, . . . [and] of good report; . . . if there be any virtue and . . . praise, think on these things.*
> PHILIPPIANS 4:8

J

JAEMARA
Following After the Lord

> Therefore be followers of God,
> . . . walk in love, as Christ also
> hath loved us, and hath given
> himself for us.
> EPHESIANS 5:1–2

JAGDISH
Following After the Lord

> Therefore be followers of God,
> . . . walk in love, as Christ also
> hath loved us, and hath given
> himself for us.
> EPHESIANS 5:1–2

JAGTAR
Following After the Lord

> Therefore be followers of God,
> . . . walk in love, as Christ also
> hath loved us, and hath given
> himself for us.
> EPHESIANS 5:1–2

JAHADI
Whom He Will Place

> But as many as recieved him, to
> them gave he power to become
> the sons of God.
> JOHN 1:12

JAHMAI
He Will Be My Defense

> The Lord is my rock, . . . my
> fortress, and my deliverer; . . .
> my strength, in whom I will
> trust.
> PSALM 18:2

JAHMAL
Following After the Lord

> Therefore be followers of God,
> . . . walk in love, as Christ also
> hath loved us, and hath given
> himself for us.
> EPHESIANS 5:1–2

JAHMICAH
Like Unto Jehovah

> I will trust, and not be afraid
> for the Lord JEHOVAH is . . . my
> salvation.
> ISAIAH 12:2

JAI
Enlightened by God

> Thy word is a lamp unto my
> feet, and a light unto my path.
> PSALM 119:105

JAIDA
Gift of God

> Every good gift and every
> perfect gift is from above and
> cometh down from the Father.
> JAMES 1:17

JAIDE
Wisdom and Love

> Let us love one another: for love
> is of God; and every one that
> loveth is born of God.
> 1 JOHN 4:7

JAIME   *also* JAMIE
Follower of Christ

> Therefore be followers of God,
> . . . walk in love, as Christ also
> hath loved us, and hath given
> himself for us.
> EPHESIANS 5:1–2

JAIR
One That Rules

> The Lord is my light and my
> salvation; . . . the strength of my
> life . . . of whom shall I be
> afraid?
> PSALM 27:1

JAIRA
Exalted One

> Thou hast given me thy . . .
> salvation: . . . thy gentleness
> hath made me great.
> PSALM 18:35

JAIRD
One that Rules

> God is my strength and power:
> and he maketh my way perfect.
> 2 SAMUEL 22:33

JAIRED   *also* JARED
One Who Rules

> God is my strength and power:
> and he maketh my way perfect.
> 2 SAMUEL 22:33

JAJIRA
One of Light

> They that be wise shall shine as
> the brightness of the firmament.
> DANIEL 12:3

JAKE
Following After the Lord

> Therefore be followers of God,
> . . . walk in love, as Christ also
> hath loved us, and hath given
> himself for us.
> EPHESIANS 5:1–2

JALA
Pure and Clear

> The commandment of the Lord
> is pure, enlightening the eyes.
> PSALM 19:8

JALAH
Pure and Clear

> The commandment of the Lord
> is pure, enlightening the eyes.
> PSALM 19:8

JALAIR
Enlightened One

> Thy testimonies are wonderful:
> therefore doth my soul keep
> them. . . . thy words giveth light.
> PSALM 119:129–130

JALAYNE
Gracious Gift of Light

> Let your light so shine before
> men, that they may see your
> good works, and glorify your
> Father in heaven.
> MATTHEW 5:16

JALENE   *also* JALINE
Radiant One

> They that be wise shall shine as
> the brightness of the firmament;
> . . . as the stars for ever and ever.
> DANIEL 12:3

JALIECE
Gracious and Devoted One

> I will meditate in thy precepts,
> . . . I will not forget thy word.
> PSALM 119:15–16

J

JALINE
Radiant One

> They that be wise shall shine as
> the brightness of the firmament;
> . . . as the stars for ever and ever.
> DANIEL 12:3

JALISA
Radiant One

> They that be wise shall shine as
> the brightness of the firmament;
> . . . as the stars for ever and ever.
> DANIEL 12:3

JALMER
Guardian Protector

> He that dwelleth in the secret
> place . . . shall abide under the
> shadow of the Almighty.
> PSALM 91:1

JALON
Peaceful Abiding

> The Lord will give strength unto
> his people; the Lord will bless
> his people with peace.
> PSALM 29:11

JAMA
Daughter

> I will praise thee, O Lord, . . .
> That I may show forth . . .
> praise in the gates of the
> daughter of Zion: I will rejoice
> in thy salvation.
> PSALM 9:1, 14

JAMAAL
Grace and Beauty

> Thy hands have made me and
> fashioned me: give me
> understanding.
> PSALM 119:73

Arabic

JAMAR
The Rejoiced In

> I will be glad and rejoice in thee:
> I will sing praise to thy name.
> PSALM 9:2

JAMEN
The Right Hand

> I have set the Lord always
> before me: . . . he is at my right
> hand, I shall not be moved.
> PSALM 16:8

JAMES
Following After the Lord

> Therefore be followers of God,
> . . . walk in love, as Christ also
> hath loved us, and hath given
> himself for us.
> EPHESIANS 5:1–2

JAMIE   also JAIME
Following After the Lord

> Therefore be followers of God,
> . . . walk in love, as Christ also
> hath loved us, and hath given
> himself for us.
> EPHESIANS 5:1–2

JAMILLA
Beautiful One

> For the lord taketh pleasure in
> his people; he will beautify the
> meek with salvation.
> PSALM 149:4

JAMION
Prosperous One

> I will sing unto the Lord,
> because he hath dealt
> bountifully with me.
> PSALM 13:6

JAMIRA
Following After the Lord

> Therefore be followers of God,
> . . . walk in love, as Christ also
> hath loved us, and hath given
> himself for us.
> EPHESIANS 5:1–2

JAN
God's Gracious Gift

> Every good gift and every
> perfect gift is from above.
> JAMES 1:17

JANA
God's Gracious Gift

> Every good gift and every
> perfect gift is from above.
> JAMES 1:17

JANCI
Grace of the Lord

> The Lord will give grace and
> glory: no good thing will he
> withhold from them that walk
> uprightly.
> PSALM 84:11

JANE
Gracious Gift of God

> Every good gift and every
> perfect gift is from above, and
> cometh down from the Father.
> JAMES 1:17

JANEL
Gracious Gift of God

> Every good gift and every
> perfect gift is from above, and
> cometh down from the Father.
> JAMES 1:17

JANELLE
God's Gracious Gift

> Every good gift and every
> perfect gift is from above, and
> cometh down from the Father.
> JAMES 1:17

JANETTA
God's Gift

> Every good gift and every
> perfect gift is from above, and
> cometh down from the Father.
> JAMES 1:17

JANICE
Gracious Gift of God

> Every good gift and every
> perfect gift is from above, and
> cometh down from the Father.
> JAMES 1:17

JANIE
Gracious Gift of God

> Every good gift and every
> perfect gift is from above, and
> cometh down from the Father.
> JAMES 1:17

J

JANIN
To Understand

*My mouth shall speak of
wisdom; and the meditation of
my heart shall be of
understanding.*
PSALM 49:3

JANINE
Gracious Gift of God

*Every good gift and every
perfect gift is from above, and
cometh down from the Father.*
JAMES 1:17

JANIS
God's Gracious Gift

*Every good gift and every
perfect gift is from above, and
cometh down from the Father.*
JAMES 1:17

JANITA
Gracious Gift of God

*Every good gift and every
perfect gift is from above, and
cometh down from the Father.*
JAMES 1:17

JANNETTE
Gracious Gift of God

*Every good gift and every
perfect gift is from above, and
cometh down from the Father.*
JAMES 1:17

JANTINA
The Violet Flower

*Thy hands have made me and
fashioned me: give me
understanding, that I may learn.*
PSALM 119:73

JANUAL
God With Us

*I love the Lord, because he hath
heard my voice and my
supplications.*
PSALM 116:1

JANUARY
The Beginning

*In the beginning was the Word,
. . . the Word was God. All things
were made by him.*
JOHN 1:1, 3

JAOCHIM
Jehovah Will Establish

*The Lord is great, and greatly to
be praised: . . . Honour and
majesty are before him.*
PSALM 96:4, 6

JARAH
Honey

*I will praise thee; for I am
fearfully and wonderfully
made: marvellous are thy
works.*
PSALM 139:14

JAREB
Of Strong Will

*I have set the Lord always
before me: . . . he is at my right
hand, I shall not be moved.*
PSALM 16:8

JARED
One That Rules

*Behold, God is my salvation; I
will trust, and not be afraid.*
ISAIAH 12:2

JAREN
The One of Rejoicing

> *I will praise thee, O Lord, . . . I will be glad and rejoice in thee.*
> PSALM 9:1–2

JARICA
One of Wise Protection

> *I will say of the Lord, He is my refuge and my fortress: my God; in him will I trust.*
> PSALM 91:2

JARIN
The One of Rejoicing

> *I will praise thee, O Lord, . . . I will be glad and rejoice in thee.*
> PSALM 9:1–2

JARIS
Sharp Spear

> *And take the helmet of salvation, and the sword of the Spirit, which is the word of God.*
> EPHESIANS 6:17

JARITA
One of Wise Protection

> *I will say of the Lord, He is my refuge and my fortress: my God; in him will I trust.*
> PSALM 91:2

JARIUS
One That Rules

> *The Lord is my light and my salvation; . . . the strength of my life; of whom shall I be afraid?*
> PSALM 27:1

JARLATH
Noble One

> *Thou hast . . . given me the shield of thy salvation: and thy gentleness hath made me great.*
> 2 SAMUEL 22:36

Old Norse

JARMA
One of Strength

> *The Lord is my rock, . . . my fortress, . . . my deliverer; my God, my strength, in whom I will trust.*
> PSALM 18:2

JARMAN
Spear Ruler of Strength

> *Take unto you the whole armour of God, the sword of the Spirit . . . which is the word of God.*
> EPHESIANS 6:13, 17

JARON
One of Rejoicing

> *I will praise thee, O Lord, . . . I will be glad and rejoice in thee.*
> PSALM 9:1–2

JARROD
The Descender

> *The Lord . . . shall descend from heaven . . . we which are alive . . . shall be caught up . . . to meet the Lord.*
> 1 THESSALONIANS 4:16–17

Hebrew

J

JARUIS
He Enlighteneth

> The Lord is my light and . . .
> salvation; . . . the strength of my
> life; of whom shall I be afraid?
> PSALM 27:1
>
> Teutonic

JARUM
Spear Keen

> Take the helmet of salvation,
> and the sword of the Spirit,
> which is the word of God.
> EPHESIANS 6:17

JARVIS
Spear Strong

> Take the helmet of salvation,
> and the sword of the Spirit,
> which is the word of God.
> EPHESIANS 6:17

JASIRI
Fervent Spirit

> I press toward the mark for the
> prize of the high calling of God
> in Christ Jesus.
> PHILIPPIANS 3:14
>
> Latin

JASIVE
God Will Increase

> The Lord thy God shall bless
> thee in all thine increase, and in
> all the works of thine hands.
> DEUTERONOMY 16:15

JASMINE
Fragrant Jasmine Flower

> I will praise thee; for I am
> fearfully and wonderfully made:
> marvellous are thy works.
> PSALM 139:14

JASON
The Healing One

> The Spirit of . . . God is upon
> me; . . . [and] hath anointed me
> to preach . . . to heal the
> brokenhearted.
> ISAIAH 61:1

JATANNA
One of Rejoicing and Grace

> The Lord will give grace and
> glory; no good thing will he
> withhold from them that walk
> uprightly.
> PSALM 84:11

JATHAN
Gift of God

> By grace are ye saved through
> faith; and that not of
> yourselves: it is the gift of God.
> EPHESIANS 2:8

JAVAN
Steadfast

> Be ye stedfast, unmovable,
> always abounding in the work
> of the Lord.
> 1 CORINTHIANS 15:58

JAVELLE
God is Gracious

> But thou, O Lord, art a God full
> of compassion, and gracious,
> longsuffering, and plenteous in
> mercy and truth.
> PSALM 86:15

JAVEN
To Understand

> My mouth shall speak of
> wisdom, and the meditation of
> my heart shall be of
> understanding.
> PSALM 49:3

JAVIER
One of Brilliant Splendor

> Thou shalt . . . be a crown of
> glory in the hand of the Lord,
> and a royal diadem.
> ISAIAH 62:3

JAWEED
Beloved One

> Love one another: for love is of
> God; and every one that loveth
> is born of God.
> 1 JOHN 4:7

JAY
Fervent One

> The effectual fervent prayer of a
> righteous man availeth much.
> JAMES 5:16

JAYA
The Rejoiced In

> I will praise thee, O Lord, . . . I
> will be glad and rejoice in thee.
> PSALM 9:1–2

JAYEL
The Rejoiced In

> I will praise thee, O Lord, . . . I
> will be glad and rejoice in thee.
> PSALM 9:1–2

JAYPEE
The Rejoiced In

> I will praise thee, O Lord, . . . I
> will be glad and rejoice in thee.
> PSALM 9:1–2

JEAN
Gracious Gift of God

> Every good gift and every
> perfect gift is from above, and
> cometh down from the Father.
> JAMES 1:17

JEANNE
God's Gracious Gift

> Every good gift and every
> perfect gift is from above, and
> cometh down from the Father.
> JAMES 1:17

JEANNETTE
Gracious Gift of God

> Every good gift and every
> perfect gift is from above, and
> cometh down from the Father.
> JAMES 1:17

JEANNINE
Gracious Gift of God

> Every good gift and every
> perfect gift is from above, and
> cometh down from the Father.
> JAMES 1:17

J

JECOLIA
Jehovah Reigns

> The Lord reigneth, he is clothed
> with majesty; the Lord is
> clothed with strength.
> PSALM 93:1

JECOLIAH
Jehovah Reigns

> The Lord reigneth, he is clothed
> with majesty; the Lord is
> clothed with strength.
> PSALM 93:1

Hebrew

JED
God is My Friend

> Greater love hath no man than
> this, that a man lay down his
> life for his friends.
> JOHN 15:13

JEETER
Strong with the Sword

> Take unto you the whole armour
> of God, the sword of the Spirit
> . . . which is the word of God.
> EPHESIANS 6:13, 17

JEFF
One of Peace and Mercy

> The wisdom that is from above
> is first pure, then peaceable, . . .
> full of mercy and good fruits.
> JAMES 3:17

JEFFERSON
Son of Peace

> Thou wilt keep him in perfect
> peace, . . . because he trusteth in
> thee.
> ISAIAH 26:3

JEFFERY   *also* GEOFFERY
One of Peace and Mercy

> The wisdom that is from above
> is first pure, then peaceable, . . .
> full of mercy and good fruits,
> . . . without hypocrisy.
> JAMES 3:17

JEFFREY   *also* GEOFFREY
One of Peace and Mercy

> The wisdom that is from above
> is first pure, then peaceable, . . .
> full of mercy and good fruits,
> . . . without hypocrisy.
> JAMES 3:17

JEHOIAKIM
Jehovah Doth Establish

> The works of the Lord are great,
> . . . He hath made his wonderful
> works to be remembered.
> PSALM 111:2, 4

Hebrew

JEHOSHA
Jehovah Is Deliverance

> I will praise thee: for thou hast
> heard me, and art become my
> salvation.
> PSALM 118:21

JEHOVAH
God Is Jehovah

> I will trust, and not be afraid:
> for the Lord JEHOVAH is my
> strength and . . . my salvation.
> ISAIAH 12:2

JEIEL
Youthful One

> For thou art my hope, O Lord
> God: thou art my trust from my
> youth.
> PSALM 71:5

JEITER
One of Excellence

> Let the words of my mouth, and
> the meditation of my heart, be
> acceptable in thy sight, O Lord.
> PSALM 19:14

JELETHA
One of Light

> Let your light so shine before
> men, that they may see your
> good works, and glorify your
> father which is in heaven.
> MATTHEW 5:16

JELIES
One of Great Strength

> The Lord is my rock, . . . my
> fortress, and my deliverer; my
> God, my strength, in whom I
> will trust.
> PSALM 18:2

JELLONT
Youthful One

> For thou art my hope, O Lord
> God: thou art my trust from my
> youth.
> PSALM 71:5

JEMEL
Desire of God

> But it is good for me to draw
> near to God: I have put my trust
> in the Lord God.
> PSALM 73:28

JEMIMA
Peaceful Dove

> Great peace have they which
> love thy law: . . . I have kept thy
> precepts and thy testimonies.
> PSALM 119:165, 168

JENESSA
Gracious Gift of God

> Every good gift and every
> perfect gift is from above and
> cometh down from the Father.
> JAMES 1:17

JENEVIEVE
Fair Lady

> Strength and honour are her
> clothing; . . . She openeth her
> mouth with wisdom; and in her
> tongue is the law of kindness.
> PROVERBS 3L:25–26

JENKINS
Gracious Gift of Jehovah

> For by grace are ye saved
> through faith; and that not of
> yourselves: it is the gift of God.
> EPHESIANS 2:8

JENNESSA
Gracious Gift of God

> Every good gift and . . . perfect
> gift is from above, and cometh
> down from the Father.
> JAMES 1:17

J

JENNIFER
Fair Lady
> Strength and honour are her
> clothing; . . . She openeth her
> mouth with wisdom; and in her
> tongue is the law of kindness.
> PROVERBS 31:25–26

JENNY
Fair Lady
> Strength and honour are her
> clothing; . . . She openeth her
> mouth with wisdom; and in her
> tongue is the law of kindness.
> PROVERBS 31:25–26

JEPTHA
God Sets Free
> Stand fast therefore in the
> liberty where with Christ hath
> made us free.
> GALATIANS 5:1

Hebrew

JEQUETTA
Following After the Lord
> Be ye therefore followers of God,
> . . . And walk in love, as Christ
> also hath loved us.
> EPHESIANS 5:1–2

JERACA
Exalted of the Lord
> Thy right hand hath holden me
> up, and thy gentleness hath
> made me great.
> PSALM 18:35

JERAH
Exalted of the Lord
> Thy right hand hath holden me
> up, and thy gentleness hath
> made me great.
> PSALM 18:35

JERALD   also GERALD
Spear Ruler of Strength
> Whatsoever ye do in word or
> deed, do all in the name of the
> Lord Jesus.
> COLOSSIANS 3:17

JERALDINE
Victorious One
> Holding forth the word of life;
> that I may rejoice in the day of
> Christ.
> PHILIPPIANS 2:16

JERAMIAH
Exalted of the Lord
> Thy right hand hath holden me
> up, and thy gentleness hath
> made me great.
> PSALM 18:35

JERANNA
Exalted and One of Grace
> No good thing will he withhold
> from them that walk uprightly.
> PSALM 84:11

JEREMIAH
Appointed of the Lord
> I am appointed a preacher, . . .
> and a teacher: . . . for I know
> whom I have believed.
> 2 TIMOTHY 1:11–12

JEREMY
Appointed of the Lord

> *I am appointed a preacher, . . .*
> *and a teacher: . . . for I know*
> *whom I have believed.*
> 2 TIMOTHY 1:11–12

JERESA
Diligent Harvester

> *Lift up your eyes, and look on*
> *the fields; for they are white*
> *already to harvest.*
> JOHN 4:35

JERICHO
Place of Fragrance

> *I will praise thee; for I am*
> *fearfully and wonderfully*
> *made: . . . How precious also are*
> *thy thoughts unto me, O God!*
> PSALM 139:14, 17

JERILYN
Exalted of the Lord

> *My servant shall deal prudently,*
> *. . . be exalted and extolled, and*
> *be very high.*
> ISAIAH 52:13

JERMAINE
One who Proclaims

> *How beautiful are the feet of*
> *them that preach the gospel of*
> *peace.*
> ROMANS 10:15

JEROME
Sacred Name

> *According to thy name, O God,*
> *so is thy praise unto the ends of*
> *the earth.*
> PSALMS 48:10

JERRAILE
Spear Ruler of Strength

> *Take unto you the whole armour*
> *of God, . . . the sword of the*
> *Spirit, which is the word of God.*
> EPHESIANS 6:13, 17

JERREL
Spear Ruler of Strength

> *Take unto you the whole armour*
> *of God, . . . the sword of the*
> *Spirit, which is the word of God.*
> EPHESIANS 6:13, 17

JERRI
Consecrated One

> *I have set the Lord . . .*
> *conscrated before me: . . . he is*
> *at my right hand, I shall not be*
> *moved.*
> PSALM 16:8

JERRIANNE
One of Consecration and Grace

> *The Lord will give grace and*
> *glory; no good thing will he*
> *withhold from them that walk*
> *uprightly.*
> PSALM 84:11

JERRIEANN
Exalted One of Grace

> *Thou hast . . . given me the*
> *shield of thy salvation: . . . thy*
> *gentleness hath made me great.*
> PSALM 18:35

J

JERRILEE
Exalted One of Peace
> *Thy right hand hath holden me up, and thy gentleness hath made me great.*
> PSALM 18:35

JERRY
Consecrated to God
> *I have set the Lord ... consecrated before me: ... he is at my right hand, I shall not be moved.*
> PSALM 16:8

JERSHON
Ruling with Strength
> *The Lord is my rock, ... my fortress, and my deliverer; my God, my strength, in whom I will trust.*
> PSALM 18:2

JERUS
Exalted of the Lord
> *Thou hast also given me the shield of thy salvation: and thy gentleness hath made me great.*
> 2 SAMUEL 22:36

JERUSALEM
Foundation of Peace
> *The Lord will give strength unto his people; the Lord will bless his people with peace.*
> PSALM 29:11

JERUSHA
One Who Is Betrothed
> *Who can find a virtuous woman? ... a woman that feareth the Lord, she shall be praised.*
> PROVERBS 31:10, 30

Hebrew

JERYL
Appointed by God
> *My servant shall deal prudently, ... be exalted and extolled, and be very high.*
> ISAIAH 52:13

JESHUA
Jehovah Is Salvation
> *Behold God is my salvation; I will trust, and not be afraid.*
> ISAIAH 12:2

Hebrew

JESIAH
Jehovah Lendeth
> *For thou, Lord, wilt bless the righteous; with favour wilt thou compass him as with a shield.*
> PSALM 5:12

JESICA
God's Grace
> *For by grace are ye saved through faith; and that not of yourselves: it is the gift of God.*
> EPHESIANS 2:8

JESIKA
God's Grace

> For by grace are ye saved
> through faith; and that not of
> yourselves: it is the gift of God.
> EPHESIANS 2:8

JESLYN
Gods Grace

> For by grace are ye saved
> through faith; and that not of
> yourselves: it is the gift of God.
> EPHESIANS 2:8

JESNER
God's Grace

> For by grace are ye saved
> through faith; and that not of
> yourselves: it is the gift of God.
> EPHESIANS 2:8

JESSA
God's Grace

> For by grace are ye saved
> through faith; and that not of
> yourselves: it is the gift of God.
> EPHESIANS 2:8

JESSAMINE
The Fragrant Jessamine

> I will praise thee; for I am
> fearfully and wonderfully
> made: marvellous are thy
> works.
> PSALM 139:14

JESSE
God's Grace

> For by grace are ye saved
> through faith; and that not of
> yourselves: it is the gift of God.
> EPHESIANS 2:8

JESSIANNE
God's Grace

> For by grace are ye saved
> through faith; and that not of
> yourselves: it is the gift of God.
> EPHESIANS 2:8

JESSICA
God 's Grace

> For by grace are ye saved
> through faith; and that not of
> yourselves: it is the gift of God.
> EPHESIANS 2:8

JESSICCA
God's Grace

> For by grace are ye saved
> through faith; and that not of
> yourselves: it is the gift of God.
> EPHESIANS 2:8

JESSIE
God's Grace

> By grace are ye saved through
> faith; and . . . that not of
> yourselves: it is the gift of God.
> EPHESIANS 2:8

JESUS
Saviour

> For he shall save his people from
> their sins.
> MATTHEW 1:21

JETAUN
One of Courage and Strength

> It is God that girdeth me with
> strength, and maketh my way
> perfect.
> PSALM 18:32

J

JETHRO
The Excellent

I press toward the mark for the prize of the high calling of God in Christ Jesus.
PHILIPPIANS 3:14

Hebrew

JEWELDEAN
Beautiful Little Gem

I will praise thee; for I am fearfully and wonderfully made: marvellous are thy works.
PSALM 139:14

JEWELL
Delightful Little Gem

I will praise thee; for I am fearfully and wonderfully made: marvellous are thy works.
PSALM 139:14

JEWELNEL
Precious Gem

I will praise thee; for I am fearfully and wonderfully made: marvellous are thy works.
PSALM 139:14

JEYNE
Gracious Gift of God

For by grace are ye saved through faith; and that not of yourselves: it is the gift of God.
EPHESIANS 2:8

JEZREEL
Sown of God

But he that received seed into the good ground is he that heareth the word.
MATTHEW 13:23

JHAMAR
Fervent One

Whatsoever ye do, do it heartily, as to the Lord, . . . for ye serve the Lord Christ.
COLOSSIANS 3:23–24

JHANNA
Gracious Gift of God

Every good gift and every perfect gift is from above, and cometh down from the Father.
JAMES 1:17

JIAH
Follower of the Lord

Therefore be followers of God, . . . walk in love, as Christ also hath loved us, and hath given himself for us.
EPHESIANS 5:2

JIHAD
He will be Praised

For the Lord is great, and greatly to be praised: . . . Honour and majesty are before him.
PSALM 96:4, 6

JILAINE
Youthful One of Grace

The Lord will give grace and glory; no good thing will he withhold from them that walk uprightly.
PSALM 84:11

JILLENE
Young at Heart

> Let no man despise thy youth;
> but be thou an example of the
> believers.
> 1 TIMOTHY 4:12

JILLIAN
Youthful One

> For thou art my hope, O Lord
> God: thou art my trust from my
> youth.
> PSALM 71:5

JILLIANNE
Youthful One of Grace

> The Lord will give grace and
> glory; no good thing will he
> withhold from them that walk
> uprightly.
> PSALM 84:11

JIM
Following the Lord

> The Lord is my rock, . . . my
> fortress, [and] my . . . strength,
> in whom I will trust.
> PSALM 18:2

JIMALEEN
Following After the Lord

> Therefore be followers of God,
> . . . walk in love, as Christ also
> hath loved us, and hath given
> himself for us.
> EPHESIANS 5:1–2

JIMBEAUX
Following After the Lord

> Therefore be followers of God,
> . . . walk in love, as Christ also
> hath loved us, and hath given
> himself for us.
> EPHESIANS 5:1–2

JIMBO
Following After the Lord

> Therefore be followers of God,
> . . . walk in love, as Christ also
> hath loved us, and hath given
> himself for us.
> EPHESIANS 5:1–2

JIMMIE
Following with Grace

> Therefore be followers of God,
> . . . walk in love, as Christ also
> hath loved us, and hath given
> himself for us.
> EPHESIANS 5:1–2

JIMMY
Following After the Lord

> Therefore be followers of God,
> . . . walk in love, as Christ also
> hath loved us, and hath given
> himself for us.
> EPHESIANS 5:1–2

JIMMYE
Following After the Lord

> Therefore be followers of God,
> . . . walk in love, as Christ also
> hath loved us, and hath given
> himself for us.
> EPHESIANS 5:1–2

J

JINA
God's Gracious Gift

> Every good gift and every
> perfect gift is from above, and
> cometh down from the Father.
> JAMES 1:17

JINDA
Humility and Excellence

> I press toward the mark for the
> prize of the high calling of God
> in Christ Jesus.
> PHILIPPIANS 3:14

JINTANA
Gracious Gift of God

> For by grace are ye saved
> through faith; and that not of
> yourselves: it is the gift of God.
> EPHESIAMS 2:8

JINX
Noble

> I will praise thee, O Lord,
> among the people: and I will
> sing praises unto thee among
> the nations.
> PSALM 108:3

JIOVANN
Gods Gracious Gift

> Every good gift and every
> perfect gift is from above, and
> cometh down from the Father.
> JAMES 1:17

JITTAUN
One of Rejoicing and Grace

> The Lord will give grace and
> glory; no good thing will he
> withhold from them that walk
> uprightly.
> PSALM 84:11

French Indian

JO
God's Gracious Gift

> Therefore will the Lord wait, that
> he may be gracious unto you.
> ISAIAH 30:18

JO ELLEN
Giving Much Light

> The Lord is my light and my
> salvation, . . . the strength of my
> life; of whom shall I be afraid?
> PSALM 27:1

JOAB
God Is My Father

> I will trust, and not be afraid:
> for the Lord JEHOVAH is my
> strength and . . . my salvation.
> ISAIAH 12:2

JOACHIM
The Lord Will Judge

> There is . . . a crown of
> righteousness, which the Lord,
> the righteous judge, shall give
> me.
> 2 TIMOTHY 4:8

JOALEA
Productive One

> The Lord thy God shall bless
> thee in all thine increase, and in
> all the works of thine hands.
> DUETERONOMY 16:15

JOAN
Gracious Gift of God

> Every good gift and every
> perfect gift is from above, and
> cometh down from the Father.
> JAMES 1:17

JOANIE
God's Gracious Gift

> Every good gift and every
> perfect gift is from above, and
> cometh down from the Father.
> JAMES 1:17

JOANN
Growing in Grace

> Grow in grace, and in the
> knowledge of our Lord and
> Saviour Jesus Christ.
> 2 PETER 3:18

JOANNA
Growing in Grace

> Grow in grace, and in the
> knowledge of our our Lord and
> Saviour Jesus Christ.
> 2 PETER 3:18

JOANNE
Growing in Grace

> Grow in grace, and in the
> knowledge of our Lord and
> Saviour Jesus Christ.
> 2 PETER 3:18

JOASH
Jehovah Is Strong

> The Lord is my rock, . . . my
> fortress, . . . my deliverer; my
> God, my strength, in whom I
> will trust.
> PSALM 18:2

JOB
Patient

> Ye have heard of the patience
> of Job.
> JAMES 5:11

JOCELYN
Joyful Spirit

> Let all those who put their trust
> in thee rejoice: . . . [and] shout
> for joy.
> PSALM 5:11

JOCILYN
Joyful Spirit

> Let all those who put their trust
> in thee rejoice: . . . let them also
> who love thy name be joyful in
> thee.
> PSALM 5:11

JOCLAIR
Productive One

> The Lord thy God shall bless
> thee in all thine increase, and in
> all the works of thine hands.
> DEUTERONOMY 16:15

JODIE
Praised of the Lord

> The Lord taketh pleasure in
> them that fear him, . . . that
> hope in his mercy.
> PSALM 147:11

J

JODY
Praised of the Lord

> The Lord taketh pleasure in
> them that fear him, . . . that
> hope in his mercy.
> PSALM 147:11

JOE
The Lord Addeth

> The Lord . . . God shall bless
> thee in all thine increase, and in
> all the works of thine hands.
> DEUTERONOMY 16:15

JOEANN
Growing in Grace

> Grow in grace, and in the
> knowledge of our Lord and
> Saviour Jesus Christ.
> 2 PETER 3:18

JOEL
Jehovah Is God

> That men may know that thou,
> whose name alone is JEHOVAH,
> art the most high.
> PSALM 83:18

JOELEA
Productive One

> The Lord thy God shall bless
> thee in all thine increase, and in
> all the works of thine hands.
> DEUTERONOMY 10:15

JOELMA
Jehovah Is God

> I will trust, and not be afraid:
> for the Lord JEHOVAH is my
> strength and : . . my salvation.
> ISAIAH 12:2

JOEQUITA
The Lord Addeth

> The Lord thy God shall bless
> thee in all thine increase, and in
> all the works of thine hands.
> DEUTERONOMY 16:15

JOETTA
Productive One

> The Lord thy God shall bless
> thee in all thine increase, and in
> all the works of thine hands.
> DEUTERONOMY 16:15

JOETTE
Productive One

> The Lord thy God shall bless
> thee in all thine increase, and in
> all the works of thine hands.
> DEUTERONOMY 16:15

JOHN
God's Gracious Gift

> The Lord make his face shine
> upon thee, and be gracious unto
> thee.
> NUMBERS 6:25

JOHN-MARK
A Mighty Warrior

> Fight the good fight of faith, lay
> hold on eternal life.
> 1 TIMOTHY 6:12

JOHNATHAN also JONATHAN
Gracious Gift of Jehovah

> Every good gift and every
> perfect gift is from above and
> cometh down from the Father.
> JAMES 1:17

JOHNATHON
Gracious Gift of God

> *Every good gift and every perfect gift is from above and cometh down from the Father.*
> JAMES 1:17

JOI
Joyful One

> *But let all those who put their trust in thee rejoice: . . . let them also that love thy name be joyful in thee.*
> PSALM 5:11

JOIAL
Jehovah is God

> *Keep not thou silence, O God: . . . That men may know that thou, . . . art the most high over all the earth.*
> PSALM 83:1, 18

JOINER
Creative Builder

> *As a wise master builder, I have laid the foundation, . . . For other foundation can no man lay than . . . Jesus Christ.*
> 1 CORINTHIANS 3:10–11

JOLA
Modest Grace

> *The Lord will give grace and glory; no good thing will he withhold from them that walk uprightly.*
> PSALM 84:11

JOLANDA
Violet Blossom

> *I will praise thee; for I am fearfully and wonderfully made: marvellous are thy works.*
> PSALM 139:14

JOLANGE
God Will Increase

> *The Lord thy God shall bless thee in all thine increase, and in all the works of thine hands.*
> DEUTERONOMY 16:15

JOLANNA
Gracious One of Light

> *Let your light so shine . . . that they may see your good works, and glorify your Father.*
> MATTHEW 5:16

JOLDIE
Precious One

> *I will praise thee; for I am fearfully and wonderfully made: . . . How precious also are thy thoughts unto me. O God!*
> PSALM 139:14, 17

JOLEAN
Pretty One

> *I will praise thee; for I am fearfully and wonderfully made: . . . How precious also are thy thoughts unto me, O God!*
> PSALM 139:14, 17

J

JOLEEN
Pretty One

For the Lord taketh pleasure in his people; he will beautify the meek with salvation.
PSALM 149:4

JOLENE
Pretty One

For the Lord taketh pleasure in his people; he will beautify the meek with salvation.
PSALM 149:4

JOLETA
Violet, Symbol of Modesty

Let the words of my mouth, and the meditation of my heart, be acceptable in thy sight, O Lord.
PSALM 19:14

JOLEY
Pretty One

I will praise thee; for I am fearfully and wonderfully made; marvellous are thy works.
PSALM 139:14

JOLI
Youthful One

For thou art my hope, O Lord God: thou art my trust from my youth.
PSALM 71:5

JOLIE
Pretty One

For the Lord taketh pleasure in his people; he will beautify the meek with salvation.
PSALM 149:4

JOLISHA
Devoted One

I will bless the Lord at all times: his praise shall continually be in my mouth.
PSALM 34:1

JOLITA
The Violet

Thy hands have made me and fashioned me: . . . that I may learn thy commandments.
PSALM 119:73

JOLLAY
Joyful and Pleasant Spirit

Thou wilt show me the path of life: in thy presence is . . . joy; at thy right hand there are pleasures evermore.
PSALM 16:11

JOLLY
Pleasant and Joyful Spirit

Thou wilt show me the path of life: in thy presence is . . . joy: at thy right hand there are pleasures evermore.
PSALM 16:11

JOMEDA
God Will Increase

The Lord thy God shall bless thee in all thine increase, and in all the works of thine hands.
DEUTERONOMY 16:15

JOMONA
One of Honor

> Thy right hand hath holden me
> up, and thy gentleness hath
> made me great.
> PSALM 18:35

JON-JON
God Is Gracious

> But thou, O Lord, art a God full
> of compassion, and gracious,
> longsuffering, and plenteous in
> mercy and truth.
> PSALM 86:15

JONA
One of Peace

> The Lord will give strength unto
> his people; the Lord will bless
> his people with peace.
> PSALM 29:11

JONAH
A Dove of Peace

> Thou wilt keep him in perfect
> peace, whose mind is stayed on
> thee: because he trusteth in thee.
> ISAIAH 26:3

JONAN
Jehovah Gracious Giver

> This is the day which the Lord
> hath made; we will rejoice and
> be glad in it.
> PSALM 118:24

JONATAN
God Has Given

> For by grace are ye saved through
> faith; . . . it is the gift of God.
> EPHESIANS 2:8

JONATHAN *also* JOHNATHAN
God's Gracious Gift

> Thou . . . art a God full of
> compassion, and gracious,
> longsuffering.
> PSALM 86:15

JONATHON *also* JOHNATHAN
God's Gracious Gift

> The Lord make his face shine
> upon thee, and be gracious unto
> thee.
> NUMBERS 6:25

JONCH
God Is Gracious

> But thou, O Lord, art a God full
> of compassion, and gracious,
> longsuffering, and plenteous in
> mercy and truth.
> PSALM 86:15

JONPAUL
God Is Gracious

> But thou, O Lord, art a God full
> of compassion, and gracious,
> longsuffering, and plenteous in
> mercy and truth.
> PSALM 86:15

JONQUIL
The Jonquil Flower

> I will praise thee; for I am
> fearfully and wonderfully
> made: marvellous are thy
> works.
> PSALM 139:14

J

JOOP
The Just One

> *Righteous art thou, O Lord, and upright art thy judgements. Thy testimonies that thou commanded are righteous.*
> PSALM 119:137–138

JOQUETTA
God Will Increase

> *The Lord thy God shall bless thee in all thine increase, and in all the works of thine hands.*
> DEUTERONOMY 16:15

JOR-EL
Spear Ruler of Strength

> *Take unto you the whole armour of God, the sword of the Spirit . . . which is the word of God.*
> EPHESIANS 6:13, 17

JORAINE
God Is Exalted

> *I will trust, and not be afraid: for the Lord JEHOVAH is my strength and . . . my salvation.*
> ISAIAH 12:2

JORAM
God Is Exalted

> *I will trust and not be afraid: for the Lord JEHOVAH is my strength and . . . my salvation.*
> ISAIAH 12:2

JORDAN
The Descender

> *The Lord . . . shall descend from heaven . . . Then we which are alive . . . shall be caught up to meet the Lord.*
> 1 THESSALONIANS 4:16–17

JOREEN
He Shall Add

> *The Lord thy God shall bless thee in all thine increase, and in all the works of thine hands.*
> DEUTERONOMY 16:15

JORETTA
Precious One

> *The Lord shall arise upon thee, and his glory shall be seen upon thee.*
> ISAIAH 60:2

JORGE *also* GEORGE
Diligent Earth Worker

> *He that tilleth his land shall have plenty . . . A faithful man shall abound with blessings.*
> PROVERBS 28:19–20

JORHETA
Precious One

> *The hands have made me and fashioned me, . . . that I may learn thy commandments.*
> PSALM 119:73

JORJANNE
Industrious One of Grace

> *No good thing will he withhold from them that walk uprightly.*
> PSALM 84:11

NAME *That* BABY!

JORMA
The Lord Is Exalted

For the Lord is great, and greatly to be praised: ... Honour and majesty are before him.
PSALM 96:4, 6

JORONDA
Strong Ruler

The Lord is my rock, ... my fortress, and my deliverer; my God, my strength, in whom I will trust.
PSALM 18:2

JOROYN
God Will Increase

The Lord thy God shall bless thee in all thine increase, and in all the works of thine hands.
DEUTERONOMY 16:15

JOSANNA
Growing in Grace

No good thing will he withhold from them that walk uprightly.
PSALM 84:11

JOSE
The Productive One

The Lord thy God shall bless thee in all thine increase, ... in all the works of thine hands.
DUETERONOMY 16:15

JOSELMA
Productive One

The Lord thy God shall bless thee in all thine increase, and in all the works of thine hands.
DEUTERONOMY 16:15

JOSEPH
The Lord Addeth

The Lord ... shall bless thee in all thine increase, ... all the works of thine hands.
DEUTERONOMY 16:15

JOSEY
He Addeth

Whereby are given unto us exceeding great and precious promises.
2 PETER 1:4

JOSHAWA
Jehovah Is Salvation

I will trust, and not be afraid: for the Lord JEHOVAH is my strength and ... my salvation.
ISAIAH 12:2

JOSHOUA
God Is my Salvation

I will trust, and not be afraid: for the Lord ... is my strength ... he ... is become my salvation.
ISAIAH 12:2

JOSHUA
God Is My Salvation

God is my salvation; I will trust, and not be afraid: for the Lord JEHOVAH is my strength.
ISAIAH 12:2

JOSIAH
God Supports

Fear thou not; for I am with thee: ... I am thy God: I will strengthen thee.
ISAIAH 41:10

J

JOSIANNE
Growing in Grace

> But grow in grace, and in the
> knowledge of our Lord and
> Saviour Jesus Christ.
> 2 PETER 3:18

JOSIAS
Jehovah Supports

> I will bless the Lord, who hath
> given me counsel: . . . I have set
> the Lord always before me.
> PSALM 16:7–8

JOSIE
Productive One

> The Lord thy God shall bless
> thee in all thine increase, and in
> all the works of thine hands.
> DEUTERONOMY 16:15

JOSIEN
God will Increase

> The Lord thy God shall bless
> thee in all thine increase, and in
> all the works of thine hands.
> DEUTERONOMY 16:15

JOSIEPHINE
Productive One

> The Lord thy God shall bless
> thee in all thine increase, and in
> all the works of thine hands.
> DEUTERONOMY 16:15

JOSLIN
The Just

> Justice and judgment are the
> habitation of thy throne: mercy
> and truth shall go before thy
> face.
> PSALM 89:14

JOSQUAN
God Is My Salvation

> I will praise thee: for thou hast
> heard me, and art become my
> salvation.
> PSALM 118:21

JOTHAM
Jehovah Is Perfect

> O Lord our Lord, how excellent
> is thy name in all the earth!
> Who hast set thy glory above the
> heavens.
> PSALM 8:1

JOU
Praise of God

> I will praise thee, O Lord, . . . I
> will be glad and rejoice in thee.
> PSALM 9:1–2

JOUETT
Youthful One

> For thou art my hope, O Lord
> God: thou art my trust from my
> youth.
> PSALM 71:5

JOURNEY
A Traveler

> As for God, his way is perfect;
> . . . God is my strength and
> power: and he maketh my way
> perfect.
> 2 SAMUEL 22:31, 33

JOUSLIN
The Just

> But the path of the just is as the
> shining light, that shineth more
> and more unto the perfect day.
> PROVERBS 4:18

NAME *That* BABY!

JOVA
God Will Establish

> *Thy right hand hath holden me up, and thy gentleness hath made me great.*
> PSALM 18:35

JOVI
One of Rejoicing

> *I will be glad and rejoice in thee: I will sing praise to thy name, O thou most High.*
> PSALM 9:2

JOVITA
One of Rejoicing and Life

> *I will show forth all thy marvellous works. I will be glad and rejoice in thee.*
> PSALM 9:1–2

JOY
Joyful One

> *Let all those that put their trust in thee rejoice: . . . let them also that love thy name be joyful in thee.*
> PSALM 5:11

JOYAL
Beautiful Gift

> *For by grace are ye saved through faith; and that not of yourselves: it is the gift of God.*
> EPHESIANS 2:8

JOYANN
One of Joy and Grace

> *No good thing will he withhold from them that walk uprightly.*
> PSALM 84:11

JOYBETH
One of Joy and Devotion

> *Thou wilt show me the path of life: in thy presence is fulness of joy; at thy right hand there are pleasures for evermore.*
> PSALM 16:11

JOYCE
Joyful One

> *Let them . . . that love thy name be joyful in thee.*
> PSALM 5:11

JOYELLE
One of Joy

> *Thou wilt show me the path of life: in thy presence is fulness of joy; at thy right hand there are pleasures for evermore.*
> PSALM 16:11

JOYLENE
One of Joy

> *I will be glad and rejoice in thee: I will sing praise to thy name.*
> PSALM 9:2

JOYMARIE
Joy and Living Fragrance

> *Thou wilt show me the path of life: in thy presence is fulness of joy; at thy right hand there are pleasures for evermore.*
> PSALM 16:11

JOZEF   *also* JOSEPH
Productive One

> *The Lord thy God shall bless thee in all thine increase, and in all the works of thine hands.*
> DEUTERONOMY 16:15

J

JOZSEF   *also* JOSEPH
Productive One
> *The Lord thy God shall bless thee in all thine increase, and in all the works of thine hands.*
> DEUTERONOMY 16:15

JSAZMA
Living Fragrance
> *I will praise thee; for I am fearfully and wonderfully made: . . . How precious also are thy thoughts unto me, O God!*
> PSALM 139:14, 17
>
>   Polynesian

JUAN
God Is Gracious
> *The Lord [is] . . . merciful and gracious, . . . abundant in goodness and truth.*
> EXODUS 34:6
>
>   Spanish

JUANITA   *also* WANITA
God's Gracious Gift
> *Every good gift and every perfect gift is from above, and cometh down from the Father.*
> JAMES 1:17

JUARD
Strong with the Spear
> *Take unto you the whole armour of God, . . . the sword of the Spirit which is the word of God.*
> EPHESIANS 6:13, 17

JUAREZ
Strong with the Spear
> *Take unto you the whole armour of God, . . . the sword of the Spirit which is the word of God.*
> EPHESIANS 6:13, 17

JUBAL
Stream of Music
> *The Lord is my strength and song, and he is become my salvation: he is my God, . . . I will exalt him.*
> EXODUS 15:2
>
>   Hebrew

JUBEL
Of Youth and Life
> *For thou art my hope, O Lord God: thou art my trust from my youth.*
> PSALM 71:5
>
>   Latin

JUBILEE
Time of Rejoicing
> *For what is our hope, or joy? Are not even ye in the presence of our Lord Jesus Christ at his coming?*
> 1 THESSALONIANS 2:19

JUCINTA
Of Precious Quality
> *Thy hands have made me and fashioned me: give me understanding, that I may learn thy commandments.*
> PSALM 119:73

JUDAH
The Praised

> *I will praise thee, O Lord, with my whole heart; . . . I will be glad and rejoice in thee.*
> PSALM 9:1–2

JUDD
Son of Praise

> *Praise ye the Lord. Praise ye the name of the Lord; praise him, O ye servants of the Lord.*
> PSALM 135:1

JUDE
Praise

> *I will praise thee, O lord, with my whole heart; I will show forth all thy marvelous works.*
> PSALM 9:1

JUDEANNE
Praised One of Grace

> *No good thing will he withhold from them that walk uprightly.*
> PSALM 84:11

JUDEMARK
Mighty Warrior of Faith

> *I will praise thee, O Lord, with my whole heart; I will show forth all thy marvellous works.*
> PSALM 9:1

JUDGE
One Who Rules

> *The mighty God, . . . hath spoken, . . . And the heavens shall declare his righteousness: for God is judge himself.*
> PSALM 50:1, 6

JUDIANNA
Praised of the Lord

> *Great is the Lord, and greatly to be praised; and his greatness is unsearchable.*
> PSALM 145:3

JUDITH
Praised of the Lord

> *Great is the Lord, and greatly to be praised; and his greatness is unsearchable.*
> PSALM 145:3

JUDSON
Song of Praise

> *I will bless the Lord at all times: his praise shall continually be in my mouth.*
> PSALM 34:1

JUDY
Praised of the Lord

> *Great is the Lord, and greatly to be praised; . . . his greatness is unsearchable.*
> PSALM 145:3

JUEL
Precious Gem

> *I will praise thee; for I am fearfully and wonderfully made: . . . How precious also are thy thoughts unto me, O God!*
> PSALM 139:14, 17

JUELL

also JUEL

Precious Gem

> I will praise thee; for I am
> fearfully and wonderfully
> made: . . . How precious also are
> thy thoughts unto me, O God!
> PSALM 139:14, 17

JUERGEN

Industrious One

> And whatsoever ye do, do it
> heartily, as to the Lord, and not
> unto men; . . . for ye serve the
> Lord Christ.
> COLOSSIANS 3:23–24

JUETTE

Little Follower of Christ

> Hold up my goings in thy paths,
> that my footsteps slip not.
> PSALM 17:5

JULE

Youthful Spirit

> For thou art my hope, O Lord
> God; thou art my trust from my
> youth.
> PSALM 71:5

JULEANN

One of Youth and Grace

> The Lord will give grace and
> glory; no good thing will he
> withhold from them that walk
> uprightly.
> PSALM 84:11

JULETTA

Youthful One

> For thou art my hope, O Lord
> God; thou art my trust from my
> youth.
> PSALM 71:5

JULIA

Youthful One

> For thou art my hope, O Lord
> God; thou art my trust from my
> youth.
> PSALM 71:5

JULIANNA

One of Youth and Grace

> For thou art my hope, O Lord
> God; thou art my trust from my
> youth.
> PSALM 71:5

JULIANNE

One of Youth and Grace

> The Lord will give grace and
> glory; no good thing will he
> withhold from them that walk
> uprightly.
> PSALM 84:11

JULIE

Youthful One

> For thou art my hope, O Lord
> God; thou art my trust from my
> youth.
> PSALM 71:5

JULIEANNE *also* JULIANNE
Youth and Grace

> The Lord will give grace and
> glory; no good thing will he
> withhold from them that walk
> uprightly.
> PSALM 84:11

JULIETTE
Youthful One

> For thou art my hope, O Lord
> God; thou art my trust from my
> youth.
> PSALM 71:5

JULY
The Youthful One

> For thou art my hope, O Lord
> God; thou art my trust from my
> youth.
> PSALM 71:5

JUMAANE
Gracious Gift

> Every good gift is from above,
> and cometh down from the
> Father.
> JAMES 1:17

Arabic

JUMAR
Divine Nature

> I will trust, and not be afraid:
> for the Lord JEHOVAH is my
> strength and . . . my song.
> ISAIAH 12:2

Muslim

JUNAZETTA
One of Youth

> For thou art my hope, O Lord
> God: thou art my trust from my
> youth.
> PSALM 71:5

JUNE
Ever Youthful

> Let no one despise thy youth;
> be thou an example of the
> believers, in word, . . . in
> charity, in spirit, in faith, in
> purity.
> 1 TIMOTHY 4:12

JUNGCLAUS
Young in Victory

> For whatsoever is born of God
> overcometh the world: and this
> is the victory that overcometh
> the world, even faith.
> 1 JOHN 5:4

German

JUNIOR
The Younger

> For thou art my hope, O Lord
> God: thou art my trust from my
> youth.
> PSALM 71:5

JUNIPER
Remaining Fresh

> Restore unto me the joy of thy
> salvation; and uphold me with
> thy free spirit.
> PSALM 51:12

J

JUOLEANNE
Youthful One of Grace

> *The Lord will give grace and glory; no good thing will he withhold from them that walk uprightly.*
> PSALM 84:11

JURATE
Noble and Devoted

> *I have set the Lord always before me: because he is at my right hand, I shall not be moved.*
> PSALM 16:8

JUREK
Noble One of Truth

> *I will meditate in thy precepts, . . . I will not forget thy word.*
> PSALM 119:15–16

JURELLE
Spear Ruler of Strength

> *Take unto you the whole armour of God, . . . taking the shield of faith, . . . the helmet of salvation, and the sword of the Spirit.*
> EPHESIANS 6:13, 16–17

JURGEN
Illustrious One

> *Now the God of peace, . . . Make you perfect in every good work to do his will, . . . that which is wellpleasing in his sight.*
> HEBREWS 13:20,24

JURPAL
One of Great Strength

> *In God is my salvation and my glory: the rock of my strength, and my refuge, is in God.*
> PSALM 62:7

JURSEY
Fighter for the Faith

> *Fight the good fight of faith, lay hold on eternal life, whereunto thou art also called.*
> 1 TIMOTHY 6:12

JURY
Tiller of the Soil

> *He that tilleth his land shall have plenty of bread: . . . A faithful man shall abound with blessings.*
> PROVERBS 28:19–20

JUSTIN
One of Justice

> *To do justice and judgment is more acceptable to the Lord than sacrifice.*
> PROVERBS 21:3

JUTTA
Great Consecration

> *I will sing unto the Lord as long as I live: I will sing praise to my God while I have my being.*
> PSALM 104:33

JUVENAL
Ever Youthful

> *Let no one despite thy youth;*
> *be thou an example of the*
> *believers, in word, . . . in*
> *charity, in spirit, in faith, in*
> *purity.*
> 1 TIMOTHY 4:12

JUWAN
God Is Gracious

> *He hath made his wonderful*
> *works to be remembered: the*
> *Lord is gracious and full of*
> *compassion.*
> PSALM 111:4

JUZEFA
The Productive One

> *The Lord thy God shall bless*
> *thee in all thine increase, and in*
> *all the works of thine hands.*
> DEUTERONOMY 16:15

JYL
Young at Heart

> *Let no one despise thy youth;*
> *be thou an example of the*
> *believers, in word, . . . in*
> *charity, in spirit, in faith, in*
> *purity.*
> 1 TIMOTHY 4:12

JYLISA
Consecrated to God

> *Give me understanding, and I*
> *shall keep thy law; yea, I shall*
> *observe it with my whole heart.*
> PSALM 119:34

JYOTHI
The Sun's Light

> *Let your light so shine before*
> *men, that they may see your*
> *good works and glorify your*
> *Father which is in heaven.*
> MATTHEW 5:16

East Indian

K

KACEY *also* KASEY
One of Purity

> Blessed are the pure in heart:
> for they shall see God.
> MATTHEW 5:8

KACY
One of Purity

> Blessed are the pure in heart:
> for they shall see God.
> MATTHEW 5:8

KALEB
Faithfulness

> I will praise thee; for thou hast
> heard me, and art become my
> salvation.
> PSALM 118:21

KALI
Heroic

> I have trusted . . . in the Lord;
> . . . I shall not slide. . . . I have
> walked in thy truth.
> PSALM 26:1, 3

KALISTE
Consecrated to God

> I delight to do thy will, O my
> God; yea, thy law is within my
> heart.
> PSALM 40:8

KALL
First Daughter

> I will praise thee; for I am
> fearfully and wonderfully
> made: marvellous are thy
> works.
> PSALM 139:14

KALLI
One of Rejoicing

> I will praise thee, O Lord, with
> my whole heart; . . . I will be
> glad and rejoice in thee: I will
> sing praise to thy name.
> PSALM 9:1–2

KALL'I
The Beauty

> I will praise thee; for I am
> fearfully and wonderfully
> made: How precious also are
> thy thoughts.
> PSALM 139:14, 17
>
> Polynesian

KA'ULA
A Prophet

> And thou, child, shalt be called
> the prophet of the Highest: for
> thou shalt go before the face of
> the Lord to prepare his ways.
> LUKE 1:76
>
> Polynesian

KARA
Pure One

> Blessed are the pure in heart:
> for they shall see God.
> MATTHEW 5:8

KAREN *also* CARRIN, KAYRON
Pure in Heart

> Blessed are the pure in heart:
> for they shall see God.
> MATTHEW 5:8

K

KARENA
Pure in Heart

> *Blessed are the pure in heart:*
> *for they shall see God.*
> MATTHEW 5:8

KARI
Pure in Heart

> *Blessed are the pure in heart:*
> *for they shall see God.*
> MATTHEW 5:8

KARIN *also* CARON
Pure One

> *With the pure thou wilt show*
> *thyself pure.*
> PSALM 18:26

KARL
Manly

> *I take pleasure . . . in*
> *persecutions, . . . for Christ's*
> *sake: for when I am weak, then*
> *am I strong.*
> 2 CORINTHIANS 12:10

KARLON
One of Great Strength

> *In God is my salvation and*
> *glory: the rock of my strength,*
> *. . . my refuge, is in God.*
> PSALM 62:7

KASEY *also* KACEY
One of Purity

> *Whatsoever things are honest,*
> *. . . just, . . . pure, . . . lovely, . . .*
> *of good report; if there be any*
> *virtue, . . . any praise, think on*
> *these things.*
> PHILIPPIANS 4:8

KATHERINE *also* CATHERINE
Pure One

> *Blessed are the pure in heart:*
> *for they shall see God.*
> MATTHEW 5:8

KATHLEEN
Pure One

> *Blessed are the pure in heart:*
> *for they shall see God.*
> MATTHEW 5:8

KATHRINA
Pure Heart

> *Blessed are the pure in heart:*
> *for they shall see God.*
> MATTHEW 5:8

KATHRINE
Pure One

> *Blessed are the pure in heart:*
> *for they shall see God.*
> MATTHEW 5:8

KATHY *also* CATHY
Pure One

> *Blessed are the pure in heart:*
> *for they shall see God.*
> MATTHEW 5:8

KATI
One of Purity

> *Blessed are the pure in heart:*
> *for they shall see God.*
> MATTHEW 5:8

KATIE
Pure One

> *Blessed are the pure in heart:*
> *for they shall see God.*
> MATTHEW 5:8

KATRINA
Pure One

> Blessed are the pure in heart:
> for they shall see God.
> MATTHEW 5:8

KATY
Pure One

> Blessed are the pure in heart:
> for they shall see God.
> MATTHEW 5:8

KATYA
Pure Heart

> Blessed are the pure in heart:
> for they shall see God.
> MATTHEW 5:8

KAUIKEOLANI
Placed on Heaven's Peak

> I will be glad and rejoice in
> thee: I will sing praise to thy
> name, O thou most High.
> PSALM 9:2
>
> Polynesian

KAULANA
One of Fame

> Wait on the Lord, and keep his
> way, and he shall exalt thee to
> inherit the land.
> PSALM 37:34

KAULO
Asked of God

> I have called upon thee, for thou
> wilt hear me, O God: incline
> thine ear unto me, and hear my
> speech.
> PSALM 17:6
>
> Polynesian

KAUPILI
Mutual Love

> Beloved, let us love one another:
> for love is of God; and every one
> that loveth is born of God, and
> knoweth God.
> 1 JOHN 4:7

KAUSHIKA
Noble and Gentle Spirit

> The fruit of the Spirit is love,
> joy, peace, longsuffering,
> gentleness, goodness, faith,
> meekness, temperance: against
> such there is no law.
> GALATIANS 5:22–23
>
> Polynesian

KAVA
Hero

> The Lord is my light and my
> salvation; whom shall I fear?
> the Lord is the strength of my
> life; of whom shall I be afraid?
> PSALM 27:1

KAVITA
Pure Heart

> The statutes of the Lord are
> right, rejoicing the heart: the
> commandment of the Lord is
> pure, enlightening the eyes.
> PSALM 19:8

KAWAILALA
Living Fragrance

> I will praise thee; for I am
> fearfully and wonderfully
> made: . . . How precious also
> are thy thoughts.
> PSALM 139:14, 17
>
> Polynesian

KAWANE
Dedication of Work

*The steps of a good man are
ordered by the Lord: and he
delighteth in his way. . . . The
law of . . . God is in his heart;
none of his steps shall slide.*
PSALM 37:23, 31

Polynesian

KAWANTA
One of Life and Joy

*Thou wilt show me the path of
life: in thy presence is fulness of
joy; at thy right hand there are
pleasures for evermore.*
PSALM 16:11

Latin

KAWANZA
Strength and Dedication

*Let the words of my mouth, and
the meditation of my heart, be
acceptable in thy sight, O Lord,
my strength, and my redeemer.*
PSALM 19:14

African

KAWIKA
Beloved One

*Beloved, let us love one another:
for love is of God; and every one
that loveth is born of God, and
knoweth God.*
1 JOHN 4:7

KAWLIGA
Dedication of Work

*The steps of a good man are
ordered by the Lord: and he
delighteth in his way. . . . The
law of his God is in his heart;
none of his steps shall slide.*
PSALM 37:23, 31

African

KAY
Pure Heart

*Blessed are the pure in heart:
for they shall see God.*
MATTHEW 5:8

KAYA
Little Sister

*I will praise thee; for I am
fearfully and wonderfully
made: . . . How precious also are
thy thoughts unto me, O God!*
PSALM 139:14, 17

KAYANNE
One of Purity and Grace

*The Lord will give grace and
glory: no good thing will he
withhold from them that walk
uprightly.*
PSALM 84:11

KAYEEN
Celebrated, Long Hoped for

*I will praise thee; for thou hast
heard me, and art become my
salvation.*
PSALM 118:21

KAYL
Crowned with Victory

> For whatsoever is born of God
> overcometh the world: and this
> is the victory that overcometh
> the world, even our faith.
> 1 JOHN 5:4

KAYLA
One of Purity

> The commandment of the Lord
> is pure, enlightening the eyes.
> PSALM 19:8

KAYLEB
Faithfulness

> I have set the Lord always
> before me: because he is at my
> right hand, I shall not be
> moved.
> PSALM 16:8

KAYLEIGH
Pure Heart

> The commandment of the Lord
> is pure, enlightening the eyes.
> PSALM 19:8

KAYRON   *also* KAREN
One of Purity

> Blessed are the pure in heart:
> for they shall see God.
> MATTHEW 5:8

KAYSHA
Safe and Pure

> I will say of the Lord, He is my
> refuge and my fortress: my God;
> in him will I trust.
> PSALM 91:2

KAZAN
Chosen Protection

> I will instruct thee and teach
> thee in the way which thou shalt
> go: I will guide thee with mine
> eye.
> PSALM 32:8

KAZIA
The Cassia Tree

> I will praise thee; for I am
> fearfully and wonderfully
> made: . . . How precious also are
> thy thoughts uno me, O God!
> PSALM 139:14, 17
>
> Hebrew

KAZIAH
God Is Salvation

> I will trust, and not be afraid:
> for the Lord JEHOVAH is my
> strength and my song; he also is
> become my salvation.
> ISAIAH 12:2
>
> Hebrew

KAZMAN
Priest of Righteousness

> Ye also, as lively stones, are
> built up a spiritual house, an
> holy priesthood, to offer up
> spiritual sacrifices, acceptable
> to God by Jesus Christ.
> 1 PETER 2:5

KAZUMI
Show Forth Peace

> The Lord will give strength unto
> his people; the Lord will bless
> his people with peace.
> PSALM 29:11

KAZUYUKI
One of Obedience

> *I have set the Lord always before me: because he is at my right hand, I shall not be moved.*
> PSALM 16:8
>
> Oriental

KEA
The Loved One

> *Beloved, let us love one another: for love is of God; and every one that loveth is born of God, and knoweth God.*
> 1 JOHN 4:7

KEAGAN
Zealous and Ardent

> *I press toward the mark for the prize of the high calling of God in Christ Jesus.*
> PHILIPPIANS 3:14

KEAH
Ardent Spirit

> *And whatsoever ye do, do it heartily, as to the Lord, and not unto men; . . . for ye serve the Lord Christ.*
> COLOSSIANS 3:23–24

KEAKA
Following After the Lord

> *Be ye therefore followers of God, as dear children; And walk in love, as Christ also hath loved us, and hath given himself for us.*
> EPHESIANS 5:1–2

KEALA
Fragrant Scent

> *I will praise thee; for I am fearfully and wonderfully made: . . . How precious also are thy thoughts.*
> PSALM 139:14, 17

KEALALAINA
Woman of the Lord

> *For thou art my rock and my fortress; therefore for thy name's sake lead me, and guide me.*
> PSALM 31:3
>
> Polynesian

KEALAN
Submissive Spirit

> *Let the words of my mouth, and the meditation of my heart, be acceptable in thy sight, O Lord, my strength, and my redeemer.*
> PSALM 19:14

KEALOHA
The Beloved One

> *Beloved, let us love one another: for love is of God; and every one that loveth is born of God, and knoweth God.*
> 1 JOHN 4:7
>
> Polynesian

KEANAN
Bold and Courageous One

> *The Lord is my rock, . . . my fortress, and my.deliverer; my God, my strength, in whom I will trust.*
> PSALM 18:2

KEARA
The Queenly One

> *I will praise thee; for I am fearfully and wonderfully made: marvellous are thy works; . . . How precious also are thy thoughts unto me, O God!*
> PSALM 139:14, 17

KEARBY
From the Church by the Village

> *I was glad when they said unto me, Let us go into the house of the Lord.*
> PSALM 122:1

KEARNEY
Victorious in Battle

> *But thanks be to God, which giveth us the victory through our Lord Jesus Christ.*
> 1 CORINTHIANS 15:57

KEASHA   *also* KEESHA
Safe and Secure

> *I will say of the Lord, He is my refuge, and my fortress: my God; in him will I trust.*
> PSALM 91:2

KEATING
Prudent and Honorable One

> *For the Lord is great, and greatly to be praised: . . . Honour and majesty are before him.*
> PSALM 96:4, 6

KEATON
One Who Came from Ketton

> *Thy word is a lamp unto my feet, and a light unto my path.*
> PSALM 119:105

KEATS
Christ Bearer

> *Ye are washed, but ye are sanctified, . . . ye are justified in the name of the Lord Jesus.*
> 1 CORINTHIANS 6:11

KECHA
One of Gladness and Joy

> *I will praise thee, O Lord, with my whole heart; . . . I will be glad and rejoice in thee: I will sing praise to thy name.*
> PSALM 9:1–2

KEDEANA
Princess of God

> *Strength and honour are her clothing; . . . . She openeth her mouth with wisdom; and in her tongue is the law of kindness.*
> PROVERBS 31:25–26

KEDRICK
Leader with Strength

> *The Lord is my strength and song, ... The right hand of the Lord is exalted: the right hand of the Lord doeth valiantly.*
> PSALM 118:14, 16

KEDRON
Compassionate Spirit

> *I will praise thee: for thou hast heard me, and art become my salvation.*
> PSALM 118:21

KEEAN-JO
Growing in Courage

> *Be strong and of a good courage; . . . for the Lord thy God is with thee withersoever thou goest.*
> JOSHUA 1:9

KEEBA
Cherished One

> *Thou wilt show me the path of life: in thy presence is fulness of joy; at thy right hand there are pleasures for evermore.*
> PSALM 16:11

KEEFE
Cherished and Gentle

> *And be ye kind one to another, tenderhearted, forgiving one another, even as God for Christ's sake hath forgiven you.*
> EPHESIANS 4:32

KEEGAN
One of Warmth and Care

> *Casting all your care upon him; for he careth for you.*
> 1 PETER 5:7

KEELA
Beautiful One

> *I will praise thee; for I am fearfully and wonderfully made: marvellous are thy works.*
> PSALM 139:14

KEELEE
The Beautiful One

> *I will praise thee; for I am fearfully and wonderfully made: marvellous are thy works.*
> PSALM 139:14

KEELIE
Heroine for the Faith

> *Fight the good fight of faith, lay hold on eternal life, whereunto thou art also called.*
> 1 TIMOTHY 6:12

KEELY
The Crest

> *Thou hast . . . given me the shield of thy salvation: . . . thy right hand hath holden me up, and thy gentleness hath made me great.*
> PSALM 18:35

KEELYN
Beauty of Spirit

> *Let the words of my mouth, and the meditation of my heart, be acceptable in thy sight, O Lord, my strength and my redeemer.*
> PSALM 19:14

KEEMA
One with Courage

> Wait on the Lord: be of good
> courage, and he shall strengthen
> thine heart: wait, I say, on the
> Lord.
> PSALM 27:14

KEERSTIN
Follower of Christ

> Ye are washed, but ye are
> sanctified, . . . ye are justified in
> the name of the Lord Jesus.
> 1 CORINTHIANS 6:11

KEESA   *also* KEASHA
Safe and Secure

> He that dwelleth in the secret
> place of the most High shall
> abide under the shadow of the
> Almighty.
> PSALM 91:1

KEETAN
Strong in Spirit

> Fight the good fight of faith, lay
> hold on eternal life, whereunto
> thou art also called.
> 1 TIMOTHY 6:12

KEGAN
Ardent Spirit

> And whatsoever ye do, do it
> heartily, as to the Lord, and not
> unto men; . . . for ye serve the
> Lord Christ.
> COLOSSIANS 3:23–24

KEHAULANI
Heavenly Dew

> For the seed shall be prosperous;
> the vine shall give her fruit, and
> the ground shall give her
> increase, and the heavens shall
> give their dew.
> ZECHARIAH 8:12

Polynesian

KEIBERA
Adoration and Delight

> I will bless the Lord at all times:
> his praise shall continually be
> in my mouth.
> PSALM 34:1

KEIHLY
Warrior for the Faith

> Fight the good fight of faith, lay
> hold on eternal life, whereunto
> thou art also called.
> 1 TIMOTHY 6:12

KEIJO
The Rejoiced In

> I will praise thee, O Lord, with
> my whole heart; I will show
> forth all thy marvelous works. I
> will be glad and rejoice in thee.
> PSALM 9:1–2

KEIL
Steadfast

> Be ye stedfast, unmovable,
> always abounding in the work
> of the Lord.
> 1 CORINTHIANS 15:58

KEILAH
Crown of Victory

> For whatsoever is born of God
> overcometh the world: and this
> is the victory that overcometh
> the world, even our faith.
> 1 JOHN 5:4

KEILEEN
Crown of Victory

> But thanks be to God, which
> giveth us the victory through
> our Lord Jesus Christ.
> 1 CORINTHIANS 15:57

KEIRA
Leader of Strength

> The Lord is my rock, and my
> fortress, and my deliverer; my
> God, my strength, in whom I
> will trust.
> PSALM 18:2

KEIRY
Protected One

> Be strong and of a good
> courage; . . . for the Lord thy
> God is with thee whithersoever
> thou goest.
> JOSHUA 1:9

KEISHA
Safe and Secure

> I will say of the Lord, He is my
> refuge and my fortress: my God;
> in him will I trust.
> PSALM 91:2

KEITH
Safe and Secure

> Thou shalt be secure, because
> there is hope; yea, . . . thou shalt
> take thy rest in safety.
> JOB 11:18

KEKALA
Radiant One

> They that be wise shall shine as
> the brightness of the firmament;
> . . . as the stars for ever and ever.
> DANIEL 12:3

KEKAPA
Of Noble Birth

> But ye are a chosen generation,
> a royal priesthood, . . . show
> forth the praises of him who
> hath called you.
> 1 PETER 2:9

Polynesian

KEKUPA'A
Steadfast One

> Therefore, my beloved brethren,
> be ye stedfast, unmovable,
> always abounding in the work
> of the Lord.
> 1 CORINTHIANS 15:58

Polynesian

KELA
A Princess

> I will praise thee; for I am
> fearfully and wonderfully
> made: . . . How precious also are
> thy thoughts unto me, O God!
> PSALM 139:14, 17

KELAN
Little, Slender One

> *I will praise thee; for I am*
> *fearfully and wonderfully*
> *made: . . . How precious also are*
> *thy thoughts unto me, O God!*
> PSALM 139:14, 17

KELANIE
One of Virtue and Grace

> *The Lord will give grace and*
> *glory: no good thing will he*
> *withhold from them that walk*
> *uprightly.*
> PSALM 84:11

KELBY
Where God Dwells

> *Then will I cause you to dwell in*
> *this place, in the land that I*
> *gave to your fathers, for ever*
> *and ever.*
> JEREMIAH 7:7

KELCEY
Peaceful One of Courage

> *The Lord will give strength unto*
> *his people; the Lord will bless*
> *his people with peace.*
> PSALM 29:11

KELDA
A Refreshing Spirit

> *The times of refreshing shall*
> *come from the presence of the*
> *Lord.*
> ACTS 3:19

KELE
Appointed by God

> *Behold, my servant shall deal*
> *prudently, he shall be exalted*
> *and extolled, and be very high.*
> ISAIAH 52:13

KELEAH
Crown of Laurel

> *But thanks be to God, which*
> *giveth us the victory through*
> *our Lord Jesus Christ.*
> 1 CORINTHIANS 15:57

KELEKULU
Maiden of Strength

> *I will trust, and not be afraid:*
> *for the Lord JEHOVAH is my*
> *strength and my song; he also is*
> *become my salvation.*
> ISAIAH 12:2

Polynesian

KELEMA
Of the Sea

> *Wherefore glorify ye the Lord in*
> *the fires, even the name of the*
> *Lord God of Israel in the isles of*
> *the sea.*
> ISAIAH 24:15

KELEMENEKE
One of Mercy and Kindness

> *For the Lord is good; his mercy*
> *is everlasting; and his truth*
> *endureth to all generations.*
> PSALM 100:5

Polynesian

KELEMIA
A Child of God

> *Whosoever shall not receive the kingdom of God as a little child shall in no wise enter therein.*
> LUKE 18:17
>
> > Polynesian

KELEN
Warrior Friend

> *Fight the good fight of faith, lay hold on eternal life, whereunto thou art also called.*
> 1 TIMOTHY 6:12

KELENAKINA
A Quiet Spirit

> *Let the words of my mouth, and the meditation of my heart, be acceptable in thy sight, O Lord, my strength, and my redeemer.*
> PSALM 19:14
>
> > Polynesian

KELEWELANA
Of the Cliff Land

> *Thy word is a lamp unto my feet, and a light unto my path.*
> PSALM 119:105
>
> > Polynesian

KELIA
Crown of Victory

> *For whatsoever is born of God overcometh the world: and this is the victory that overcometh the world, even our faith.*
> 1 JOHN 5:4

KELIN
Noble and Kind

> *And be ye kind one to another, tenderhearted, forgiving one another, even as God for Christ's sake hath forgiven you.*
> EPHESIANS 4:32

KELITA
One of Light

> *Let your light so shine before men, that they may see your good works, and glorify your Father which is in heaven.*
> MATTHEW 5:16

KELL
From the Spring

> *The Lord is my shepherd; I shall not want. He maketh me to lie down in green pastures: he leadeth me beside the still waters.*
> PSALM 23:1–2

KELLAN
Strong in the Faith

> *Fight the good fight of faith, lay hold on eternal life, whereunto thou art also called.*
> 1 TIMOTHY 6:12

KELLAND
Warrior for the Faith

> *Fight the good fight of faith, lay hold on eternal life, whereunto thou art also called.*
> 1 TIMOTHY 6:12

KELLEN
Warrior for the Faith

> *Fight the good fight of faith, lay hold on eternal life, whereunto thou art also called.*
> 1 TIMOTHY 6:12

KELLETT
From the Peaceful Meadow

> *The Lord is my shepherd; I shall not want. He maketh me to lie down in green pastures: he leadeth me beside the still waters.*
> PSALM 23: 1–2

KELLEY
Sustainer of Virture

> *Who are kept by the power of God through faith unto salvation, ready to be revealed in the last time.*
> 1 PETER 1:5

KELLI
Sustainer of Virtue

> *Who are kept by the power of God through faith unto salvation, ready to be revealed in the last time.*
> 1 PETER 1:5

KELLIS
Jehovah Is God

> *Behold, God is my salvation; I will trust and not be afraid: for the Lord JEHOVAH is my strength and my song.*
> ISAIAH 12:2

KELLY
Sustainer of Virtue

> *Who are kept by the power of God through faith unto salvation, ready to be revealed in the last time.*
> 1 PETER 1:5

KELLYANN
One of Virtue and Grace

> *Whatever things are true, . . . honest, . . . pure, . . . if there be any virtue, . . . think on these things.*
> PHILIPPIANS 4:8

KELMA
Chosen Protection

> *The Lord thy God hath chosen thee to be a special people unto himself.*
> DEUTERONOMY 7:6

KELPHEN
One of Kindness

> *And be ye kind one to another, tenderhearted, forgiving one another.*
> EPHESIANS 4:32

KELROY
Red-haired Son

> *My son, attend unto my wisdom, and bow thine ear to my understanding.*
> PROVERBS 5:1

KELVA
Warrior Friend
> *Fight the good fight of faith, lay hold on eternal life, whereunto thou art also called.*
> 1 TIMOTHY 6:12

KELWOOD
Warrior for the Faith
> *Fight the good fight of faith, lay hold on eternal life, whereunto thou art also called.*
> 1 TIMOTHY 6:12

KEM
Royal Courageous Champion
> *Whatsoever is born of God overcometh the world; and this is the victory . . . even our faith.*
> 1 JOHN 5:4

KEMIA
One of Honor and Truth
> *I will meditate in thy precepts, . . . I will delight myself in thy statutes.*
> PSALM 119:15–16

KEMILIA
Noble Messenger of Truth
> *How beautiful are the feet of them that preach the gospel of peace.*
> ROMANS 10:15
>
> Polynesian

KEMIN
One of Honor
> *For the Lord is great, and greatly to be praised.*
> PSALM 96:4

KEMP
A Champion
> *Whatsoever is born of God overcometh the world; and this is the victory . . . even our faith.*
> 1 JOHN 5:4

KEN
Courageous Champion
> *Whatsoever is born of God overcometh the world: and this is the victory . . . even our faith.*
> 1 JOHN 5:4

KENA
Courageous Champion
> *Whatsoever is born of God overcometh the world: and this is the victory . . . even our faith.*
> 1 JOHN 5:4

KENALYN
Brave Helmet
> *I will say of the Lord, He is my refuge and my fortress.*
> PSALM 91:2

KENAN
Strong Leader
> *God is my strength and power: and he maketh my way perfect.*
> 2 SAMUEL 22:33

KENDA
Child of Clear Peaceful Water
> *The Lord is my shepherd; . . . He leadeth me beside still waters.*
> PSALM 23:1–2

KENDAHL
Strong and Courageous

> *Whatsoever is born of God overcometh the world: and this is the victory . . . even our faith.*
> 1 JOHN 5:4

KENDAL
Strong and Courageous

> *Whatsoever is born of God overcometh the world: and this is the victory . . . even our faith.*
> 1 JOHN 5:4

KENDRA
One of Understanding

> *My mouth shall speak of wisdom; and the meditation of my heart shall be of understanding.*
> PSALM 49:3

KENDRICK
Royal King

> *For the Lord is great, and greatly to be praised.*
> PSALM 96:4

KENEFRA
One of Great Freedom

> *Stand fast therefore in the liberty wherewith Christ hath made us free.*
> GALATIANS 5:1

KENETTER
Courageous Champion

> *Whatsoever is born of God overcometh the world: and this is the victory . . . even our faith.*
> 1 JOHN 5:4

KENEWIWE
Fair Lady

> *I will praise thee; for I am fearfully and wonderfully made: marvellous are thy works.*
> PSALM 139:14

KENNA
Love

> *Beloved, let us love one another: for love is of God, and every one that loveth is born of God.*
> 1 JOHN 4:7

KENNAH
Love

> *Beloved, let us love one another: for love is of God, and every one that loveth is born of God.*
> 1 JOHN 4:7

KENNARD
Bold and Strong

> *The Lord is my rock, . . . my fortress, . . . my deliverer; my God, my strength, in whom I will trust.*
> PSALM 18:2

KENNEDY
Courageous Champion

> *Whatsoever is born of God overcometh the world: and this is the victory . . . even our faith.*
> 1 JOHN 5:4

KENNEL
Learned Man
> For the Lord giveth wisdom: out
> of his mouth cometh knowldege
> and understanding.
> PROVERBS 2:6

KENNETH
Courageous Champion
> Whatsoever is born of God
> overcometh the world: and this
> is the victory . . . even our faith.
> 1 JOHN 5:4

KENNY
Courageous in Battle
> Wait on the Lord: be of good
> courage, and he shall strengthen
> thine heart.
> PSALM 27:14

KENON
Courageous Champion
> Thou hast . . . given me the
> shield of thy salvation: . . . thy
> gentleness hath made me great.
> PSALM 18:35

KENSLEY
Royally Brave
> I have set the Lord always
> before me: . . . he is at my right
> hand, I shall not be moved.
> PSALM 16:8

KENT
Leader of Justice
> Justice and judgment are the
> habitation of thy throne.
> PSALM 89:14

KEOHOKALOLE
Divine Gift
> Every good gift and every
> perfect gift is from above, and
> cometh down from the Father.
> JAMES 1:17
>
> Polynesian

KEOINA
Fellowship
> I will say of the Lord, He is my
> refuge and my fortress: my God.
> PSALM 91:2

KEOKI
Tiller of the Soil
> He that tilleth his land shall
> have plenty of bread: . . . A
> faithful man shall abound with
> blessings.
> PROVERBS 28:19–20
>
> Polynesian

KEOKIA
Industrious One
> And whatsoever ye do, do it
> heartily, as to the Lord, . . . for
> ye serve the Lord Christ.
> COLOSSIANS 3:23–24B

KEOKOLO
Divine Gift
> Every good gift and every
> perfect gift is from above, and
> cometh down from the Father.
> JAMES 1:17

NAME *That* BABY!

KEOLA-MAI-IKAIKA
Strength for Healing

> The Spirit of the Lord God is
> upon me; because the Lord hath
> anointed me.
> ISAIAH 61:1
>
> Polynesian

KEPA
Strong as a Rock

> In God is my salvation and my
> glory: the rock of my strength,
> and my refuge.
> PSALM 62:7

KEPOLA
Loyal Messenger of Truth

> Let the words of my mouth, . . .
> be acceptable in thy sight,
> O Lord.
> PSALM 19:14

KERALA
Strong in the Lord

> The Lord is my rock, . . . my
> fortress, . . . my deliverer; my
> God, my strength.
> PSALM 18:2

KERIN
One of Leadership

> God is my strength and power:
> and he maketh my way perfect.
> 2 SAMUEL 22:33

KERMIT
Free Man

> For he that is called in the Lord,
> being a servant, is the Lord's
> freeman.
> 1 CORINTHIANS 7:22

KERRI
Seeker of Light

> I am the light of the world: . . .
> he that followeth me . . . shall
> have the light of life.
> JOHN 8:12

KERRY
Seeker of Light

> I am the light of the world: he
> that followeth me, . . . shall have
> the light of life.
> JOHN 8:12

KERSTIN
Follower of Christ

> Be ye therefore followers of God,
> as dear children; And walk in
> love, as Christ also hath loved
> us.
> EPHESIANS 5:1–2

KESHENA
Swift in Flight

> Thy word is a lamp unto my
> feet, and a light unto my path.
> . . . I hope in thy word.
> PSALM 119:105, 114

KESHIA
One of Gladness and Joy

> I will praise thee, O Lord, with
> my whole heart; . . . I will be
> glad and rejoice in thee.
> PSALM 9:1–2

KESI
Gladness and Joy

> I will praise thee, O Lord, with
> my whole heart; . . . I will be
> glad and rejoice in thee.
> PSALM 9:1–2

KET
One of Praise

> *My lips shall utter praise, . . .*
> *My tongue shall speak of thy*
> *word.*
> PSALM 119:171–172

KETHA
Safe and Secure

> *I have set the Lord always*
> *before me: . . . he is at my right*
> *hand, . . . I shall not be moved.*
> PSALM 16:8

KETTY
Mistress of the Home

> *Through wisdom is a house*
> *builded; and by understanding*
> *it is established.*
> PROVERBS 24:3

KETURAH
One of Praise

> *My lips shall utter praise, . . . My*
> *tongue shall speak of thy word.*
> PSALM 119:171–172
>
> Hebrew

KEU
The Rejoiced In

> *I will praise thee, O Lord, with*
> *my whole heart; . . . I will be*
> *glad and rejoice in thee.*
> PSALM 9:1–2

KEVIN
One of Kindness

> *Be ye kind one to another,*
> *tenderhearted, forgiving one*
> *another, . . . as God . . . hath*
> *forgiven you.*
> EPHESIANS 4:32

KEVIRA
Kind and Faithful

> *I love the Lord, because he hath*
> *heard my voice and my*
> *supplications.*
> PSALM 116:1

KEYNA
Precious Jewel

> *I will praise thee; for I am*
> *fearfully and wonderfully*
> *made: marvellous are thy*
> *works.*
> PSALM 139:14

KEYRA
Of the Royal Throne

> *I will praise thee; for I am*
> *fearfully and wonderfully*
> *made: marvellous are thy*
> *works.*
> PSALM 139:14

KEZIA
Chosen Protection

> *Ye have not chosen me, but I*
> *have chosen you, and ordained*
> *you, that you should go bring*
> *forth fruit.*
> JOHN 15:16

KHA
A Friend

> *A man that hath friends must*
> *show himself friendly.*
> PROVERBS 18:24

KHAI
One of Royal Nobility

> *Ye are a chosen generation, a*
> *royal priesthood . . . that ye*
> *should show forth the praises of*
> *him who hath called you.*
> 1 PETER 2:9

KHALIL
Good Friend

> *Ye are my friends, if ye do*
> *whatsoever I command you.*
> JOHN 15:14

> Arabic

KHALILAH
Friend

> *A man that hath friends must*
> *show himself friendly.*
> PROVERBS 18:24

KHAMPHANH
Loved by God

> *For God so loved the world, that*
> *he gave his only begotten Son.*
> JOHN 3:16

KHENNETH
Leader with Courage

> *Be strong and of a good*
> *courage; . . . for the Lord thy*
> *God is with thee.*
> JOSHUA 1:9

KHIVA
Rock of Strength

> *He only is my rock and my*
> *salvation: . . . In God is my*
> *salvation and my glory: the rock*
> *of my strength.*
> PSALM 62:6–7

KHOURY
The Helmet

> *Take unto you the whole armour*
> *of God, . . . And take the helmet*
> *of salvation.*
> EPHESIANS 6:13, 17

KHYVA
Protected by God

> *The beloved of the Lord shall*
> *dwell in safety by him; and the*
> *Lord shall cover him.*
> DEUTERONOMY 33:12

KIA
One of Victory

> *Whatsoever is born of God*
> *overcometh the world . . . this is*
> *the victory that overcometh, . . .*
> *even our faith.*
> 1 JOHN 5:4

KIAH
Ardent Spirit

> *Whatsoever ye do, do it heartily,*
> *as to the Lord, . . . for ye serve*
> *the Lord Christ.*
> COLOSSIANS 3:23–24

> Polynesian

KIANA
Divine One

> *[There] are given unto us . . .*
> *great and precious promises:*
> *that . . . ye might be partakers*
> *of the divine nature.*
> 2 PETER 1:4

KIANI
Divine One

*[There] are given unto us . . .
great and precious promises:
that . . . ye might be partakers
of the divine nature.*
2 PETER 1:4

KIARA
Radiant One

*Let your light so shine . . . that
they may see your good works,
and glorify your Father in
heaven.*
MATTHEW 5:16

KICE
Brave and Strong

*The Lord is my rock, . . . my
fortress, . . . my deliverer; my
God, my strength, in whom I
will trust.*
PSALM 18:2

KIDRA
One of Power and Strength

*Thou hast also given me the
shield of thy salvation: and thy
right hand hath holden me up.*
PSALM 18:35

KIDRON
One of Compassion

*The Lord is gracious and full of
compassion.*
PSALM 111:4

KIELA
Fragrant Blossom

*I will praise thee; for I am
fearfully and wonderfully made.*
PSALM 139:14

KIELI
Laurel of Victory

*For whatsoever is born of God
overcometh the world: and this
is the victory . . . even our faith.*
1 JOHN 5:4

KIENAN
Chosen of God

*Ye have not chosen me, but I
have chosen you, and ordained
you, that ye should go and bring
forth fruit.*
JOHN 15:16

KIERNAN
Leader of Strength

*The Lord is my rock, . . . my
fortress, and my deliverer; my
God, my strength, in whom I
will trust.*
PSALM 18:2

KIESA
One of Purity

*Blessed are the pure in heart:
for they shall see God.*
MATTHEW 5:8

KIFFEN
Kind and Tenderhearted

*And be ye kind one to another,
tenderhearted, forgiving one
another.*
EPHESIANS 4:32

KIKIONA
Of Great Strength and Might

> The Lord is my rock, . . . my
> fortress, . . . my deliverer; my
> God, my strength, in whom I
> will trust.
> PSALM 18:2

Polynesian

KIKO
Safely Protected

> He that dwelleth in the . . . place
> of the most High shall abide
> under the shadow of the
> Almighty.
> PSALM 91:1

KILA
Of Good Character

> My hands also will I lift up unto
> thy commandments, which I
> have loved.
> PSALM 119:48

KILAKILA
Majestic

> For the Lord is great, and
> greatly to be praised: . . .
> Honour and majesty are before
> him.
> PSALM 96:4, 6

Polynesian

KILBURN
Strong Foundation

> The Lord is my rock, and my
> fortress, and my deliverer; my
> God, my strength.
> PSALM 18:2

KILBY
From the Farmstead by the Spring

> Through wisdom is an house
> builded; and by understanding
> it is established.
> PROVERBS 24:3

KILE
A Chapel

> I will praise thee, O Lord my
> God, with all my heart: and I
> will glorify thy name for
> evermore.
> PSALM 86:12

KILEY
Full of Grace

> The Lord will give grace and
> glory: no good thing will he
> withhold.
> PSALM 84:11

KILLIAN
Strong in the Faith

> Fight the good fight of faith, lay
> hold on eternal life, whereunto
> thou art also called.
> 1 TIMOTHY 6:12

KILOHOKU
The Star Gazer

> They that be wise shall shine as
> the brightness of the firmament;
> . . . as the stars for ever and ever.
> DANIEL 12:3

KILPATRICK
Noble Son

> Thou hast also given me the
> shield of thy salvation: . . . thy
> gentleness hath made me great.
> PSALM 18:35

KIM
One of Honor

> I will be glad and rejoice in
> thee: I will sing praise to thy
> name, O thou most high.
> PSALM 9:2

KIMALISHEA
One of Honor and Truth

> For the Lord is great, and greatly
> to be praised: . . . Honour and
> majesty are before him.
> PSALM 96:4, 6

KIMBA
Royally Brave

> He only is my rock and my
> salvation: he is my defence; I
> shall not be moved.
> PSALM 62:6

KIMBERLEE
One of Honor

> Strength and honour are her
> clothing; and . . . she shall be
> praised.
> PROVERBS 31:25, 30

KIMBERLI
One of Honor

> Strength and honour are her
> clothing; and . . . she shall be
> praised.
> PROVERBS 31:25, 30

KIMBERLY
One of Honor

> The Lord is great, and greatly to
> be praised: . . . Honour and
> majesty are before him.
> PSALM 96:4, 6

KIMBI
Noble One of Honor

> The Lord is great, and greatly to
> be praised: . . . Honour and
> majesty are before Him.
> PSALM 96:4, 6

KIMCHI
Noble and Sovereign One

> Ye have not chosen me, but I have
> chosen you, and ordained you.
> JOHN 15:16

KIMONA
The Lord Hath Heard

> I will bless the Lord at all times:
> his praise shall continually be
> in my mouth.
> PSALM 34:1

KIN
Golden

> I will praise thee; for I am
> fearfully and wonderfully made.
> PSALM 139:14

KINCAID
Leader of Strength

> In God is my salvation and my
> glory: the rock of my strength,
> and my refuge, is in God.
> PSALM 62:7

KINDER
One Who is Kind

> And be ye knd one to another,
> tenderhearted, forgiving one
> another.
> EPHESIANS 4:32

KING
One of Royal Nobility

> But ye are a chosen generation,
> a royal priesthood, . . . that ye
> should show forth . . . praises.
> 1 PETER 2:9

KINGSTON
From the Royal House

> I was glad when they said unto
> me, Let us go into the house of
> the Lord.
> PSALM 122:1

KINLEY
Fair Hero

> Thou hast also given me the
> shield of thy salvation: . . . thy
> right hand hath holden me up.
> PSALM 18:35

KINOIKE
The Petite One

> I will priase thee; for I am
> fearfully and wonderfully
> made: marvellous are thy
> works.
> PSALM 139:14

KINOINI
Crowned One

> When the chief Shepherd shall
> appear, ye shall receive a crown
> of glory that fadeth not.
> 1 PETER 5:4

KINSELLA
Precious Heritage

> The Lord is the portion of mine
> inheritance and of my cup: . . . I
> have a goodly heritage.
> PSALM 16:5–6

KINTA
One of Grace

> The Lord will give grace and
> glory: no good thing will he
> withhold from them that walk
> uprightly.
> PSALM 84:11

KIONA
Honored One

> For the Lord is great, and
> greatly to be praised: . . .
> Honour and majesty are before
> him.
> PSALM 96:4, 6

KIORA
One of Light

> And they that be wise shall
> shine as the brightness of the
> firmament.
> DANIEL 12:3

KIP
High Dweller

> Surely goodness and mercy shall
> follow me all the days of my life:
> and I will dwell in the house of
> the Lord for ever.
> PSALM 23:6

KIPLEY
High Dweller

> Surely goodness and mercy shall
> follow me all the days of my life:
> and I will dwell in the house of
> the Lord for ever.
> PSALM 23:6

KIRA
Radiant Light

> And they that be wise shall
> shine as the brightness of the
> firmament; . . . as the stars for
> ever and ever.
> DANIEL 12:3

KIRIEL
Majestic One

> For the Lord is great, and greatly
> to be praised: . . . Honour and
> majesty are before him.
> PSALM 96:4, 6

KIRK
Worshipful Spirit

> Give unto the Lord the glory due
> unto his name; worship the Lord
> in the beauty of holiness.
> PSALM 29:2
>
> Scottish

KIRKLAND
Worshipful Spirit

> Give unto the Lord the glory due
> unto his name; worship the Lord
> in the beauty of holiness.
> PSALM 29:2

KIRKWOOD
Dweller at the Church

> I was glad when they said unto
> me, Let us go into the house of
> the Lord.
> PSALM 122:1

KISHAWNA
God Is Gracious

> But thou, O Lord, art a God full
> of compassion, and gracious,
> longsuffering, and plenteous in
> mercy.
> PSALM 86:15
>
> African

KIVA
Guardian Protector

> He that dwelleth in the secret
> place . . . shall abide under the
> shadow of the Almighty.
> PSALM 91:1

KIYOMI
Pure Beauty

> Thy hands have made me and
> fashioned me: give me
> understanding that I may learn
> thy commandments.
> PSALM 119:73

KIYONO
The Rejoiced In

> I will praise thee, O Lord, with
> my whole heart; . . . I will be
> glad and rejoice in thee.
> PSALM 9:1–2

KIZZIE
Pure Heart

> The commandment of the Lord
> is pure, enlightening the eyes.
> PSALM 19:8

KJERSTEN
A Christian

> Ye are washed, but ye are
> sanctified, . . . ye are justified in
> the name of the Lord Jesus.
> 1 CORINTHIANS 6:11

KLAMPHANH
Loved by God

> God so loved the world, that he
> gave his only begotten Son,
> that whosoever believeth in him
> should have everlasting life.
> JOHN 3:16
>
> Chinese

KLEILA
Loyal

> I have set the Lord always
> before me: . . . he is at my right
> hand, I shall not be moved.
> PSALM 16:8

KLENZ
Peaceful Dweller

> The Lord is my shepherd; I shall
> not want. . . . he leadeth me
> beside the still waters.
> PSALM 23:1–2

KLETA
Chosen and Called

> Ye have not chosen me, but I have
> chosen you, and ordained you,
> that you should go and bring
> forth fruit.
> JOHN 15:16

KLISTIA
Consecrated to God

> I will bless the Lord at all times:
> his praise shall continually be
> in my mouth.
> PSALM 34:1

KNIGHT
Warrior Strength

> The Lord is my light and my
> salvation; whom shall I fear? the
> Lord is the strength of my life.
> PSALM 27:1

KNISH
Blessed Food

> The works of the Lord are great,
> . . . His work is . . . glorious: . . .
> He hath given meat.
> PSALM 111:2, 3, 5

KNOX
Peaceful Dweller

> The Lord is my shepherd; I shall
> not want. He maketh me to lie
> down in green pastures.
> PSALM 23:1–2

KOAN
Courageous and Brave

> Be strong and of a good
> courage; . . . for the Lord thy
> God is with thee.
> JOHSUA 1:9

KODI
Victorious One

> For whatsoever is born of God
> overcometh the world: and this
> is the victory that overcometh
> the world, even our faith.
> 1 JOHN 5:4

KOE
Exalted One

> Thou hast also given me the
> shield of thy salvation . . . thy
> gentleness hath made me great.
> PSALM 18:35

KOELLENA
One of Light

> They that be wise shall shine as
> the brightness of the firmament;
> . . . as the stars for ever and ever.
> DANIEL 12:3

KOFI
Special One

> Thy hands have made me and
> fashioned me; give me
> understanding.
> PSALM 119:73

KOHN
Brave

> The Lord is my strength and my
> shield; my heart trusted in him.
> PSALM 28:7

KOIER
One of Fellowship

> I will say of the Lord, He is my
> refuge, and my fortress: . . . in
> him will I trust.
> PSALM 91:2

KOINONIA
Fellowship

> I will say of the Lord, He is my
> refuge and my fortress: . . . in
> him will I trust.
> PSALM 91:2
>
> Greek

KOLBIE
Of Rich Earth

> O Lord, how manifold are thy
> works! . . . the earth is full of
> thy riches.
> PSALM 104:24

KOLEENA
Girl of Virtue

> Whatsoever things are true, . . .
> honest, . . . just, . . . [and] pure,
> lovely . . of good report, if there
> be any virtue . . . think on these
> things.
> PHILIPPIANS 4:8

KOLEKA
Gift of God

> For by grace are ye saved
> through faith; and that not of
> yourselves: it is the gift of God.
> EPHESIANS 2:8

KOLIKA
Bountiful

> I will sing unto the Lord,
> because he hath dealt
> bountifully with me.
> PSALM 13:6

KOLOMONA
One of Peace

> The Lord will give strength to
> his people; the Lord will bless
> his people with peace.
> PSALM 29:11

KOMA
A Twin, One of Equality

> For God so loved the world, that
> he gave his only . . . Son.
> JOHN 3:16

KONANE
Bright as Moon Light

> *Let your light so shine . . . that*
> *they may see your good works,*
> *and glorify your Father in*
> *heaven.*
> MATTHEW 5:16

KONE
Loyal Devotion

> *I have set the Lord always*
> *before me: because he is at my*
> *right hand, I shall not be*
> *moved.*
> PSALM 16:8

KONI
Loyal Devotion

> *I have set the Lord always*
> *before me: because he is at my*
> *right hand, I shall not be*
> *moved.*
> PSALM 16:8

KONITA
Wise Counsel

> *I will bless the Lord, who hath*
> *given me counsel: . . . he is at my*
> *right hand.*
> PSALM 16:7–8

KONNAMIJA
Giver of Wise and Bold Counsel

> *I will bless the Lord, who hath*
> *given me counsel: . . . he is at my*
> *right hand.*
> PSALM 16:7–8

Dutch

KOO
Cherished One

> *Let the words of my mouth, and*
> *the meditation of my heart, be*
> *acceptable in thy sight.*
> PSALM 19:14

KOPAIA
One of Wisdom

> *For the Lord giveth wisdom: out*
> *of his mouth cometh knowledge.*
> PROVERBS 2:6

Polynesian

KORAL
Small Pebble by the Sea

> *Thy hands have made me and*
> *fashioned me: . . . give me*
> *understanding that I may learn*
> *thy commandments.*
> PSALM 119:73

KORBAN
One of Valor

> *Thou hast . . . given me the*
> *shield of thy salvation: . . . thy*
> *right hand hath holden me up.*
> PSALM 18:35

KORI
One of Youth

> *For thou art my hope, O Lord*
> *God: thou art my trust from my*
> *youth.*
> PSALM 71:5

KORLON
Majestic and Strong

> *The Lord is my rock, . . . my*
> *fortress, . . . my deliverer; my*
> *God, my strength.*
> PSALM 18:2

KORSI
One of Strength

> The Lord is my light and my
> salvation; . . . the Lord is the
> strength of my life.
> PSALM 27:1

KOSHIE
Quiet and Peaceful

> The Lord will give strength unto
> his people; the Lord will bless
> with peace.
> PSALM 29:11

KOSSI
Firm of Purpose

> I have set the Lord always
> before me: because he is at my
> right hand, I shall not be
> moved.
> PSALM 16:8

KOUJI
God will Strengthen

> The Lord is my rock, . . . my
> fortress, . . . my deliverer; my
> God, my strength.
> PSALM 18:2

KOUKLA
Life of Victory

> Whatsoever is born of God
> overcometh the world: . . . this is
> the victory . . . even our faith.
> 1 JOHN 5:4
> German

KOWANA
Walking with the Lord

> Thy word is a lamp unto my
> feet, and a light unto my path.
> PSALM 119:105
> American Indian

KREHL
Warrior for the Faith

> Fight the good fight of faith, lay
> hold on eternal life, whereunto
> thou art also called.
> 1 TIMOTHY 6:12
> German

KRES
A Christian

> Ye are washed, . . . sanctified,
> . . . [and] justified in the name
> of the Lord Jesus.
> 1 CORINTHIANS 6:11

KRISSI
A Christian

> Ye are washed, . . . sanctified,
> . . . [and] justified in the name
> of the Lord Jesus.
> 1 CORINTHIANS 6:11

KRISTEN
A Christian

> Ye are washed, . . . sanctified,
> . . . [and] justified in the name
> of the Lord Jesus.
> 1 CORINTHIANS 6:11

KRISTI
also KRYSTI

A Christian

> Ye are washed, . . . sanctified,
> . . . [and] justified in the name
> of the Lord Jesus.
> 1 CORINTHIANS 6:11

KRISTIN   *also* CHRISTIN
A Christian

> *Ye are washed, . . . sanctified,*
> *. . . [and] justified in the name*
> *of the Lord Jesus.*
> 1 CORINTHIANS 6:11

KRISTINA   *also* CHRISTINA
A Christian

> *Ye are washed, . . . sanctified,*
> *. . . [and] justified in the name*
> *of the Lord Jesus.*
> 1 CORINTHIANS 6:11

KRISTINE   *also* CHRISTINE
Follower of Christ

> *Ye are washed, . . . sanctified,*
> *. . . [and] justified in the name*
> *of the Lord Jesus.*
> 1 CORINTHIANS 6:11

KRISTOFER
Steadfast for Christ

> *Be ye stedfast, unmovable,*
> *always abounding in the work*
> *of the Lord.*
> 1 CORINTHIANS 15:58

KRISTOFOR
Steadfast for Christ

> *Be ye stedfast, unmovable,*
> *always abounding in the work*
> *of the Lord.*
> 1 CORINTHIANS 15:58

KRISTOPHER
also CHRISTOPHER
Steadfast for Christ

> *Be ye stedfast, unmovable,*
> *always abounding in the work*
> *of the Lord.*
> 1 CORINTHIANS 15:58

KRISTY   *also* CHRISTIE
A Christian

> *Ye are washed, . . . sanctified,*
> *. . . [and] justified in the name*
> *of the Lord Jesus.*
> 1 CORINTHIANS 6:11

KRSITA
A Christian

> *Ye are washed, . . . sanctified,*
> *. . . [and] justified in the name*
> *of the Lord Jesus.*
> 1 CORINTHIANS 6:11

KRUGER
Keeper of the Inn

> *And whatsoever ye do, do it*
> *heartily, as to the Lord, . . . for*
> *ye serve the Lord Christ.*
> COLOSSIANS 3:23–24

KRYSIA
A Christian

> *Ye are washed, . . . sanctified,*
> *. . . [and] justified in the name*
> *of the Lord Jesus.*
> 1 CORINTHIANS 6:11

KRYSTAL
Brilliantly Pure

> *Unto the pure all things are pure.*
> TITUS 1:15

KRYSTI
A Christian

> Ye are washed, . . . sanctified,
> . . . [and] justified in the name
> of the Lord Jesus.
> 1 CORINTHIANS 6:11

KRYSTINA
A Follower of Christ

> Ye are washed, . . . sanctified,
> . . . [and] justified in the name
> of the Lord Jesus.
> 1 CORINTHIANS 6:11

KRYSTLENE
Brilliantly Pure

> The commandment of the Lord
> is pure, enlightening the eyes.
> PSALM 19:8

KRYSTN   *also* KRISTIN
A Christian

> Ye are washed, . . . sanctified,
> . . . [and] justified in the name
> of the Lord Jesus.
> 1 CORINTHIANS 6:11

KSANKA
Beautiful One

> I will praise thee; for I am
> fearfully and wonderfully made:
> marvellous are thy works.
> PSALM 139:14

KSENIJA
Pure Heart

> Blessed are the pure in heart:
> for they shall see God.
> MATTHEW 5:8

Teutonic

KSHE
Joy and Gladness

> I will praise thee, O Lord, with
> my whole heart, . . . I will be
> glad.
> PSALM 9:1–2

KUCENSKI
One of Light

> Let your light so shine before
> men, that they may see your
> good works and glorify your
> Father . . . in heaven.
> MATTHEW 5:16

Slavic

KUHIO
Youthful One

> For thou art my hope, O Lord
> God: thou art my trust from my
> youth.
> PSALM 71:5

KUKER
Symbol of Pure Heart

> Blessed are the pure in heart:
> for they shall see God.
> MATTHEW 5:8

KUMAR
One of Noble Royalty

> But ye are a chosen generation,
> a royal priesthood, . . . that ye
> should show forth the praises
> of him.
> 1 PETER 2:9

Pakistan

KUMUDHA
Resting Place

> Take my yoke upon you, and
> learn of me; for I am meek and
> lowly in heart . . . and ye shall
> find rest.
> MATTHEW 11:29
>
> Muslim

KUNIKO
Country-born Child

> I will praise thee; for I am
> fearfully and wonderfully made:
> marvellous are thy works.
> PSALM 139:14
>
> Japanese

KUNTA
One of Strong Counsel

> I have set the Lord always
> before me: because he is at my
> right hand, I shall not be
> moved.
> PSALM 16:8

KU'ULEILANI
My Royal Child

> I will bless the Lord at all times:
> his praise shall continually be
> in my mouth.
> PSALM 34:1
>
> Polynesian

KUWANNA
God's Gracious Gift

> For by grace are ye saved
> through faith; . . . it is the gift of
> God.
> EPHESIANS 2:8

KWABENA
Born on Monday

> I will praise thee; for I am
> fearfully and wonderfully made:
> marvellous are thy works.
> PSALM 139:14
>
> African

KWAI
God Is Gracious

> He hath made his wonderful
> works to be remembered: the
> Lord is gracious.
> PSALM 111:4
>
> Zuni Indian

KWAME
Born on Saturday

> Thy hands have made me and
> fashioned me: give me
> understanding.
> PSALM 119:73
>
> African

KWASI
Born on Sunday

> Thou hast also given me the
> shield of thy salvation.
> PSALM 18:35
>
> African

KWESI
Born on Sunday

> Let the words of my mouth, and
> the meditation of my heart, be
> acceptable in thy sight.
> PSALM 19:14

KWINSI
The Wise

> For the Lord giveth wisdom: out
> of his mouth cometh knowledge.
> PROVERBS 2:6

KYDIA
Crown of Victory

> Whatsoever is born of God
> overcometh the world: . . . this is
> the victory . . . even our faith.
> 1 JOHN 5:4

KYELAYA
Crown with Laurel

> Whatsoever is born of God
> overcometh the world: and this
> is the victory . . . even our faith.
> 1 JOHN 5:4

KYIA
Crown of Victory

> Whatsoever is born of God
> overcometh the world: . . . this is
> the victory . . . even our faith.
> 1 JOHN 5:4

KYJAWA
Crowned with Victory

> Whatsoever is born of God
> overcometh the world: . . . this is
> the victory . . . even our faith.
> 1 JOHN 5:4

KYLE
Walk Uprightly

> He who walketh uprightly, and
> . . . that doeth these things shall
> never be moved.
> PSALM 15:2–5

KYLELAYA
Crowned with Laurel

> Whatsoever is born of God
> overcometh the world: . . . this is
> the victory . . . even our faith.
> 1 JOHN 5:4

KYLIE
A Refreshing Spirit

> The times of refreshing shall
> come from the presence of the
> Lord.
> ACTS 3:19

KYNAN
One Who Is Wise

> The fear of the Lord is the
> beginning of wisdom.
> PSALM 111:10

KYNDRA
One of Understanding

> The meditation of my heart
> shall be of understanding.
> PSALM 49:3

KYONG
Brightness

> They that be wise shall shine as
> the brightness of the firmament;
> . . . as the stars for ever and ever.
> DANIEL 12:3
>
> Korean

KYRA
Noble Strength

> The Lord is my rock, and my
> fortress, . . . my deliverer; . . .
> my strength.
> PSALM 18:2

KYRALISSA
Sovereign Nobility

> *Thou hast also given me the*
> *shield of thy salvation.*
> 2 SAMUEL 22:36

KYRIAKOS
Belonging to the Lord

> *I have set the Lord always*
> *before me: because he is at my*
> *right hand, I shall not be*
> *moved.*
> PSALM 16:8

Greek

KYRITA
Wearing a Crown

> *When the chief Shepherd shall*
> *appear, ye shall receive a crown*
> *of glory.*
> 1 PETER 5:4

Hindu

KYROUZ
Eternal

> *I will praise thee: for thou hast*
> *heard me, and art become my*
> *salvation.*
> PSALM 118:21

German

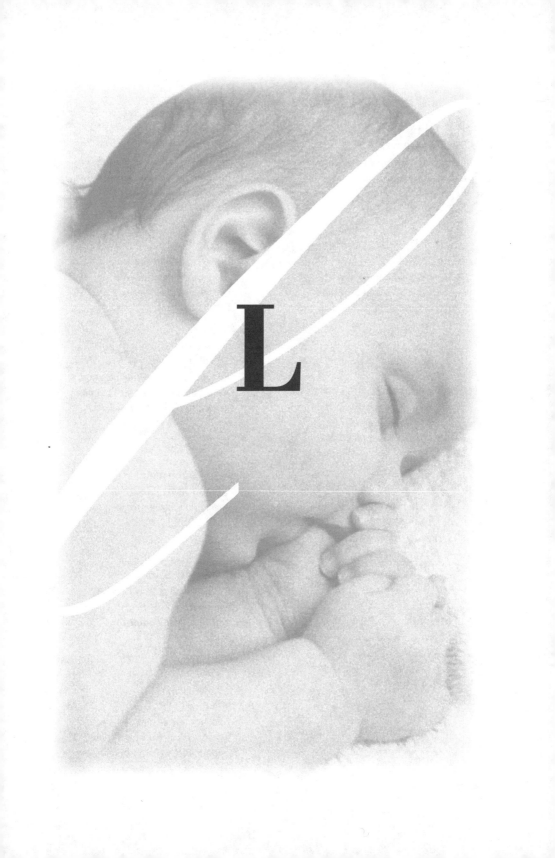

L

LABETH
The Devoted One

> *I will bless the Lord at all times:*
> *his praise shall continually be*
> *in my mouth.*
> PSALM 34:1

LABOMIR
One of Royal Nobility

> *Ye have not chosen me, but I*
> *have chosen you, and ordained*
> *you, that ye should go and bring*
> *forth fruit.*
> JOHN 15:16

LACEANN
Excellent Countenance and Grace

> *The Lord will give grace and*
> *glory: no good thing will he*
> *withhold from them that walk*
> *uprightly.*
> PSALM 84:11

LACEY
Excellent Countenance

> *A merry heart maketh a*
> *cheerful countenance.*
> PROVERBS 15:13

LACHELE
One of Strength

> *The Lord is my rock, . . . my*
> *fortress, and my deliverer; my*
> *God, my strength, . . . whom I*
> *will trust.*
> PSALM 18:2

LACHONEUS
Warrior for the Faith

> *Fight the good fight of faith, lay*
> *hold on eternal life, whereunto*
> *thou art also called.*
> 1 TIMOTHY 6:12

LACIE
Excellent Countenance

> *A merry heart maketh a*
> *cheerful countenance.*
> PROVERBS 15:13

LACRETIA
One of Light

> *Let your light so shine before*
> *men, that they may see . . . good*
> *works, and glorify your Father.*
> MATTHEW 5:16

LACY
Excellent Countenance

> *A merry heart maketh a*
> *cheerful countenance.*
> PROVERBS 15:13

LADAERE
Compassionate Spirit

> *I will praise thee, O Lord my*
> *God, with all my heart: . . . I*
> *will glorify thy name for*
> *evermore.*
> PSALM 86:12

LADIMER
A Scholar

> *Instruct a wise man, and he will*
> *be yet wiser: teach a just man,*
> *and he will increase in learning.*
> PROVERBS 9:9

L

LADONNA
The Lady of Honor

> *A gracious woman retaineth honor.*
> PROVERBS 11:16

LADRINA
The Helper

> *I bless the Lord, who gave me counsel: . . . I shall not be moved.*
> PSALM 16:7–8

LADYE
Cherished and Beloved One

> *Beloved, let us love one another: . . . every one that loveth is born of God, and knoweth God.*
> 1 JOHN 4:7

LAEL
Gift of God

> *Every good gift and every perfect gift is from above, and cometh down from the Father.*
> JAMES 1:17

LAENI
True and Faithful

> *I will bless the Lord at all times: his praise shall continually be in my mouth.*
> PSALM 34:1

LAFAYETTE
Peaceful Dweller

> *The Lord is my shepherd; I shall not want. He maketh me to lie down in green pastures.*
> PSALM 23:1

LAFEISE
One of Nobility

> *Ye are a chosen generation, a royal priesthood, . . . ye should show forth the praises of him who hath called you.*
> 1 PETER 2:9

LAFOGAULA
One of Nobility

> *Strength and honour are her clothing; . . . a woman that feareth the Lord, she shall be praised.*
> PROVERBS 31:25, 30

Polynesian

LAHOMA
Noble One

> *Thou hast . . . given me the shield of salvation: . . . thy right hand hath holden me up, . . . thy gentleness hath made me great.*
> PSALM 18:35

LAHONA
One of Honor

> *I will call upon the Lord, who is worthy to be praised.*
> PSALM 18:3

North American Indian

LAI
Calm and Tranquil

> *Thou wilt keep him in perfect peace, whose mind is stayed on thee: because he trusteth in thee.*
> ISAIAH 26:3

Polynesian

LAIFE
Faith

> Make me to go in the path of thy
> commandments; for therein do I
> delight.
> PSALM 119:35
>
> Old French

LAILA
Devoted to the Lord

> The Lord is my rock, . . . my
> fortress, and my deliverer; my
> God, my strength, in whom I
> will trust.
> PSALM 18:2
>
> Hebrew

LAIMITE
Blessing

> The blessing of the Lord, it
> maketh rich, and he addeth no
> sorrow with it.
> PROVERBS 10:22
>
> Teutonic

LAINA
One of Light

> Let your light so shine before
> men, that they may see . . . good
> works, and glorify your Father
> . . . in heaven.
> MATTHEW 5:16

LAIONELA
A Little Lion

> The righteous are bold as a lion.
> When righteous men do rejoice,
> there is great glory.
> PROVERBS 28:1; 12
>
> Polynesian

LAIRD
Guardian Protector

> He that dwelleth in the secret
> place . . . shall abide under the
> shadow of the Almighty.
> PSALM 91:1
>
> Scottish

LAJUAN
God Is Gracious

> But thou, O Lord, art a God full
> of compassion, and gracious,
> longsuffering.
> PSALM 86:15

LAKEISHA
One of Purity

> Blessed are the pure in heart:
> for they shall see God.
> MATTHEW 5:8
>
> African-American

LAKEITTSHIA
One of Joy and Gladness

> I will praise thee, O Lord, with
> my whole heart; . . . I will be
> glad and rejoice in thee: I will
> sing praise to thy name.
> PSALM 9:1–2
>
> African-American

LAKHVINDE
To Conquer

> For whatsoever is born of God
> overcometh the world: . . . this is
> the victory that overcometh the
> world, even our faith.
> 1 JOHN 5:4
>
> Teutonic

L

LALA
Crown of Victory

> For whatsoever is born of God overcometh the world: . . . the victory that overcometh the world, even our faith.
> 1 JOHN 5:4
>
> Polynesian

LALANIA
Heavenly Child

> Thou hast . . . given me the shield of thy salvation: . . . thy right hand hath holden me up.
> PSALM 18:35

LALAPA
The Protector

> He that dwelleth in the secret place of the most High shall abide under the shadow of the Almighty.
> PSALM 91:1

LALEL
He Is God's

> I have set the Lord always before me: . . . he is at my right hand, I shall not be moved.
> PSALM 16:8

LALITA
Cherished One

> Beloved, let us love one another: for love is of God; . . . every one that loveth is born of God, and knoweth God.
> 1 JOHN 4:7

LALLA
Of the Lowlands

> He maketh me to lie down in green pastures: he leadeth me beside the still waters.
> PSALM 23:2
>
> Scottish

LAMA
One of Strength

> The Lord is my rock, . . . my fortress, and my deliverer; my God, my strength, in whom I will trust.
> PSALM 18:2
>
> Hebrew

LAMAR
A Refreshing Spirit

> The times of refreshing shall come from the presence of the Lord.
> ACTS 3:19

LAMBERT
Beautiful Lamb

> Ye know that ye were not redeemed with corruptible things, . . . But with the precious blood of Christ.
> 1 PETER 1:18–19

LAMOND
One Who Is Wise

> The Lord giveth wisdom: out of his mouth cometh knowledge and understanding.
> PROVERBS 2:6

LAMONT
One of Noble Truth

> *He shall cover thee with his feathers, and under his wings shalt thou trust.*
> PSALM 91:4

LAMOYA
One of Greatness and Merit

> *The Lord is my rock, . . . my fortress, and my deliverer; . . . my strength, in whom I will trust.*
> PSALM 18:2

Greek

LANA
True and Faithful

> *Draw near with a true heart in full assurance of faith, . . . Let us hold fast the profession of our faith without wavering.*
> HEBREWS 10:22–23

LANAKILA
Victorious

> *But thanks be to God, which giveth us the victory through our Lord Jesus Christ.*
> 1 CORINTHIANS 15:57

Polynesian

LANCE
He Who Serves

> *What doth the Lord . . . require of thee, but . . . to walk in all his ways, and to love him, and to serve the Lord . . . with all thy heart and . . . soul.*
> DEUTERONOMY 10:12

LANDELL
Peaceful Dweller

> *The Lord is my shepherd; I shall not want. He maketh me to lie down in green pastures.*
> PSALM 23:1–2

LANDIE
A Strong Leader

> *Thou hast . . . given me the shield of thy salvation: and thy right hand hath holden me up.*
> PSALM 18:35

LANDON
Quiet and Peaceful

> *The Lord is my shepherd; I shall not want. He maketh me to lie down in green pastures.*
> PSALM 23:1–2

LANDREW
One of Great Courage

> *Be strong and of a good courage; . . . for the Lord thy God is with thee whithersoever thou goest.*
> JOSHUA 1:9

LANE
Wayfarer

> *Thy word is a lamp unto my feet, and a light unto my path.*
> PSALM 119:105

LANEE
From the Narrow Road

> *Thy word is a lamp unto my feet, and a light unto my path.*
> PSALM 119:105

LANESSA
A Little Bypath

> *As for God, his way is perfect:*
> *. . . It is God that girdeth me*
> *with strength, and maketh my*
> *way perfect.*
> PSALM 18:30, 32

LANETTE
A Little Bypath

> *As for God, his way is perfect:*
> *. . . It is God that girdeth me*
> *with strength, and maketh my*
> *way perfect.*
> PSALM 18:30, 32

LANEY
Wayfarer

> *Thy word is a lamp unto my*
> *feet, and a light unto my path.*
> PSALM 119:105

LANG
Tall in Stature

> *Thou hast . . . given me the*
> *shield of thy salvation: . . . thy*
> *right hand hath holden me up.*
> PSALM 18:35

LANGFORD
Wise One

> *The fear of the Lord is the*
> *beginning of wisdom: a good*
> *understanding have all they*
> *that do his commandments.*
> PSALM 111:10

LANGSTON
Rock of Strength

> *In God is my salvation and my*
> *glory: the rock of my strength,*
> *and my refuge, is in God.*
> PSALM 62:7

LANIER
A Weaver

> *And whatsoever ye do, do it*
> *heartily, as to the Lord, and not*
> *unto men; . . . for ye serve the*
> *Lord Christ.*
> COLOSSIANS 3:23–24

LANIKA
Majesty and Heavenly

> *Thou hast . . . given me the*
> *shield of thy salvation: . . . thy*
> *right hand hath holden me up,*
> *. . . thy gentleness hath made me*
> *great.*
> PSALM 18:35

LANIPUAKEA
Fair Flower from Heaven

> *I will praise thee, for I am*
> *fearfully and wonderfully*
> *made: marvellous are thy*
> *works.*
> PSALM 139:14

Polynesian

LANITA
A Shining Light

> *Let your light so shine . . . that*
> *they may see your good works,*
> *and glorify your Father.*
> MATTHEW 5:16

LANNETTE
A Little Path

> Thy word is a lamp unto my
> feet, and a light unto my path.
> PSALM 119:105

LANSON
Crown of Victory

> But thanks be to God, which
> giveth us the victory through
> our Lord Jesus Christ.
> 1 CORINTHIANS 15:57

LANTY
Fame of the Land

> Wait on the Lord, and keep his
> way and he shall exalt thee to
> inherit the land.
> PSALM 37:34

LANTZ
Ruler of the Land

> Wait on the Lord, and keep his
> way, and he shall exalt thee to
> inherit the land.
> PSALM 37:34

LANVIN
Fame of the Land

> Wait on the Lord, and keep his
> way, and he shall exalt thee to
> inherit the land.
> PSALM 37:34

LAODICE
One of Justice

> The days come, saith the Lord,
> . . . a King shall reign and
> prosper, and shall execute
> judgment and justice in the earth.
> JEREMIAH 23:5

Greek

LAPAELA
God Hath Healed

> Wait on the Lord: be of good
> courage, and he shall strengthen
> thine heart.
> PSALM 27:14

Polynesian

LAPINO
Watchful One

> In all things, endure afflictions,
> do the work of an evangelist,
> make full proof of thy ministry.
> 2 TIMOTHY 4:5

LAQUETTA
Precious to God

> I will praise thee; for I am
> fearfully and wonderfully
> made: marvellous are thy
> works.
> PSALM 139:14

LAQUINDRA
Precious One

> Thy hands have made me and
> fashioned me: give me
> understanding, that I may learn
> thy commandments.
> PSALM 119:73

LARABETH
One of Victory and Consecration

> For whatsoever is born of God
> overcometh the world: and this
> is the victory . . . even our faith.
> 1 JOHN 5:4

LARANDA
Crown of Victory

> For whatsoever is born of God
> overcometh the world: and this
> is the victory . . . even our faith.
> 1 JOHN 5:4

LAREEDIA
Crown of Victory

> But thanks be to God, which
> giveth us the victory through
> our Lord Jesus Christ.
> 1 CORINTHIANS 15:57

LARIANNE
Victory and Grace

> For whatsoever is born of God
> overcometh the world: and this
> is the victory . . . even our faith.
> 1 JOHN 5:4

LARISA
Cheerful and Happy

> Thou wilt show me the path of
> life: in thy presence is fulness of
> joy.
> PSALM 16:11

LARK
Crown of Victory

> Thanks be to God, which giveth
> us the victory through our Lord
> Jesus Christ.
> 1 CORINTHIANS 15:57

LARMONT
One of Wisdom

> For the Lord giveth wisdom: out
> of his mouth cometh knowledge
> and understanding.
> PROVERBS 2:6

LARNELLE
One of Victory

> For whatsoever is born of God
> overcometh the world: and this
> is the victory . . . even our faith.
> 1 JOHN 5:4

LARON
Mighty Power

> As for God, his way is perfect; . . .
> God is my strength and power:
> and he maketh my way perfect.
> 2 SAMUEL 22:31, 33

LARRIANE
Of Victory and Grace

> The Lord will give grace and
> glory: no good thing will he
> withhold from them that walk
> uprightly.
> PSALM 84:11

LARRILEE
Victory and Peace

> The Lord will give strength unto
> his people; the Lord will bless
> his people with peace.
> PSALM 29:11

LARRILYN
Victorious

> For whatsoever is born of God
> overcometh the world: and this
> is the victory . . . even our faith.
> 1 JOHN 5:4

LARRY
Victorious

> But thanks be to God, which
> giveth us the victory through
> our Lord Jesus Christ.
> 1 CORINTHIANS 15:57

LARUE
The River

> He shall be like a tree planted
> by the rivers of water, ...
> whatsoever he doeth shall
> prosper.
> PSALM 1:3

Teutonic

LASHAN
God Hath Helped

> I love the Lord, because he hath
> heard my voice and my
> supplications.
> PSALM 116:1

LASHAWN
God Is Gracious

> But thou, O Lord, art a God full
> of compassion, and gracious,
> longsuffering, and plenteous in
> mercy and truth.
> PSALM 86:15

LASHONDRA
God Is Gracious

> But thou, O Lord, art a God full
> of compassion, and gracious,
> longsuffering, and plenteous in
> mercy and truth.
> PSALM 86:15

LASSIE
Little Maid

> I will praise thee; for I am
> fearfully and wonderfully made:
> marvellous are thy works.
> PSALM 139:14

LASTICE
The Shining One

> They that be wise shall shine as
> the brightness of the firmament;
> ... as the stars for ever and ever.
> DANIEL 12:3

LASZLO
God Is Helper

> I will lift up mine eyes unto the
> hills ... whence cometh my
> help. My help cometh from the
> Lord, which made heaven and
> earth.
> PSALM 121:1–2

LATASHA
One of Prayer and Peace

> The Lord will give strength unto
> his people; the Lord will bless
> his people with peace.
> PSALM 29:11

LATEE
One of Joy and Gladness

> Thou hast put gladness in my
> heart, ... let all those that put
> their trust in thee rejoice.
> PSALM 4:7; 5:11

LATEEF
Pure Peace

> The Lord will give strength unto
> his people; the Lord will bless
> his people with peace.
> PSALM 29:11

LATEFA
Pure Heart

> Blessed are the pure in heart:
> for they shall see God.
> MATTHEW 5:8

L

LATHAN
Faithful One

I have set the Lord always before me: because he is at my right hand, I shall not be moved.
PSALM 16:8

LATIE
Divine One

Whereby are given unto us exceeding great and precious promises: that by these ye might be partakers of the divine nature.
2 PETER 1:4

LATISHA
One of Joy and Gladness

Thou wilt show me the path of life: in thy presence is fulness of joy; at thy right hand there are pleasures for evermore.
PSALM 16:11

LATONIA
Beyond Praise

The Lord is great, and greatly to be praised: . . . Honour and majesty are before him.
PSALM 96:4, 6

LATONYA
Beyond Praise

The Lord is great, and greatly to be praised: . . . Honour and majesty are before him.
PSALM 96:4, 6

LATRISHA
Full of Honor

The Lord is great, and greatly to be praised: . . . Honour and majesty are before him.
PSALM 96:4, 6

LATTIE
Little Girl

I will praise thee; for I am fearfully and wonderfully made: marvellous are thy works.
PSALM 139:14

LAUDER
Famous Warrior

Fight the good fight of faith, lay hold on eternal life, whereunto thou art also called.
1 TIMOTHY 6:12

LAUGHLIN
One of Serenity

I have set the Lord . . . before me: . . . I shall not be moved.
PSALM 16:8

LAULENEKE
Victorious

But thanks be to God, which giveth us the victory through our Lord Jesus Christ.
1 CORINTHIANS 15:57

Polynesian

LAURA
Lady of Victory

Thanks be to God, which giveth us the victory through our Lord Jesus Christ.
1 CORINTHIANS 15:57

LAURAANNE
Victory and Grace

> *Whatsoever is born of God overcometh the world: . . . this is the victory that overcometh the world, even our faith.*
> 1 JOHN 5:4

LAUREN
Victorious

> *Whatsoever is born of God overcometh the world: . . . this is the victory that overcometh the world, even our faith.*
> 1 JOHN 5:4

LAURIE   *also* LORI
Crown of Victory

> *Whatsoever is born of God overcometh the world: . . . even our faith.*
> 1 JOHN 5:4

LAUTHER
Illustrious Warrior

> *The Lord is my rock, . . . my fortress, and my deliverer; my God, my strength, in whom I will trust.*
> PSALM 18:2

LAVAGA
One of Courage and Strength

> *Thy right hand hath holden me up, . . . thy gentleness hath made me great.*
> PSALM 18:35

LAVINIA
Pure Heart

> *Blessed are the pure in heart: for they shall see God.*
> MATTHEW 5:8

LAVONE
Bringer of Victory

> *Whatsoever is born of God overcometh the world: and this is the victory that overcometh the world, even our faith.*
> 1 JOHN 5:4

LAVONIA
Bringer of Victory

> *Whatsoever is born of God overcometh the world: and this is the victory that overcometh the world, even our faith.*
> 1 JOHN 5:4

LAVONYA
Bringer of Victory

> *Whatsoever is born of God overcometh the world: and this is the victory that overcometh the world, even our faith.*
> 1 JOHN 5:4

LAVOYNNE
Bringer of Victory

> *Whatsoever is born of God overcometh the world: and this is the victory that overcometh the world, even our faith.*
> 1 JOHN 5:4

L

LAVRELLO
Leader of Strength

> Thou hast . . . given me the
> shield of thy salvation: . . . thy
> gentleness hath made me great.
> PSALM 18:35

LAWLER
One of Knowledge

> Through wisdom is an house
> builded; . . . And by knowledge
> shall the chambers be filled with
> all . . . riches.
> PROVERBS 24:3–4

LAWRENCE
Victorious

> But thanks be to God, which
> giveth us the victory through
> our Lord Jesus Christ.
> 1 CORINTHIANS 15:57

LAWRIE
Victorious One

> But thanks be to God, which
> giveth us the victory through
> our Lord Jesus Christ.
> 1 CORINTHIANS 15:57

LAWSON
Victorious One

> Whatsoever is born of God
> overcometh the world: and this
> is the victory that overcometh
> the world, even our faith.
> 1 JOHN 5:4

LAWTHER
Illustrious Warrior

> Fight the good fight of faith, lay
> hold on eternal life, whereunto
> thou art also called.
> 1 TIMOTHY 6:12

LAWTON
From the Meadow Hill

> The Lord is my shepherd; I shall
> not want. He maketh me to lie
> down in green pastures: he
> leadeth me beside still waters.
> PSALM 23:1–2

LAWYER
One of Strong Counsel

> I have set the Lord always
> before me: . . . I shall not be
> moved.
> PSALM 16:8

LAYLA
Inner Beauty

> Give unto the Lord the glory due
> unto his name; worship the Lord
> in the beauty of holiness.
> PSALM 29:2

LAYTON
One of Peace

> My son, forget not my law; but
> let thine heart keep my
> commandments.
> PROVERBS 3:1

LAZAROS   *also* LAZARUS
The Lord's Help

> Thou hast . . . given me the
> shield of thy salvation: . . . thy
> right hand hath holden me up.
> PSALM 18:35

LAZARUS
The Lord's Help

> Thou hast . . . given me the
> shield of thy salvation: . . . thy
> right hand hath holden me up,
> . . . thy gentleness hath made me
> great.
> PSALM 18:35

LAZVIMINDA
The Lord Will Help

> I will praise thee: for thou hast
> heard me, and art become my
> salvation.
> PSALM 118:21

Polynesian

LEAH
Contentment

> I have set the Lord . . . before
> me: . . . he is at my right hand, I
> shall not be moved.
> PSALM 16:8

LEANDER
One of Courage

> Be strong and of a good
> courage; . . . for the Lord thy
> God is with thee whithersoever
> thou goest.
> JOSHUA 1:9

LEANNA
Consecrated One

> It is good for me to draw near to
> God: I have put my trust in the
> Lord God, that I may declare all
> thy works.
> PSALM 73:28

LEANNE
Consecrated One

> It is good for me to draw near to
> God: I have put my trust in the
> Lord God, that I may declare all
> thy works.
> PSALM 73:28

LEANORA
One of Courage

> The Lord is my light and my
> salvation; whom shall I fear?
> the Lord is the strength of my
> life; of whom shall I be afraid?
> PSALM 27:1

LEANORD
One of Courage

> Be strong and of a good
> courage; . . . for the Lord thy
> God is with thee whithersoever
> thou goest.
> JOSHUA 1:9

LEARMON
Of the Peaceful Meadow

> The Lord is my shepherd; I shall
> not want. He maketh me to lie
> down in green pastures.
> PSALM 23:1–2

LEATHA
Forgetfulness

> Forgetting those things which
> are behind, . . . reaching forth
> unto those things . . . before, I
> press toward the prize of the
> high calling of God in Christ
> Jesus.
> PHILIPPIANS 3:13–14

Teutonic

LEAVITT
Joined in Harmony

> *Let the words of my mouth, and the meditation of my heart, be acceptable in thy sight.*
> PSALM 19:14

LECIA
Consecrated to God

> *Give me understanding, and I shall keep thy law; [and] observe it with my whole heart.*
> PSALM 119:34

LECKADIA
Exalted and Noble One

> *Thou hast . . . given me the shield of thy salvation: . . . thy right hand hath holden me up, . . . thy gentleness hath made me great.*
> PSALM 18:35
>
> Slavic

LECOLA
Brave and Victorious

> *But thanks be to God, which giveth us the victory through our Lord Jesus Christ.*
> 1 CORINTHIANS 15:57

LEDILLON
The Faithful One

> *I will bless the Lord, . . . I have set the Lord . . . before me: . . . he is at my right hand, I shall not be moved.*
> PSALM 16:7–8

LEE
One of Peace

> *The Lord will give strength unto his people; the Lord will bless his people with peace.*
> PSALM 29:11

LEE ANN
Peaceful and Contented

> *It is good for me to draw near to God: I have put my trust in the Lord God, . . . I may declare all thy works.*
> PSALM 73:28

LEGOLIA
Protector

> *He that dwelleth in the secret place of the most High shall abide under the shadow of the Almighty.*
> PSALM 91:1
>
> Teutonic

LEIANNE
Of Victory and Grace

> *The Lord will give grace and glory: no good thing will he withhold from them that walk uprightly.*
> PSALM 84:11

LEICHA
God Is My Salvation

> *I will praise thee: for thou hast heard me, and art become my salvation.*
> PSALM 118:21
>
> Teutonic

LEIDA
Rich Raiment

> Bless the Lord, O my soul. O Lord
> my God, thou art very great.
> PSALM 104:1

LEIF
One of Love

> Beloved, let us love one another:
> for love is of God; and every one
> that loveth is born of God and
> knoweth God.
> 1 JOHN 4:7
>
> Teutonic

LEIGH
From the Peaceful Meadow

> He maketh me to lie down in
> green pastures: He leadeth me
> beside the still waters. He
> restoreth my soul.
> PSALM 23:2–3

LEIGHANN
Contented One of Grace

> The Lord will give grace and
> glory: . . . no good thing will he
> withhold from them that walk
> uprightly.
> PSALM 84:11

LEIGHANN
Contented One

> It is good for me to draw near to
> God: I have put my trust in the
> Lord God.
> PSALM 73:28

LEILA
Inner Beauty

> Give unto the Lord . . . glory; . . .
> worship the Lord in the beauty
> of holiness.
> PSALM 29:2

LEILANI
Heavenly Child

> Thy hands have made me and
> fashioned me: give me
> understanding, that I may learn
> thy commandments.
> PSALM 119:73
>
> Polynesian

LEIMANA
Wise Protector

> He that dwelleth in the secret
> place of the most High shall
> abide under the shadow of the
> Almighty.
> PSALM 91:1

LEKE
A King

> I will praise thee; for I am
> fearfully and wonderfully made:
> marvellous are thy works.
> PSALM 139:14

LEKINALA
Strong Ruler

> Thou hast . . . given me the
> shield of thy salvation: . . . thy
> right hand hath holden me up,
> . . . thy gentleness hath made me
> great.
> PSALM 18:35
>
> Polynesian

L

LELAN
From the Meadowland

The Lord is my shepherd; I shall not want. He maketh me to lie down in green pastures.
PSALM 23:1–2

LELAND
From the Meadowland

The Lord is my shepherd; I shall not want. He maketh me to lie down in green pastures.
PSALM 23:1–2

LELL
Faithful and Loyal

Thou wilt show me the path of life: in thy presence is fulness of joy; at thy right hand . . . are pleasures for evermore.
PSALM 16:11

LELLA
Seeker of Light

Then spoke Jesus . . . I am the light of the world: . . . he that followeth me shall . . . have the light of life.
JOHN 8:12

LELLUS
Noble One of Strength

The Lord is my light and my salvation; whom shall I fear? The Lord is the strength of my life; of whom shall I be afraid?
PSALM 27:1

LELONIE
Fighter for the Faith

Fight the good fight of faith, lay hold on eternal life, whereunto thou art also called.
1 TIMOTHY 6:12

LEMONT
One of Noble Truth

He shall cover thee with his feathers, and under his wings shalt thou trust.
PSALM 91:4

LEMUEL
God Is with Them

For thou, Lord, wilt bless the righteous; with favour wilt thou compass him as with a shield.
PSALM 5:12

Greek

LENA
Bright One

And he shall bring forth thy righteousness as the light.
PSALM 37:6

LENAY
One of Light

Let your light so shine . . . that they may see your good works, and glorify your Father which is in heaven.
MATTHEW 5:16

LENDIS
Shining Gift

For by grace are ye saved through faith; and that not of yourselves: it is the gift of God.
EPHESIANS 2:8

LENDLE
Peaceful Dweller

> The Lord will give strength unto
> his people; the Lord will bless
> his people with peace.
> PSALM 29:11

LENDOORA
Shining Gift

> They that be wise shall shine as
> the brightness of the firmament;
> . . . as the stars for ever and ever.
> DANIEL 12:3

LENDWARD
Bold One of Courage

> The Lord is my light and my
> salvation; whom shall I fear?
> the lord is the strength of my
> life; of whom shall I be afraid?
> PSALM 27:1

LENEVA
Gentle One

> Be ye kind one to another,
> tenderhearted, forgiving . . .
> even as God for Christ's sake
> hath forgiven you.
> EPHESIANS 4:32

LENG
One Who Stands Tall

> Thou hast also given me the
> shield of thy salvation: and thy
> gentleness hath made me great.
> 2 SAMUEL 22:36

LENINA
One of Light

> Let your light so shine . . . that
> they may see your good works,
> and glorify your Father which is
> in heaven.
> MATTHEW 5:16

LENIONELL
One of Courage

> Be strong and of a good courage;
> . . . for the Lord thy God is with
> thee whithersoever thou goest.
> JOSHUA 1:9

LENIS
A Tranquil Spirit

> The Lord will give strength unto
> his people; the Lord will bless
> his people with peace.
> PSALM 29:11

LENITA
Light

> Thy word is a lamp unto my
> feet, and a light unto my path.
> PSALMS 119:105

LENKE
Fame of the Land

> Wait on the Lord, and keep his
> way, and he shall exalt thee to
> inherit the land.
> PSALM 37:34

L

LENNIE
Courageous Leader

> Thou hast also given me the
> shield of thy salvation: . . . thy
> right hand hath holden me up,
> . . . thy gentleness hath made me
> great.
> PSALM 18:35

LENNOX
Chief in Courage

> Be strong and of a good
> courage; be not afraid, . . . the
> Lord . . . is with thee
> whithersoever thou goest.
> JOSHUA 1:9

LENNY
Bold One

> The Lord is my light and my
> salvation; whom shall I fear?
> the Lord is the strength of my
> life; of whom shall I be afraid?
> PSALM 27:1

LENORE
Lady of Splendor

> By humility and the fear of the
> Lord are riches, and honour,
> and life.
> PROVERBS 22:4

LENSON
One Who Has Courage

> Be of good courage, and he shall
> strengthen your heart, all ye
> that hope in the Lord.
> PSALM 31:24

LENTISHA
One of Light

> And they that be wise shall
> shine as the brightness of the
> firmament; and they that turn
> many to righteousness as the
> stars for ever and ever.
> DANIEL 12:3

LENWARD
Brave and Courageous

> Be strong and of a good
> courage; . . . for the Lord thy
> God is with thee whithersoever
> thou goest.
> JOSHUA 1:9

LENWOOD
From the Hidden Wood

> He that dwelleth in the secret
> place of the most High shall
> abide under the shadow of the
> Almighty.
> PSALM 91:1

LEO
The Lion

> God is my salvation; I will trust,
> and not be afraid: for the Lord
> JEHOVAH is my strength and
> my song; . . . my salvation.
> ISAIAH 12:2

LEOKADIA
One of Lion Strength

> In God is my salvation and my
> glory: the rock of my strength,
> and my refuge, is in God.
> PSALM 62:7

German

LEOLANI
Heavenly Voice

> *The voice of rejoicing and*
> *salvation is in the tabernacles of*
> *the righteous: the right hand of*
> *the Lord doeth valiantly.*
> PSALM 118:15
>
> Hawaiian

LEON
Lion of Boldness

> *The Lord is my light and . . .*
> *salvation; . . . the strength of my*
> *life; of whom shall I be afraid?*
> PSALM 27:1

LEONA
Lady of Courage

> *Be strong and of a good*
> *courage; . . . the Lord . . . is with*
> *thee whithersoever thou goest.*
> JOSHUA 1:9

LEONALA
One of Courage

> *I will say of the Lord, He is my*
> *refuge and my fortress: . . . in*
> *him will I trust.*
> PSALM 91:2

LEONARD
Bold One

> *The Lord is my light and my*
> *salvation; . . . the strength of my*
> *life; of whom shall I be afraid?*
> PSALM 27:1

LEONARDO
One of Courage

> *The Lord thy God is with thee*
> *whithersoever thou goest.*
> JOSHUA 1:9

LEONORA
One of Light

> *Let your light so shine before*
> *men, that they may see your*
> *good works and glorify . . .*
> *Father, who is in heaven.*
> MATTHEW 5:16

LEONTHENA
Bold with Courage

> *The Lord is my light and my*
> *salvation; whom shall I fear?*
> *the Lord is the strength of my*
> *life; of whom shall I be afraid?*
> PSALM 27:1

LEONZA
Lion Strong

> *The Lord is my rock, . . . my*
> *fortress, and my deliverer; my*
> *God, my strength, in whom I*
> *will trust.*
> PSALM 18:2

LEOPOLD
Defender of the People

> *For whatsoever is born of God*
> *overcometh the world: and this*
> *is the victory that overcometh*
> *the world, even our faith.*
> 1 JOHN 5:4

LEOTA
Lady of Courage

> *Wait on the Lord; be of good*
> *courage, and he shall strengthen*
> *thine heart.*
> PSALM 27:14

LEOVIGILDO
Lion Strong

> *In God is my salvation and my
> glory: the rock of my strength,
> and my refuge, is in God.*
> PSALM 62:7

Teutonic

LEPHA
Joy and Gladness

> *I will praise thee, O Lord, with
> my whole heart; . . . I will be
> glad and rejoice in thee: I will
> sing praise to thy name.*
> PSALM 9:1–2

Teutonic

LEQUETTA
Precious to God

> *I will praise thee; for I am
> fearfully and wonderfully
> made: . . . How precious . . . are
> thy thoughts unto me, O God!*
> PSALM 139:14, 17

LEREY
The Royal and Sovereign

> *Thou hast . . . given me the
> shield of thy salvation: . . . thy
> right hand hath holden me up,
> . . . thy gentleness hath made me
> great.*
> PSALM 18:35

LERMISSOT
Royal Nobility

> *Thou hast . . . given me the
> shield of thy salvation: . . . thy
> right hand hath holden me up,
> . . . thy gentleness hath made me
> great.*
> PSALM 18:35

LESCIL
Consecrated to God

> *Let the words of my mouth, and
> the meditation of my heart, be
> acceptable in thy sight.*
> PSALM 19:14

Teutonic

LESHENNE
God Is Gracious

> *He that walketh uprightly, and
> worketh righteousness, and
> speaketh the truth in his heart.*
> PSALM 15:2

LESLIANNA
Calm Spirit and Grace

> *The Lord will give strength unto
> his people; the Lord will bless
> his people with peace.*
> PSALM 29:11

LESLIE
Calm Spirit

> *Show me thy ways, O Lord; . . .
> Lead me in thy truth, . . . on
> thee do I wait all the day.*
> PSALM 25:4–5

LESSE
From the Stronghold

> *In God is my salvation and my
> glory: the rock of my strength,
> and my refuge, is in God.*
> PSALM 62:7

LESTER
Shining

> *Let your light so shine . . . that
> they may see your good works,
> and glorify your Father.*
> MATTHEW 5:16

LESTIA
Shining With Honor

> For thou, Lord, wilt bless the
> righteous; with favour wilt thou
> compass him as with a shield.
> PSALM 5:12

LETA
One of Light and Gladness

> I will praise thee, O Lord, with
> my whole heart; . . . I will be
> glad and rejoice in thee: I will
> sing praise to thy name.
> PSALM 9:1–2

LETHA
Dreamy One

> And the angel of God spake unto
> me in a dream, . . . And I said,
> Here am I.
> GENESIS 31:11

LETICIA
One of Joy and Gladness

> Thou hast put gladness in my
> heart, . . . let them also that love
> thy name be joyful in thee.
> PSALM 4:7; 5:11

LETITIA
One of Gladness and Joy

> Thou hast put gladness in my
> heart, . . . let all those who love
> thy name be joyful in thee.
> PSALM 4:7; 5:11

LETSON
The Shining One

> Let your light so shine before
> men, that they may see your
> good works, and glorify your
> Father which is in heaven.
> MATTHEW 5:16

LEVAN
The Rising Sun

> Let your light so shine before
> men, that they may see your
> good works, and glorify your
> Father which is in heaven.
> MATTHEW 5:16

LEVAR
Laurel of Victory

> But thanks be to God, which
> giveth us the victory through
> our Lord Jesus Christ.
> 1 CORINTHIANS 15:57

LEVEN
One of Youthful Strength

> The Lord is my light and my
> salvation; whom shall I fear?
> the Lord is the strength of my
> life; of whom shall I be afraid?
> PSALM 27:1

LEVETRA
To Rise

> [The] wise shall shine as the
> brightness of the firmament; . . .
> they that turn many to
> righteousness as stars for ever
> and ever.
> DANIEL 12:3

L

LEVI
United

> Endeavouring to keep the unity of the Spirit in the bond of peace.
> EPHESIANS 4:3

LEVITA
Sacred Understanding

> The entrance of thy words giveth light; it giveth understanding unto the simple.
> PSALM 119:130

LEVITICUS
Strong Alliance

> The Lord is my rock, . . . my fortress, and my deliverer; my God, my strength, in whom I will trust.
> PSALM 18:2

Hebrew

LEYLAHND
From the Meadowland

> The Lord is my shepherd; . . . He maketh me to lie down in green pastures.
> PSALM 23:1–2

LEYNA
Cheerful One of Light

> And they that be wise shall shine as the brightness of the firmament.
> DANIEL 12:3

LEYTON
One of Peace .

> Thou wilt keep him in perfect peace, whose mind is stayed on thee.
> ISAIAH 26:3

LIAN
An Alliance

> The Lord is my rock, . . . my fortress, and my deliverer; my God, my strength.
> PSALM 18:2

LIATT
One Who Brings Good News

> How beautiful are the feet of them that preach the gospel of peace.
> ROMANS 10:15

LIBBY
Consecrated to God

> Give me understanding, and I shall keep thy law; yea, I shall observe it with my whole heart.
> PSALM 119:34

LIBERTY
One of Freedom

> Stand fast therefore in the liberty wherewith Christ hath made us free.
> GALATIANS 5:1

LIBON
Life

> The Lord is my light and my salvation; . . . the Lord is the strength of my life.
> PSALM 27:1

Yiddish

LIDICE
Happy

> Thou wilt show me the path of
> life: in thy presence is fulness of
> joy.
> PSALM 16:11

LIDNEY
Beloved of People

> Beloved, let us love one another:
> for love is of God.
> 1 JOHN 4:7

LIEALOHA
Beloved One

> Whatsoever is born of God
> overcometh the world: and this
> is the victory . . . even our faith.
> 1 JOHN 5:4

LIEBE
To Hold Dear

> Beloved, let us love one another:
> for love is of God.
> 1 JOHN 4:7

LIEF
One of Love

> Beloved, let us love one another:
> for love is of God and every one
> that loveth is born of God and
> knoweth God.
> 1 JOHN 4:7

LIGAYA
One of Joy

> Thou wilt show me the path of
> life: in thy presence is fulness of
> joy.
> PSALM 16:11

Polynesian

LIGIA
One of Joy

> Thou wilt show me the path of
> life: in thy presence is fulness of
> joy.
> PSALM 16:11

LIGON
Spear Sharp

> Take unto you the whole armour
> of God, . . . taking the shield of
> faith . . . and . . . the sword of
> the Spirit, which is the word of
> God.
> EPHESIANS 6:13, 16–17

LIGOR
A Gem

> Thy hands have made me and
> fashioned me: give me
> understanding that I may learn
> thy commandments.
> PSALM 119:73

Teutonic

LIL-LANI
Lily of the Heavenly Sky

> Thy hands have made me and
> fashioned me: give me
> understanding that I may learn
> thy commandments.
> PSALM 119:73

LILA
Peaceful and Quiet

> Blessed are the peacemakers;
> for they shall be called the
> children of God.
> MATTHEW 5:9

L

LILI
Lily of Purity

The commandment of the Lord is pure, enlightening the eyes.
PSALM 19:8

LILIANA
Belonging to God

For we are labourers together with God: ye are God's husbandry, . . . God's building.
1 CORINTHIANS 3:9

LILIANNE
Lily of Grace

The Lord will give grace and glory: no good thing will he withhold from them.
PSALM 84:11

LILIBETH
One of Purity and Consecration

I will bless the Lord at all times: his praise shall continually be in my mouth.
PSALM 34:1

LILLIE
Belonging to God

As ye have therefore received Christ Jesus the Lord, so walk in him.
COLOSSIANS 2:6

LINCOLN
Prosperous One

I will sing unto the Lord, because he hath dealt bountifully with me.
PSALM 13:6

LINDA
Beautiful One

For the Lord taketh pleasure in his people: he will beautify the meek with salvation.
PSALM 149:4

LINDSEY
Of Gentle Speech

The wise in heart shall be called prudent: and the sweetness of the lips increaseth learning.
PROVERBS 16:21

LINRICO
From the Peaceful Meadow

The Lord is my shepherd; . . . He maketh me to lie down in green pastures.
PSALM 23:1–2

LINSTER
The Shining One

They that be wise shall shine as the brightness of the firmament; . . . as the stars for ever and ever.
DANIEL 12:3

LINTON
From the Flax Enclosure

The earth is the Lord's, and the fullness thereof.
PSALM 24:1

LINVILLE
One of Strength and Peace

Be of good courage, and he shall strengthen your heart, all ye that hope.
PSALM 31:24

LIONEL
The Little Lion

> The righteous are bold as a lion.
> . . . [and] righteous men do
> rejoice.
> PROVERBS 28:1B, 12

LIORAH
I Have Light

> Let your light so shine before
> men, that they may see your
> good works, and glorify your
> Father which is in heaven.
> MATTHEW 5:16

Hebrew

LIPANO
Strength and Courage

> In God is my salvation and my
> glory: the rock of my strength.
> PSALM 62:7

LIPHUS
Bringer of Light

> They that be wise shall shine as
> the brightness of the firmament;
> . . . as the stars for ever and ever.
> DANIEL 12:3

LIQUINTA
The Wise One

> For the Lord giveth wisdom: out
> of his mouth cometh knowledge.
> PROVERBS 2:6

LIRIA
Tender and Delicate

> And be ye kind one to another,
> tenderhearted, forgiving one
> another.
> EPHESIANS 4:32

LISA
Consecrated to God

> I will bless the Lord at all times:
> his praise shall continually be
> in my mouth.
> PSALM 34:1

LISSETTE
Consecrated to God

> God is the strength of my heart,
> and my portion for ever.
> PSALM 73:26

LISTON
Innovative One

> It is God that girdeth me with
> strength, and maketh my way
> perfect.
> PSALM 18:32

LITA
Vineyard and Fruitfield

> Ye have not chosen me, but I
> have chosen you, . . . that ye
> should . . . bring forth fruit.
> JOHN 15:16

Spanish

LITO
God's Vineyard

> I am the vine, ye are the
> branches: He that abideth in
> me, . . . bringeth forth much
> fruit.
> JOHN 15:5

LITTLE
The Little

> O Lord my God, thou hast made
> thy servant . . . and I am but a
> little child.
> 1 KINGS 3:7

L

LITTON
A Little Town

> And thou Bethlehem, . . . out of
> thee shall come a Governor.
> MATTHEW 2:6

LIZ
Consecrated to God

> I have put my trust in the Lord
> God, that I may declare all thy
> works.
> PSALM 73:28

LIZA
Consecrated to God

> Give me understanding, and I
> shall keep thy law; . . . I shall
> observe it with my whole heart.
> PSALM 119:34

LLEWELLYN
One of Sovereign Light

> Let your light so shine before
> men, that they may see your
> good works and glorify your
> Father which is in heaven.
> MATTHEW 5:16

LLOYD
One of Authority

> Let no man despise thy youth;
> but be thou an example . . . in
> word.
> 1 TIMOTHY 4:12

LLUVIA
Little Beloved One

> Beloved, let us love one another:
> for love is of God: and every one
> that loveth is born of God and
> knoweth God.
> 1 JOHN 4:7

LOIS
Desirable One

> Being born again, . . . by the
> word of God, which liveth and
> abideth forever.
> 1 PETER 1:23

LOLLY
Crown of Victory

> Whatsoever is born of God
> overcometh the world: and this
> is the victory that overcometh
> the world, even our faith.
> 1 JOHN 5:4

LONDON
One of Honor

> I will say of the Lord, He is my
> refuge and my fortress: my God;
> in him will I trust.
> PSALM 91:2

LORA
One of Light

> Let your light so shine . . . that
> they may see your good works,
> and glorify your Father which is
> in heaven.
> MATTHEW 5:16

LORENA
Lady of Victory

> Thanks be to God, which giveth
> us the victory through our Lord
> Jesus Christ.
> 1 CORINTHIANS 15:57

LORETTA
One of Wisdom and Truth

> The Lord giveth wisdom: out of
> his mouth cometh knowledge
> and understanding.
> PROVERBS 2:6

LORETTE
Wisdom and Truth

> For thou art my hope, O Lord
> God: thou art my trust from my
> youth.
> PSALM 71:5

LORI
also LAURIE
Victorious

> Thanks be to God, which giveth
> us the victory through our Lord
> Jesus Christ.
> 1 CORINTHIANS 15:57

LORIA
One of Victory

> Thanks be to God, which giveth
> us the victory through our Lord
> Jesus Christ.
> 1 CORINTHIANS 15:57

LORIE
also LORI
Victorious

> Thanks be to God, which giveth
> us the victory through our Lord
> Jesus Christ.
> 1 CORINTHIANS 15:57

LORNE
One of Victory

> Thanks be to God, which giveth
> us the victory through our Lord
> Jesus Christ.
> 1 CORINTHIANS 15:57

LORRIE
also LAURIE
Victorious

> Thanks be to God, which giveth
> us the victory through our Lord
> Jesus Christ.
> 1 CORINTHIANS 15:57

LOTANYA
A Fairy Queen

> I will praise thee; for I am
> fearfully and wonderfully
> made: marvellous are thy
> works.
> PSALM 139:14

LOTTIE
A Woman of the Lord

> I will bless the Lord at all time:
> his praise shall continually be
> in my mouth.
> PSALM 34:1

LOUISE
Victorious Love

> Whatsoever is born of God
> overcometh the world: and this
> is the victory that overcometh
> the world, even our faith.
> 1 JOHN 5:4

Teutonic

LOURDE
Exalted One

> Thou art my God, and I will
> praise thee, . . . I will exalt thee.
> PSALM 118:28

LOURDES
The Exalted One

> Thou art my God, and I will
> praise thee, . . . I will exalt thee.
> PSALM 118:28

Spanish

LOURDINE
The Exalted One

> Thou art my God, and I will
> praise thee; . . . I will exalt thee.
> PSALM 118:28

L

LOURENE
Victorious

> *Whatsoever is born of God overcometh the world: and this is the victory that overcometh the world, even our faith.*
> 1 JOHN 5:4

LOVA
Heroine for the Faith

> *Fight the good fight of faith, lay hold on eternal life, whereunto thou art also called.*
> 1 TIMOTHY 6:12

LOVE
God is Love

> *God so loved the world, that he gave his only begotten Son, that whosoever believeth in him should not perish, but have everlasting life.*
> JOHN 3:16

LOVECHILD
Cherished One

> *I will praise thee; for I am fearfully and wonderfully made: marvellous are thy works.*
> PSALM 139:14

LOVEDA
Cherished Affection

> *Beloved, let us love one another: for love is of God; and every one that loveth is born of God and knoweth God.*
> 1 JOHN 4:7

LOVELLA
Woman of Wisdom

> *She openeth her mouth with wisdom; and in her tongue is the law of kindness.*
> PROVERBS 31:26

LOVERTA
To Hold Dear

> *Beloved, let us love one another: for love is of God; and every one that loveth is born of God and knoweth God.*
> 1 JOHN 4:7

LOVEY
Cherished Affection

> *I will sing unto the Lord as long as I live: . . . I will be glad in the Lord.*
> PSALM 104:33–34

LOVISA
One of Victory

> *But thanks be to God, which giveth us the victory through our Lord Jesus.*
> 1 CORINTHIANS 15:57

LOWAINE
Famous Warrior

> *Fight the good fight of faith, lay hold on eternal life; whereunto thou art also called.*
> 1 TIMOTHY 6:12

LOWANNA
Graceful Warrior

> *Fight the good fight of faith, lay hold on eternal life; whereunto thou art also called.*
> 1 TIMOTHY 6:12

LOWELL
Beloved of God

> *Beloved, let us love one another:*
> *for love is of God; and every one*
> *that loveth is born of God and*
> *knoweth God.*
> 1 JOHN 4:7

LOWERY
Crown of Victory

> *Whatsoever is born of God*
> *overcometh the world: and this*
> *is the victory . . . even our faith.*
> 1 JOHN 5:4

LOWTHER
Illustrious Warrior

> *Fight the good fight of faith, lay*
> *hold on eternal life; whereunto*
> *thou art also called.*
> 1 TIMOTHY 6:12

LOYAL
The Faithful

> *I have set the Lord always*
> *before me: . . . I shall not be*
> *moved.*
> PSALM 16:8

LOYCE
Desirable One

> *Let the words of my mouth, and*
> *the meditation of my heart, be*
> *acceptable in thy sight.*
> PSALM 19:14

LOYOLA
Faithful One

> *Thy hands have made me and*
> *fashioned me: give me*
> *understanding; that I may learn*
> *thy commandments.*
> PSALM 119:73

LUBA
Dearly Beloved

> *Beloved, let us love one another:*
> *for love is of God; and every one*
> *that loveth is born of God and*
> *knoweth God.*
> 1 JOHN 4:7

English

LUBERTHA
One of Radiant Light

> *Let your light so shine before*
> *men, that they may see your*
> *good works and glorify your*
> *Father which is in heaven.*
> MATTHEW 5:16

LUCADA
Bearer of Light

> *Let your light so shine before*
> *men, that they may see your*
> *good works and glorify your*
> *Father which is in heaven.*
> MATTHEW 5:16

LUCAS
Bearer of Light

> *Let your light so shine before*
> *men, that they may see your*
> *good works and glorify your*
> *Father which is in heaven.*
> MATTHEW 5:16

Spanish

LUCIA
Gracious Light

> *Let your light so shine before*
> *men, that they may see your*
> *good works and glorify your*
> *Father which is in heaven.*
> MATTHEW 5:16

L

LUCIANNE
One of Light and Grace

> They that be wise shall shine as
> the brightness of the firmament;
> . . . as the stars for ever and ever.
> DANIEL 12:3

LUCIENNE
One of Light

> Let your light so shine before
> men, that they may see your
> good works and glorify your
> Father which is in heaven.
> MATTHEW 5:16

LUCILE
One of Light

> The Lord is my light and my
> salvation; . . . the Lord is the
> strength of my life; of whom
> shall I be afraid?
> PSALM 27:1

LUCILLE
Bringer of Light

> The Lord is my light and my
> salvation; . . . the Lord is the
> strength of my life; of whom
> shall I be afraid?
> PSALM 27:1

LUCKIE
Hoped For

> And now, Lord, what wait I for?
> My hope is in thee.
> PSALM 39:7

LUCRECIA
Prosperous One

> I will sing unto the Lord,
> because he hath dealt
> bountifully with me.
> PSALM 13:6

LUCRETIA
Prosperous One

> I will sing unto the Lord,
> because he hath dealt
> bountifully with me.
> PSALM 13:6

LUCY
Bringer of Light

> The Lord is my light and my
> salvation; . . . the Lord is the
> strength of my life; of whom
> shall I be afraid?
> PSALM 27:1

LUDEAN
Famous Warrior

> Fight the good fight of faith, lay
> hold on eternal life, whereunto
> thou art also called.
> 1 TIMOTHY 6:12

LUDER
Illustrious Warrior

> The Lord is my light and my
> salvation; . . . the Lord is the
> strength of my life; of whom
> shall I be afraid?
> PSALM 27:1

NAME *That* BABY!

LUDON
From the Low Valley

> The Lord is my shepherd; I shall
> not want. He leadeth me beside
> the still waters.
> PSALM 23:1–2

LUDWIG
Victorious Love

> Whatsoever is born of God
> overcometh the world: and this
> is the victory that overcometh
> the world, ever our faith.
> 1 JOHN 5:4

LUGENE
One of Nobility

> But ye are a chosen generation,
> a royal priesthood.
> 1 PETER 2:9

LUIGI   *also* LUDWIG
Victorious Love

> Whatsoever is born of God
> overcometh the world: and this
> is the victory that overcometh
> the world, even our faith.
> 1 JOHN 5:4

LUIS
Famous Warrior

> Thou therefore endure hardness,
> as a good soldier of Jesus Christ.
> 2 TIMOTHY 2:3

LUKE
Bringer of Light and Truth

> Let your light so shine before
> men, that they may see your
> good works and glorify your
> Father which is in heaven.
> MATTHEW 5:16

LULA
Devoted One

> I will bless the Lord at all times:
> his praise shall . . . be in my
> mouth.
> PSALM 34:1

LUM
Dweller Near Peaceful Meadow

> The Lord is my shepherd; I shall
> not want. He leadeth me beside
> the still waters.
> PSALM 23:1–2

LUMING
Radiant One

> They that be wise shall shine as
> the brightness of the firmament;
> . . . as the stars for ever and ever.
> DANIEL 12:3

LUNA
Little Shining One

> They that be wise shall shine as
> the brightness of the firmament;
> . . . as the stars for ever and ever.
> DANIEL 12:3

LUNDEEN
Shining One

> Let your light so shine before
> men, that they may see your
> good works and glorify your
> Father which is in heaven.
> MATTHEW 5:16

LUNUEL
The Lion Strong

> In God is my salvation and my
> glory: the rock of my salvation,
> and my refuge.
> PSALM 62:7

LUNYE
Shining One

> Let your light so shine before men, that they may see your good works and glorify your Father which is in heaven.
> MATTHEW 5:16

LUNZY
Strong in Spirit

> I press toward the mark for the prize of the high calling of God in Christ.
> PHILIPPIANS 3:14

LUONA
Strong in the Faith

> Fight the good fight of faith, lay hold on eternal life, whereunto thou art also called.
> 1 TIMOTHY 6:12

LUOUKIA
Leader of Strength

> The Lord is my rock, . . . my fortress, and my deliverer; my God, my strength.
> PSALM 18:2

LUPE
Compassionate Spirit

> I will praise thee: for thou hast heard me, and art become my salvation.
> PSALM 118:21

LUPTON
Courageous One

> Be strong and of a good courage; . . . for the Lord thy God is with thee.
> JOSHUA 1:9

LURAE
Crown of Victory

> Whatsoever is born of God overcometh the world: and this is the victory that overcometh the world, even our faith.
> 1 JOHN 5:4

LURALEE
Victory and Peace

> But thanks be to God, which giveth us the victory through our Lord Jesus.
> 1 CORINTHIANS 15:57

LURETA
The Alluring One

> Let the words of my mouth, and the meditation of my heart, be acceptable in thy sight.
> PSALM 19:14

LURLEEN
Alluring One

> Thou wilt show me the path of life: in thy presence is fulness of joy.
> PSALM 16:11

LURLINE
Alluring One

> Thou wilt show me the path of life: in thy presence is fulness of joy.
> PSALM 16:11

LUSHANYA
One of Radiance

> They that be wise shall shine as the brightness of the firmament; . . . as the stars for ever and ever.
> DANIEL 12:3

LUTREL
Illustrious Warrior

> Fight the good fight of faith, lay
> hold on eternal life, whereunto
> thou art also called.
> 1 TIMOTHY 6:12

LUTRICIA
One of Light and Nobility

> Let your light so shine before
> men, that they may see your
> good works and glorify your
> Father which is in heaven.
> MATTHEW 5:16

LUTSKE
Bringer Of Light

> Let your light so shine before
> men, that they may see your
> good works and glorify your
> Father which is in heaven.
> MATTHEW 5:16

LUVEENA
To Hold Dear

> Beloved, let us love one another:
> for love is of God; and every one
> that loveth is born of God and
> knoweth God.
> 1 JOHN 4:7

LUVELLE
Victorious

> But thanks be to God, which
> giveth us the victory through
> our Lord Jesus.
> 1 CORINTHIANS 15:57

LUVISA
One of Victory

> Whatsoever is born of God
> overcometh the world: and this
> is the victory that overcometh
> the world, even our faith.
> 1 JOHN 5:4

LUWANDA
God is Gracious

> The Lord God, merciful and
> gracious, longsuffering, and
> abundant in goodness and
> truth.
> EXODUS 34:6

LYAL
One of Purity

> Whatsoever things are true, . . .
> honest, . . . just, . . . [and] pure,
> . . . think on these things.
> PHILIPPIANS 4:8

LYANN
Strong Alliance

> The Lord is my rock, . . . my
> fortress, and my deliverer; my
> God, my strength.
> PSALM 18:2

LYCRUSIA
One Who Brings Light

> They that be wise shall shine as
> the brightness of the firmament;
> . . . as the stars for ever and ever.
> DANIEL 12:3

L

LYDEN
Protected One

> He that dwelleth in the secret
> place of the most High shall
> abide under the shadow of the
> Almighty.
> PSALM 91:1

LYDIA
Worshiper of God

> I will praise thee; . . . How
> precious . . . are thy thoughts
> unto me, O God!
> PSALM 139:14, 17

LYGIA
Fighter for the Faith

> Fight the good fight of faith, lay
> hold on eternal life, whereunto
> thou art also called.
> 1 TIMOTHY 6:12

LYLE
One of Purity

> Whatsoever things are true, . . .
> honest, . . . just, . . . [and] pure,
> . . . think on these things.
> PHILIPPIANS 4:8

LYN   *also* LYNN
A Refreshing Spirit

> The times of refreshing shall
> come from the presence of the
> Lord.
> ACTS 3:19

LYNANNE
Refreshing Spirit and Grace

> The Lord will give grace and
> glory: no good thing will he
> withhold from them that walk
> uprightly.
> PSALM 84:11

LYNDALL
Peaceful Dweller

> The Lord is my shepherd; I shall
> not want. He leadeth me beside
> the still waters.
> PSALM 23:1–2

LYNDELLE
A Refreshing Spirit

> The times of refreshing shall
> come from the presence of the
> Lord.
> ACTS 3:19

LYNDEN
From the Peaceful Valley

> The Lord is my shepherd; I shall
> not want. He leadeth me beside
> the still waters.
> PSALM 23:1–2

LYNDSEY
Of Gentle Speech

> The sweetness of the lips
> increaseth learning.
> PROVERBS 16:21

LYNEEN
A Refreshing Spirit

> The times of refreshing shall
> come from the presence of the
> Lord.
> ACTS 3:19

LYNELLE
A Refreshing Spirit

> The times of refreshing shall come from the presence of the Lord.
> ACTS 3:19

LYNETHIA
A Refreshing Spirit

> I will praise thee, O Lord, with my whole heart; . . . I will be glad and rejoice.
> PSALM 9:1–2

LYNETTE
A Refreshing Spirit

> The times of refreshing shall come from the presence of the Lord.
> ACTS 3:19

LYNFORD
From the Peaceful Valley

> The Lord is my shepherd; I shall not want. He leadeth me beside the still waters.
> PSALM 23:1–2

LYNN
A Refreshing Spirit

> The times of refreshing shall come from the presence of the Lord.
> ACTS 3:19

LYNNANNE
Refreshing Spirit and Grace

> The Lord will give grace and glory: no good thing will he withhold.
> PSALM 84:11

LYNNELLE
A Refreshing Spirit

> The times of refreshing shall come from the presence of the Lord.
> ACTS 3:19

also LYNN

LYNNETTA
A Refreshing Spirit

> The times of refreshing shall come from the presence of the Lord.
> ACTS 3:19

also LYNN

LYNSEY
Refreshing One

> And whosoever will, let him take the water of life freely.
> REVELATION 22:17

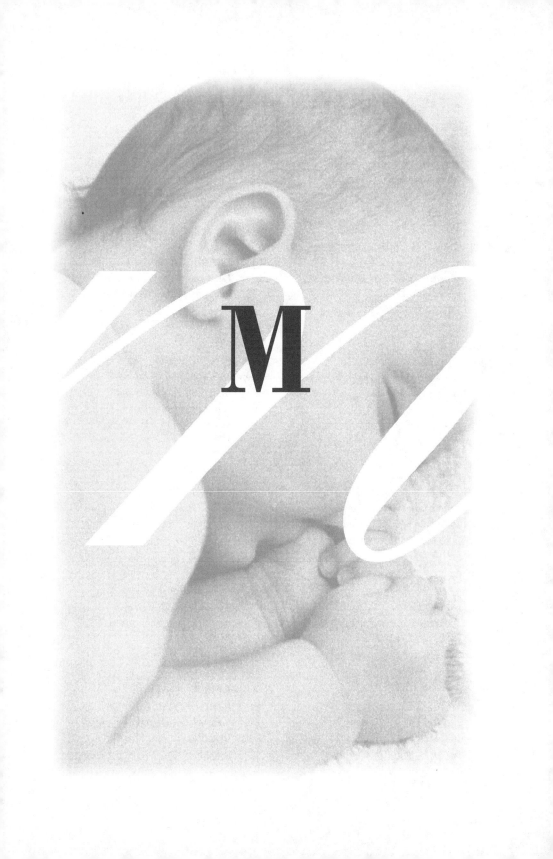

M

MABEL
Loveable One

> For the Father himself loveth
> you, because ye have loved me.
> JOHN 16:27

MABETH
Consecrated to God

> I will bless the Lord at all times:
> his praise shall continually be
> in my mouth.
> PSALM 34:1

MABREY
One of Joy

> Thou wilt show me the path of
> life: in thy presence is fulness of
> joy.
> PSALM 16:11

MAC
Beloved Heir

> Beloved, let us love one another:
> for love is of God; and every one
> that loveth is born of God and
> knoweth God.
> 1 JOHN 4:7

MACAELA
Like Unto the Lord

> I will trust, and not be afraid:
> for the Lord JEHOVAH is my
> strength.
> ISAIAH 12:2

MACALL
Strong in the Faith

> Fight the good fight of faith, lay
> hold on eternal life, whereunto
> thou art also called.
> 1 TIMOTHY 6:12

MACAME
One of Radiant Light

> They that be wise shall shine as
> the brightness of the firmament;
> . . . as the stars for ever and ever.
> DANIEL 12:3

MACARIO
Fighter for the Faith

> Fight the good fight of faith, lay
> hold on eternal life, whereunto
> thou art also called.
> 1 TIMOTHY 6:12

MACARTHUR
One of Valor

> Be strong and of a good
> courage; be not afraid, neither
> be thou dismayed.
> JOSHUA 1:9

MACAYLA
Rock of Strength

> In God is my salvation and my
> glory: the rock of my strength.
> PSALM 62:7

MACE
Gift of Jehovah

> Every good gift and every
> perfect gift is from above.
> JAMES 1:17

MACEL
Like Unto the Lord

> I will trust, and not be afraid:
> for the Lord JEHOVAH is my
> strength.
> ISAIAH 12:2

M

MACHIA
Great Protector

The Lord is my light and my salvation; whom shall I fear?
PSALM 27:1

MACHREE
Love

God so loved the world, that he gave his only . . . Son.
JOHN 3:16

MACILLE
Gift of Jehovah

Every good gift and every perfect gift is from above.
JAMES 1:17

MACKENZIE
Radiant One

Let your light so shine . . . that they may see your good works, and glorify your Father . . . in heaven.
MATTHEW 5:16

MACKINTOSH
Son of the Leader

Thou hast also given me the shield of thy salvation . . . thy gentleness hath made me great.
PSALM 18:35

MACLAINE
Son of the Servant

Rejoice the soul of thy servant: for unto thee, O Lord, do I lift up my soul.
PSALM 86:4

MACON
One of Strength

In God is my salvation and my glory: the rock of my strength.
PSALM 62:7

MACRAM
One of Perseverance

I press toward the mark for the prize of the high calling of God in Christ Jesus.
PHILIPPIANS 3:14

MACRINA
Strong in the Faith

Fight the good fight of faith, lay hold on eternal life, whereunto thou art also called.
1 TIMOTHY 6:12

MADELAINE
A High Tower

The Lord is my rock, and my fortress, and my deliverer; my God.
PSALM 18:2

MADEMOISELLE
Lady of Honor

Strength and honour are her clothing; and she shall rejoice in time to come.
PROVERBS 31:25

French

MADGE
A Precious Pearl

I will praise thee; for I am fearfully and wonderfully made.
PSALM 139:14

MADIGAN
Tower of Strength

> *In God is my salvation and my glory: the rock of my strength.*
> PSALM 62:7

MADISON
Son of Matthew

> *For by grace are ye saved through faith; and that not of yourselves: it is the gift of God.*
> EPHESIANS 2:8

MADONNA
My Lady

> *I delight to do thy will, O my God: yea, thy law is within my heart.*
> PSALM 40:8

MADORA
The Healing One

> *The Spirit of the Lord God is upon me; . . . the Lord hath anointed me to preach.*
> ISAIAH 61:1

MAGALI
My High Tower

> *The Lord is my rock, . . . my fortress, and my deliverer; my God, my strength.*
> PSALM 18:2

MAGALY
Devotion

> *I will offer to thee the sacrifice of thanksgiving, and will call upon the Lord.*
> PSALM 116:17

MAGAN
Exalted One

> *My servant . . . shall be exalted and extolled, and be very high.*
> ISAIAH 52:13

MAGNOLIA
One of Greatness

> *Let all those that seek thee rejoice and be glad in thee.*
> PSALM 40:16

MAGRUDER
Watchful One

> *But watch thou in all things, endure afflictions, do the work of an evangelist, make full proof of thy ministry.*
> 2 TIMOTHY 4:5
>
> Teutonic

MAHALIA
Woman

> *Strength and honour are her clothing; and she shall rejoice in time to come.*
> PROVERBS 31:25

MAHAN
I Rejoice

> *I will praise thee, O Lord, with my whole heart.*
> PSALM 9:1–2

MAHESH
Great and Noble One

> *Thou hast also given me the shield of thy salvation . . . thy gentleness hath made me great.*
> PSALM 18:35

M

MAHLON
I Rejoice
> I will praise thee, O Lord, with
> my heart; . . . I will be glad and
> rejoice.
> PSALM 9:1–2

Hebrew

MAIGHDLIN
Tower of Devotion
> The Lord is my rock, . . . my
> fortress, and my deliverer; my
> God, my strength.
> PSALM 18:2

MAIJA
One of Greatness
> For the Lord is great, and
> greatly to be praised.
> PSALM 96:4

MAILA
Living Fragrance
> I will praise thee; for I am
> fearfully and wonderfully made:
> marvellous are thy works.
> PSALM 139:14

Polynesian

MAILE
Crown of Victory
> Whatsoever is born of God
> overcometh the world: and this
> is the victory.
> 1 JOHN 5:4

MAILINDA
Gentle One
> Thou hast . . . given me the
> shield of thy salvation: . . . thy
> gentleness hath made me great.
> PSALM 18:35

MAIRA
Living Fragrance
> I will praise thee; for I am
> fearfully and wonderfully made:
> marvellous are thy works.
> PSALM 139:14

MAIRAGI
Gift from Heaven
> Every good gift and every
> perfect gift is from above and
> cometh down from the Father.
> JAMES 1:17

MAISON
Master Builder
> As a wise masterbuilder, I have
> laid the foundation, . . . which is
> Jesus Christ.
> 1 CORINTHIANS 3:10–11

MAITHILI
Rare Earth
> He causeth the grass to grow for
> the cattle, and herb for the
> service of man.
> PSALM 104:14

MAJEL
One of Great Promise
> If that which ye have heard . . .
> shall remain in you, . . . this is
> the promise.
> 1 JOHN 2:24–25

MAJELLA
Glorious
> For the Lord is great, and
> greatly to be praised.
> PSALM 96:4

MAJOR
One of Greatness

> *Thou hast . . . given me the shield of thy salvation: . . . thy gentleness hath made me great.*
> PSALM 18:35

MAKALA
Like Unto the Lord

> *The Lord is my strength and song, and he is become my salvation.*
> EXODUS 15:2
>
> Polynesian

MAKALEHA
Seeking One

> *But seek ye first the kingdom of God, and his righteousness.*
> MATTHEW 6:33
>
> Polynesian

MAKALEKA
A Pearl

> *I will praise thee; for I am fearfully and wonderfully made: marvellous are thy works.*
> PSALM 139:14
>
> Polynesian

MAKANANI
Gift of God

> *Every good gift and every perfect gift is from above and cometh down from the Father.*
> JAMES 1:17

MAKEDA
Shepherd Leader

> *I will set up shepherds over them which shall feed them.*
> JEREMIAH 23:4

MAKEMAE
Precious One

> *I will praise thee; for I am fearfully and wonderfully made: marvellous are thy works.*
> PSALM 139:14

MAKENNA
One of Understanding

> *My mouth shall speak of wisdom; and the meditation of my heart shall give understanding.*
> PSALM 49:3

MAKI
From the Mountain

> *They that trust in the Lord shall be as mount Zion, which cannot be removed.*
> PSALM 125:1

MAKIA
Greatest in Excellence

> *I press toward the mark for the prize of the high calling of God in Christ.*
> PHILIPPIANS 3:14

MAKINI
A Mighty Warrior

> *Fight the good fight of faith, lay hold on eternal life, whereunto thou art also called.*
> 1 TIMOTHY 6:12

MAKOA
Gracious Gift of Jehovah

> *The Lord will give grace and glory: no good thing will he withhold.*
> PSALM 84:11
>
> Polynesian

M

MAKOTO
Truth

> *I will meditate in thy precepts,*
> *. . . [and] delight myself in thy*
> *statutes.*
> PSALM 119:15–16
>
> Japanese

MAKRAM
Strong in the Faith

> *Fight the good fight of faith, lay*
> *hold on eternal life, whereunto*
> *thou art also called.*
> 1 TIMOTHY 6:12

MALACHI
Messenger

> *How beautiful are the feet of*
> *them that preach the gospel of*
> *peace.*
> ROMANS 10:15

MALAKOMA
Dove of Peace

> *The Lord will give strength unto*
> *his people; the Lord will bless*
> *his people with peace.*
> PSALM 29:11

MALARY
A Strong Counselor

> *I have set the Lord always*
> *before me: because he is at my*
> *right hand, I shall not be moved.*
> PSALM 16:8

MALCOM
The Dove

> *Jesus, when he was baptized, . . .*
> *saw the Spirit of God*
> *descending like a dove.*
> MATTHEW 3:16

MALDON
Noble and Majestic

> *I will praise thee, O Lord, with*
> *my whole heart; . . . I will be*
> *glad.*
> PSALM 9:1–2

MALDWYN
Quiet Meadowland

> *The Lord is my shepherd; . . . He*
> *maketh me to lie down in green*
> *pastures.*
> PSALM 23:1–2

MALEKO
A Mighty Warrior

> *Fight the good fight of faith, lay*
> *hold on eternal life, whereunto*
> *thou art also called.*
> 1 TIMOTHY 6:12

MALHAB
Always Burning

> *I have fought a good fight, I*
> *have finished my course.*
> 2 TIMOTHY 4:7

MALIA
Living Fragrance

> *I will praise thee; for I am*
> *fearfully and wonderfully made.*
> PSALM 139:14

MALIAKA
God's Messenger

> *Ye have not chosen me, but I*
> *have chosen you, and ordained*
> *you, that you should go forth*
> *and bear fruit.*
> JOHN 15:16
>
> African

MALINDA
One Who Is Gentle

> Thou hast . . . given me the
> shield of thy salvation: . . . thy
> gentleness hath made me great.
> PSALM 18:35

MALULANI
Under Heaven's Protection

> He that dwelleth in the secret
> place of the most High shall
> abide under . . . the Almighty.
> PSALM 91:1

MALVIS
Respect and Leadership

> Thou hast also given me the
> shield of thy salvation: thy
> gentleness hath made me great.
> PSALM 18:35

MAME
Living Fragrance

> Thy hands have made me
> and fashioned me: give me
> understanding that I may
> learn thy commandments.
> PSALM 119:73

MAMO
Yellow Bird

> I will praise thee; for I am
> fearfully and wonderfully made:
> marvellous are thy works.
> PSALM 139:14

MANCE
God's Guidance

> I have set the Lord always
> before me, I shall not be moved.
> PSALM 16:8

MANFRED
One of Peace

> The Lord will give strength unto
> his people; the Lord will bless
> his people.
> PSALM 29:11

MANITA
One of Peace

> The Lord will give strength unto
> his people; the Lord will bless
> his people.
> PSALM 29:11

MANJA
A Song

> I will praise thee, O Lord, with
> my whole heart; . . . I will be
> glad and rejoice.
> PSALM 9:1–2

Hebrew

MANLEY
A Man of God

> I delight to do thy will, O my
> God: yea, thy law is within my
> heart.
> PSALM 40:8

MANNA
It Is Manna

> When the children of Israel saw
> it, they said . . . It is manna.
> EXODUS 16:15

MANNY
Strength and Peace

> The Lord will give strength unto
> his people; the Lord will bless
> his people with peace.
> PSALM 29:11

MANOHARAN
Rest and Quiet
> *Thou wilt keep him in perfect peace, whose mind is stayed on thee.*
> ISAIAH 26:3

MANOLA
God is With Us
> *Be strong and of a good courage; . . . for the Lord thy God is with thee.*
> JOSHUA 1:9

MANTON
The Greatest
> *For the Lord is great, and greatly to be praised.*
> PSALM 96:4

MANUEL
God With Us
> *The Lord is my defence; and my God is the rock of my refuge.*
> PSALM 94:22

MANUS
Public Testimony
> *I . . . have taught you publicly, and . . . testifying . . . repentance toward God.*
> ACTS 20:20–21

MAPLE
Sweet and Lovable
> *Thy hands have made me and fashioned me: give me understanding that I may learn thy commandments.*
> PSALM 119:73

MAPU
A Rising Fragrance
> *I will praise thee; for I am fearfully and wonderfully made: marvellous are thy works.*
> PSALM 139:14

MAPUANA
Sending Forth Fragrance
> *And whatsoever ye do, do it heartily ,as to the Lord . . . for ye serve the Lord Christ.*
> COLOSSIANS 3:23–24

MARA
Living Fragrance
> *I will offer to thee the sacrifice of thanksgiving, and . . . call upon the . . . Lord.*
> PSALM 116:17

MARABELLE
Living Fragrance and Beauty
> *The Lord is my strength and my shield; my heart trusted in him.*
> PSALM 28:7

MARABETH
Living Fragrance and Devotion
> *I will bless the Lord at all times: his praise shall continually be in my mouth.*
> PSALM 34:1

MARALISE
Living Fragrance and Devotion
> *I have set the Lord always before me: because he is at my right hand, I shall not be moved.*
> PSALM 16:8

MARALTA
Peaceful

> The Lord will give strength unto
> his people; the Lord will bless
> his people with peace.
> PSALM 29:11

MARANATHA
The Lord Comes

> I am the Alpha and Omega, the
> Beginning and the End.
> REVELATION 1:8

MARBINE
A Notable Friend

> The Lord is my strength and
> song, and is become my
> salvation.
> PSALM 118:14

MARBURY
From the Strong Fortress

> The Lord is my rock, . . . my
> fortress, and my deliverer; my
> God, my strength.
> PSALM 18:2

MARC   *also* MARK
A Mighty Warrior

> Fight the good fight of faith, lay
> hold on eternal life, whereunto
> thou art also called.
> 1 TIMOTHY 6:12

MARCA
Strong in the Faith

> Fight the good fight of faith, lay
> hold on eternal life, whereunto
> thou art also called.
> 1 TIMOTHY 6:12

MARCEILE
Strong in Faith

> Fight the good fight of faith, lay
> hold on eternal life, whereunto
> thou art also called.
> 1 TIMOTHY 6:12

MARCELINA
Strong in the Faith

> Fight the good fight of faith, lay
> hold on eternal life, whereunto
> thou art also called.
> 1 TIMOTHY 6:12

MARCELLA
A Brave Heart

> My defence is of God, which
> saveth the upright in heart.
> PSALM 7:10

MARCEY
Heroine of Faith

> Fight the good fight of faith, lay
> hold on eternal life.
> 1 TIMOTHY 6:12

MARCH
Mighty Warrior

> Fight the good fight of faith, lay
> hold on eternal life, whereunto
> thou art also called.
> 1 TIMOTHY 6:12

MARCHANT
Mighty Warrior

> Fight the good fight of faith, lay
> hold on eternal life, whereunto
> thou art also called.
> 1 TIMOTHY 6:12

M

MARCHETA
Strong in the Faith
> Fight the good fight of faith, lay
> hold on eternal life, whereunto
> thou art also called.
> 1 TIMOTHY 6:12

MARCIANNE
Graceful Heroine of Faith
> The Lord will give grace and
> glory: no good thing will he
> withhold.
> PSALM 84:11

MARCIE
Heroine of Faith
> Fight the good fight of faith, lay
> hold on eternal life, whereunto
> thou art also called.
> 1 TIMOTHY 6:12

MARCUS
Mighty Warrior
> Give unto the Lord, O ye mighty,
> give unto the Lord glory and
> strength.
> PSALM 29:1

MARCY   *also* MARSIE
Heroine of Faith
> Fight the good fight of faith, lay
> hold on eternal life, whereunto
> thou art also called.
> 1 TIMOTHY 6:12

MARDEN
From the Quiet Meadow
> The Lord is my shepherd; . . . He
> maketh me to lie down in green
> pastures.
> PSALM 23:1–2

MARDETTE
From the Water in the Valley
> The Lord is my shepherd, . . . he
> leadeth me beside the still waters.
> PSALM 23:1–2

MARDO
One of Greatness
> Thou hast also given me the
> shield of thy salvation . . .thy
> gentleness hath made me great.
> PSALM 18:35

MARDOQUEO
Famous Master
> For the Lord is great, and
> greatly to be praised.
> PSALM 96:4

MARESADEANN
Living Fragrance and Radiance
> Let your light so shine before
> men, that they may see your
> good works and glorify your
> Father which is in heaven.
> MATTHEW 5:16

MARGARET
A Pearl
> I will praise thee; for I am
> fearfully and wonderfully
> made: . . . How precious also are
> thy thoughts.
> PSALM 139:14, 17

MARGARITA
A Pearl
> I will praise thee; for I am
> fearfully and wonderfully
> made: . . . How precious also are
> thy thoughts.
> PSALM 139:14, 17

MARGERITE
A Pearl

> *I will praise thee; for I am fearfully and wonderfully made: . . . How precious also are thy thoughts.*
> PSALM 139:14, 17

MARGIE
A Precious Pearl

> *I will praise thee; for I am fearfully and wonderfully made: . . . How precious also are thy thoughts.*
> PSALM 139:14, 17

MARGIEANN
Pearl of Grace

> *The Lord will give grace and glory: no good thing will he withhold.*
> PSALM 84:11

MARGO
A Precious Pearl

> *I will praise thee; for I am fearfully and wonderfully made: . . . How precious also are thy thoughts.*
> PSALM 139:14, 17

MARIA
Living Fragrance

> *I will praise thee; for I am fearfully and wonderfully made: marvellous are thy works.*
> PSALM 139:14

MARIAH
Living Fragrance

> *I will praise thee; for I am fearfully and wonderfully made: marvellous are thy works.*
> PSALM 139:14

MARIAN
Living Fragrance

> *I will praise thee; for I am fearfully and wonderfully made: marvellous are thy works.*
> PSALM 139:14

MARIANNA
Living Fragrance and Grace

> *I will praise thee; for I am fearfully and wonderfully made: marvellous are thy works.*
> PSALM 139:14

MARIBELLE
Living Fragrance and Beautiful

> *I will praise thee; for I am fearfully and wonderfully made: marvellous are thy works.*
> PSALM 139:14

MARIBETH
Living Fragrance, Consecration

> *I will bless the Lord at all times: his praise shall continually be in my mouth.*
> PSALM 34:1

MARIE
Living Fragrance

> *I will praise thee; for I am fearfully and wonderfully made: marvellous are thy works.*
> PSALM 139:14

MARIGRACE
Living Fragrance and Grace

> *The Lord will give grace and glory: no good thing will he withhold.*
> PSALM 84:11

MARIJANE
Living Fragrance and Grace

> *The Lord will give grace and glory: no good thing will he withhold.*
> PSALM 84:11

MARILDA
Famous One

> *Thou hast also given me the shield of thy salvation . . . thy gentleness hath made me great.*
> PSALM 18:35

MARILYN
Living Fragrance

> *I will praise thee; for I am fearfully and wonderfully made: marvellous are thy works.*
> PSALM 139:14

MARINER
Of the Sea

> *The works of the Lord are great, . . . His work is honourable.*
> PSALM 111:2–3

MARINI
One Who Brings Joy

> *Thou wilt show me the path of life: in thy presence is fulness of joy.*
> PSALM 16:11

MARINIQUE
Warrior of Strength

> *The Lord is my light and my salvation; . . . the Lord is the strength of my life.*
> PSALM 27:1

MARIO
A Mighty Warrior

> *Fight the good fight of faith, lay hold on eternal life, whereunto thou art also called.*
> 1 TIMOTHY 6:12

MARION
One of Grace

> *The Lord God is a sun and shield: . . . [He] will give grace and glory.*
> PSALM 84:11

MARIPAT
Exalted Nobility

> *Ye are a chosen generation, a royal priesthood . . . show forth the praises of him.*
> 1 PETER 2:9

MARIS
Of the Sea

> *The works of the Lord are great, . . . His work is honourable.*
> PSALM 111:2–3

MARISEL
Strong in the Faith

> *Fight the good fight of faith, lay hold on eternal life, whereunto thou art also called.*
> 1 TIMOTHY 6:12

MARISOL
Living Radiant Fragrance

> Thy hands have made me and
> fashioned me: give me
> understanding, that I may
> learn.
> PSALM 119:73

MARIT
The Deserving One

> Let the words of my mouth, and
> the meditation of my heart, be
> acceptable in thy sight.
> PSALM 19:14

MARJORY
A Pearl

> I will praise thee; for I am
> fearfully and wonderfully
> made; . . . How precious also
> are thy thoughts.
> PSALM 139:14, 17

MARK   *also* MARC
A Mighty Warrior

> Fight the good fight of faith, lay
> hold on eternal life, whereunto
> thou art also called.
> 1 TIMOTHY 6:12

MARKAELA
Strong in the Faith

> Fight the good fight of faith, lay
> hold on eternal life, whereunto
> thou art also called.
> 1 TIMOTHY 6:12

MARKHAM
Warrior for the Faith

> Fight the good fight of faith, lay
> hold on eternal life, whereunto
> thou art also called.
> 1 TIMOTHY 6:12

MARLA
Living Fragrance

> I will praise thee; for I am
> fearfully and wonderfully made.
> PSALM 139:14

MARLENE
A High Watchtower

> The name of the Lord is a strong
> tower: the righteous runneth
> into it, and are safe.
> PROVERBS 18:10

MARLEY
The Pleasant One

> I will praise thee, O Lord, with
> my whole heart.
> PSALM 9:1

MARLIN
Grand Leader

> The Lord is my light and
> salvation; whom shall I fear?
> PSALM 27:1

MARLISA
Living Fragrance and Consecration

> I will bless the Lord at all times:
> his praise shall continually be
> in my mouth.
> PSALM 34:1

M

MARLON
Wise Leader

> The Lord is my light and my salvation; . . . the Lord is the strength of my life; of whom shall I be afraid?
> PSALM 27:1

MARLOW
From the Peaceful Meadow

> The Lord is my shepherd; . . . He maketh me to lie down in green pastures.
> PSALM 23:1–2

MARLYN
Skill in Leadership

> Thou hast . . . given me the shield of thy salvation: . . . thy gentleness hath made me great.
> PSALM 18:35

MARLYSE
Living Fragrance

> I will praise thee; for I am fearfully and wonderfully made: marvellous are thy works.
> PSALM 139:14

MARNETTE
One of Rejoicing

> I will praise thee, . . . with my whole heart . . . I will sing praise to thy name.
> PSALM 9:1–2

MARNIE
One Who Brings Joy

> I will praise thee, O Lord, with my whole heart; . . . I will be glad.
> PSALM 9:1–2

MAROO
Skilled in Service

> And whatsoever ye do, do it heartily, as to the Lord, . . . for ye serve the Lord Christ.
> COLOSSIANS 3:23–24

MARSHA
Heroine of Faith

> Fight the good fight of faith, lay hold on eternal life, whereunto thou art . . . called.
> 1 TIMOTHY 6:12

MARSHALL
Commander

> Behold, I have given him for a witness to the people.
> ISAIAH 55:4

MARSHANNE
One of Courage and Grace

> For the Lord God is a sun and shield: the Lord will give grace and glory.
> PSALM 84:11

MARSIE   *also* MARCY
Heroine for the Faith

> Fight the good fight of faith, lay hold on eternal life, whereunto thou art also called.
> 1 TIMOTHY 6:12

MARSTON
From the Farm on the Lake

> Thy word is a lamp unto my feet, and a light unto my path.
> PSALM 119:105

MARTEUS
Victorious Warrior

> *I can do all things through*
> *Christ which strengtheneth me.*
> PHILIPPIANS 4:13

MARTHA
Compassionate Spirit

> *Now abideth faith, hope,*
> *charity, these three, but the*
> *greatest of these is charity.*
> 1 CORINTHIANS 13:13

MARTHALYN
Lady of High Esteem

> *Strength and honour are her*
> *clothing; and she shall rejoice in*
> *time to come.*
> PROVERBS 31:25

MARTIN
A Mighty Warrior

> *Fight the good fight of faith, lay*
> *hold on eternal life, whereunto*
> *thou art also called.*
> 1 TIMOTHY 6:12

MARTINA
Heroine of Faith

> *Fight the good fight of faith, lay*
> *hold on eternal life, whereunto*
> *thou art called.*
> 1 TIMOTHY 6:12

MARTY
A Mighty Warrior

> *Fight the good fight of faith, lay*
> *hold on eternal life, unto which*
> *thou art also called.*
> 1 TIMOTHY 6:12

MARVALENE
The Wondrous

> *For the Lord is great, and*
> *greatly to be praised.*
> PSALM 96:4

MARVEE
Wonderful One

> *I will praise thee; for I am*
> *fearfully and wonderfully made:*
> *marvellous are thy works.*
> PSALM 139:14

MARVIN
A Notable Friend

> *Ye are my friends, if ye do*
> *whatsoever I command you.*
> JOHN 15:14

MARVINA
Notable Friend

> *Ye are my friends, if ye do*
> *whatsoever I command you.*
> JOHN 15:14

MARWOOD
Famous Friend

> *A man that hath friends must*
> *show himself friendly.*
> PROVERBS 18:24

MARY
Living Fragrance

> *I will praise thee; for I am*
> *fearfully and wonderfully*
> *made; . . . How precious also are*
> *thy thoughts unto me.*
> PSALM 139:14, 17

MARY RUTH
Living Fragrance and Compassion
> *I will praise thee; for I am*
> *fearfully and wonderfully made:*
> *marvellous are thy works.*
> PSALM 139:14

MARY-JO
Living Fragrance
> *I will praise thee; for I am*
> *fearfully and wonderfully made:*
> *marvellous are thy works.*
> PSALM 139:14

MARYA
Living Fragrance
> *I will praise thee; for I am*
> *fearfully and wonderfully made:*
> *marvellous are thy works.*
> PSALM 139:14

MARYANN
Living Fragrance and Grace
> *The Lord will give grace and*
> *glory: no good thing will he*
> *withhold from them.*
> PSALM 84:11

MARYANNA
Living Fragrance and Grace
> *I will praise thee; for I am*
> *fearfully and wonderfully made:*
> *marvellous are thy works.*
> PSALM 139:14

MARYANNE
Living Fragrance and Grace
> *I will praise thee; for I am*
> *fearfully and wonderfully made:*
> *marvellous are thy works.*
> PSALM 139:14

MARYBELLE
Living Fragrance and Beautiful
> *I will praise thee; for I am*
> *fearfully and wonderfully made:*
> *marvellous are thy works.*
> PSALM 139:14

MARYBETH
Living Fragrance and Devotion
> *I will praise thee; for I am*
> *fearfully and wonderfully made:*
> *marvellous are thy works.*
> PSALM 139:14

MARYLOU
Living Fragrance and Victorious
> *I will praise thee; for I am*
> *fearfully and wonderfully made:*
> *marvellous are thy works.*
> PSALM 139:14

MARYNELL
Living Fragrance and Light
> *Let your light so shine before*
> *men that they may see your*
> *good works, and glorify your*
> *Father which is in heaven.*
> MATTHEW 5:16

MASAHIRO
Long and Generous Life
> *I will praise thee: for thou hast*
> *heard me, and art become my*
> *salvation.*
> PSALM 118:21

MASAKO
Lady of Grace
> *The Lord will give grace and*
> *glory: no good thing will he*
> *withhold.*
> PSALM 84:11

MASHADI
Of Strong Determination

> I press toward the mark for the prize of the high calling of God in Christ Jesus.
> PHILIPPIANS 3:14

MASHARIO
Of Noble Family

> Ye are a chosen generation, a royal priesthood . . . that ye should show forth the praises of him.
> 1 PETER 2:9

Japanese

MASHUN
Rock of Strength

> In God is my salvation and my glory: the rock of my strength, and my refuge.
> PSALM 62:7

MASIL
Gift of Jehovah

> For by grace are ye saved through faith; and that not of yourselves: it is the gift of God.
> EPHESIANS 2:8

Teutonic

MASIRAY
Gift of Jehovah

> For by grace are ye saved through faith; and that not of yourselves, it is the gift of God.
> EPHESIANS 2:8

MASON
Master Builder

> As a wise masterbuilder, I have laid the foundation, . . . which is Jesus Christ.
> 1 CORINTHIANS 3:10–11

MASOOD
Majestic One

> For the Lord is great, and greatly to be praised: . . . Honour and majesty are before him.
> PSALM 96:4, 6

MATHIEU
Gift of Jehovah

> Every good gift and every perfect gift is from above and cometh down from the Father.
> JAMES 1:17

MATHILDE
A Noble Lady

> Strength and honour are her clothing; and she shall rejoice in time to come.
> PROVERBS 31:25

MATT
Gift of God

> By grace are ye saved through faith; and that not of yourselves: it is the gift of God.
> EPHESIANS 2:8

MATTHEW
Gift of God

> I will praise thee: for thou hast heard me, and art become my salvation.
> PSALM 118:21

MATTIE
Gift of the Lord

> *Every good gift and every*
> *perfect gift is from above and*
> *cometh down from the Father.*
> JAMES 1:17

MATTIE LEE
Gift of Jehovah

> *By grace are ye saved through*
> *faith; . . . it is the gift of God.*
> EPHESIANS 2:8

MAUDE
Mighty in Battle

> *For thou hast girded me with*
> *strength unto the battle.*
> PSALM 18:39

MAULDIN
Noble and Majestic

> *For the Lord is great, and*
> *greatly to be praised.*
> PSALM 96:4

MAUNA
Of Wise Counsel

> *I will bless the Lord, who hath*
> *given me counsel: . . . I have set*
> *the Lord . . . before me.*
> PSALM 16:7–8

MAUREEN
Great

> *Only fear the Lord, and serve*
> *him in truth with all your heart.*
> 1 SAMUEL 12:24

MAUREY
One of Endurance and Greatness

> *Thou hast also given me the*
> *shield of thy salvation.*
> PSALM 18:35

MAURICIA
Endurance and Greatness

> *Thou hast . . . given me the*
> *shield of thy salvation: . . . thy*
> *gentleness hath made me great.*
> PSALM 18:35

MAURICIO
Endurance and Greatness

> *Thou hast . . . given me the*
> *shield of thy salvation: . . . thy*
> *gentleness hath made me great.*
> PSALM 18:35

MAURY
One of Endurance and Greatness

> *Thou hast given me . . . the*
> *shield of thy salvation: . . . thy*
> *gentleness hath made me great.*
> PSALM 18:35

MAVERICK
Of Joy

> *Thou wilt show me the path of*
> *life: in thy presence is fulness of*
> *joy.*
> PSALM 16:11

MAWII
Essence of Life

> *The Lord is my light and my*
> *salvation; . . . the Lord is the*
> *strength of my life; of whom*
> *shall I be afraid?*
> PSALM 27:1

African

MAWIYAH
Essence of Life

> The Lord is my light and my
> salvation; . . . the Lord is the
> strength of my life; of whom
> shall I be afraid?
> PSALM 27:1

Arabic

MAX
The Greatest

> He that shall humble himself
> shall be exalted.
> MATTHEW 23:12

MAXANNE
Of Most High Grace

> The Lord will give grace and
> glory: no good thing will he
> withhold from them that walk
> uprightly.
> PSALM 84:11

MAXEY
The Greatest

> Thou hast . . . given me the
> shield of thy salvation: . . . thy
> gentleness hath made me great.
> PSALM 18:35

MAXFIELD
The Great Field

> Jesus saith . . . behold, I say
> unto you, Lift up your eyes, and
> look on the fields.
> JOHN 4:34–35

MAXIMILIAN
The Greatest

> Now abideth faith, hope,
> charity, these three; but the
> greatest of these is charity.
> 1 CORINTHIANS 13:13

MAXINE
Full of Honor

> Strength and honour are her
> clothing; and she shall rejoice in
> time to come.
> PROVERBS 31:25

MAXWELL
The Greatest

> Now abideth faith, hope,
> charity, these three; but the
> greatest of these is charity.
> 1 CORINTHIANS 13:13

MAY
A Pearl

> I will praise thee; for I am
> fearfully and wonderfully
> made; marvelous are thy works.
> PSALM 139:14

MAYA
One of Great Wisdom

> The Lord giveth wisdom: out of
> his mouth cometh knowledge
> and understanding.
> PROVERBS 2:6

MAYBELLE
Pearl of Beauty

> I will praise thee; for I am
> fearfully and wonderfully made:
> marvellous are thy works.
> PSALM 139:14

M

MAYNARD
Mightily Brave

> I have fought a good fight, I
> have finished my course.
> 2 TIMOTHY 4:7

MAYRA
Living Fragrance

> I will praise thee; for I am
> fearfully and wonderfully made:
> marvellous are thy works.
> PSALM 139:14

MEADE
Pressing Toward the Goal

> I press toward the mark for the
> prize of the high calling of God.
> PHILIPPIANS 3:14

MEAGAN
Exalted One

> Humble yourselves . . . under
> the mighty hand of God, that he
> may exalt you.
> 1 PETER 5:6

MEARA
From the Quiet Brook

> The Lord is my shepherd; . . . he
> leadeth me beside the still
> waters.
> PSALM 23:1–2

MEDARD
Pearl of Wisdom

> For the Lord giveth wisdom: out
> of his mouth cometh knowledge.
> PROVERBS 2:6

MEDEA
The Healing One

> The Lord hath anointed me to
> preach good tidings unto the
> meek . . . to heal the
> brokenhearted.
> ISAIAH 61:1

MEDFORD
One of Strength

> But they that wait upon the
> Lord shall renew their strength.
> ISAIAH 40:31

MEESHA
Deliverance

> I will praise thee: for thou hast
> heard me, and art become my
> salvation.
> PSALM 118:21

MEG
Exalted One

> Humble yourselves . . . under
> the mighty hand of God, that he
> may exalt you in due time.
> 1 PETER 5:6

MEGAL
One of Strength

> The Lord is my light . . . my
> salvation; [and] . . . the strength
> of my life; of whom shall I be
> afraid?
> PSALM 27:1

MEGAN
Exalted One

> Humble yourselves . . . under
> the mighty hand of God, that he
> may exalt you in due time.
> 1 PETER 5:6

MEGHAN
A Pearl

> *I will praise thee; for I am*
> *fearfully and wonderfully made:*
> *marvellous are thy works.*
> PSALM 139:14

MEIER
Servant of Light

> *They that be wise shall shine as*
> *the brightness of the firmament;*
> *. . . as the stars for ever and ever.*
> DANIEL 12:3

MEINRAD
Mightily Brave

> *Thou hast also given me the*
> *shield of thy salvation: and thy*
> *gentleness hath made me great.*
> 2 SAMUEL 22:36

MEIPALA
One of Joy

> *Thou wilt show me the path of*
> *life: in thy presence is fulness of*
> *joy; at thy right hand there are*
> *pleasures for evermore.*
> PSALM 16:11

MEIPELA
Precious and Beautiful Pearl

> *I will praise thee; for I am*
> *fearfully and wonderfully made:*
> *marvellous are thy works.*
> PSALM 139:14
>
> Polynesian

MEKEL
Follower

> *Be ye therefore followers of*
> *God, as dear children; And*
> *walk in Love, as Christ also*
> *hath loved us.*
> EPHESIANS 5:1–2

MELA
God's Vineyard

> *I am the vine, ye are the*
> *branches: He that abideth in*
> *me, and I in him, the same*
> *bringeth forth much fruit.*
> JOHN 15:5

MELANIE
Always Kind

> *Be ye kind one to another,*
> *tenderhearted, forgiving one*
> *another.*
> EPHESIANS 4:32

MELANIE ANN
Joy and Grace

> *In thy presence is fulness of joy;*
> *at thy right hand . . . are*
> *pleasures for evermore.*
> PSALM 16:11

MELBA
One of Strength

> *The Lord is my light and my*
> *salvation; whom shall I fear?*
> *the Lord is the strength of my*
> *life; of whom shall I be afraid?*
> PSALM 27:1

MELBOURNE
One of Strength and Courage

> *The Lord is my light and my salvation; whom shall I fear? the Lord is the strength of my life; of whom shall I be afraid?*
> PSALM 27:1

MELBY
Noble and Strong

> *The Lord is my rock, and my fortress, and my deliverer; my God, my strength.*
> PSALM 18:2

MELE
A Song

> *I will praise thee; O Lord, with my whole heart; . . . I will be glad and rejoice in thee: I will sing praise to thy name.*
> PSALM 9:1–2

MELELANI
Song from Heaven

> *I will be glad and rejoice in thee: I will sing praise to thy name, O thou most High.*
> PSALM 9:2

MELINDA
One of Wisdom

> *The fear of the Lord is the beginning of wisdom: . . . his praise endureth forever.*
> PSALM 111:10

MELISA
Honeybee

> *How sweet are thy words unto my taste! yea, sweeter than honey to my mouth!*
> PSALM 119:103

MELISSA
Honeybee

> *How sweet are thy words unto my taste! yea, sweeter than honey to my mouth!*
> PSALM 119:103

MELODY
Joyful Life

> *Therefore with joy shall ye draw water out of the wells of salvation.*
> ISAIAH 12:3

MELONI
Joyful Life

> *Thou wilt show me the path of life; in thy presence is fulness of joy.*
> PSALM 16:11

MELRITA
Honey of a Pearl

> *I will praise thee; for I am fearfully and wonderfully made: . . . How precious also are thy thoughts unto me, O God!*
> PSALM 139: 14,17

MELROSE
Devoted Rose

> *Thy hands have made me and fashioned me: give me understanding, that I may learn thy commandments.*
> PSALM 119:73

MELTON
From the Peaceful Homestead

> *The Lord will give strength unto his people; the Lord will bless his people with peace.*
> PSALM 29:11

MELVALINE
One of Strength

> *The Lord is my light and my salvation; whom shall I fear? the Lord is the strength of my life; of whom shall I be afraid?*
> PSALM 27:1

MELVIN
Steadfast Chief

> *Be ye stedfast, unmovable, always abounding in the work of the Lord.*
> 1 CORINTHIANS 15:58

MEME
Protecting One

> *Thou art my hiding place and my shield: I hope in thy word . . . Hold thou me up, and I shall be safe.*
> PSALM 119:114, 117

MEMRIE
Beautiful Thoughts

> *Whatsoever things are true, . . . honest, . . . just, . . . pure, . . . lovely, . . . of good report; if there be any virtue, and . . . any praise, think on these things.*
> PHILIPPIANS 4:8

MENAHEM
Comforter

> *I will pray the Father, and he shall give you another Comforter, that he may abide with you for ever.*
> JOHN 14:16

MENDE
One of Wisdom and Love

> *My mouth shall speak of wisdom; and the meditation of my heart shall be of understanding.*
> PSALM 49:3

MENDEL
Of the Mind

> *Fulfil ye my joy, that ye be likeminded, having the same love, being of one accord, of one mind . . . Let this mind be in you, which was also in Christ Jesus.*
> PHILIPPIANS 2:2, 5

MENERVIA
One of Wisdom and Purpose

> *For the Lord giveth wisdom: out of his mouth cometh knowledge and understanding.*
> PROVERBS 2:6

MENITA
Divine Strength

> *He that dwelleth in the secret place of the most High shall abide under the shadow of the Almighty.*
> PSALM 91:1

M

MENZO
One of Joy
> I will bless the Lord, who hath given me counsel.
> PSALM 16:7

MERCEDES
Compassionate Spirit
> I will praise thee: for thou hast heard me, and art become my salvation.
> PSALM 118:21
>
> Spanish

MERCY
Compassionate Spirit
> Thou, O Lord, art a God full of compassion, and gracious, longsuffering, and plenteous in mercy and truth.
> PSALM 86:15

MEREDITH
Blessed of God
> I am the Lord thy God which teacheth thee to profit, which leadeth thee by the way that thou shouldest go.
> ISAIAH 48:17

MERENA
Majestic One
> For the Lord is great, and greatly to be praised: . . . Honour and majesty are before him.
> PSALM 96:4, 6

MERIANNA
Living Fragrance and Grace
> The Lord will give grace and glory: no good thing will he withhold from them that walk uprightly.
> PSALM 84:11

MERIBETH
One of Devotion
> I delight to do thy will, O my God: yea, thy law is within my heart.
> PSALM 40:8

MERIC
Ruling with Strength
> In God is my salvation and my glory: the rock of my strength; and my refuge, is in God.
> PSALM 62:7

MERIDEN
From the Quiet Meadow
> The Lord is my shepherd; I shall not want. He maketh me to lie down in green pastures: he leadeth me beside the still waters.
> PSALM 23:1–2

MERONICA
True Image
> For whom he did foreknow, he also did predestinate to be conformed to the image of his Son, that he might be the firstborn among many brethren.
> ROMANS 8:29

MERRIANNE
One of Joy and Grace

> The Lord will give grace and
> glory: no good thing will he
> withhold from them that walk
> uprightly.
> PSALM 84:11

MERRIE
Joyful

> I will praise thee, . . . with my
> whole heart; . . . I will be glad
> and rejoice . . . I will sing praise
> to thy name.
> PSALM 9:1–2

MERRILL
Illustrious One

> Make you perfect in every good
> work to do his will, working in
> you that which is wellpleasing
> in his sight, through Jesus
> Christ.
> HEBREWS 13:21

MERROW
Famous Power

> Thou hast also given me the
> shield of thy salvation: and thy
> right hand hath holden me up,
> . . . thy gentleness hath made
> me great.
> PSALM 18:35

MERRY
Joyful One

> Thou wilt show me the path of
> life: in thy presence is fulness of
> joy; at thy right hand there are
> pleasures for evermore.
> PSALM 16:11

META
Pressing Toward the Goal

> Reaching forth unto those things
> which are before, I press toward
> the mark for the prize of the high
> calling of God in Christ Jesus.
> PHILIPPIANS 3:13–14

METHERION
Gift of Jehovah

> For by grace are ye saved
> through faith; and that not of
> yourselves: it is the gift of God.
> EPHESIANS 2:8

METHODIA
Firm of Purpose

> I will bless the Lord, who hath
> given me counsel, . . . I have set
> the Lord always before me.
> PSALM 16:7–8

MIA
Like Unto the Lord

> The Lord is my strength and
> song, and he is become my
> salvation: he is my God, . . . I
> will exalt him.
> EXODUS 15:2

MICAH
Like Unto Jehovah

> The Lord is my strength and
> song, and he is become my
> salvation: he is my God, . . . I
> will exalt him.
> EXODUS 15:2

M

MICHAEL
also MICHAL, MICHEL

Like Unto the Lord

> *The Lord is my strength and*
> *song, and he is become my*
> *salvation: he is my God, . . . I*
> *will exalt him.*
> EXODUS 15:2

MICHAL
also MICHAEL

Like Unto the Lord

> *The Lord is my strength and*
> *song, and he is become my*
> *salvation: he is my God, . . . I*
> *will exalt him.*
> EXODUS 15:2

MICHEL

Like Unto the Lord

> *The Lord is my strength and*
> *song, and he is become my*
> *salvation: he is my God, . . . I*
> *will exalt him.*
> EXODUS 15:2

MICHELLE

Like Unto the Lord

> *The Lord is my strength and*
> *song, and he is become my*
> *salvation: he is my God, . . . I*
> *will exalt him.*
> EXODUS 15:2

MICKEY

Like Unto the Lord

> *The Lord is my strength and*
> *song, and he is become my*
> *salvation: he is my God, . . . I*
> *will exalt him.*
> EXODUS 15:2

MIDDLETON

The Town Near the Meadow

> *The Lord is my shepherd; I shall*
> *not want. He maketh me to lie*
> *down in green pastures: he*
> *leadeth me beside the still*
> *waters.*
> PSALM 23:1–2

MIDGE

Strong in Spirit

> *In God is my salvation and my*
> *glory: the rock of my strength,*
> *and my refuge, is in God.*
> PSALM 62:7

MIECZYSLAW

Bright Sword Edge

> *Put on the whole armour of*
> *God, . . . And take the helmet of*
> *salvation, and the sword of the*
> *Spirit, which is the word of God.*
> EPHESIANS 6:11, 17
>
> Slavic

MIESHA

Industrious One

> *Whatsoever ye do, do it heartily,*
> *as to the Lord, . . . for ye serve*
> *the Lord Christ.*
> COLOSSIANS 3:23–24

MIETEK

Touched by God

> *Thou hast also given me the*
> *shield of thy salvation.*
> PSALM 18:35

MIGNON
Small and Pretty

> *I will praise thee; for I am*
> *fearfully and wonderfully*
> *made: . . . How precious also are*
> *thy thoughts unto me, O God!*
> PSALM 139:14–17

MIGUEL
Like Unto the Lord

> *The Lord is my strength and*
> *song, and he is become my*
> *salvation: he is my God, . . . I*
> *will exalt him.*
> EXODUS 15:2

MIKE
Like Unto the Lord

> *The Lord is my strength and*
> *song, and he is become my*
> *salvation: he is my God, . . . I*
> *will exalt him.*
> EXODUS 15:2

MIKINLEY
Fair Hero

> *Thou hast also given me the*
> *shield of thy salvation: and thy*
> *right hand hath holden me up,*
> *. . . thy gentleness hath made me*
> *great.*
> PSALM 18:35

MILAM
Of Gentle Strength

> *Thou hast also given me the*
> *shield of thy salvation: and thy*
> *right hand hath holden me up,*
> *. . . thy gentleness hath made me*
> *great.*
> 2 SAMUEL 22:36

MILBERT
From the Mill

> *The Lord is my shepherd; I shall*
> *not want. He maketh me to lie*
> *down in green pastures: he*
> *leadeth me beside the still*
> *waters.*
> PSALM 23:1–2

MILBURN
From the Mill on the Brook

> *Thy word is a lamp unto my*
> *feet, and a light unto my path.*
> PSALM 119:105

MILDRED
Gentle Counselor

> *I have set the Lord . . . before*
> *me: . . . he is at my right hand, I*
> *shall not be moved.*
> PSALM 16:8

MILEAH
Industrious One

> *Whatsoever ye do, do it heartily,*
> *as to the Lord, . . . for ye serve*
> *the Lord Christ.*
> COLOSSIANS 3:23–24

MILFORD
From the Mill by the Ford

> *The Lord is my shepherd; I shall*
> *not want. He maketh me to lie*
> *down in green pastures: he*
> *leadeth me beside the still*
> *waters.*
> PSALM 23:1–2

M

MILIA
Of Quiet Power

> Thou hast also given me the
> shield of thy salvation: and thy
> right hand hath holden me up,
> . . . thy gentleness hath made
> me great.
> PSALM 18:35

MILILANI
Gentle Counselor in Grace

> The Lord will give grace and
> glory: no good thing will he
> withhold from them that walk
> uprightly.
> PSALM 84:11

Polynesian

MILLER
One Who Grinds

> I will bless the Lord at all times:
> his praise shall continually be
> in my mouth.
> PSALM 34:1

MILLIE
Gentle Counselor

> I will speak of excellent things;
> and the opening of my lips shall
> be right things. . . . [and] speak
> truth.
> PROVERBS 8:6–7

MILTON
Prosperous One

> I will sing unto the Lord,
> because he hath dealt
> bountifully with me.
> PSALM 13:6

MIMI
Chosen Protection

> Thou hast also given me the
> shield of thy salvation: and thy
> right hand hath holden me up.
> PSALM 18:35

MINDEL
One Who Is Wise

> Continue thou in the things
> which thou hast learned . . .
> from a child thou hast known
> the holy scriptures, which are
> able to make thee wise unto
> salvation through faith . . . in
> Christ Jesus.
> 2 TIMOTHY 3:14–15

MINDIE
Love

> In this was manifested the love
> of God . . . [who] sent his only
> begotten Son into the world.
> 1 JOHN 4:9

MINDOZIER
From the Mountain

> They that trust in the Lord shall
> be as mount Zion, which cannot
> be removed, but abideth forever.
> PSALM 125:1

MINDRA
Love and Protection

> In this was manifested the love
> of God toward us, because that
> God sent his only begotten Son
> into the world, that we might
> live.
> 1 JOHN 4:9

MINDY
Beloved One

> Beloved, let us love one another:
> for love is of God; and every one
> that loveth is born of God, and
> knoweth God.
> 1 JOHN 4:7

MINERVA
One of Wisdom and Purpose

> The Lord giveth wisdom: out of
> his mouth cometh knowledge
> and understanding.
> PROVERBS 2:6

MINOLA
Chosen Protection

> Ye have not chosen me, but I
> have chosen you, and ordained
> you, that ye should go and bring
> forth fruit.
> JOHN 15:16

MINOR
Youthful One

> For thou art my hope, O Lord
> God: thou art my trust from my
> youth.
> PSALM 71:5

MINOS
One of Nobel Lineage

> Ye are a chosen generation, a
> royal priesthood, . . . show forth
> the praises of him who hath
> called you.
> 1 PETER 2:9

MIRACLE
Wonderful

> I will praise thee; for I am
> fearfully and wonderfully made:
> marvellous are thy works.
> PSALM 139:14

MIRANDA
Deserving of Admiration

> The Lord shall . . . come to be
> glorified in his saints, and to be
> admired in all them that
> believe.
> 2 THESSALONIANS 1:9–10

MIRENE
One of Nobility

> Ye have not chosen me, but I
> have chosen you, and ordained
> you, that ye should go and bring
> forth fruit.
> JOHN 15:16

MIRIAM
Living Fragrance

> I will offer to thee the sacrifice
> of thanksgiving, and will call
> upon the name of the Lord.
> PSALM 116:17

MIRLE
Wonderful

> The Lord taketh pleasure in
> them that fear him, in those that
> hope in his mercy.
> PSALM 147:11

MISSY
Honeybee

> The Lord hath made all things
> for himself.
> PROVERBS 16:4

MISTIQUE
Seeking Knowledge

> *For the Lord giveth wisdom: out*
> *of his mouth cometh knowledge*
> *and understanding.*
> PROVERBS 2:6

MISTY
Beloved One

> *Behold, what manner of love the*
> *Father hath bestowed upon us.*
> 1 JOHN 3:1

MITCHELL
Like unto the Lord

> *The Lord is my strength and*
> *song, and he is become my*
> *salvation: he is my God, . . . I*
> *will exalt him.*
> EXODUS 15:2

MITHRAN
Defender of the Truth

> *I will sing of the mercies of the*
> *Lord for ever: with my mouth*
> *will I make known thy*
> *faithfulness to all generations.*
> PSALM 89:1

MITSUKO
Faithful Child

> *I have set the Lord always*
> *before me: because he is at my*
> *right hand, I shall not be*
> *moved.*
> PSALM 16:8

Japanese

MITTIE
Living Fragrance

> *I will praise thee; for I am*
> *fearfully and wonderfully made:*
> *marvellous are thy works.*
> PSALM 139:14

MITZI
Living Fragrance

> *I will praise thee; for I am*
> *fearfully and wonderfully made:*
> *marvellous are thy works.*
> PSALM 139:14

MITZIE
Living Fragrance

> *I will praise thee; for I am*
> *fearfully and wonderfully made:*
> *marvellous are thy works.*
> PSALM 139:14

MIYOKO
Beautiful Generation Child

> *For thou art my hope, O Lord*
> *God: thou art my trust from my*
> *youth.*
> PSALM 71:5

MOBLEY
Of Sacred Fame

> *Wait on the Lord, and keep his*
> *way, and he shall exalt thee to*
> *inherit the land.*
> PSALM 37:34

MOBY
Devoted and Loyal One

> *I have set the Lord always*
> *before me: because he is at my*
> *right hand, I shall not be*
> *moved.*
> PSALM 16:8

MODELL
One of Knowledge

> For the Lord giveth wisdom: out
> of his mouth cometh knowledge.
> PROVERBS 2:6

MODESTE
The Modest

> The fruit of the Spirit is love,
> joy, peace, longsuffering,
> gentleness.
> GALATIANS 5:22

MODISE
Saved

> For by grace are ye saved
> through faith; and that not of
> yourselves: it is the gift of God.
> EPHESIANS 2:8

MOE
Saved from the Water

> He sent from above, he took me;
> he drew me out of many waters.
> 2 SAMUEL 22:17

MOHAMMED
One of Praise

> The Lord is great, and greatly to
> be praised: . . . Honour and
> majesty are before him.
> PSALM 96:4, 6
>
> Africa

MOICA
Strength in Counsel

> I have set the Lord always
> before me: because he is at my
> right hand.
> PSALM 16:8

M'KAILA
Source of Joy

> Thou wilt show me the path of
> life: in thy presence is fulness of
> joy.
> PSALM 16:11
>
> Polynesian

MOLLY
Living Fragrance

> I will offer to thee the sacrifice
> of thanksgiving, and . . . call
> upon the name of the Lord.
> PSALM 116:17

MOMIR
Excellent and High Degree

> He that dwelleth in the secret
> place of the most High shall
> abide under the shadow of the
> Almighty.
> PSALM 91:1

MONA
Lady of Honor

> A gracious woman retaineth
> honour.
> PROVERBS 11:16

MONACO
Noble and One of Honor

> The Lord liveth; and blessed be
> my rock; and let the God of my
> salvation be exalted.
> PSALM 18:46

MONALISA
Lady of Honor and Consecration

> I delight to do thy will, O my
> God: yea, thy law is within my
> heart.
> PSALM 40:8

MONCIE
One of Strong Counsel

> *I will bless the Lord, who hath given me counsel: . . . I have set the Lord always before me.*
> PSALM 16:7–8

MONDAY
Faithful Servant

> *I will bless the Lord, who hath given me counsel: . . . he is at my right hand.*
> PSALM 16:7–8

MONICA
Advisor

> *For the Lord giveth wisdom: out of his mouth cometh knowledge and understanding.*
> PROVERBS 2:6

MONIQUE
Advisor

> *For the Lord giveth wisdom: out of his mouth cometh knowledge and understanding.*
> PROVERBS 2:6

MONNIE
The Advisor

> *For the Lord giveth wisdom: out of his mouth cometh knowledge and understanding.*
> PROVERBS 2:6

MONROE
Peaceful Dweller

> *Thou wilt keep him in perfect peace, whose mind is stayed on thee.*
> ISAIAH 26:3

MONTANA
Of the Mountain

> *They that trust in the Lord shall be as mount Zion, which cannot be removed.*
> PSALM 125:1

MONTEL
From the Mountain

> *They that trust in the Lord shall be as mount Zion, which cannot be removed.*
> PSALM 125:1

MONTFORD
Mountain Ford

> *They that trust in the Lord shall be as mount Zion, which cannot be removed.*
> PSALM 125:1

MONTGOMERY
Seeking One

> *But seek ye first the kingdom of God, and his righteousness.*
> MATTHEW 6:33

MONWAELA
Just and Great Chief

> *The Lord is my rock, . . . my fortress, and my deliverer; my God.*
> PSALM 18:2

MOODY
Victorious Mind

> *My mouth shall speak of wisdom; and the meditation of my heart shall be understanding.*
> PSALM 49:3

MOORE
Peaceful Dweller

> The Lord will give strength unto
> his people; the Lord will bless
> his people.
> PSALM 29:11

MORALICA
God Is My Teacher

> I am thy servant; give me
> understanding, that I may know
> thy testimonies.
> PSALM 119:125

MOREA
Majestic One

> Thou hast also given me the
> shield of thy salvation: . . . thy
> right hand hath holden me up.
> PSALM 18:35

MOREH
Teacher

> I will bless the Lord, who hath
> given me counsel.
> PSALM 16:7

MORELAND
From the Moor Land

> Thy word is a lamp unto my
> feet, and a light unto my path.
> PSALM 119:105

MORELLE
Strong in Perseverance

> I can do all things through
> Christ which strengtheneth me.
> PHILIPPIANS 4:13

MORENA
Little Mary

> I will praise thee; for I am
> fearfully and wonderfully made:
> marvellous are thy works.
> PSALM 139:14

MORENIKE
One of Warrior Strength

> Fight the good fight of faith, lay
> hold on eternal life, whereunto
> thou art also called.
> 1 TIMOTHY 6:12

MORETTA
The Great One

> The Lord is my rock, and my
> fortress, . . . I will call upon the
> Lord.
> PSALM 18:2–3

MORGAN
Born by the Sea

> I will praise thee; for I am
> fearfully and wonderfully made:
> marvellous are thy works.
> PSALM 139:14

MORGANA
Born by the Sea

> I will praise thee: for I am
> fearfully and wonderfully made.
> PSALM 139:14

MORGANNE
Born by the Sea

> Thy hands have made me and
> fashioned me: give me
> understanding.
> PSALM 119:73

MORIAH
God Is My Teacher

> I will instruct thee and teach
> thee in the way which thou shalt
> go.
> PSALM 32:8

MORIE
God Is My Teacher

> I will instruct thee and teach
> thee in the way which thou shalt
> go.
> PSALM 32:8

MORLEY
Dweller by the Meadow

> The Lord is my shepherd; I shall
> not want. He maketh me to lie
> down in green pastures.
> PSALM 23:1–2

MORNING
Break Of Day

> This is the day which the Lord
> hath made; we will rejoice and
> be glad in it.
> PSALM 118:24

MORREY
Majestic and Honored

> I will praise thee, O Lord, with
> my whole heart; I will show
> forth all thy marvellous works.
> PSALM 9:1

MORRIS
Trust

> It is good for me to draw near to
> God: I have put my trust in the
> Lord God.
> PSALM 73:28

MORRISON
Endurance and Greatness

> I press toward the mark for the
> prize of the high calling of God
> in Christ Jesus.
> PHILIPPIANS 3:14

MORTIMER
Cheerful Nobility

> Let all those who seek thee
> rejoice and be glad in thee.
> PSALM 40:16

MOSIAH
Great Leader

> Be thou exalted, Lord, in thine
> own strength.
> PSALM 21:13

MOTTRIE
Leader of Strength

> Be strong and of a good
> courage; be not afraid, neither
> be thou dismayed.
> JOSHUA 1:9

MOYLE
One of Great Merit

> Thou hast also given me the
> shield of thy salvation: . . . thy
> right hand hath holden me up.
> PSALM 18:35

MOZELLE
A Refreshing Spirit

> The times of refreshing shall
> come from the presence of the
> Lord.
> ACTS 3:19

MRYTLE
Crown of Victory

> *Whatsoever is born of God overcometh the world: and this is the victory, . . . even our faith.*
> 1 JOHN 5:4

MUFFETT
Cherished One

> *Beloved, let us love one another: for love is of God; and every one that loveth is born of God and knoweth God.*
> 1 JOHN 4:7

MUNIRA
Gifts

> *For by grace are ye saved through faith; and that not of yourselves: it is the gift of God.*
> EPHESIANS 2:8

MURCHISON
Little One

> *My God, thou hast made thy servant . . . and I am but a little child.*
> 1 KINGS 3:7–9
>
> English

MURDELL
Blessed of God

> *Thou hast also given me the shield of thy salvation . . . thy gentleness hath made me great.*
> PSALM 18:35

MURDOCH
Sea Protector

> *He that dwelleth in the secret place of the most High shall abide under the shadow of the Almighty.*
> PSALM 91:1

MURIEL
Illustrious One

> *Make you perfect in every good work to do his will.*
> HEBREWS 13:21

MURLENE
A Watchtower

> *The name of the Lord is a strong tower: the righteous runneth into it, and are safe.*
> PROVERBS 18:10

MURNEY
Strength and Honour

> *For the Lord is great, and greatly to be praised: . . . Honour and majesty are before him.*
> PSALM 96:4, 6

MURPHY
Sea Warrior

> *Fight the good fight of faith, lay hold on eternal life, whereunto thou art also called.*
> 1 TIMOTHY 6:12

MURRAY
One of Endurance

> *But watch thou in all things, endure affliction, do the work of an evangelist, make full proof of thy ministry.*
> 2 TIMOTHY 4:5

M

MUSETTE
To Play Music

> *I will praise thee, O Lord, with my whole heart; . . . I will be glad and rejoice in thee.*
> PSALM 9:1–2

MUSTFA
Chosen

> *Ye have not chosen me, but I have chosen you, and ordained you that ye should go and bring forth fruit.*
> JOHN 15:16

MUTSUKO
Faithful Child

> *I have set the Lord always before me: because he is at my right hand, I shall not be moved.*
> PSALM 16:8
>
> Japanese

MYERS
One Who Oversees

> *Take heed . . . to all the flock, over . . . which the Holy Ghost hath made you overseers.*
> ACTS 20:28

MYLA
Beloved One

> *Beloved, let us love one another: for love is of God; and every one that loveth is born of God and knoweth God.*
> 1 JOHN 4:7

MYLIE
Fighter for the Faith

> *Fight the good fight of faith, lay hold on eternal life, whereunto thou art also called.*
> 1 TIMOTHY 6:12

MYOKIA
Beautiful Generation Child

> *Thy hands have made me and fashioned me: give me understanding.*
> PSALM 119:73

MYONG SUM
Strength and Courage

> *The Lord is my light and my salvation; whom shall I fear? the Lord is the strength of my life; of whom shall I be afraid?*
> PSALM 27:1
>
> Korean

MYOUNG
One of Strength

> *The Lord is my rock, . . . my fortress, and my deliverer; my God, my Strength.*
> PSALM 18:2
>
> Korean

MYRIAM
Living Fragrance

> *I will praise thee; for I am fearfully and wonderfully made: marvellous are thy works.*
> PSALM 139:14

MYRNA
Of a Gentle Spirit

> *Wisdom . . . from above is . . .*
> *pure, then peaceable, gentle,*
> *and easy to be intreated.*
> JAMES 3:17

MYRNI
Of a Gentle Spirit

> *Wisdom . . . from above is . . .*
> *pure, then peaceable, gentle,*
> *and easy to be intreated.*
> JAMES 3:17

MYRON
A Refreshing Spirit

> *The times of refreshing shall*
> *come from the presence of the*
> *Lord.*
> ACTS 3:19

MYRTICE
Crown of Victory

> *Whatsoever is born of God*
> *overcometh the world: and this*
> *is the victory that overcometh*
> *the world, even our faith.*
> 1 JOHN 5:4

MYRTLE
Crown of Victory

> *Whatsoever is born of God*
> *overcometh the world: and this*
> *is the victory that overcometh*
> *the world, even our faith.*
> 1 JOHN 5:4

MYSIE
Little Miss

> *Thy hands have made me and*
> *fashioned me: give me*
> *understanding that I may learn*
> *thy commandments.*
> PSALM 119:73

MYUNG
New Spirit

> *Let the words of my mouth, and*
> *the meditation of my heart, be*
> *acceptable in thy sight.*
> PSALM 19:14

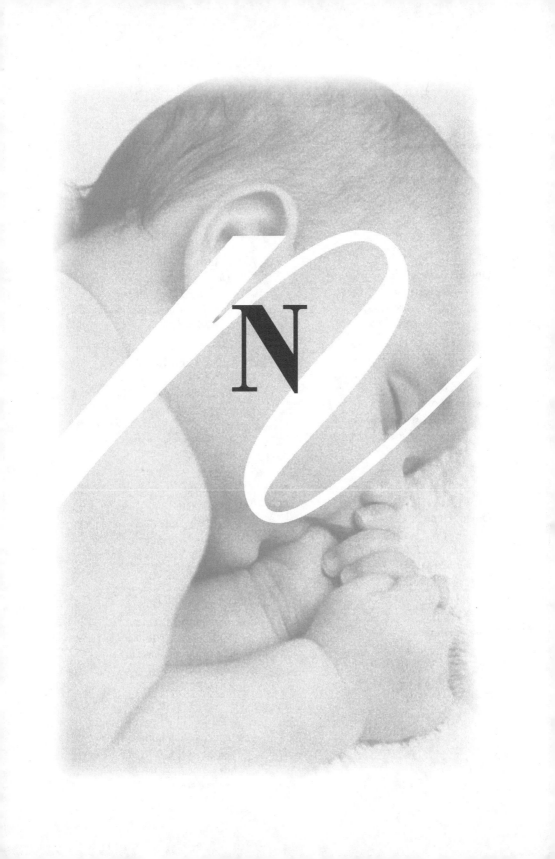

N

NAAMAN
One of Delight and Pleasantness

> *I will delight myself in thy statutes: I will not forget thy words.*
> PSALM 119:16

Hebrew

NABIL
One of Noble Birth

> *I will praise thee; for I am fearfully and wonderfully made: marvellous are thy works.*
> PSALM 139:14

Arabic

NACHEM
Rich in Comfort Is God

> *I will praise thee: for thou hast heard me, and art become my salvation.*
> PSALM 118:21

NADEAN
One of Hope

> *Trust ye in the Lord for ever: for in the Lord JEHOVAH is everlasting strength.*
> ISAIAH 26:4

NADELITA
One of Hope

> *Trust ye in the Lord for ever: for in the Lord JEHOVAH is everlasting strength.*
> ISAIAH 26:4

NADENE
One of Hope

> *Trust ye in the Lord for ever: for in the Lord JEHOVAH is everlasting strength.*
> ISAIAH 26:4

NADER
A Rare Jewel

> *There is gold, and a multitude of rubies: but the lips of knowledge are a precious jewel.*
> PROVERBS 20:15

NADEREH
Precious One

> *I will praise thee; for I am fearfully and wonderfully made: . . . How precious also are thy thoughts unto me, O God!*
> PSALM 139:14, 17

NADIJKA
Prosperous One

> *I will sing unto the Lord, because he hath dealt bountifully with me.*
> PSALM 13:6

NAEEM
Rich in Comfort Is God

> *I love the Lord, because he hath heard my voice and my supplications.*
> PSALM 116:1

NAEHAL
Courageous Champion

> *Whatsoever is born of God overcometh the world: and this is the victory.*
> 1 JOHN 5:4

NAHAMAN
Compassionate Comforter

> *I will praise thee: for thou hast heard me, and art become my salvation.*
> PSALM 118:21

NAHEEL
Courageous Champion

> *The Lord is my light and my salvation; whom shall I fear? the Lord is the strength of my life; of whom shall I be afraid?*
> PSALM 27:1

NAHJLA
Excellent and Noble Virtue

> *Whatsoever things are true, honest, . . . just, . . . [and] of good report . . . if there be any virtue and praise, . . . think on these things.*
> PHILIPPIANS 4:8
> Arabic

NAHTANHA
Gift of the Lord

> *Every good gift and every perfect gift is from above.*
> JAMES 1:17
> American Indian

NAIM
Comforter

> *The Lord is my strength and song, and is become my salvation. . . . I will praise thee; for thou hast heard me.*
> PSALM 118:14, 21

NAIRN
From the River

> *He shall be like a tree . . . that bringeth forth his fruit in his season.*
> PSALM 1:3

NAJA
Great Success

> *I can do all things through Christ which strengtheneth me.*
> PHILIPPIANS 4:13
> Arabic

NAJI
Saviour

> *And she shall bring forth a son, and thou shalt call his name JESUS.*
> MATTHEW 1:21
> Arabic

NAJIYAH
Safe and Secure

> *The Lord is my light and my salvation; . . . the Lord is the strength of my life.*
> PSALM 27:1
> Arabic

NAKANIELA
Gift of Our Lord

> *Every good gift and every perfect gift is from above, and cometh down from the Father.*
> JAMES 1:17
> Polynesian

NAKEA
Bringer of Victory

> But thanks be to God, which giveth us the victory through our Lord Jesus Christ.
> 1 CORINTHIANS 15:57

NAKEISHA
One of Victory

> For whatsoever is born of God overcometh the world: and this is the victory that overcometh the world, even our faith.
> 1 JOHN 5:4

NAKESHIA
One of Victory

> Whatsoever is born of God overcometh the world: and this is the victory that overcometh the world, even our faith.
> 1 JOHN 5:4

NAKITA
One of Victory

> For whatsoever is born of God overcometh the world: and this is the victory that overcometh the world, even our faith.
> 1 JOHN 5:4

NAKITI
One of Victory

> Whatsoever is born of God overcometh the world: and this is the victory that overcometh the world, even our faith.
> 1 JOHN 5:4

NALANI
From Heaven

> Thou shalt guide me with thy counsel, and afterward receive me to glory.
> PSALM 73:24

Polynesian

NALEDRA
Happy Spirit

> Thou wilt show me the path of life: in thy presence is fulness of joy.
> PSALM 16:11

NALITA
One of Truth

> Let the words of my mouth, and the meditation of my heart, be acceptable in thy sight.
> PSALM 19:14

NAN
One of Grace

> The Lord will give grace and glory: no good thing will be withhold from them that walk uprightly.
> PSALM 84:11

NANA
One of Grace

> The Lord will give grace and glory: no good thing will be withhold from them that walk uprightly.
> PSALM 84:11

NANCIANNE
One of Grace

> The Lord will give grace and
> glory: no good thing will he
> withhold from them that walk
> uprightly.
> PSALM 84:11

NANCY
One of Grace

> The Lord will give grace and
> glory: no good thing will he
> withhold from them that walk
> uprightly.
> PSALM 84:11

NANETTA
One of Grace

> The Lord will give grace and
> glory: no good thing will he
> withhold from them that walk
> uprightly.
> PSALM 84:11

NANETTE
One of Grace

> The Lord will give grace and
> glory: no good thing will he
> withhold from them that walk
> uprightly.
> PSALM 84:11

NANILOHA
One of Glory and Splendor

> For the Lord is great, and
> greatly to be praised: . . .
> Honour and majesty are before
> him.
> PSALM 96:4, 6

Polynesian

NANNIE-KATE
One of Grace and Purity

> The Lord will give grace and
> glory: no good thing will he
> withhold from them that walk
> uprightly.
> PSALM 84:11

NAOMI
My Delight

> I delight to do thy will, O my
> God: yea, thy law is within my
> heart.
> PSALM 40:8

NAPANEE
Strength and Courage

> Be strong and of a good
> courage; . . . for the Lord thy
> God is with thee.
> JOSHUA 1:9

NAPHTALI
Warrior of Strength

> The Lord is my light and my
> salvation; . . . the Lord is the
> strength of my life.
> PSALM 27:1

Hebrew

NAPOLEON
Forest Lion of Courage

> The Lord is my light and my
> salvation; whom shall I fear?
> the Lord is the strength of my
> life; of whom shall I be afraid?
> PSALM 27:1

NARA
Girl of Our Hearts

> Blessed are the pure in heart:
> for they shall see God.
> MATTHEW 5:8

NARCINA
Peace and Beauty

> The Lord will give strength unto
> his people; the Lord will bless
> his people.
> PSALM 29:11

NARCISSUS
One of Peace and Beauty

> The Lord will give strength unto
> his people; the Lord will bless
> his people.
> PSALM 29:11

NARDO
Strong Counsel

> I will bless the Lord, who hath
> given me counsel: . . . I have set
> the Lord always before me.
> PSALM 16:7, 8

NAREDA
God Lights My Pathway

> Thy word is a lamp unto my
> feet, and a light unto my path.
> PSALM 119:105

NARENDRA
Happy and Joyous One

> Thou wilt show me the path of
> life: in thy presence is fulness of
> joy.
> PSALM 16:11

NARSINGH
Of Victory and Protection

> He that dwelleth in the secret
> place of the most High shall
> abide under the shadow of the
> Almighty.
> PSALM 91:1

Hindu

NARU
Firm and Persevering

> I press toward the mark for the
> prize of the high calling of God
> in Christ Jesus.
> PHILIPPIANS 3:14

NARVELLE
One of Inspired Wisdom

> For the Lord giveth wisdom: out
> of his mouth cometh knowledge.
> PROVERBS 2:6

NASHELSKY
One of Victory

> Whatsoever is born of God
> overcometh the world: and this
> is the victory that overcometh
> the world, even our faith.
> 1 JOHN 5:4

German

NASHIA
Divine Favor

> The Lord will give grace and
> glory: no good thing will he
> withhold from them that walk
> uprightly.
> PSALM 84:11

NASIYAH
Divine Favor

> The Lord will give grace and glory: no good thing will he withhold from them that walk uprightly.
> PSALM 84:11

NASTASHA
Birthday of the Lord

> Unto you is born this day in the city of David a Saviour, which is Christ the Lord. . . . Glory to God in the highest.
> LUKE 2:11, 14

NASTASSIA
Birthday of Our Lord

> Unto you is born this day in the city of David a Saviour, which is Christ the Lord. . . . Glory to God in the highest.
> LUKE 2:11, 14

NASYA
Miracle of God

> When he was in Jerusalem at the passover, . . . many believed in his name, when they saw the miracles which he did.
> JOHN 2:23

NATACHA
Christmas Born

> Unto you is born this day in the city of David a Saviour, which is Christ the Lord. . . . Glory to God in the highest.
> LUKE 2:11, 14

NATACIA
Birthday of Our Lord

> Unto you is born this day in the city of David a Saviour, which is Christ the Lord. . . . Glory to God in the highest.
> LUKE 2:11, 14

NATALE
Birthday of Our Lord

> Unto you is born this day in the city of David a Saviour, which is Christ the Lord. . . . Glory to God in the highest.
> LUKE 2:11, 14

NATALIA
Birthday of Our Lord

> Unto you is born this day in the city of David a Saviour, which is Christ the Lord. . . . Glory to God in the highest.
> LUKE 2:11, 14

NATASHA
Birthday of Our Lord

> Unto you is born this day in the city of David a Saviour, which is Christ the Lord. . . . Glory to God in the highest.
> LUKE 2:11, 14

NATE
Gift

> Every good gift and every perfect gift is from above and cometh down from the Father.
> JAMES 1:17

NAME *That* BABY!

NATHAN
Given of God

> Ye are my witnesses, saith the
> Lord, and my servant whom I
> have chosen.
> ISAIAH 43:10

NATHANAEL
Gift of the Lord

> Every good gift and every
> perfect gift is from above and
> cometh down from the Father.
> JAMES 1:17

NATILIE
Birthday of our Lord

> For unto you is born this day in
> the city of David a Saviour,
> which is Christ the Lord.
> LUKE 2:11

NATIVIDAD
Christmas Child

> And she shall bring forth a son,
> and thou shalt call his name
> Jesus.
> MATTHEW 1:21

NAUSHMA
Pure Heart

> The statutes of the Lord are
> right, rejoicing the heart: the
> commandment of the Lord is
> pure.
> PSALM 19:8

NAVAR
From the Peaceful Meadow

> The Lord is my shepherd; . . . He
> maketh me to lie down in green
> pastures.
> PSALM 23:1–2

NAWAL
Safe and Secure

> He that dwelleth in the secret
> place of the most High shall
> abide under the shadow of the
> Almighty.
> PSALM 91:1

NAZAREE
Consecrated to God

> I will bless the Lord at all times:
> his praise shall continually be
> in my mouth.
> PSALM 34:1

NAZLEEN
Vowed to the Lord's Service

> I have set the Lord always before
> me: . . . I shall not be moved.
> PSALM 16:8

NAZZARENO
Guardian Protector

> He that dwelleth in the secret
> place of the most High shall
> abide under the shadow of the
> Almighty.
> PSALM 91:1

NEAL
Champion

> I press toward the mark for the
> prize of the high calling of God
> in Christ Jesus.
> PHILIPPIANS 3:14

NEBOJSA
His Prophecy

> Blessed is he that readeth, and
> they that hear the words of this
> prophecy.
> REVELATION 1:3

NED
Guardian of Property

*My soul, wait thou only upon
God; for my expectation is from
him.*
PSALM 62:5

NEDRA
Written Word

*Every word of God is pure: he is
a shield unto them that put
their trust in him.*
PROVERBS 30:5

NEELTJE
Courage and Light

*Let your light so shine before
men, that they may see your
good works and glorify your
Father which is in heaven.*
MATTHEW 5:16

NEFERTITI
One of Purity and Honor

*Blessed are the pure in heart:
for they shall see God.*
MATTHEW 5:8

NEFRETITI
Comforted by Jehovah

*I will lift up mine eyes unto the
hills, . . . My help cometh from
the Lord.*
PSALM 121:1–2

NEFTALI
Laurel of Victory

*Whatsoever is born of God
overcometh the world: and this
is the victory that overcometh
the world, even our faith.*
1 JOHN 5:4

NEGUSSY
Rejoicing and Blessing

*I will praise thee, O Lord, with
my whole heart; . . . I will be
glad and rejoice.*
PSALM 9:1–2

NEHEMIAH
Comforted by Jehovah

*I will lift up mine eyes unto the
hills, . . . My help cometh from
the Lord.*
PSALM 121:1–2

NEIKA
Life of Victory

*Whatsoever is born of God
overcometh the world: and this
is the victory that overcometh
the world, even our faith.*
1 JOHN 5:4

NEIL
Champion

*I can do all things through
Christ which strengtheneth me.*
PHILIPPIANS 4:13

NELCIE
Shining with Light

*Light is sown for the righteous,
and gladness for the upright in
heart.*
PSALM 97:11

NELDIA
One of Contentment

*I will bless the Lord at all times:
his praise shall continually be
in my mouth.*
PSALM 34:1

NELLY
Happy

> Whoso trusteth in the Lord,
> happy is he.
> PROVERBS 16:20

NELSON
The Courageous

> Be strong and of a good
> courage; . . . for the Lord thy
> God is with thee.
> JOSHUA 1:9

NENA   *also* NINA
One of Grace

> The Lord will give grace and
> glory: no good thing will he
> withhold from them that walk
> uprightly.
> PSALM 84:11

NEOMA
My Delight

> I delight to do thy will, O my
> God: yea, thy law is within my
> heart.
> PSALM 40:8

NERINE
Of the Sea

> Thy word is a lamp unto my
> feet, and a light unto my path.
> PSALM 119:105

NERMA
One of High Degree

> Thou hast also given me the
> shield of thy salvation: . . . thy
> right hand hath holden me up,
> and thy gentleness hath made
> me great.
> PSALM 18:35

NESSIE
One of Purity

> The statutes of the Lord are
> right, rejoicing the heart: the
> commandment of the Lord is
> pure, enlightening the eyes.
> PSALM 19:8

NESTAR
One of Wisdom

> For the Lord giveth wisdom: out
> of his mouth cometh knowledge
> and understanding.
> PROVERBS 2:6

NETRA
Leader of Strength

> In God is my salvation and my
> glory: the rock of my strength,
> and my refuge, is in God.
> PSALM 62:7

NETTIE
One of Purity and Grace

> The Lord will give grace and
> glory: no good thing will he
> withhold from them that walk
> uprightly.
> PSALM 84:11

NEVA   *also* NIVA
White as Snow

> Purge me with hyssop, and I
> shall be clean: wash me, and I
> shall be whiter than snow.
> PSALM 51:7

NEVILLE
From the New Town

> I am returned unto Zion, . . .
> Jerusalem shall be called a city
> of truth.
> ZECHARIAH 8:3

NEWSOM
From the New Town

> I am returned unto Zion, . . .
> Jerusalem shall be called a city
> of truth.
> ZECHARIAH 8:3

NEWTON
From the New Town

> They shall dwell in the midst of
> Jerusalem: and they shall be my
> people, and I will be their God.
> ZECHARIAH 8:8

NIA
Purpose

> I have set the Lord . . . before
> me: . . . I shall not be moved.
> PSALM 16:8

NICENE
Victorious

> But thanks be to God, which
> giveth us the victory through
> our Lord Jesus Christ.
> 1 CORINTHIANS 15:57

NICHOLAS
Victory of the People

> This is the victory that
> overcometh the world, even our
> faith, that overcometh the
> world, even our faith.
> 1 JOHN 5:4

NICK
Victory of the People

> For whatsoever is born of God
> overcometh the world: and this
> is the victory, that overcometh
> the world, even our faith.
> 1 JOHN 5:4

NICOLE
Victorious Heart

> The Lord liveth; . . . blessed be
> my rock; and let the God of my
> salvation be exalted.
> PSALM 18:46

NICOLETTE
One of Victory

> Whatsoever is born of God
> overcometh the world: and this
> is the victory that overcometh
> the world, even our faith.
> 1 JOHN 5:4

NIDA
Refuge

> He is my refuge and my fortress:
> my God; in him will I trust.
> PSALM 91:2

NIDELVIA
Refuge

> He that dwelleth in the secret
> place of the most High shall
> abide under the shadow of the
> Almighty.
> PSALM 91:1

NIDIA
Happy Guardian

*In thy presence is fulness of joy;
at thy right hand . . . are
pleasures for evermore.*
PSALM 16:11

NIDRA
The Written Word

*Every word of God is pure: he is
a shield unto them that put
their trust in him.*
PROVERBS 30:5

Spanish

NIEL
Courageous Champion

*I press toward the mark for the
prize of the high calling of God
in Christ Jesus.*
PHILIPPIANS 3:14

NIESHA
Of the Resurrection

*And this is the Father's will . . . I
will raise him up at the last day.*
JOHN 6:39–40

NIEVES
Snow

*Purge me with hyssop, and I
shall be clean: wash me, and I
shall be whiter than snow.*
PSALM 51:7

Spanish

NIGEL
Consecrated to God

*I have set the Lord always
before me: because he is at my
right hand, I shall not be moved.*
PSALM 16:8

NIGERIAN
Native of Nigeria

*Thy hands have made me and
fashioned me: give me
understanding.*
PSALM 119:73

NIKITA
Crown of Victory

*Whatsoever is born of God
overcometh the world: and this
is the victory.*
1 JOHN 5:4

NIKOLAI
Victory of the People

*For whatsoever is born of God
overcometh the world: . . . the
victory that overcometh the
world, even our faith.*
1 JOHN 5:4

NILA
Champion Leader

*Thou hast also given me the
shield of thy salvation: . . . thy
gentleness hath made me great.*
PSALM 18:35

NILANE
Of the Nest

*He that dwelleth in the secret
place of the most High shall
abide under the shadow of the
Almighty.*
PSALM 91:1

NILDA
One of Peace

> The Lord will give strength unto
> his people; . . . [and] bless his
> people with peace.
> PSALM 29:11

NILES
One of Victory

> Whatsoever is born of God
> overcometh the world: and this
> is the victory that overcometh
> the world, even our faith.
> 1 JOHN 5:4

NILS
One of Victory

> Whatsoever is born of God
> overcometh the world: and this
> is the victory that overcometh
> the world, even our faith.
> 1 JOHN 5:4

NILSA
One of Victory

> Whatsoever is born of God
> overcometh the world: and this
> is the victory that overcometh
> the world, even our faith.
> 1 JOHN 5:4

NIMA
Blessings

> Blessed are they that keep his
> testimonies, and that seek him
> with the whole heart.
> PSALM 119:2

NIMOS
One of Adventure

> How sweet are thy words unto
> my taste! yea, sweeter than
> honey to my mouth!
> PSALM 119:103

NIMOTCHKA
Endeared One

> Beloved, let us love one another:
> for love is of God.
> 1 JOHN 4:7

NIMROD
Valiant

> Fight the good fight of faith, lay
> hold on eternal life, whereunto
> thou art also called.
> 1 TIMOTHY 6:12

NINA   *also* NENA
One of Grace

> The Lord will give grace and
> glory: no good thing will he
> withhold from those that walk
> uprightly.
> PSALM 84:11

NINOCHKA
Little Darling

> Beloved, let us love one another:
> for love is of God; and every one
> that loveth is born of God and
> knoweth God.
> 1 JOHN 4:7

NINORTCHAKA
One of Grace

> *The Lord will give grace and glory: no good thing will he withhold from those that walk uprightly.*
> PSALM 84:11

NIQUITA
Victory of the People

> *Whatsoever is born of God overcometh the world: this is the victory that overcometh the world, even our faith.*
> 1 JOHN 5:4

NIRAH
Light

> *They that be wise shall shine as the brightness of the firmament; . . . as the stars for ever and ever.*
> DANIEL 12:3

NISHA
Cherished and Beloved One

> *Beloved, let us love one another: for love is of God; and every one that loveth is born of God and knoweth God.*
> 1 JOHN 4:7

NITA
One of Grace

> *The Lord will give grace and glory: no good thing will he withhold from them that walk uprightly.*
> PSALM 84:11

NITZA
One of Light

> *Let your light so shine before men, that they may see your good works and glorify your Father which is in heaven.*
> MATTHEW 5:16

NIURKA
One of Victory

> *Whatsoever is born of God overcometh the world: this is the victory that overcometh the world, even our faith.*
> 1 JOHN 5:4

NIVA   *also* NEVA
White as Snow

> *Purge me with hyssop, and I will be clean: . . . I shall be whiter than snow.*
> PSALM 51:7

NIYOKIA
Gem Treasure

> *Thy hands have made me and fashioned me: give me understanding.*
> PSALM 119:73

NO
Quiet Peace

> *Thou wilt keep him in perfect peace, whose mind is stayed on thee.*
> ISAIAH 26:3

NOA
Rest and Comfort

> *Come unto me, all ye that labour . . . and I will give you rest.*
> MATTHEW 11:28

NOAH
Rest and Comfort

> Thou, . . . art a God full of
> compassion, and gracious, . . .
> thou, Lord, hast helped me, and
> comforted me.
> PSALM 86:15, 17

NOBLE
Noble One

> Blessed is the man that feareth
> the Lord, that delighteth greatly
> in his commandments.
> PSALM 112:1

NOEL
Birthday of Our Lord

> For unto you is born this day in
> the city of David a Saviour,
> which is Christ the Lord.
> LUKE 2:11

NOELIA
Birthday of Our Lord

> For unto you is born this day in
> the city of David, a Saviour,
> which is Christ the Lord.
> LUKE 2:11

NOHEA
Loveliness

> I will praise thee; for I am
> fearfully and wonderfully made.
> PSALM 139:14

NOKOMIS
Moon Daughter

> Let your light so shine . . . that
> they may see your good works,
> and glorify your Father which is
> in heaven.
> MATTHEW 5:16

NOLAND
Noble and Famous

> Wait on the Lord, and keep his
> way, and he shall exalt thee to
> inherit the land.
> PSALM 37:34

NONA
The Ninth

> I would seek unto God, . . .
> which doeth great and . . .
> marvellous things without
> number.
> JOB 5:8–9

NONOY
Little Boy

> Thy hands have made me and
> fashioned me: give me
> understanding that I may learn
> thy commandments.
> PSALM 119:73

NORA
Shining with Honor

> They that be wise shall shine as
> the brightness of the firmament.
> DANIEL 12:3

NORALEE
Shining with Honor

> Strength and honour are her
> clothing; . . . a woman that
> feareth the Lord, she shall be
> praised.
> PROVERBS 31:25, 30

NORBERTA
Divine Brightness

> *They that be wise shall shine as the brightness of the firmament; . . . as the stars for ever and ever.*
> DANIEL 12:3

NORDAHL
Divine Image

> *For whom he did foreknow, he also did predestinate to be conformed to the image his son.*
> ROMANS 8:29

NOREEN
Shining with Honor

> *They that be wise shall shine as the brightness of the firmament; . . . as the stars for ever and ever.*
> DANIEL 12:3

NOREENE
Shining with Honor

> *They that be wise shall shine as the brightness of the firmament; . . . as the stars for ever and ever.*
> DANIEL 12:3

NORENE
Shining with Honor

> *Strength and honour are her clothing; and she shall rejoice in time to come.*
> PROVERBS 31:25

NORIS
The Guardian

> *He that dwelleth in the secret place of the most High shall abide under [His] shadow.*
> PSALM 91:1

NORLEY
Brilliant Hero

> *Thou hast also given me the shield of thy salvation: . . . thy right hand hath holden me up.*
> PSALM 18:35

NORM-ANNE
Example of Grace

> *The Lord will give grace and glory: no good thing will he withhold from those that walk uprightly.*
> PSALM 84:11

NORMA
The Example

> *Be thou an example of the believers, in word, in conversation.*
> 1 TIMOTHY 4:12

NORMAN
Man of Strength

> *Be strong and of a good courage; . . . for the Lord thy God is with thee.*
> JOSHUA 1:9

NORRELL
Divine Strength

> *In God is my salvation and my glory, the rock of my strength.*
> PSALM 62:7

NORRIS
The Guardian

> *Humble yourselves therefore under the mighty hand of God, that he may exalt you.*
> 1 PETER 5:6

NORTHA
From the North

> Thy word is a lamp unto my
> feet, and a light unto my path.
> PSALM 119:105

NORTON
From the North Town

> I will walk before the Lord in
> the land of the living.
> PSALM 116:9

NORVA
Divine Strength

> The Lord is my rock, . . . my
> fortress, and my deliverer; my
> God, my strength.
> PSALM 18:2

NORVELLE
Divine Strength

> In God is my salvation and my
> glory, the rock of my strength.
> PSALM 62:7

NORWOOD
Guardian

> Be strong in the Lord, and in the
> power of his might.
> EPHESIANS 6:10

NOUNOC
Messenger

> How beautiful are the feet of
> them that preach the gospel of
> peace.
> ROMANS 10:15

French

NOVA
Radiant One

> They that be wise shall shine as
> the brightness of the firmament;
> . . . as the stars for ever and ever.
> DANIEL 12:3

NOVELLA
Christmas Child

> Unto you is born this day in the
> city of David a Saviour, which is
> Christ the Lord.
> LUKE 2:11

NOWELL
Birthday of Our Lord

> Unto you is born this day in the
> city of David a Saviour, which is
> Christ.
> LUKE 2:11

NOYLE
From the High Mountain

> They that trust in the Lord shall
> be as mount Zion, which cannot
> be removed.
> PSALM 125:1

NUALA
Fair Shoulders

> Cast thy burden upon the Lord,
> and he shall sustain thee.
> PSALM 55:22

NUBIA
A Cloud

> Thy mercy, O Lord, is in the
> heavens; and thy faithfulness
> reacheth unto the clouds.
> PSALM 36:5

NUNZIO
Bearer of News

> As it is written, "How beautiful
> are the feet of them that preach
> the gospel."
> ROMANS 10:15

NURISHA
One of Light

> Let your light so shine before
> men, that they may see your
> good works and glorify your
> Father which is in heaven.
> MATTHEW 5:16

NYANDI
New and Strong One

> The Lord is my rock, . . . my
> fortress, and my deliverer; my
> God, my strength.
> PSALM 18:2
>
> Teutonic

NYASANU
An Imperial Ordinance

> Preserve me, O God: for in thee
> do I put my trust.
> PSALM 16:1

NYLAND
Young at Heart

> I will praise thee; for I am
> fearfully and wonderfully
> made: marvellous are thy
> works.
> PSALM 139:14

NYLENE
Of the Nest

> He that dwelleth in the secret
> place of the most High shall
> abide under the shadow of the
> Almighty.
> PSALM 91:1

NYOKA
Tiller of the Soil

> And whatsoever ye do, do it
> heartily, as to the Lord, . . . for
> ye serve the Lord Christ.
> COLOSSIANS 3:23–24

NYONA
Sweetness and Pleasantness

> I will bless the Lord at all times:
> his praise shall continually be
> in my mouth.
> PSALM 34:1

NYSSA
One of Purity

> The commandment of the Lord
> is pure, enlightening the eyes.
> PSALM 19:8

OAKIE
One of Strength

> *God is my salvation and my glory: the rock of my strength, . . . my refuge, is in God.*
> PSALM 62:7

OAMON
Faithful

> *They that wait upon the Lord shall renew their strength; they shall mount up with wings as eagles.*
> ISAIAH 40:31

OB
Servant Of The Lord

> *Thy hands have made me and fashioned me: give me understanding, that I may learn thy commandments.*
> PSALM 119:73

OBADIAH
Servant of the Lord

> *I am thy servant; give me understanding, that I may know thy testimonies.*
> PSALM 119:125

OBEDIAH
Serving Jehovah

> *I am thy servant; give me understanding, that I may know thy testimonies.*
> PSALM 119:125

OBELEA
Pillar of Strength

> *The Lord is my rock, . . . my fortress, and my deliverer; my God, my strength, in whom I will trust.*
> PSALM 18:2

OBELIA
Of Great Strength

> *Thou hast . . . given me the shield of thy salvation: . . . thy gentleness hath made me great.*
> PSALM 18:35

Greek

OBERA
Brilliant and Illustrious One

> *Make you perfect in every good work to do his will, working in you that which is wellpleasing.*
> HEBREWS 13:21

OBERIA
Brilliant and Illustrious One

> *The God of peace, . . . Make you perfect in . . . good work to do his will, working in you.*
> HEBREW 13:20–21

OBET
One of Radiance

> *They that be wise shall shine as the brightness of the firmament; . . . as the stars for ever and ever.*
> DANIEL 12:3

German

O

OBIE
Servant of the Lord

> *Thy hands have made me and fashioned me: give me understanding, that I may learn thy commandments.*
> PSALM 119:73

OCE
Divine Power

> *The Lord is my rock, . . . my fortress, and my deliverer; my God, my strength, in whom I will trust.*
> PSALM 18:2

OCIA
Divine Power

> *The Lord is my rock, . . . my fortress, and my deliverer; my God, my strength, in whom I will trust.*
> PSALM 18:2

OCIE
New Seed

> *For the seed shall be prosperous; the vine shall give her fruit, and the ground shall give her increase.*
> ZECHARIAH 8:12

OCTAVIA
The Eighth

> *I would seek unto God, . . . which doeth great and marvellous things without number.*
> JOB 5:8–9

Latin

OCTOBER
Special Child

> *Which doeth great things and unsearchable; marvellous things without number.*
> JOB 5:9

ODAS
Diligent to Listen

> *My hands . . . will I lift up unto thy commandmants, which I have loved.*
> PSALM 119:48

ODDIS   *also* OTTIS
Diligently Hearkening

> *Hearken diligently unto me, . . . Incline your ear, . . . hear, and your soul shall live.*
> ISAIAH 55:2–3

ODEAN
Champion of Heroes

> *Thou hast . . . given me the shield of thy salvation: and.thy right hand hath holden me up.*
> PSALM 18:35

ODEDE
Noble and Prosperous

> *The Lord thy God shall bless thee in all thine increase, and in all the works of thine hands.*
> DEUTERONOMY 16:15

ODELL
Of Noble Rank

> *But ye are a chosen generation, a royal priesthood, . . . that ye should show forth the praises of him who hath called you.*
> 1 PETER 2:9

ODELLE
Of Noble Rank

> Ye are a chosen generation, a
> royal priesthood, . . . show forth
> the praises of him who hath
> called you.
> 1 PETER 2:9

ODEN
Prosperous One

> The Lord thy God shall bless
> thee in all thine increase, and in
> all the works of thine hands.
> DEUTERONOMY 16:15

ODENE
From the Peaceful Valley

> The Lord is my shepherd; I shall
> not want. He maketh me to lie
> down in green pastures: he
> leadeth me beside the still
> waters.
> PSALM 23:1–2

ODESSA
One of Wisdom

> The Lord giveth wisdom: out of
> his mouth cometh knowledge
> and understanding.
> PROVERBS 2:6

ODEST
One of Wisdom

> For the Lord giveth wisdom: out
> of his mouth cometh knowledge
> and understanding.
> PROVERBS 2:6

ODETTA
I Will Praise God

> I will praise thee, O Lord, with
> my whole heart; . . . I will be
> glad and rejoice in thee: I will
> sing praise to thy name.
> PSALM 9:1–2

ODETTE
The Nobly Rich

> I will sing unto the Lord,
> because he hath dealt
> bountifully with me.
> PSALM 13:6

ODIE
Noble and Prosperous One

> I will sing unto the Lord,
> because he hath dealt
> bountifully with me.
> PSALM 13:6

ODIS   *also* OTTIS
Diligently Listening

> Incline your ear, . . . hear, and
> your soul shall live; and I will
> make an everlasting covenant
> with you.
> ISAIAH 55:3

ODMAN
Rich Protector

> In God is my salvation and my
> Glory: the rock of my strength,
> and my refuge, is in God.
> PSALM 62:7

O

ODUS
Diligent to Listen

> *I will praise thee: for thou hast heard me, and art become my salvation.*
> PSALM 118:21

ODYSSEY
One of Wisdom

> *For the Lord giveth wisdom: out of his mouth cometh knowledge and understanding.*
> PROVERBS 2:6

OGBURN
Peaceful Dweller

> *The Lord is my shepherd; . . . He maketh me to lie down in green pastures.*
> PSALM 23:1–2

OGRETTA
A Precious Pearl

> *I will praise thee; for I am fearfully and wonderfully made: . . . How precious also are thy thoughts unto me, O God!*
> PSALM 139:14, 17

OKALANI
Of the Heavens

> *O Lord our Lord, how excellent is thy name in all the earth! who hast set thy glory above the heavens.*
> PSALM 8:1

OKEY
Divine Spearman

> *Take unto you the whole armour of God, . . . take the helmet of salvation, and the sword of the spirit, which is the word of God.*
> EPHESIANS 6:13, 17

OKEYNA
Praised of the Hills

> *They that trust in the Lord shall be as mount Zion, which cannot be removed, but abideth for ever.*
> PSALM 125:1

OKIE
From the Oak Tree Meadow

> *The Lord is my shepherd: I shall not want. He maketh me to lie down in green pastures: he leadeth me beside the still waters.*
> PSALM 23:1–2

OLA
One of Peace

> *The Lord will give strength unto his people; the Lord will bless his people with peace.*
> PSALM 29:11

OLAF
Peace

> *Thou wilt keep him in pefect peace, whose mind is stayed on thee: because he trusteth in thee.*
> ISAIAH 26:3

Teutonic

OLAMAE
One of Peace

> The Lord will give strength unto
> his people; the Lord will bless
> his people with peace.
> PSALM 29:11

OLAN
One of Peace

> The Lord will give strength unto
> his people; the Lord will bless
> his people with peace.
> PSALM 29:11

OLAND
A Blessed Heritage

> Come, ye blessed of my Father,
> inherit the kingdom prepared
> for you from the foundation of
> the world.
> MATTHEW 25:34

OLANTHA
One of Truth

> The statutes of the Lord are
> right, rejoicing the heart: the
> commandment of the Lord is
> pure, enlightening the eyes.
> PSALM 19:8

OLAY
One of Peace

> The Lord will give strength unto
> his people; the Lord will bless
> his people with peace.
> PSALM 29:11

OLE
One of Peace

> The Lord will give strength unto
> his people; the Lord will bless
> his people with peace.
> PSALM 29:11

OLEAN
Blessed Heritage

> Come, ye blessed of my Father,
> inherit the kingdom prepared
> for you from the foundation of
> the world.
> MATTHEW 25:34

OLEDA
One of Gladness

> I will praise thee, O Lord, with
> my whole heart; . . . I will be
> glad and rejoice in thee: I will
> sing praise to thy name.
> PSALM 9:1–2

OLEETA
One of Gladness

> I will praise thee, O Lord, with
> my whole heart; . . . I will be
> glad and rejoice in thee: I will
> sing praise to thy name.
> PSALM 9:1–2

OLEG
The Holy

> I will praise thee, O Lord, with
> my whole heart; . . . I will be
> glad and rejoice in thee: I will
> sing praise to thy name.
> PSALM 9:1–2

O

OLEN
A Blessed Heritage

> *Come, ye blessed of my Father,*
> *inherit the kingdom prepared*
> *for you from the foundation of*
> *the world.*
> MATTHEW 25:34

OLIN
The Inheritance of Christ

> *Ye shall receive the reward of*
> *the inheritance: for ye serve the*
> *Lord Christ.*
> COLOSSIANS 3:24

OLIVE
Lady of Peace

> *Be perfect, be of good comfort,*
> *be of one mind, live in peace;*
> *and the God of love and peace*
> *shall be with you.*
> 2 CORINTHIANS 13:11

OLIVER
Man of Peace

> *Be perfect, be of good comfort,*
> *be of one mind, live in peace;*
> *and the God of love and peace*
> *shall be with you.*
> 2 CORINTHIANS 13:11

OLIVETTE
One Of Peace

> *The Lord will give strength unto*
> *his people; the Lord will bless*
> *his people with peace.*
> PSALM 29:11

OLIVIA
One of Peace

> *Be perfect, be of good comfort,*
> *be of one mind, live in peace;*
> *and the God of love and peace*
> *shall be with you.*
> 2 CORINTHIANS 13:11

OLSON
Son of Peace

> *Be perfect, be of good comfort,*
> *be of one mind, live in peace;*
> *and the God of love and peace*
> *shall be with you.*
> 2 CORINTHIANS 13:11

OLUFEMI
God Loves Me

> *God sent his only begotten Son*
> *into the world, that we might*
> *live through him.*
> 1 JOHN 4:9

OLUREMI
God Comforts Me

> *Come unto me, all ye that*
> *labour and are heavy laden,*
> *and I will give you rest.*
> MATTHEW 11:28

OMA
Orator

> *I will bless the Lord at all times:*
> *his praise shall continually be*
> *in my mouth.*
> PSALM 34:1

OMAH
Most High One

> *The Lord is great, . . . Honour*
> *and majesty are before him.*
> PSALM 96:4, 6

OMARYUMAR
One of High Esteem

> Thou hast . . . given me the
> shield of thy salvation: . . . thy
> gentleness hath made me great.
> PSALM 18:35

OMEGA
The Last

> I am Alpha and Omega, the
> beginning and the ending, saith
> the Lord.
> REVELATION 1:8

OMRA
The Praised One

> The Lord is great, . . . Honour
> and majesty are before him.
> PSALM 96:4, 6

ONA
One of Strength

> In God is my salvation and my
> glory: the rock of my strength,
> and my refuge, is in God.
> PSALM 62:7

ONAONA
Soft, Sweet Fragrance

> I will praise thee; I am fearfully,
> and wonderfully made:
> marvellous are thy works.
> PSALM 139:14, 17

ONAS
Peaceful Friend

> The Lord will give strength unto
> his people; the Lord will bless
> his people with peace.
> PSALM 29:11

ONDRAY
Brave and Courageous

> God . . . girdeth me with strength,
> and maketh my way perfect.
> PSALM 18:32

ONEDA
The Expected One

> Wait on the Lord: be of good
> courage, and he shall strengthen
> thine heart: wait, I say, on the Lord.
> PSALM 27:14

ONEIDA
The Expected One

> Wait on the Lord: be of good
> courage, and he shall strengthen
> thine heart: wait, I say, on the
> Lord.
> PSALM 27:14

ONEZIMA
One Jewel

> I will praise thee; I am fearfully,
> wonderfully made: marvellous
> are thy works.
> PSALM 139:14

ONNIE
One of Peace and Truth

> Let us therefore follow after the
> things which make for peace,
> and things wherewith one may
> edify another.
> ROMANS 14:19

ONNIG
Prosperous One

> I will sing unto the Lord, . . . he
> hath dealt bountifully with me.
> PSALM 13:6

Teutonic

ONOFRE
Champion of the Peace

> The Lord will give strength, the Lord will bless his people with peace.
> PSALM 29:11

ONWUNTA
Good Prophet

> I will give . . . thanks in the great congregation: . . . [and] praise thee among much people. . . . all the day long.
> PSALM 35:18, 28
>
> North American Indian

OPAL
A Precious Gem

> I will praise thee; for I am fearfully and wonderfully made: marvellous are thy works.
> PSALM 139:14

OPHELIA
Wise One

> The Lord giveth wisdom: out of his mouth cometh knowledge and understanding.
> PROVERBS 2:6
>
> Greek

OPIE
A Quiet Spirit

> Thou wilt keep him in perfect peace, whose mind is stayed on thee: because he trusteth in thee.
> ISAIAH 26:3

OPPIE
A Quiet Spirit

> Thou wilt keep him in perfect peace, whose mind is stayed on thee: because he trusteth in thee.
> ISAIAH 26:3

OPRAH
Fawn

> Thy hands have made me . . . give me understanding that I may learn thy commandments.
> PSALM 119:73
>
> Greek

OPTIMUM
The Most Favorable

> Remember me, O Lord, with the favour . . . thou bearest unto thy people.
> PSALM 106:4

OPUARLEODIA
Precious

> I will praise thee; for I am fearfully and wonderfully made: . . . How precious also are thy thoughts unto me, O God!
> PSALM 139:14, 17

OPUS
Song of Joy

> Thou wilt show me the path of life: in thy presence is fulness of joy; at thy right hand are pleasures for evermore.
> PSALM 16:11

ORA
Pray

> *Continue in prayer, and watch in the same with thanksgiving.*
> COLOSSIANS 4:2

ORA LEE
Prayer and Peace

> *Continue in prayer, and watch in the same with thanksgiving; . . . the Lord will bless his people with peace.*
> COLOSSIANS 4:2; PSALM 29:11

ORAL
Consecration of Speech

> *I will be glad and rejoice in thee: I will sing praise to thy name.*
> PSALM 9:2

ORANETTA
Symbol of Strength and Purity

> *The statutes of the Lord are right . . . the commandment of the Lord is pure.*
> PSALM 19:8

ORBIE
Celestial Path

> *Thy word is a lamp unto my feet, and a light unto my path.*
> PSALM 119:105

ORBIT
Celestial Path

> *Thy word is a lamp unto my feet, and a light unto my path.*
> PSALM 119:105

ORDEAN
Spear Strength

> *Take unto you the . . . shield of faith, . . . the helmet of salvation, and the sword of the Spirit.*
> EPHESIANS 6:13, 16–17

ORELIA
Heavenly Messenger

> *How beautiful are the feet of them that . . . bring glad tidings of good things!*
> ROMANS 10:15

OREST
Prayer

> *I will praise thee: for thou hast heard me, and art become my salvation.*
> PSALM 118:21

ORESTES
Prayer

> *I will praise thee: for thou hast heard me, and art become my salvation.*
> PSALM 118:21

ORETA
Little Honored One

> *The Lord is great, . . . Honour and majesty are before him.*
> PSALM 96:4, 6

ORI
One of Light

> *Let your light so shine before men, that they may see your good works, and glorify your Father which is in heaven.*
> MATTHEW 5:16

O

ORIENT
Radiant One

> They that be wise shall shine as
> the brightness of the firmament;
> . . . as the stars for ever and ever.
> DANIEL 12:3

ORIN
Radiant Light

> Let your light so shine before
> men, that they may see your
> good works, and glorify your
> Father which is in heaven.
> MATTHEW 5:16

ORIOLE
The Golden One

> I will praise thee; for I am
> fearfully and wonderfully made:
> marvellous are thy works.
> PSALM 139:14

ORIS
God's Gift

> Every good gift and every
> perfect gift is from above, and
> cometh down from the Father.
> JAMES 1:17

ORIVILLE   also ORVILLE
Of the Rich Town

> The blessing of the Lord, it
> maketh rich, and he addeth no
> sorrow with it.
> PROVERBS 10:22

ORLANDO
Fame of the Land

> Wait on the Lord, and keep his
> way, and he shall exalt thee to
> inherit the land.
> PSALM 37:34

ORLENE
Fame of the Land

> Wait on the Lord, and keep his
> way, and he shall exalt thee to
> inherit the land.
> PSALM 37:34

ORMOND
Guardian Protector

> Be strong and of a good
> courage; . . . for the Lord thy
> God is with thee.
> JOSHUA 1:9

ORNAN
Make Ye to Shine

> They that be wise shall shine as
> the brightness of the firmament;
> . . . as the stars for ever and ever.
> DANIEL 12:3

ORPHA
Lively Maiden

> My lips shall greatly rejoice
> when I sing unto thee; and my
> soul, which thou hast redeemed.
> PSALM 71:23

ORRIN
Arise with Light and Radiance

> They that be wise shall shine as
> the brightness of the firmament;
> . . . as the stars for ever and ever.
> DANIEL 12:3

ORVILLE
Prosperous One

> The blessing of the Lord, it
> maketh rich, and he addeth no
> sorrow with it.
> PROVERBS 10:22

OSAMA
From the Sun's Splendor

> Let them that love him be as the sun when he goeth forth in his might.
> JUDGES 5:31

OSANNA
Strength of the Lord

> Thou hast . . . given me the shield of thy salvation: . . . thy gentleness hath made me great.
> PSALM 18:35

OSBERT
Of Godly Brightness

> Let your light so shine before men that they may see your good works, and glorify your Father which is in heaven.
> MATTHEW 5:16

OSBORNE
Divinely Strong

> The Lord is my light and my salvation; whom shall I fear? the Lord is the strength of my life; of whom shall I be afraid?
> PSALM 27:1

OSCAR
Bounding Warrior

> Fight the good fight of faith, lay hold on eternal life, whereunto thou art also called.
> 1 TIMOTHY 6:12

OSIE
Having Power from God

> The Lord is my rock, . . . my fortress, and my deliverer; . . . my strength, in whom I will trust.
> PSALM 18:2

OSMOND
Divine Protector

> He that dwelleth in the secret place of the most high shall abide under the shadow of the Almighty.
> PSALM 91:1

OSWALD
Divine Power

> They that wait upon the Lord shall renew their strength.
> ISAIAH 40:31

OTHA
One of Elevation

> God . . . hath raised us up together, and made us sit together in heavenly places.
> EPHESIANS 2:4, 6

OTTILIA
I Will Praise God

> Every day will I bless thee; I will praise thy name for ever and ever.
> PSALM 145:2

OTTILIE
I Will Praise God

> Every day will I bless thee; I will praise thy name for ever and ever.
> PSALM 145:2

O

OTTIS
Diligently Hearkening

> Hearken diligently unto me, . . .
> Incline your ear . . . hear . . .
> I will make an everlasting
> covenant with you.
> ISAIAH 55:2–3

OUIDA
Victorious Love

> This is the victory that
> overcometh the world, even our
> faith.
> 1 JOHN 5:4

OWEN
Mighty Warrior

> Give unto the Lord, O ye mighty,
> give unto the Lord glory and
> strength.
> PSALM 29:1

OZELLE
Having Power from God

> It is God that girdeth me with
> strength, and maketh my way
> perfect.
> PSALM 18:32

P

PABLITA
Little One

> I am but a little child: . . . Give
> . . . thy servant an
> understanding heart.
> 1 KINGS 3:7, 9

PABLO
Humble

> God . . . girdeth me with
> strength, . . . thy gentleness hath
> made me great.
> PSALM 18:32, 35

PADDY
Noble One

> But ye are a chosen generation,
> a royal priesthood, . . . that ye
> should show forth the praises of
> him who hath called you.
> 1 PETER 2:9

PADGETT
One Who Serves

> Serve the Lord with gladness:
> come before his presence with
> singing.
> PSALM 100:2

PAGE
Servant of the Lord

> Thy hands have made me and
> fashioned me: give me
> understanding, that I may learn
> thy commandments.
> PSALM 119:73

PAIGE
Servant of the Lord

> My mouth shall show forth thy
> righteousness and thy salvation
> all the day.
> PSALM 71:15

PAISLEY
From the Quiet Meadow

> The Lord is my shepherd; . . . He
> maketh me to lie down in green
> pastures.
> PSALM 23:1–2

PAL
Symbol of Victory

> My sons, be not now negligent:
> for the Lord hath chosen you to
> stand before him, to serve him.
> 2 CHRONICLES 29:11

PALANI
One of Freedom

> Stand fast therefore in the
> liberty wherewith Christ hath
> made us free.
> GALATIANS 5:1

PALMA
Pilgrim

> Sojourn in this land, and I will
> be with thee, and will bless thee.
> GENESIS 26:3

PALMER
A Palm Bearer

> I will praise thee; for I am
> fearfully and wonderfully
> made: marvellous are thy
> works.
> PSALM 139:14

P

PALMIRA
Palm-bearing Pilgrim

> *I will instruct thee and teach thee in the way which thou shalt go.*
> PSALM 32:8

PAM
Sweet as Honey

> *Pleasant words are as an honeycomb, sweet to the soul, and health to the bones.*
> PROVERBS 16:24

PAMELA
Sweet as Honey

> *Pleasant words are as an honeycomb, sweet to the soul, and health to the bones.*
> PROVERBS 16:24

PANAGIOTA
Crowned One

> *When the chief Shepherd shall appear, ye shall receive a crown of glory that fadeth not away.*
> 1 PETER 5:4
> Greek

PANCHITO
One of Freedom

> *Stand fast therefore in the liberty wherewith Christ hath made us free.*
> GALATIANS 5:1

PANCHO
One of Freedom

> *Stand fast therefore in the liberty wherewith Christ hath made us free.*
> GALATIANS 5:1

PANDA
All Gifted

> *Having then gifts differing according to the grace that is given to us, . . . let us prophesy according to the proportion of faith.*
> ROMANS 12:6

PANDORA
All Gifted

> *Having then gifts differing according to the grace that is given to us, . . . let us prophesy according to the proportion of faith.*
> ROMANS 12:6

PANNELL
Famed Patriot

> *Wait on the Lord, and keep his way, he shall exalt thee to inherit the land.*
> PSALM 37:34

PANOLA
Gifted One of Peace

> *Thou wilt keep him in perfect peace, whose mind is stayed on thee: . . . because he trusteth in thee.*
> ISAIAH 26:3

PANSY
Beautiful Thoughts

> *Whatsoever things are true, . . . honest, . . . just, . . . pure, . . . lovely, . . . of good report; if there be any virtue, [and] praise, think on these things.*
> PHILIPPIANS 4:8

PANSYE
Beautiful Thoughts

> Let the words of my mouth, and
> the meditation of my heart, be
> acceptable in thy sight, O Lord,
> my strength, and my redeemer.
> PSALM 19:14

PANTHEA
In God's Honor

> The Lord is great, . . . strength
> and beauty are in his sanctuary.
> PSALM 96:4, 6

PAOLA
Little One

> I will praise thee; for I am
> fearfully and wonderfully made:
> marvellous are thy works.
> PSALM 139:14

PAOLO
Humble One

> I will praise thee; for I am
> fearfully and wonderfully made:
> marvellous are thy works.
> PSALM 139:14

PAPATHANASIOU
Noble Warrior

> Fight the good fight of faith, lay
> hold on eternal life, whereunto
> thou art also called.
> 1 TIMOTHY 6:12
>
> Greek

PARADISE
Heavenly Abode

> In my Father's house are many
> mansions: . . . I go to prepare a
> place for you. . . . that where I
> am, there ye may be.
> JOHN 14:2–3

PARIS
Peaceful Dweller

> The Lord is my shepherd; I shall
> not want. He maketh me to lie
> down in green pastures.
> PSALM 23:1–2

PARISH
From the Church

> I will praise thee; for I am
> fearfully and wonderfully made:
> marvellous are thy works.
> PSALM 139:14

PARK
Guardian

> He that dwelleth in the secret
> place of the most High shall
> abide under the shadow of the
> Almighty.
> PSALM 91:1

PARKER
Keeper of the Park

> And whatsoever ye do, do it
> heartily, as to the Lord, . . . for
> ye serve the Lord Christ.
> COLOSSIANS 3:23–24

PARMILEE
Holy Land Pilgrim

> I will instruct thee and teach thee
> in the way which thou shalt go.
> PSALM 32:8

PARR
Guardian Protector

> *He that dwelleth in the secret place of the most High shall abide under the shadow of the Almighty.*
> PSALM 91:1

PARRY
Guardian Protector

> *He that dewelleth in the secret place of the most High shall abide under the shadow of the Almighty.*
> PSALM 91:1

PARSONS
A Clergyman

> *I will give thee thanks in the great congregation: I will praise thee among much people.*
> PSALM 35:18

PASCAL
Of the Passover

> *For even Christ our passover is sacrificed for us: . . . let us keep the feast, . . . with the unleavened bread of sincerity and truth.*
> 1 CORINTHIANS 5:7–8

PASQUALE
Child of the Passover

> *For even Christ our passover is sacrificed for us: . . . let us keep the feast, . . . with the unleavened bread of sincerity and truth.*
> 1 CORINTHIANS 5:7–8

PAT
Full of Honor

> *In God is my salvation and glory: the rock of my strength, . . . my refuge, is in God.*
> PSALM 62:7

PATIENCE
Quiet Endurance and Patient

> *The trying of your faith worketh patience. . . . let patience have her perfect work.*
> JAMES 1:3–4

PATON
One of Nobility

> *Thou hast also given me the shield of thy salvation: and thy right hand hath holden me up, . . . thy gentleness hath made me great.*
> PSALM 18:35

PATRICE
Noble One

> *But ye are a chosen generation, a royal priesthood, . . . show forth the praises of him who hath called you.*
> 1 PETER 2:9

PATRICIA
Noble One

> *But ye are a chosen generation, a royal priesthood, . . . show forth the praises of him who hath called you.*
> 1 PETER 2:9

PATRICK
Noble One

> Ye are a chosen generation, a
> royal priesthood, . . . show forth
> the praises of him who hath
> called you.
> 1 PETER 2:9

PATSY
Full Of Honor

> In God is my salvation and my
> glory: the rock of my strength,
> and my refuge, is in God.
> PSALM 62:7

PATTERSON
One of Nobility

> But ye are a chosen generation,
> a royal priesthood, . . . show
> forth the praises of him who
> hath called you.
> 1 PETER 2:9

PATTI
Full of Honor

> In God is my salvation and my
> glory: the rock of my strength,
> and my refuge, is in God.
> PSALM 62:7

PATTY
Full of Honor

> In God is my salvation and my
> glory: the rock of my strength,
> and my refuge, is in God.
> PSALM 62:7

PAUL
Little One

> O Lord my God, thou hast made
> thy servant . . . I am but a little
> child: . . . Give . . . thy servant
> an understanding heart.
> 1 KINGS 3:7, 9

PAULENE
Little One

> O Lord my God, thou hast made
> thy servant . . . I am but a little
> child: . . . Give . . . thy servant
> an understanding heart.
> 1 KINGS 3:7, 9

PAXTON
One of Peace

> The Lord will give strength unto
> his people; the Lord will bless
> his people with peace.
> PSALM 29:11

PAYNE
Country Man

> The Lord is my rock, . . . my
> fortress, and my deliverer; my
> God, my strength, in whom I
> will trust.
> PSALM 18:2

PAYTON
Noble One

> But ye are a chosen generation,
> a royal priesthood, . . . ye should
> show forth the praises of him
> who hath called you.
> 1 PETER 2:9

P

PEACE
Quiet and Calm
> The Lord will give strength unto
> his people; the Lord will bless
> his people with peace.
> PSALM 29:11

PEACH
Precious Endearment
> Thy hands have made me and
> fashioned me: give me
> understanding, that I may learn
> thy commandments.
> PSALM 119:73

PEACHIE
Beloved One
> Beloved, let us love one another:
> for love is of God; and every one
> that loveth is born of God, and
> knoweth God.
> 1 JOHN 4:7

PEACHY
Beloved One
> Beloved, let us love one another:
> for love is of God; and every one
> that loveth is born of God, and
> knoweth God.
> 1 JOHN 4:7

PEARCE
Rock of Strength
> In God is my salvation and my
> glory: the rock of my strength,
> and my refuge, is in God.
> PSALM 62:7

PEARL
Pure Heart
> Blessed are the pure in heart:
> for they shall see God.
> MATTHEW 5:8

PEARLANN
Precious Pearl of Grace
> The Lord will give grace and
> glory: no good thing will he
> withhold from them that walk
> uprightly.
> PSALM 84:11

PEBBLE
A Small Stone
> The stone which the builders
> refused is become the head stone
> of the corner.
> PSALM 118:22

PEBBLES
Cherished
> That ye might walk worthy of
> the Lord . . . being fruitful in
> every good work.
> COLOSSIANS 1:10

PECOLA
Sounding for the Lord
> I will praise thee, O Lord, with
> my whole heart; . . . I will be
> glad and rejoice in thee.
> PSALM 9:1–2

PEDRO
Rock of Strength
> In God is my salvation and my
> glory: the rock of my strength,
> and my refuge, is in God.
> PSALM 62:7

PEE WEE
Cherished One

> *Beloved, let us love one another: for love is of God; and every one that loveth is born of God, and knoweth God.*
> 1 JOHN 4:7

PEG
A Pearl

> *I will praise thee; for I am fearfully and wonderfully made: . . . How precious . . . are thy thoughts unto me, O God!*
> PSALM 139:14, 17

PEGGY
A Pearl

> *I will praise thee; for I am fearfully and wonderfully made: . . . How precious . . . are thy thoughts unto me, O God!*
> PSALM 139:14, 17

PEILING
Supreme Being

> *For the Lord is great, and greatly to be praised: . . . Honour and majesty are before him.*
> PSALM 96:4, 6

PELA
Beautiful One

> *I will praise thee; for I am fearfully and wonderfully made: . . . How precious also are thy thoughts unto me, O God!*
> PSALM 139:14, 17

PELE
A Precious Pearl

> *I will praise thee; for I am fearfully and wonderfully made: . . . How precious . . . are thy thoughts unto me, O God!*
> PSALM 139:14, 17

PELEKILA
Of Long Life

> *The gift of God is eternal life through Jesus Christ our Lord.*
> ROMANS 6:23

PELLEGRINO
A Pilgrim

> *Thy word is a lamp unto my feet, and a light unto my path.*
> PSALM 119:105

PENELOPE
Creative

> *Give her of the fruit of her hands; and let her own works praise her in the gates.*
> PROVERBS 31:31

PENNIE
Creative Spirit

> *Create in me a clean heart, O God and renew a right spirit within me.*
> PSALM 51:10

PENNY
Creative Spirit

> *Give her of the fruit of her hands; and let her own works praise her in the gates.*
> PROVERBS 31:31

P

PENTICA
The Fifth Child

I would seek unto God, . . .
which doeth great things . . .
without number.
JOB 5:8–9

PEPPER
Spirited one

Thou wilt show me the path of
life: . . . at thy right hand there
are pleasures for evermore.
PSALM 16:11

PERCIVAL
One of Great Understanding

For the Lord giveth wisdom: out
of his mouth cometh knowledge
and understanding.
PROVERBS 2:6

PERCY
Stalwart

But thou, O man of God, . . .
follow after righteousness,
godliness, faith, love, patience,
meekness.
1 TIMOTHY 6:11

PERIWINKLE
Emblem of Love

In this was manifested the love
of God toward us, . . . that we
might live through him.
1 JOHN 4:9

PERLA
A Pearl

I will praise thee; for I am
fearfully and wonderfully made.
PSALM 139:14

PERPETUA
The Everlasting

In thy presence is fullness of joy;
at thy right hand there are
pleasures for evermore.
PSALM 16:11

PERRIN
Rock of Strength

In God is my salvation and my
glory: the rock of my strength,
. . . my refuge, is in God.
PSALM 62:7

PERRY
Strong in Spirit

Wait on the Lord: . . . and he
shall strengthen thine heart:
wait, I say, on the Lord.
PSALM 27:14

PERSIA
Famed Hero

Thou hast also given me the
shield of thy salvation: . . . thy
gentleness hath made me great.
PSALM 18:35

PERSIS
Woman

Strength and honour are her
clothing; and she shall rejoice in
time to come.
PROVERBS 31:25

PETA
Rock of Strength

In God is my salvation and my
glory: the rock of my strength,
and my refuge, is in God.
PSALM 62:7

PETAL
One of Youth

> For thou art my hope, O Lord
> God: thou art my trust from my
> youth.
> PSALM 71:5

PETE
Rock of Strength

> In God is my salvation and my
> glory: the rock of my strength,
> and my refuge, is in God.
> PSALM 62:7

PETER
Rock of Strength

> In God is my salvation and my
> glory: the rock of my strength,
> and my refuge, is in God.
> PSALM 62:7

PETERSON
Rock of Strength

> In God is my salvation and my
> glory: the rock of my strength,
> and my refuge, is in God.
> PSALM 62:7

PETRILLA
Rock of Strength

> In God is my salvation and my
> glory: the rock of my strength,
> and my refuge, is in God.
> PSALM 62:7

PETRONELLA
A Little Stone

> In God is my salvation and my
> glory: the rock of my strength,
> and my refuge, is in God.
> PSALM 62:7

Greek

PHEADRE
Bright and Shining

> They that be wise shall shine as
> the brightness of the firmament;
> . . . as the stars for ever and ever.
> DANIEL 12:3

PHENORIS
Upright One

> Be glad in the Lord, and rejoice,
> ye righteous: and shout for joy,
> all ye that are upright in heart.
> PSALM 32:11

PHEOBE
The Wise, Shining One

> Let your light so shine before
> men, that they may see your
> good works, and glorify your
> Father which is in heaven.
> MATTHEW 5:16

PHEOBIA
Wise Shining One

> Let your light so shine before
> men, that they may see your
> good works, and glorify your
> Father which is in heaven.
> MATTHEW 5:16

PHEROBY
Gift of God

> Every good gift and every
> perfect gift is from above, and
> cometh down from the father of
> lights.
> JAMES 1:17

P

PHIL
Lover of Power and Majesty
> *The voice of the Lord is powerful; the voice of the Lord is full of majesty.*
> PSALM 29:4

PHILEMON
Of Loving Mind
> *Beloved, let us love one another: for love is of God; and every one that loveth is born of God, and knoweth God.*
> 1 JOHN 4:7

PHILIP
Lover of Power and Majesty
> *The voice of the Lord is powerful; the voice of the Lord is full of majesty.*
> PSALM 29:4

PHILIPPA
Lover of Power and Majesty
> *The voice of the Lord is powerful; the voice of the Lord is full of majesty.*
> PSALM 29:4

PHILLIP
Lover of Power and Majesty
> *The voice of the Lord is powerful; the voice of the Lord is full of majesty.*
> PSALM 29:4

PHILOMENA
Of Loving Mind
> *Beloved, let us love one another: for love is of God; and every one that loveth is born of God, and knoweth God.*
> 1 JOHN 5:7

PHOEBE JO
He Increaseth Thy Light
> *That ye might walk worthy of the Lord unto all pleasing, being fruitful in every good work.*
> COLOSSIANS 1:10

PHYLISS
Young and Strong
> *For thou art my hope, O Lord God: thou art my trust from my youth.*
> PSALM 71:5

PHYLLIS
Young and Strong
> *For thou art my hope, O Lord God: thou art my trust from my youth.*
> PSALM 71:5

PIERCE
Rock of Strength
> *In God is my salvation and my glory: the rock of my strength, and my refuge, is in God.*
> PSALM 62:7

PILAN
Supreme One of Honor
> *For the Lord is great and greatly to be praised: . . . Honour and majesty are before him.*
> PSALM 96:4, 6

PILAR
Heavenly Sorrow

> The Lord is nigh unto them that
> are of a broken heart; and
> saveth such as be of a contrite
> spirit.
> PSALM 34:18

PINCKNEY
Traveler

> Thy word is a lamp unto my
> feet, and a light unto my path.
> PSALM 119:105

PINKY
Consecration of Speech

> I will praise thee, O Lord, with
> my whole heart; . . . I will sing
> praise to thy name.
> PSALM 9:1–2

PIPER
Player of the Pipe

> I will praise the name of God
> with a song, and will magnify
> him with thanksgiving.
> PSALM 69:30

PIUS
Devout Reverence for God

> I will meditate in thy precepts,
> and have respect unto thy ways.
> . . . I will not forget thy word.
> PSALM 119:15–16

PIXIE
Little Spirit

> The fruit of the Spirit is love,
> joy, peace, longsuffering,
> gentleness, goodness, faith, . . .
> against such there is no law.
> GALATIANS 5:22–23

POET
Expressing Beauty

> Blessed are they that keep his
> testimonies, . . . I will praise
> thee with uprightness of heart.
> PSALM 119:2, 7

POLLY
Living Fragrance

> I love the Lord, . . . he hath
> heard my voice and my
> supplications.
> PSALM 116:1

POLLYANNA
Living Fragrance and Grace

> The Lord will give grace and
> glory: no good thing will he
> withhold from them that walk
> uprightly.
> PSALM 84:11

POMEROY
Apple of the King

> I will praise thee; for I am
> fearfully and wonderfully
> made: marvellous are thy
> works.
> PSALM 139:14

PONCIE
The Fifth Son

> I would seek unto God, . . .
> which doeth . . . marvellous
> things without number.
> JOB 5:8–9

PONI
The Good and Blessed

> Blessed are they that keep his
> testimonies, and that seek him
> with the whole heart.
> PSALM 119:2

POPPY
Fragrance of the Poppy

> All things were made by him;
> and without him was not
> anything made that was made.
> JOHN 1:3

PORTER
Keeper of the Gate

> And whatsoever ye do, do it
> heartily, as to the Lord, and not
> unto men; . . . for ye serve the
> Lord Christ.
> COLOSSIANS 3:23–24

PORTIA
An Offering

> Let the words of my mouth, and
> the meditation of my heart, be
> acceptable in thy sight, . . . my
> strength, and my redeemer.
> PSALM 19:14

POSEY
Little Flower

> I will praise thee; for I am
> fearfully and wonderfully
> made: marvellous are thy
> works.
> PSALM 139:14

POST
Majestic Position

> For the Lord is great, and
> greatly to be praised: . . .
> Honour and majesty are before
> him.
> PSALM 96:4, 6

PRECIOUS
Beloved One

> Beloved, let us love one another:
> for love is of God; and every one
> that loveth is born of God, and
> knoweth God.
> 1 JOHN 4:7

PRENTICE
Prudent Learner

> Give instruction to a wise man,
> and he will be yet wiser: teach a
> just man, and he will increase in
> learning.
> PROVERBS 9:9

PRESLEY
Peaceful Dweller

> The Lord is my Shepherd; I
> shall not want. He maketh me to
> lie down in green pastures.
> PSALM 23:1–2

PRESTON
Serving the Lord

> He that doeth the will of God
> abideth forever.
> 1 JOHN 2:17

PRICE
One of Value

> Let it be the hidden man of the heart, . . . a meek and quiet spirit, which is in the sight of God of great price.
> 1 PETER 3:4

PRIMAVERA
First in Excellence

> Thou hast also given me the shield of thy salvation: . . . thy gentleness hath made me great.
> PSALM 18:35

PRIMROSE
First Rose

> Thy hands have made me and fashioned me: give me understanding, that I may learn thy commandments.
> PSALM 119:73

PRINCE
One of Royalty

> Ye have not chosen me, but I have chosen you, and ordained you, that you may go and bring forth fruit.
> JOHN 15:16

PRINCESS
Of Noble Rank

> Ye are a chosen generation, a royal priesthood, . . . show forth the praises of him who hath called you.
> 1 PETER 2:9

PRISCILLA
Of Long Life

> The gift of God is eternal life through Jesus Christ our Lord.
> ROMANS 6:23

PROCTOR
Of Good Counsel

> The Lord is the portion of mine inheritance . . . I will bless the Lord, who hath given me counsel.
> PSALM 16:5, 7

PROMISE
A Pledge

> Confess with thy mouth the Lord Jesus, . . . believe . . . that God hath raised him from the dead, [and] thou shalt be saved.
> ROMANS 10:9

PROSPER
The Successful and Prosperous

> I have trusted in thy mercy; my heart shall rejoice in thy salvation.
> PSALM 13:5

PRUITT
The Valiant Man

> I press toward the mark for the prize of the high calling of God in Christ Jesus.
> PHILIPPIANS 3:14

PRYOR
Superior Leader

> As for God, his way is perfect; . . . God is my strength and power.
> 2 SAMUEL 22:31, 33

PSALM
Sacred Song

> *I will praise thee, O Lord, with*
> *my whole heart; . . . I will sing*
> *praise to thy name.*
> PSALM 9:1–2

PUALANI
Heavenly Flower

> *I will praise thee; for I am*
> *fearfully and wonderfully made.*
> PSALM 139:14

PULA
My Strength Is in God

> *In God is my salvation and my*
> *glory: the rock of my strength,*
> *and my refuge is in God.*
> PSALM 62:7

PURIFICATION
Pure and Clean

> *The statutes of the Lord are*
> *right, . . . the commandment of*
> *the Lord is pure, enlightening*
> *the eyes.*
> PSALM 19:8

Q

QIANA
One of Wisdom and Grace

> For the Lord giveth wisdom: out
> of his mouth cometh knowledge
> and understanding.
> PROVERBS 2:6

QIAVA
One of Victory and Grace

> The Lord will give grace and
> glory: no good thing will he
> withold from them that walk
> uprightly.
> PSALM 84:11

QUADE
Rock of Strength

> In God is my salvation and my
> glory: the rock of my strength,
> and my refuge, is in God.
> PSALM 62:7

QUAN
God Is Gracious

> But thou, O Lord, art a God full
> of compassion, and gracious,
> longsuffering, and plenteous in
> mercy and truth.
> PSALM 86:15

QUANDRA
Companion and Friend

> Ye are my friends, if ye do
> whatsoever I command you.
> JOHN 15:14

QUANINA
Noble and Royal

> Thy hands have made me and
> fashioned me: give me
> understanding, that I may learn
> thy commandments.
> PSALM 119:73

QUASI
Special Child

> I will praise thee; for I am
> fearfully and wonderfully made.
> PSALM 139:14

QUAWN
Royal and Noble Companion

> Ye are my friends, if ye do
> whatsoever I command you.
> JOHN 15:14

QUAY
Rock of Stength

> The Lord is my rock, . . . my
> fortress, . . . my deliverer; my
> God, my strength, in whom I
> will trust.
> PSALM 18:2

QUE
Beloved One

> Beloved, let us love one another:
> for love is of God; and every one
> that loveth is born of God, and
> knoweth God.
> 1 JOHN 4:7

QUEENA
One of Royalty

> Ye have not chosen me, but I
> have chosen you, and ordained
> you, that you may go and bring
> forth fruit.
> JOHN 15:16

QUEENELLA
One of Sovereign Nobility

> But ye are a chosen generation,
> a royal priesthood, . . . show
> forth the praises of him who
> hath called you.
> 1 PETER 2:9

QUEENIE
One of Sovereign Nobility

> But ye are a chosen generation,
> a royal priesthood, . . . show
> forth the praises of him who
> hath called you.
> 1 PETER 2:9

QUENTIN
The Fifth

> I would seek unto God, . . .
> which doeth great things and
> . . . marvellous things without
> number.
> JOB 5:8–9

QUEST
Seeking One of Truth

> Ask, and it shall be given you;
> seek, and ye shall find; knock,
> and it shall be opened unto you.
> MATTHEW 7:7

QUEWANNCOII
Beloved One

> The Lord hath appeared of old
> unto me, saying, Yea, I have
> loved thee with an everlasting
> love.
> JEREMIAH 31:3

Spanish/
North American Indian

QUEZELLA
Zealous and Ardent

> And whatsoever ye do in word
> or deed, do all in the name of
> the Lord Jesus, giving thanks to
> God.
> COLOSSIANS 3:17

QUI
Victorious Love

> For whatsoever is born of God
> overcometh the world: and this
> is the victory that overcometh
> the world, even our faith.
> 1 JOHN 5:4

QUILLA
Shield Bearer

> Take unto you the whole armour
> of God, . . . taking the shield of
> faith, . . . the helmet of
> salvation, and the sword of the
> Spirit, which is the word of God.
> EPHESIANS 6:13, 16–17

QUINCY
Wise One

> For the Lord giveth wisdom: out
> of his mouth cometh knowledge
> and understanding.
> PROVERBS 2:6

QUINETTE
The Wise

> *For the Lord giveth wisdom: out of his mouth cometh knowledge and understanding.*
> PROVERBS 2:6

QUINN
One of Wisdom

> *For the Lord giveth wisdom: out of his mouth cometh knowledge and understanding.*
> PROVERBS 2:6

QUINT
The Fifth

> *I would seek unto God, and unto God would I commit my cause: Which doeth great things . . . without number.*
> JOB 5:8–9

QUNION
One of Wisdom

> *For the Lord giveth wisdom: out of his mouth cometh knowledge and understanding.*
> PROVERBS 2:6

QURAN
Beloved One

> *Beloved, let us love one another: for love is of God; and every one that loveth is born of God, and knoweth God.*
> 1 JOHN 4:7

R

RABIA
Guardian Protector

> He that dwelleth in the secret
> place of the most High shall
> abide under the shadow of the
> Almighty.
> PSALM 91:1

RACHEAL
Gentle Lamb

> The Lord God will come with
> strong hand, . . . He shall feed
> his flock like a shepherd: he
> shall gather the lambs with his
> arm, and carry them.
> ISAIAH 40:10–11

RACHEL
Lamb

> The Lord God will come with
> strong hand, . . . He shall feed
> his flock like a shepherd: he
> shall gather the lambs with his
> arm, and carry them.
> ISAIAH 40:10–11

RACINE
Enthusiastic and Ardent

> I press toward the mark for the
> prize of the high calling of God
> in Christ Jesus.
> PHILIPPIANS 3:14

RACQUEL
A Lamb

> The Lord God will come with
> strong hand, . . . He shall feed
> his flock like a shepherd: he
> shall gather the lambs with his
> arm, and carry them.
> ISAIAH 40:10–11

RADA
Bright Counsel

> I will bless the Lord, who hath
> given me counsel . . . because he
> is at my right hand, I shall not
> be moved.
> PSALM 16:7–8

RADAEL
God Hath Healed

> Wait on the Lord: be of good
> courage, and he shall strengthen
> thine heart.
> PSALM 27:14

RADD
Bright Counsel

> I will bless the Lord, who hath
> given me counsel: my reins also
> instruct me in the night seasons.
> PSALM 16:7

RADENA
Radiant One

> They that be wise shall shine as
> the brightness of the firmament;
> . . . as the stars for ever and ever.
> DANIEL 12:3

RADFORD
From the Red Ford

> Thy word is a lamp unto my
> feet, and a light unto my path.
> PSALM 119:105

RADIANT
One of Radiance

> They that be wise shall shine as
> the brightness of the firmament;
> . . . as the stars for ever and ever.
> DANIEL 12:3

R

RADOMIR
Love of Peace

> The Lord will give strength unto
> his people; the Lord will bless
> his people with peace.
> PSALM 29:11

RADONNA
Counselor with Honor

> I will bless the Lord, who hath
> given me counsel.
> PSALM 16:7

RAEANN
Little Lamb of Grace

> The Lord God will come with
> strong hand, . . . He shall feed
> his flock like a shepherd: he
> shall gather the lambs with his
> arm, and carry them.
> ISAIAH 40:10–11

RAEANNA
Lamb of Grace

> The Lord will give grace and
> glory: no good thing will he
> withold from them that walk
> uprightly.
> PSALM 84:11

RAEANNE
Little Lamb of Grace

> The Lord God will come with
> strong hand, . . . He shall feed
> his flock like a shepherd: he
> shall gather the lambs with his
> arm, and carry them.
> ISAIAH 40:10–11

RAEL
Wise Protection

> He that dwelleth in the secret
> place of the most High shall
> abide under the shadow of the
> Almighty.
> PSALM 91:1

RAFAELA
God Hath Healed

> For thou, Lord, art good, and
> ready to forgive; and plenteous
> in mercy unto all them that call
> upon thee.
> PSALM 86:5

RAFIK
Companion

> But it is good for me to draw
> near to God: . . . that I may
> declare all thy works.
> PSALM 73:28

RAFORD
Wise Protector

> In God is my salvation and my
> glory: . . . my refuge: is in God.
> PSALM 62:7

RAGEN
A Strong Leader

> Thou hast . . . given me the
> shield of thy salvation: . . . thy
> gentleness hath me great.
> PSALM 18:35

RAGENHILD
One of Strength

> In God is my salvation and my
> glory: the rock of my strength,
> and my refuge, is in God.
> PSALM 62:7

RAGNHILD
One of Strength

> In God is my salvation and my
> glory: the rock of my strength,
> and my refuge, is in God.
> PSALM 62:7

Teutonic

RAHNEIDA
The Royal One

> Ye have not chosen me, but I
> have chosen you, and ordained
> you that ye should go and bring
> forth fruit.
> JOHN 15:16

Polynesian

RAIMO
Wise Protection

> The Lord is my rock, . . . my
> fortress, and my deliverer; my
> God, my strength, in whom I
> will trust.
> PSALM 18:2

RAINEE
Royal and Noble

> Ye are a chosen generation, a
> royal priesthood, . . . show forth
> the praises of him who hath
> called you.
> 1 PETER 2:9

RAINER
One of Royalty

> Ye have not chosen me, but I
> have chosen you, and ordained
> you, that ye should go and bring
> forth fruit.
> JOHN 15:16

RAISA
Beautiful Rose

> Thy hands have made me and
> fashioned me: give me
> understanding, that I may learn
> thy commandments.
> PSALM 119:73

Yiddish

RAJAI
Warrior for the Faith

> Fight the good fight of faith, lay
> hold on eternal life, whereunto
> thou art also called.
> 1 TIMOTHY 6:12

RAJEEV
Priceless Gift

> For by grace are ye saved
> through faith; and that not of
> yourselves: it is the gift of God.
> EPHESIANS 2:8

Arabic

RAJHON
Compassionate Ruler

> He that ruleth over men must be
> just, ruling in the fear of God.
> 2 SAMUEL 23:3

R

RALEIGH
Ruler with Strength

> *The Lord is my light and my
> salvation; whom shall I fear?
> the Lord is the strength of my
> life; of whom shall I be afraid?*
> PSALM 27:1

Teutonic

RALENE
Radiant One

> *Let your light so shine before
> men, that they may see your
> good works, and glorify your
> Father which is in heaven.*
> MATTHEW 5:16

RALF
The Protector

> *There shall not any man be able
> to stand before thee all the days
> of thy life: . . . I will be with
> thee: I will not fail thee, nor
> forsake thee.*
> JOSHUA 1:5

RALPH
The Protector

> *There shall not any man be able
> to stand before thee all the days
> of thy life: . . . I will be with
> thee: I will not fail thee, nor
> forsake thee.*
> JOSHUA 1:5

RAMAEL
Of Wise Protecton

> *He that dwelleth in the secret
> place of the most High shall
> abide under the shadow of the
> Almighty.*
> PSALM 91:1

RAMAH
A High Place

> *The Lord is my rock, . . . my
> fortress, and my deliverer; my
> God, my strength, in whom I
> will trust.*
> PSALM 18:2

Hebrew

RAMALE
Whom Jehovah Adorned

> *God is my salvation; I will trust
> and not be afraid: for the Lord
> JEHOVAH is my strength and
> my song.*
> ISAIAH 12:2

RAMBERTO
Bright Counsel

> *I have set the Lord always
> before me: because he is at my
> right hand, I shall not be
> moved.*
> PSALM 16:8

German

RAMBO
Strong and Handsome

> *The Lord is my rock, . . . my
> fortress, and my deliverer; my
> God, my strength, in whom I
> will trust.*
> PSALM 18:2

RAMEY
Guardian Protector

> *The Lord is my rock, . . . my
> fortress, and my deliverer; my
> God, my strength, in whom I
> will trust.*
> PSALM 18:2

French

RAMIAH
Jehovah Hath Exalted

> *For the Lord is great, and greatly to be praised: . . . Honour and majesty are before him.*
> PSALM 96:4, 6

RAMIRO
Wise Protector

> *Trust ye in the Lord for ever: for in the Lord JEHOVAH is everlasting strength.*
> ISAIAH 26:4

RAMON
Wise Protector

> *The Lord is my strength and my shield; my heart trusted in him, and I am helped.*
> PSALM 28:7

RAMONA   *also* ROMONA
Wise Protector

> *The Lord is my strength and my shield; my heart trusted in him, and I am helped.*
> PSALM 28:7

Spanish

RAMOTH
Exalted One

> *Bless the Lord, O my soul. O Lord my God, . . . thou art clothed with honour and majesty.*
> PSALM 104:1

RAMSAY
The Strong

> *The Lord is my light and my salvation; whom shall I fear? the Lord is the strength of my life; of whom shall I be afraid?*
> PSALM 27:1

RAMSEY
The Strong

> *The Lord is my light and my salvation; whom shall I fear? the Lord is the strength of my life; of whom shall I be afraid?*
> PSALM 27:1

RANAE
Royal Nobility

> *But ye are a chosen generation, a royal priesthood, . . . show forth the praises of him who hath called you.*
> 1 PETER 2:9

RANATA
Song and Joy

> *I will praise thee, O Lord, with my whole heart; . . . I will sing praise to thy name.*
> PSALM 9:1–2

RANDAHL
Loyal Protector

> *The Lord is my rock, . . . my fortress, and my deliverer; my God, my strength, in whom I will trust.*
> PSALM 18:2

R

RANDAL
Protector

> In God is my salvation and my glory: the rock of my strength, and my refuge, is in God.
> PSALM 62:7

RANDOLPH
Protector

> Be strong and of good courage; be not afraid, . . . for the Lord thy God is with thee whithersoever thou goest.
> JOSHUA 1:9

RANDY
The Protector

> I will be with thee: I will not fail thee, nor forsake thee.
> JOSHUA 1:5

RANFORD
Strong Shield

> The Lord is my strength and my shield; my heart trusted in him, . . . my heart greatly rejoiceth; and with . . . song will I praise him.
> PSALM 28:7

RANITA
Firm of Purpose

> I will bless the Lord, who hath given me counsel: . . . I have set the Lord always before me: . . . I shall not be moved.
> PSALM 16:7–8

RANNER
Of Strong Counsel

> I have set the Lord always before me: because he is at my right hand, I shall not be moved.
> PSALM 16:8

RANOTA
Joy and Song

> I will praise thee, O Lord, with my whole heart; . . . I will be glad and rejoice in thee: I sing praise to thy name.
> PSALM 9:1–2

RANSAY
Royal Nobility

> But ye are a chosen generation, a royal priesthood, . . . show forth the praises of him who hath called you.
> 1 PETER 2:9

RANSFORD
Brave Courage

> He that dwelleth in the secret place of the most High shall abide under the shadow of the Almighty.
> PSALM 91:1

RANSOM
Redemption

> All we like sheep have gone astray; we turned every one to his own way; and the Lord hath laid on him the inquity of us all.
> ISAIAH 53:6

RAOUL
Wise Counsel

> I will bless the Lord, who hath given me counsel: . . . I have set the Lord always before me.
> PSALM 16:7–8

RAPHAEL
God Hath Healed

> Wait on the Lord: be of good courage, and he shall strengthen thine heart.
> PSALM 27:14

RAQUEL
Gentle Lamb

> The fruit of the Spirit is love, joy, peace, longsuffering, gentleness, goodness, faith.
> GALATIANS 5:22

RASA
Dew

> Therefore God give thee of the dew of heaven.
> GENESIS 27:28

RASHAAD
Noble Ruler

> Thou hast also given me the shield of thy salvation: and thy gentleness hath made me great.
> 2 SAMUEL 22:36

RASHAE
Majestic One

> Thou art my God, and I will praise thee: thou art my God, I will exalt thee.
> PSALM 118:28

RASHEED
Ruler with Power

> As for God, his way is perfect; . . . God is my strength, power: and he maketh my way perfect.
> 2 SAMUEL 22:31, 33
>
> Arabic

RASHEENA
Noble Gracious Gift

> Every good gift and every perfect gift is from above, and cometh down from the Father of lights.
> JAMES 1:17

RASHIDA
A Mighty Ruler

> Thou hast also given me the shield of thy salvation: . . . and thy gentleness hath made me great.
> PSALM 18:35

RASHIDI
Of Good Counsel

> I will bless the Lord, who hath given me counsel: . . . because he is at my right hand, I shall not be moved.
> PSALM 16:7–8
>
> Arabic

RASHIEM
A Noble Name

> A good name is rather to be chosen than great riches, and loving favour rather than silver and gold.
> PROVERBS 22:1

R

RASHMI
Royal Love

> Beloved, let us love one another:
> for love is of God; and every one
> that loveth is born of God, and
> knoweth God.
> 1 JOHN 4:7

RASHON
The Secret of the Lord

> He that dwelleth in the secret
> place of the most High shall
> abide under the shadow of the
> Almighty.
> PSALM 91:1

RASMUS
Worthy to be Loved

> Beloved, let us love one another:
> for love is of God.
> 1 JOHN 4:7

RATHE
Advice and Counsel

> I will bless the Lord, who hath
> given me counsel: my reins also
> instruct me in the night seasons.
> PSALM 16:7

RAUDEL
Helper Commander

> In God is my salvation and my
> glory: the rock of my strength,
> and my refuge, is in God.
> PSALM 62:7

RAUL
The Protector

> Be strong and of a good courage;
> ... the Lord thy God is with thee
> whithersoever thou goest.
> JOSHUA 1:9

RAUN
Mighty Ruler

> Thou hast ... given me the
> shield of thy salvation: and thy
> right hand hath holden me up,
> ... thy gentleness hath made me
> great.
> PSALM 18:35

RAUNIE
A Strong Ruler

> Thou hast ... given me the
> shield of thy salvation: and thy
> right hand hath holden me up,
> ... thy gentleness hath made me
> great.
> PSALM 18:35

RAUSTIN
Shield and Protector

> He that dwelleth in the secret
> place of the most High shall
> abide under the shadow of the
> Almighty.
> PSALM 91:1

RAVEENA
Radiant One

> They that be wise shall shine as
> the brightness of the firmament;
> ... as the stars for ever and ever.
> DANIEL 12:3

RAVEL
God's Healing

> Heal me, O Lord, and I shall be
> healed; save me, and I shall be
> saved: for thou art my praise.
> JEREMIAH 17:14

RAVEN
Prosperous and Good

> *I will sing unto the Lord,*
> *because he hath dealt*
> *bountifully with me.*
> PSALM 13:6

RAVIN
Prosperous and Good

> *I will sing unto the Lord,*
> *because he hath dealt*
> *bountifully with me.*
> PSALM 13:6

RAWLE
From the Peaceful Meadow

> *The Lord is my shepherd; I shall*
> *not want. He maketh me to lie*
> *down in green pastures.*
> PSALM 23:1

RAWLINS
Shield and Protector

> *I will say of the Lord, He is my*
> *refuge and my fortress: my God;*
> *in him will I trust.*
> PSALM 91:2

RAWN
From the Strong Fort

> *The Lord is my rock, . . . my*
> *fortress, and my deliverer; my*
> *God, my strength, in whom I*
> *will trust.*
> PSALM 18:2

RAY
Wise One

> *I have taught thee in the way of*
> *wisdom; I have led thee in right*
> *paths.*
> PROVERBS 4:11

RAYANN
The Lamb of Grace

> *He giveth power to the faint;*
> *and to those that have no might*
> *he increaseth strength.*
> ISAIAH 40:29

RAYANNE   *also* RAEANNE
Lamb of Grace

> *The Lord God will come with*
> *strong hand, . . . He shall feed*
> *his flock like a shepherd: he*
> *shall gather the lambs with his*
> *arm, and carry them.*
> ISAIAH 40:10–11

RAYBURN
Peaceful Dweller

> *Thou wilt keep him in perfect*
> *peace, whose mind is stayed on*
> *thee, because he trusteth in thee.*
> ISAIAH 26:3

RAYDONNA
Lamb of Honor

> *The Lord God will come with*
> *strong hand, . . . He shall feed*
> *his flock like a shepherd: he*
> *shall gather the lambs with his*
> *arm, and carry them.*
> ISAIAH 40:10–11

RAYETTA
Lamb of Radiant Light

> *The Lord God will come with*
> *strong hand, . . . He shall feed*
> *his flock like a shepherd: he*
> *shall gather the lambs with his*
> *arm, and carry them.*
> ISAIAH 40:10–11

R

RAYHFEAL
God Hath Healed

*For thou, Lord, art good, and
ready to forgive; plenteous in
mercy unto all them that call
upon thee.*
PSALM 86:5

RAYLETTA
Wise Protector

*The Lord is my light and my
salvation; whom shall I fear?
the Lord is the strength of my
life; of whom shall I be afraid?*
PSALM 27:1

RAYMA
Wise Protection

*The Lord is my light and my
salvation; whom shall I fear?
the Lord is the strength of my
life; of whom shall I be afraid?*
PSALM 27:1

RAYMELL
Wise Protection

*In God is my salvation and my
glory: the rock of my strength,
and my refuge, is in God.*
PSALM 62:7

RAYMOND
Wise Protector

*When wisdom entereth into
thine heart, and knowledge is
pleasant ... Discretion shall
preserve thee.*
PROVERBS 2:10–11

RAYNALDO
A Strong Ruler

*God is my strength and power:
and he maketh my way perfect.*
2 SAMUEL 22:33

RAYNARD
Strong Counsel

*I will bless the Lord, who hath
given me counsel: ... I have set
the Lord always before me: ... I
shall not be moved.*
PSALM 16:7–8

RAYNE
Warrior for the Faith

*Fight the good fight of faith, lay
hold on eternal life, whereunto
thou art also called.*
1 TIMOTHY 6:12

RAYNELDA
Wise and Strong Protector

*The Lord is my light and my
salvation; whom shall I fear?
the Lord is the strength of my
life; of whom shall I be afraid?*
PSALM 27:1

RAYNER
Strong Counsel

*I will bless the Lord, who hath
given me counsel: ... I have set
the Lord always before me: ... I
shall not be moved.*
PSALM 16:7–8

RAYNOR
Strong Counsel

> I will bless the Lord, who hath given me counsel: . . . I have set the Lord always before me: . . . I shall not be moved.
> PSALM 16:7–8

RAZIEL
God's Divine Secret

> The secret of the Lord is with them that fear him; and he will show them his covenant.
> PSALM 25:14
>
> Hebrew-Aramaic

REAGAN
One of Royalty

> Ye have not chosen me, but I have chosen you, and ordained you, that ye should go and bring forth fruit.
> JOHN 15:16

REAH
The Lord Hath Seen

> Thou art my hiding place and my shield: I hope in thy word.
> PSALM 119:114

REALITY
One of Truth

> Thou art near, O Lord; and all thy commandments are truth.
> PSALM 119:151

REANNE
Lamb of Grace

> The Lord God shall come with strong hand, . . . He shall feed his flock like a shepherd: he shall gather the lambs with his arm, and carry them.
> ISAIAH 40:10–11

REATHA
A Pearl

> I will praise thee; for I am fearfully and wonderfully made: marvellous are thy works.
> PSALM 139:14

REATHIA
A Pearl

> I will praise thee; for I am fearfully and wonderfully made: marvellous are thy works.
> PSALM 139:14

REAVER
To Gain Strength

> In God is my salvation and my glory: the rock of my strength, and my refuge, is in God.
> PSALM 62:7

REAVES
One Who Leads

> As for God, his way is perfect; . . . God is my strength and power: and he maketh my way perfect.
> 2 SAMUEL 22:31, 33

R

REBA
Earnest Devotee

> It is good for me to draw near to
> God: I have put my trust in the
> Lord God.
> PSALM 73:28

REBBEKAH
Steadfast and Faithful

> Be ye stedfast, unmovable,
> always abounding in the work
> of the Lord.
> 1 CORINTHIANS 15:58

REBECCA
Steadfast and Faithful

> Be ye stedfast, unmovable,
> always abounding in the work
> of the Lord.
> 1 CORINTHIANS 15:58

REBEKAH
Steadfast and Faithful

> Be ye stedfast, unmovable,
> always abounding in the work
> of the Lord.
> 1 CORINTHIANS 15:58

REBEL
Lively Spirit

> And whatsoever ye do, do it
> heartily, as to the Lord, and not
> unto men, for ye serve the Lord
> Christ.
> COLOSSIANS 3:23–24

RED
The Protector

> Be strong and of a good
> courage; . . . for the Lord thy
> God is with thee whithersoever
> thou goest.
> JOSHUA 1:9

REDEAIL
Redeemed

> The Lord liveth, who hath
> redeemed my soul out of all
> adversity.
> 2 SAMUEL 4:9

REDELLA
Wise Counsel

> I will instruct thee and teach thee
> in the way which thou shalt go;
> I will guide thee with mine eye.
> PSALM 32:8

REDEMPTA
Saviour

> I will praise thee: for thou hast
> heard me, and have become my
> salvation.
> PSALM 118:21

REDFORD
From the Red River Crossing

> Thy word is a lamp unto my
> feet, and a light unto my path.
> PSALM 119:105

REDMOND
Counsel and Protection

> I will bless the Lord, who hath
> given me counsel: . . . I have set
> the Lord always before me: . . . I
> shall not be moved.
> PSALM 16:7

REDRIC
Rich in Counsel

> I will bless the Lord, who hath given me counsel: . . . I have set the Lord always before me: . . . I shall not be moved.
> PSALM 16:7

REECE
Enthusiastic and Ardent

> I will praise thee, O Lord my God, with all my heart: and I will glorify thy name for evermore.
> PSALM 86:12

REED
One of Courage

> Be strong and of a good courage; . . . for the Lord thy God is with thee whithersoever thou goest.
> JOSHUA 1:9

REEFE
Leader of Strength

> In God is my salvation and my glory: the rock of my strength, and my refuge, is in God.
> PSALM 62:7

REESE
Enthusiastic and Ardent

> I will praise thee, O Lord my God, . . . and I will glorify thy name for evermore.
> PSALMS 86:12

REGAL
Noble and Brave

> I will say of the Lord, He is my refuge and my fortress: my God; in him will I trust.
> PSALM 91:2

REGAN
A Queen

> I will praise thee; for I am fearfully and wonderfully made: marvellous are thy works.
> PSALM 139:14

REGGIE
Of Mighty Power

> God is my strength and power: and he maketh my way perfect.
> 2 SAMUEL 22:33

REGINA
A Queen

> Let the words of my mouth, and the meditation of my heart, be acceptable in thy sight, O Lord.
> PSALM 19:14

REGINALD
Of Mighty Power

> God is my strength and power: and he maketh my way perfect.
> 2 SAMUEL 22:33

REGINETTE
To Reign as a Queen

> I will praise thee; for I am fearfully and wonderfully made: marvellous are thy works.
> PSALM 139:14

R

REGIS
One of Power

Thou hast also given me the shield of thy salvation: and thy right hand hath holden me up.
PSALM 18:35

REHEMA
Strong Counsel

The counsel of the Lord standeth forever, the thoughts of his hearts to all generations.
PSALM 33:11

East Africa

REHTA
Words of Wisdom

My mouth shall speak of wisdom; and the meditation of my heart shall be of understanding.
PSALM 49:3

REI
My Friend

I have taught thee in the way of wisdom; I have led thee in right paths.
PROVERBS 4:11

REID
One of Wise Protection

Thou hast also given me the shield of thy salvation; and thy right hand hath holden me up.
PSALM 18:35

REIKO
Gratitude

I will praise the Lord according to his righteousness . . . will sing praise to the name of the Lord most high.
PSALM 7:17

Japanese

REILLEY
An Ardent Spirit

I press toward the mark for the prize of the high calling of God in Christ Jesus.
PHILIPPIANS 3:14

REILLY
One of Great Strength

And he said unto me, "My grace is sufficient for thee."
2 CORINTHIANS 12:9

REINA
Of Wise Protection

Thou hast also given me the shield of thy salvation; thy right hand hath holden me up, . . . thy gentleness hath made me great.
PSALM 18:35

REINALDO
Mighty Ruler

As for God, his way is perfect; . . . God is my strength and power.
2 SAMUEL 22:31, 33

REINHARDT
Firm of Purpose

> I have set the Lord always before me: . . . he is at my right hand, I shall not be moved.
> PSALM 16:8
>
> German

REINO
Strong Counsel

> I will bless the Lord, who hath given me counsel.
> PSALM 16:7

REJ
One of Radiant Royalty

> I will go in the strength of the Lord God: I will make mention of thy righteousness.
> PSALM 71:16

REJINA
To Reign as a Queen

> I will praise thee; for I am fearfully and wonderfully made.
> PSALM 139:14

REKEM
Steadfast and One of Honor

> Therefore, my beloved brethren, be ye stedfast, unmovable, always abounding in the work of the Lord.
> 1 CORINTHIANS 15:58

RELENE
Wise Protection

> The Lord is my light and my salvation; whom shall I fear? the Lord is the strength of my life; of whom shall I be afraid?
> PSALM 27:1

RELK
Of Power and Peace

> The Lord will give strength unto his people; the Lord will bless his people with peace.
> PSALM 29:11

RELLA
The Listener

> I will praise thee: for thou hast heard me, and art become my salvation.
> PSALM 118:21

RELLAND
Noble and Wise Protection

> He that dwelleth in the secret place of the most High shall abide under the shadow of the Almighty.
> PSALM 91:1

RELLO
Fame of the Land

> Wait on the Lord, and keep his way, and he shall exalt thee to inherit the land.
> PSALM 37:34

RELMINA
Strong Counsel

> The Lord liveth; and blessed be my rock; and let the God of my salvation be exalted.
> PSALM 18:46

REMA
Devoted Words of Praise

> Let the words of my mouth, and the meditation of my heart be acceptable in thy sight, O Lord.
> PSALM 19:14

R

REME
Lifted Up to Jehovah

> This is the day which the Lord
> hath made; we will rejoice and
> be glad in it.
> PSALM 118:24

REMEMBER
Pleasant Thoughts

> Whatsoever things are true, . . .
> honest, . . . just, . . . [and] of
> good report; if there be any
> virtue, and . . . any praise, think
> on these things.
> PHILIPPIANS 4:8

REMI
Lifted Up to Jehovah

> This is the day which the Lord
> hath made; we will rejoice and
> be glad in it.
> PSALM 118:24

REMIGIO
Guardian Protector

> The Lord is my light and my
> salvation; whom shall I fear?
> the Lord is the strength of my
> life; of whom shall I be afraid?
> PSALM 27:1

REMIGIUS
Guardian Protector

> The Lord is my light and my
> salvation; whom shall I fear?
> the Lord is the strength of my
> life; of whom shall I be afraid?
> PSALM 27:1

REMINGTON
From the Raven Estate

> Thy word is a lamp unto my
> feet, and a light unto my path.
> PSALM 119:105

RENA
Born Anew

> I have longed for thy salvation,
> O Lord; and thy law is my
> delight.
> PSALM 119:174
>
> North American Indian

RENA
Messenger of Peace

> How beautiful are the feet of
> them that preach the gospel of
> peace, and bring glad tidings of
> good things!
> ROMANS 10:15
>
> Latin

RENAE
Born Anew

> I have longed for thy salvation,
> O Lord; and thy law is my
> delight.
> PSALM 119:174

RENALDO
A Strong Ruler

> God is my strength and power:
> and he maketh my way perfect.
> 2 SAMUEL 22:33

RENARD
Strong Counsel

> I will bless the Lord, who hath
> given me counsel.
> PSALM 16:7

RENATA
Born Anew

> I have longed for thy salvation,
> O Lord; and thy law is my
> delight.
> PSALM 119:174

RENDIE
Protecting One

> In God is my salvation and my
> glory: the rock of my strength,
> and my refuge, is in God.
> PSALM 62:7

RENELDA
Strong Ruler

> God is my strength and power:
> and he maketh my way perfect.
> 2 SAMUEL 22:33

RENELL
Of Mighty Power

> God is my strength and power:
> and he maketh my way perfect.
> 2 SAMUEL 22:33

RENETTA
Firm of Purpose

> I have set the Lord always
> before me: because he is at my
> right hand, I shall not be
> moved.
> PSALM 16:8

RENETTE
One of Peace

> The Lord will give strength unto
> his people; the Lord will bless
> his people with peace.
> PSALM 29:11

RENFRO
Peaceful One

> The Lord will give strength unto
> his people; the Lord will bless
> his people with peace.
> PSALM 29:11

RENIE
Strong Counsel

> I will bless the Lord, who hath
> given me counsel: . . . I have set
> the Lord always before me: . . . I
> shall not be moved.
> PSALM 16:7–8

RENITA
Firm of Purpose

> I will bless the Lord, who hath
> given me counsel: . . . I have set
> the Lord always before me: . . . I
> shall not be moved.
> PSALM 16:7–8

RENNARD
One of Firm Counsel

> I will bless the Lord, who hath
> given me counsel.
> PSALM 16:7

RENO
A Quiet Spirit

> Thou wilt show me the path of
> life: in thy presence is fulness of
> joy; at thy right hand there are
> pleasures for evermore.
> PSALM 16:11

R

RENOTTA
Firm of Purpose

*I have set the Lord always
before me: because he is at my
right hand, I shall not be moved.*
PSALM 16:8

RENSE
Laurel of Victory

*But thanks be to God, which
giveth us the victory through
our Lord Jesus Christ.*
1 CORINTHIANS 15:57

German

RENWICK
Raven's Nest

*Thy hands have made me and
fashioned me: give me
understanding, that I may learn
thy commandments.*
PSALM 119:73

Teutonic

REONA
Pure and Clean

*The statutes of the Lord are
right, rejoicing the heart: the
commandment of the Lord is
pure, enlightening the eyes.*
PSALM 19:8

REQUITTA
Precious to God

*I will praise thee; for I am
fearfully and wonderfully
made: . . . How precious also are
thy thoughts unto me, O God!*
PSALM 139:14, 17

RESSA
Diligent Harvester

*Jesus saith . . . "Lift up your eyes,
and look on the fields; for they
are white already to harvest."*
JOHN 4:34–35

RESSIE
Diligent Harvester

*Jesus saith . . . "Lift up your eyes,
and look on the fields; for they
are white already to harvest."*
JOHN 4:34–35

RESTON
Peace and Contentment

*The Lord will give strength unto
his people; the Lord will bless
his people with peace.*
PSALM 29:11

RETA
A Pearl

*I will praise thee; for I am
fearfully and wonderfully
made: . . . How precious also are
thy thoughts unto me, O God!*
PSALM 139:14, 17

RETONJA
Beyond Praise

*For the Lord is great, and greatly
to be praised: . . . Honour and
majesty are before him.*
PSALM 96:4, 6

REUBEN
Behold a Son

*For unto us a child is born, unto
us a son is given.*
ISAIAH 9:6

Hebrew

REUEL
God Is My Friend

> *Behold, God is my salvation; I will trust, and not be afraid: for the Lord JEHOVAH is my strength and my song; . . . my salvation.*
> ISAIAH 12:2
>
> Hebrew

REVALEE
One of Joy

> *Thou wilt show me the path of life: in thy presence is fulness of joy; at thy right hand there are pleasures for evermore.*
> PSALM 16:11

REVIS
Enthusiastic and Ardent

> *I will praise thee, O Lord my God, with all my heart: and I will glorify thy name for evermore.*
> PSALM 86:12

REVOE
To Gain Strength

> *The Lord is my light and my salvation; whom shall I fear? the Lord is the strength of my life; of whom shall I be afraid?*
> PSALM 27:1

REVONA
One of Victory

> *For whatsoever is born of God overcometh the world: and this is the victory that overcometh the world, even our faith.*
> 1 JOHN 5:4

REX
Man of Authority

> *The righteous also shall hold on his way, and he that hath clean hands shall be stronger.*
> JOB 17:9

REXANN
Of Royal Grace

> *For by grace are ye saved through faith; and that not of yourselves: it is the gift of God.*
> EPHESIANS 2:8

REXANNA
Of Royal Grace

> *For by grace are ye saved through faith; and that not of yourselves: it is the gift of God.*
> EPHESIANS 2:8

REXFORD
Of Royal Nobility

> *Ye are a chosen generation, a royal priesthood . . . show forth the praises of him who hath sent you.*
> 1 PETER 2:9

REYBURN
Wise Protection

> *He that dwelleth in the secret place of the most High shall abide under the shadow of the Almighty.*
> PSALM 91:1

R

REYLENE
Majestic One

> I will lift up mine eyes unto the
> hills, from whence cometh my
> help. My help cometh from the
> Lord.
> PSALM 121:1–2

REYNA
To Be Born Anew and Reign

> I have longed for thy salvation, O
> Lord; and thy law is my delight.
> PSALM 119:174

REYNALD
A Strong Leader

> But thou, O Lord, art a God full
> of compassion, and gracious,
> longsuffering, and plenteous in
> mercy and truth.
> PSALM 86:15

REYNALDO
Of Mighty Power

> Thou hast also given me the
> shield of thy salvation: and thy
> gentleness hath made me great.
> 2 SAMUEL 22:36

REYNARD
Upright

> Light is sown for the righteous,
> and gladness for the upright in
> heart.
> PSALM 97:11

REYNAUD
Firm of Purpose

> I will bless the Lord, who hath
> given me counsel: . . . I have set
> the Lord always before me: . . . I
> shall not be moved.
> PSALM 16:7–8

RHASHAD
Noble Ruler

> Thou hast also given me the
> shield of thy salvation: . . . thy
> gentleness hath made me great.
> PSALM 18:35

RHEBA
Ernest Devotee

> But it is good for me to draw
> near to God: I have put my trust
> in the Lord God.
> PSALM 73:28

RHEEM
Devoted Word of Praise

> Let the words of my mouth, and
> the meditation of my heart, be
> acceptable in thy sight.
> PSALM 19:14

RHEMA
Devoted Words of Praise

> Let the words of my mouth, and
> the meditation of my heart be
> acceptable in thy sight, . . . my
> strength, and my redeemer.
> PSALM 19:14

Greek

RHETT
Words of Wisdom

> *I will sing of the mercies of the Lord for ever: with my mouth will I make known thy faithfulness.*
> PSALM 89:1

RHETTA
Words of Wisdom

> *I will sing of the mercies of the Lord for ever: with my mouth will I make known thy faithfulness to all generations.*
> PSALM 89:1

RHIAN
Of Noble and Royal Birth

> *Ye are a chosen generation, a royal priesthood, . . . show forth the praises of him who hath called you.*
> 1 PETER 2:9

RHIANON
Joyous and Noble One

> *Ye have not chosen me, but I have chosen you, and ordained you, that ye should go and bring forth fruit.*
> JOHN 15:16

Latin

RHILES
Valiant Hero

> *Thou hast also given me the shield of thy salvation: and thy right hand hath holden me up, . . . thy gentleness hath made me great.*
> PSALM 18:35

RHOBENA
Illustrious One

> *Thou hast also given me the shield of thy salvation: and thy right hand hath holden me up, . . . thy gentleness hath made me great.*
> PSALM 18:35

RHODA
The Rose

> *Thy hands have made me and fashioned me: . . . give me understanding, that I may learn thy commandments.*
> PSALM 119:73

RHODEA
Fragrant Spirit

> *I will freely sacrifice unto thee: I will praise thy name, O Lord; for it is good.*
> PSALM 54:6

RHOMA
Fighter for the Faith

> *Fight the good fight of faith, lay hold on eternal life, whereunto thou art also called.*
> 1 TIMOTHY 6:12

RHONDA
Illustrious One

> *The God of peace make you perfect in every good work to do his will, working in you that which is well pleasing in his sight.*
> HEBREWS 13:21

R

RHU
One Hath Obtained Mercy
*All the paths of the Lord are
mercy and truth unto such as
keep his covenant and his
testimonies.*
PSALM 25:10

RHUEL
God Is His Friend
*Ye are my friends, if ye do
whatsoever I command you.*
JOHN 15:14

RHUNETTE
Compassionate One
*But thou, O Lord, art a God full
of compassion, and gracious,
longsuffering, and plenteous in
mercy and truth.*
PSALM 86:15

RIA
A Small River
*I will praise thee; for I am
fearfully and wonderfully
made: . . . How precious also are
thy thoughts unto me.*
PSALM 139:14, 17

Spanish

RICARDO
Power and Strength
*The Lord is my rock, . . . my
fortress, and my deliverer; . . .
my strength, in whom I will
trust.*
PSALM 18:2

RICH
A Mighty Ruler
*God is my strength and power:
and he maketh my way perfect.*
2 SAMUEL 22:33

RICHARD
A Mighty Ruler
*Thou hast also given me the
shield of thy salvation: and thy
right hand holden me up, . . .
thy gentleness made me great.*
PSALM 18:35

RICHEA
Mighty Ruler
*Thou hast also given me the
shield of thy salvation: and thy
right hand holden me up, . . .
thy gentleness made me great.*
PSALM 18:35

RICHELLE
Leader of Strength
*The Lord is my rock, and my
fortress, . . . my deliverer; my
God, my strength, in whom I
will trust.*
PSALM 18:2

RICHIE
One Who is Brave
*For God hath not given us the
spirit of fear, but of power, and
of love, and of a sound mind.*
2 TIMOTHY 1:7

RICHMOND
King Protector

> The Lord is my rock, and my
> fortress, . . . my deliverer; my
> God, my strength, in whom I
> will trust.
> PSALM 18:2

RICKY
Mighty Ruler

> God is my strength and power:
> and he maketh my way perfect.
> 2 SAMUEL 22:33

RIDGE
From the Mountain Crest

> I will extol thee, O Lord; for
> thou hast lifted me up, . . . Lord,
> by thy favour thou hast made
> my mountain to stand strong.
> PSALM 30:1, 7

RIDGELY
From the Mountain Crest

> I will extol thee, O Lord; for
> thou hast lifted me up, . . . Lord,
> by thy favour thou hast made
> my mountain to stand strong.
> PSALM 30:1, 7

RIDLEY
From the Meadow

> The Lord is my shepherd; I shall
> not want. He maketh me to lie
> down in green pastures.
> PSALM 23:1–2

RIEF
Ruler with Peace

> The Lord will give strength unto
> his people; the Lord will bless
> his people with peace.
> PSALM 29:11

German

RILDA
Valiant and Brave

> Be strong and of a good
> courage; be not afraid, . . . the
> Lord . . . is with thee
> whithersoever thou goest.
> JOSHUA 1:9

RILEY
One of Great Strength

> My grace is sufficient for thee:
> for my strength is made perfect
> in weakness.
> 2 CORINTHIANS 12:9

RILLA
Peaceful Brook

> The Lord is my shepherd; I shall
> not want. He maketh me to lie
> down in green pastures.
> PSALM 23:1–2

RINAH
One of Song and Joy

> The Lord is my strength and
> song, . . . he is become my
> salvation: he is my God, and . . .
> I will exalt him.
> EXODUS 15:2

Hebrew

R

RINALDA
One Who Rules with Strength

The Lord is my rock, . . . my fortress, . . . my deliverer; my God, my strength, in whom I will trust.
PSALM 18:2

RINAT
Joy and Song

I will praise thee, O Lord, with my whole heart; . . . I will be glad and rejoice in thee: I will sing praise to thy name.
PSALM 9:1–2

RINDA
The Protector

In God is my salvation and my glory: the rock of my strength, my refuge, is in God.
PSALM 62:7

RINNIE
To Be Born Again

God so loved the world, that he gave his only begotten Son, that whosoever believeth in him should not perish, but have everlasting life.
JOHN 3:16

RIO
A Stream

And he shall be like a tree planted by the rivers of water, that bringeth forth his fruit in his season.
PSALM 1:3

RIP
Illustrious One

The God of peace make you perfect in every good work to do his will, working in you that which is wellpleasing in his sight.
HEBREWS 13:21

RIPLEY
Dweller at the Meadow

The Lord is my shepherd; I shall not want. He maketh me to lie down in green pastures.
PSALM 23:1–2

RISE
Strong and Brave

The Lord is my light and my salvation; whom shall I fear? the Lord is the strength of my life; of whom shall I be afraid?
PSALM 27:1

RIT
Firm Ruler

He that ruleth over men must be just, ruling in the fear of God.
2 SAMUEL 23:3

RITA
A Pearl

I will praise thee; for I am fearfully and wonderfully made.
PSALM 139:14

RITCH
One of Power and Strength

In God is my salvation and my glory: the rock of my strength, and my refuge, is in God.
PSALM 62:7

RIVA
Steadfast and Faithful

> Therefore, my beloved brethren,
> be ye stedfast, unmovable,
> always abounding in the work
> of the Lord.
> 1 CORINTHIANS 15:58

RIVAN
River of Water

> He shall be like a tree . . .
> that bringeth forth his fruit . . .
> and whatsoever he doeth shall
> prosper.
> PSALM 1:3

RIVER
Dweller by the River

> He shall be like a tree planted
> by the river of water that
> bringeth forth his fruit in his
> season; . . . and whatsoever he
> doeth shall prosper.
> PSALM 1:3

RIVKAH
Steadfast

> Be ye stedfast, unmovable,
> always abounding in the work
> of the Lord.
> 2 CORINTHIANS 15:58
>
> Hebrew

RIVO
Steadfast and Faithful

> Be ye stedfast, unmovable,
> always abounding in the work
> of the Lord.
> 1 CORINTHIANS 15:58

ROANNE
Celebrated Grace

> For by grace are ye saved
> through faith; and that not of
> yourselves: it is the gift of God.
> EPHESIANS 2:8

ROARY
Of Strong Fame

> Thou hast also given me the
> sheild of thy salvation: . . . thy
> right hand holden me up, and
> thy gentleness made me great.
> PSALM 18:35

ROASVELL
From the Rose Field

> I will praise thee; for I am
> fearfully and wonderfully
> made: marvellous are thy
> works.
> PSALM 139:14

ROB
Illustrious One

> The God of peace, . . . Make you
> perfect in every good work to do
> his will, working in you that
> which is wellpleasing in his
> sight.
> HEBREWS 13:20–21

ROBENA
Bright in Fame

> Wait on the Lord, and keep his
> way, and he shall exalt thee to
> inherit the land.
> PSALM 37:34

R

ROBERT
Illustrious One

> The God of peace, ... make you perfect in every good work to do his will, working in you that which is wellpleasing in his sight.
> HEBREWS 13:20–21

ROBERTA
Illustrious

> The God of peace, ... make you perfect in every good work to do his will, working in you that which is wellpleasing in his sight.
> HEBREWS 13:20–21

ROBERTSON
Illustrious One

> The God of peace, ... make you perfect in every good work to do his will, working in you that which is wellpleasing in his sight.
> HEBREWS 13:20–21

ROBIN
Illustrious One

> Make you perfect in every good work to do his will, working in you that which is wellpleasing in his sight.
> HEBREWS 13:21

ROCCI
Rock of Strength

> In God is my salvation and my glory: the rock of my strength, and my refuge, is in God.
> PSALM 62:7

ROCHELLE
Little Rock

> The Lord ... is my rock.
> PSALM 92:15

ROCID
From the Strong Fortress

> The Lord is my rock, and my fortress, and my deliverer; my God, my strength, in whom I will trust.
> PSALM 18:2

ROCK
Rock of Strength

> In God is my salvation and my glory: the rock of my strength, and my refuge, is in God.
> PSALM 62:7

ROCKEFELLER
Dweller Near the Field

> Jesus saith ... "Lift up your eyes, and look on the fields; for they are white already to harvest."
> JOHN 4:34–35

ROCKFORD
Rock of Strength

> The Lord is my rock, and my fortress, ... my strength, in whom I will trust.
> PSALM 18:2

ROCKY
Pride in Strength

> I will go in the strength of the Lord God: I will make mention of thy righteousness.
> PSALM 71:16

RODCITA
Esteemed One

> And whatsoever ye do in word or deed, do all in the name of our Lord Jesus, giving thanks to God.
> COLOSSIANS 3:17

RODELLA
Rich in Fame

> Thou hast ... given me the shield of thy salvation ... thy gentleness hath made me great.
> PSALM 18:35

RODERICK
Famous Ruler

> Thou hast ... given me the shield of thy salvation: ... thy right hand hath holden me up, and thy gentleness hath made me great.
> PSALM 18:35

RODERLYN
Rich in Counsel

> The Lord is the portion of mine inheritance and of my cup: ... I will bless the Lord.
> PSALM 16:5, 7

RODGERS
Heroic Soldier

> Thou therefore endure hardness, as a good soldier of Jesus Christ.
> 2 TIMOTHY 2:3

RODNEY
One of Esteem

> There is none like him in the earth, a perfect and an upright man, one that feareth God.
> JOB 2:3

RODRICK
Rich in Counsel

> I will bless the Lord, who hath given me counsel.
> PSALM 16:7

ROENA
Well-Known Friend

> I will bless the Lord, who hath given me counsel.
> PSALM 16:7

ROGELIO
Strong in the Faith

> Fight the good fight of faith, lay hold on eternal life, whereunto thou art also called.
> 1 TIMOTHY 6:12

ROGER
Heroic Soldier

> Thou therefore endure hardness, as a good soldier of Jesus Christ.
> 2 TIMOTHY 2:3

ROHLFF
The Protector

> Be strong and of a good courage; be not afraid, neither be thou dismayed: for the Lord thy God is with thee.
> JOSHUA 1:9

ROJANN
Noble One of Grace

> The Lord will give grace and glory: no good thing will he withhold from them that walk uprightly.
> PSALM 84:11

R

ROLANDA
Fame of the Land

> Wait on the Lord, and keep his
> way, and he shall exalt thee to
> inherit the land.
> PSALM 37:34

ROLANDO
Fame of the Land

> Wait on the Lord, and keep his
> way, and he shall exalt thee to
> inherit the land.
> PSALM 37:34

ROMAGENE
Noble Pilgrim

> Thy word is a lamp unto my
> feet, and a light unto my path.
> PSALM 119:105

ROMAN
Wise Protector

> Thou hast . . . given me the shield
> of thy salvation and: . . . and thy
> gentleness hath made me great.
> PSALM 18:35

ROME
Pilgrim to Rome

> Thy word is a lamp unto my
> feet, and a light unto my path.
> PSALM 119:105

ROMONA   *also* RAMONA
Wise Protecton

> I will instruct thee and teach
> thee in the way which thou
> shalt go: I will guide thee with
> mine eye.
> PSALM 32:8

ROMULIS
Strength and Power

> Thou hast also given me the
> shield of thy salvation: . . . thy
> right hand hath holden me up,
> and thy gentleness hath made
> me great.
> PSALM 18:35

RONALD
Mighty Power

> God is my strength and power:
> and he maketh my way perfect.
> 2 SAMUEL 22:33

RONITA
Of Mighty Power

> The Lord is my rock, . . . my
> fortress, and my deliverer; my
> God, my strength, in whom I
> will trust.
> PSALM 18:2

RONSON
Powerful One

> Thou hast . . . given me the
> shield of thy salvation: . . . thy
> gentleness hath made me great.
> PSALM 18:35

ROONEY
Brave Hero

> The Lord is my light and my
> salvation; whom shall I fear?
> the Lord is the strength of my
> life; whom shall I be afraid?
> PSALM 27:1

ROOSEVELT
From the Rosefield

> *I will praise thee; for I am*
> *fearfully and wonderfully made:*
> *marvellous are thy works.*
> PSALM 139:14

ROREY
Famous Ruler

> *Thou hast also given me the*
> *shield of thy salvation: and thy*
> *gentleness hath made me great.*
> PSALM 18:35

ROSALEA
Most Beautiful Rose

> *I will praise thee; for I am*
> *fearfully and wonderfully made:*
> *marvellous are thy works.*
> PSALM 139:14

ROSALENE
Rose of Light

> *They that be wise shall shine as*
> *the brightness of the firmament;*
> *. . . as the stars for ever and ever.*
> DANIEL 12:3

ROSALIA
The Rose

> *I will praise thee; for I am*
> *fearfully and wonderfully made:*
> *marvellous are thy works.*
> PSALM 139:14

ROSALINDA
Pretty Rose

> *I will praise thee; for I am*
> *fearfully and wonderfully*
> *made: . . . How precious also are*
> *thy thoughts unto me, O God.*
> PSALM 139:14, 17

ROSAMARIA
Rose of Living Fragrance

> *I will praise thee; for I am*
> *fearfully and wonderfully made:*
> *marvellous are thy works.*
> PSALM 139:14

ROSAMUND
Rose of the World

> *Thy hands have made me and*
> *fashioned me: . . . that I may*
> *learn thy commandments.*
> PSALM 119:73

ROSCOE
One of Strength

> *The Lord is my light and my*
> *salvation; whom shall I fear?*
> *the Lord is the strength of my*
> *life; of whom shall I be afraid?*
> PSALM 27:1

ROSEANNE
Rose of Grace

> *Let your speech be always with*
> *grace, . . . that ye may know how*
> *ye ought to answer every man.*
> COLOSSIANS 4:6

ROSELIE
The Rose

> *I will praise thee; for I am*
> *fearfully and wonderfully made.*
> PSALM 139:14

ROSELLA
The Rose

> *I will praise thee; for I am*
> *fearfully and wonderfully*
> *made: marvellous are thy*
> *works.*
> PSALM 139:14

R

ROSEMARIE
Beautiful Living Fragrance

> *I will praise thee; for I am*
> *fearfully and wonderfully*
> *made: marvellous are thy*
> *works.*
> PSALM 139:14

ROSEMARY
Beautiful Living Fragrance

> *I will praise thee; for I am*
> *fearfully and wonderfully made.*
> PSALM 139:14

ROSI
Giver of Love

> *Now abideth faith, hope,*
> *charity, . . . but the greatest of*
> *these is charity.*
> 1 CORINTHIANS 13:13

ROSIE
Beautiful

> *The Lord hath made all things*
> *for himself.*
> PROVERBS 16:4

ROSITA
Beautiful Rose

> *I will praise thee; for I am*
> *fearfully and wonderfully*
> *made: . . . How precious also are*
> *thy thoughts unto me, O God!*
> PSALM 139:14, 17

ROSLYN
Beautiful Rose

> *I will praise thee; for I am*
> *fearfully and wonderfully*
> *made: marvellous are thy*
> *works.*
> PSALM 139:14

ROSS
One of Strength

> *The Lord is my light and my*
> *salvation; whom shall I fear? the*
> *Lord is the strength of my life; of*
> *whom shall I be afraid?*
> PSALM 27:1

ROSWELL
One of Strength

> *In God is my salvation and my*
> *glory: the rock of my strength,*
> *and my refuge; is in God.*
> PSALM 62:7

ROTHER
From the Strong Fortress

> *The Lord is my rock, and my*
> *fortress, and my deliverer; my*
> *God, my strength, in whom I*
> *will trust.*
> PSALM 18:2

ROURKE
Strong Ruler

> *Thou hast also given me the*
> *shield of thy salvation: . . . thy*
> *gentleness hath made me great.*
> PSALM 18:35

ROVIDA
Famous Friend

> *Ye are my friends, if ye do*
> *whatsoever I command you.*
> JOHN 15:14

ROWAN
The Famed One

> *Wait on the Lord, and keep his*
> *way, and he shall exalt thee to*
> *inherit the land.*
> PSALM 37:34

ROWENDA
Famed Friend

> Ye are my friends, if ye do
> whatsoever I command you.
> JOHN 15:14

ROXANA
Dawn of Day

> I will praise the name of God
> with a song, and will magnify
> him with thanksgiving.
> PSALM 69:30

ROXIE
Dawn of Day

> The Lord's mercies . . . are new
> every morning: great is thy
> faithfulness.
> LAMENTATIONS 3:22–23

ROYAL
The Kingly

> I will praise thee; for I am
> fearfully and wonderfully
> made: . . . How precious also are
> thy thoughts unto me.
> PSALM 139:14, 17

ROYDEN
From the King's Hill

> Who shall ascend into the hill of
> the Lord? . . . He that hath clean
> hands, and a pure heart.
> PSALM 24:3–4

ROYSE
One of Nobility

> But ye are a chosen generation,
> a royal priesthood, . . . that ye
> should show forth the praises of
> him who hath called you.
> 1 PETER 2:9

ROZEANN
Rose of Grace

> The Lord will give grace and
> glory: no good thing will he
> withhold from them that walk
> uprightly.
> PSALM 84:11

RUAIRI
Gem of Precious Quality

> I will praise thee; for I am
> fearfully and wonderfully made:
> marvellous are thy works.
> PSALM 139:14

Japanese

RUANN
Compassionate One of Grace

> But thou, O Lord, art a God full
> of compassion, and gracious,
> longsuffering, and plenteous in
> mercy and truth.
> PSALM 86:15

RUBIE   *also* RUBYE
A Precious Jewel

> I will praise thee; for I am
> fearfully and wonderfully made:
> marvellous are thy works.
> PSALM 139:14

RUBLE
Of Precious Quality

> I will praise thee; for I am
> fearfully and wonderfully made.
> PSALM 139:14

R

RUBYE
A Precious Jewel

*I will praise thee; for I am
fearfully and wonderfully made:
marvellous are thy works.*
PSALM 139:14

RUDOLPH
Bright in Fame

*I press toward the mark for the
prize of the high calling of God
in Christ Jesus.*
PHILIPPIANS 3:14

RUE
The Compassionate One

*God so loved the world, that he
gave his only begotten son, that
whosoever believeth in him
should not perish, but have
everlasting life.*
JOHN 3:16

RUEBEN
Behold a Son

*For unto us a child is born, . . . a
son is given: . . . The mighty
God, The everlasting Father,
The Prince of Peace.*
ISAIAH 9:6

RUEL
God Is His Friend

*Ye are my friends, if ye do
whatsoever I command you.*
JOHN 15:14

RUFINA
Red Haired

*I will praise thee; for I am
fearfully and wonderfully made:
marvellous are thy works.*
PSALM 139:14

RUFUS
Prosperous One

*Thou shalt meditate therein day
and night, . . . then thou shalt
have good success.*
JOSHUA 1:8

RUGBY
Strong Warrior

*Fight the good fight of faith, lay
hold on eternal life, whereunto
thou art also called.*
1 TIMOTHY 6:12

RUHAMAH
She Hath Obtained Mercy

*O give thanks unto the Lord; for
he is good: because his mercy
endureth for ever.*
PSALM 118:1

RUMIKO
Glorious Leader

*Thou hast also given me the
shield of thy salvation: and thy
gentleness hath made me great.*
2 SAMUEL 22:36

RUMYRTLE
Compassion and Victory

*For whatsoever is born of God
overcometh the world: this is the
victory that overcometh the
world, even our faith.*
1 JOHN 5:4

RUNETTE
Secret

*When thou prayest, . . . pray to
thy Father: which is in secret . . .
thy Father shall reward thee
openly.*
MATTHEW 6:6

RUNYON
Precious to God

> I will praise thee; for I am
> fearfully and wonderfully made:
> marvellous are thy works.
> PSALM 139:14

RUSH
Dwelling in Safety

> I will both lay me down in
> peace, and sleep: for thou, Lord,
> only makest me dwell in safety.
> PSALM 4:8

RUSSELL
Vigilant One

> Watch . . . for ye know neither
> the day nor the hour wherein
> the Son of man cometh.
> MATTHEW 25:13

RUSTIN
The Vigilant One

> Watch . . . for ye know neither
> the day nor the hour wherein
> the Son of man cometh.
> MATTHEW 25:13

RUSTY
Vigilant One

> Watch . . . for ye know neither
> the day nor the hour wherein
> the Son of man cometh.
> MATTHEW 25:13

RUTH
Compassionate One

> I will praise thee: for thou hast
> heard me, and art become my
> salvation.
> PSALM 118:21

RUTHANNE
Compassionate One of Grace

> The Lord will give grace and
> glory: no good thing will he
> withhold from them that walk
> uprightly.
> PSALM 84:11

RUTHERFORD
From the River Crossing

> He shall be like a tree planted
> by the river of water, that
> bringeth forth his fruit in his
> season; . . . and whatsoever he
> doeth shall prosper.
> PSALM 1:3

RYAN
Joyous King

> In thy presence is fulness of joy;
> at thy right hand . . . are
> pleasures forevermore.
> PSALM 16:11

RYDEL
Guardian Protector

> The Lord is my rock, and my
> fortress, . . . my deliverer; my
> God, my strength, in whom I
> will trust.
> PSALM 18:2

RYDER
Mounted Guardian of a Forest

> Thy word is a lamp unto my
> feet, and a light unto my path.
> PSALM 119:105

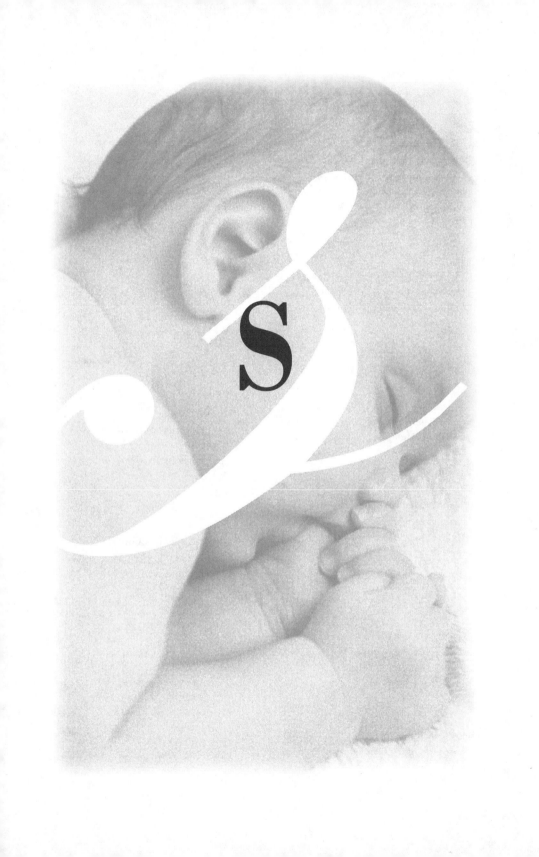

S

SAAD
One of Wisdom

> *My mouth shall speak of wisdom; and the meditation of my heart shall be of understanding.*
> PSALM 49:3

SABASTIAN
Majesty and Reverence

> *Honour and majesty are before him: strength and beauty are in his sanctuary.*
> PSALM 96:6

SABEIDA
Wise One

> *For the Lord giveth wisdom: out of his mouth cometh knowledge and understanding.*
> PROVERBS 2:6

SABIN
Honor and Esteem

> *Teach me, . . . the way of thy statutes; and I shall keep it unto the end.*
> PSALM 119:33

SABRE
To Rest

> *Come unto me, all ye that labour and are heavy laden, and I will give you rest.*
> MATTHEW 11:28

SABRINA
Daughter of the King

> *Kings' daughters were among thy honourable women.*
> PSALM 45:9

SACHA
Helper of Mankind

> *The God of peace . . . make you perfect in every good work to do his will, working in you that which is well-pleasing.*
> HEBREWS 13:21

SACHIKO
Bliss Child

> *Thy hands have made me and fashioned me. . . give me understanding that I may learn thy commandments.*
> PSALM 119:73

Japanese

SADAO
True to One's Self

> *Let the words of my mouth and the meditation of my heart, be acceptable in thy sight.*
> PSALM 19:14

Japanese

SADAYOSHI
Good and Respectful One

> *It is God that girdeth me with strength, and maketh my way perfect.*
> PSALM 18:32

Japanese

SADIE
A Princess

> *Ye are a chosen generation, a royal priesthood, . . . show forth the praises of him who hath called you.*
> 1 PETER 2:9

SAEMA
God Hath Heard

> *I have called upon thee, for thou will hear me, O God.*
> PSALM 17:6

SAFFRON
From the Quiet Meadow

> *The Lord is my shepherd; . . . He maketh me to lie down in green pastures.*
> PSALM 23:1–2

SAGA
One of Wisdom

> *For the Lord giveth wisdom: out of his mouth cometh knowledge and understanding.*
> PROVERBS 2:6

SAGE
Wise and Learned One

> *The fear of the Lord is the beginning of wisdom.*
> PSALM 111:10

SAHAR
Dawn of Day

> *This is the day which the Lord hath made; we will rejoice and be glad in it.*
> PSALM 118:24

SAHRA
A Noble Princess

> *But ye are a chosen generation, a royal priesthood.*
> 1 PETER 2:9

SAIJI
One of Great Strength

> *In God is my salvation and my glory: the rock of my strength.*
> PSALM 62:7

Japanese

SAINTILMA
Pure and Upright in Heart

> *The Lord will give grace and glory: no good thing will he withhold from them that walk uprightly.*
> PSALM 84:11

SAJAUNA
God's Gracious Gift

> *Every good gift and every perfect gift is from above, and cometh down from the Father.*
> JAMES 1:17

SAJID
One of Nobility

> *But ye are a chosen generation, a royal priesthood.*
> 1 PETER 2:9

Japanese

SAKAI
Protected One

> *He that dwelleth in the secret place of the most high, shall abide under the shadow of the Almighty.*
> PSALM 91:1

Hawaiian

SAKIYA
One of Nobility

> *I will praise thee; for I am fearfully and wonderfully made: marvellous are thy works.*
> PSALM 139:14

NAME *That* BABY!

SALA
Blessings and Peace

> The Lord will give strength unto his people; the Lord will bless his people with peace.
> PSALM 29:11

SALAFORE
Of the Saviour

> But God commendeth his love toward us, . . . Christ died for us.
> ROMANS 5:8

SALATORE
Of the Saviour

> But God commendeth his love toward us, . . . Christ died for us.
> ROMANS 5:8

SALEM
One of Nobility

> Ye are a chosen generation, a royal priesthood, . . . show forth the praises of him who hath called you.
> 1 PETER 2:9

SALETA
A Rock of Strength

> The Lord is my rock, and my fortress, . . . my strength, in whom I will trust.
> PSALM 18:2

SALINA
Pure Radiance

> Let your light so shine before men . . . glorify your Father which is in heaven.
> MATTHEW 5:16

SALLEEM
Safe and Secure

> He that dwelleth in the secret place of the most high, shall abide under the shadow of the Almighty.
> PSALM 91:1

Arabic

SALLY
A Princess

> Ye are a chosen generation, a royal priesthood, . . . show forth the praises of him who hath called you.
> 1 PETER 2:9

SALOME
One of Wisdom and Grace

> The Lord will give strength unto his people; the Lord will bless his people with peace.
> PSALM 29:11

SALOMON
One of Peace

> The Lord will give strength unto his people; the Lord will bless his people with peace.
> PSALM 29:11

SALVADORE
Saviour

> But God commendeth his love toward us, . . . Christ died for us.
> ROMANS 5:8

SALVINA
In Safe Protection

> *The Lord is my light and my salvation; whom shall I fear? the Lord is the strength of my life; of whom shall I be afraid?*
> PSALM 27:1

SAM
Heard by God

> *I will praise thee: for thou hast heard me, and art become my salvation.*
> PSALM 118:21

SAMAD
The Lord Hath Heard

> *I will bless the Lord at all times: . . . I sought the Lord, and he heard me.*
> PSALM 34:1–4

SAMANATHA
One Who Listens

> *I will praise thee: for thou hast heard me, and art become my salvation.*
> PSALM 118:21

SAMANTHA
One Who Listens

> *The heart of the prudent getteth knowledge; and the ear of the wise seeketh knowledge.*
> PROVERBS 18:15

SAMARIA
A Guardian

> *Be strong and of a good courage; . . . for the Lord thy God is with thee whithersoever thou goest.*
> JOSHUA 1:9

SAMER
Ruled by God

> *God is my strength and power: and he maketh my way perfect.*
> 2 SAMUEL 22:33

SAMIEH
God Hath Heard

> *I will praise thee: for thou hast heard me, and art become my salvation.*
> PSALM 118:21

SAMMIE
Heard by God

> *I will praise thee: for thou hast heard me, and art become my salvation.*
> PSALM 118:21

SAMMY
Heard by God

> *I will praise thee: for thou hast heard me, and art become my salvation.*
> PSALM 118:21

SAMONA
Gentle Counselor

> *I will bless the Lord, who hath given me counsel: . . . he is at my right hand, I shall not be moved.*
> PSALM 16:7–8

SAMONE
Gracious Hearing

> I will praise thee: for thou hast heard me, and art become my salvation.
> PSALM 118:21

SAMOY
Guarded by God

> He that dwelleth in the secret place of the most High shall abide under the shadow of the Almighty.
> PSALM 91:1

SAMPSON
Little Sun

> Let your light so shine before men, that they may see your good works, and glorify your Father which is in heaven.
> MATTHEW 5:16

SAMUEL
Heard by God

> I will praise thee: for thou hast heard me, and art become my salvation.
> PSALM 118:21

SANCHA
Holy and Devoted to God

> I will bless the Lord at all times: his praise shall continually be in my mouth.
> PSALM 34:1

SANCHERA
Child of God

> I will praise thee: for thou hast heard me, and art become my salvation.
> PSALM 118:21

SANCTINE
Holy and Sanctified

> But ye are washed, . . . sanctified, . . . [and] justified in the name of the Lord Jesus.
> 1 CORINTHIANS 6:11

SANCTUARY
The Lord's Haven

> I was glad when they said unto me, "Let us go into the house of the Lord."
> PSALM 122:1

SANDEE
Helper of Mankind

> The Lord is my helper, and I will not fear what man shall do unto me.
> HEBREWS 13:6

SANDRA
also SONDRA, XANDRA

Helper of Mankind

> Let us . . . come boldly unto the throne . . . obtain mercy, and find grace to help in time of need.
> HEBREWS 4:16

SANFORD
From the Sandy River Crossing

> Thy word is a lamp unto my feet, and a light unto my path.
> PSALM 119:105

SANTA
Divine Protection

> *Be strong and of a good courage; . . . the Lord thy God is with thee whithersoever thou goest.*
> JOSHUA 1:9

SANTIAGO
Following After the Lord

> *Be ye therefore followers of God, . . . And walk in love, as Christ also hath loved us, and hath given himself for us.*
> EPHESIANS 5:1–2

SANTINO
The Saint

> *Ye are washed, . . . sanctified, . . . [and] justified in the name of the Lord Jesus.*
> 1 CORINTHIANS 6:11
>
> Spanish

SANTOS
The Sanctified

> *Ye are washed, . . . sanctified, . . . [and] justified in the name of the Lord Jesus.*
> 1 CORINTHIANS 6:11

SARA
A Princess

> *But ye are a chosen generation, a royal priesthood, . . . show forth the praises of him who hath called you.*
> 1 PETER 2:9

SARABETH
Consecrated Princess

> *I will bless the Lord, who hath given me counsel: . . . he is at my right hand, I shall not be moved.*
> PSALM 16:7–8

SARAH
A Princess

> *But ye are a chosen generation, a royal priesthood, . . . show forth the praises of him who hath called you.*
> 1 PETER 2:9

SARAI
A Princess

> *But ye are a chosen generation, a royal priesthood, . . . show forth the praises of him who hath called you.*
> 1 PETER 2:9

SARAN
Of Royal Nobility

> *But ye are a chosen generation, a royal priesthood, . . . show forth the praises of him who hath called you.*
> 1 PETER 2:9

SAREPTA
Great and Strong Spirit

> *He that dwelleth in the secret place of the most High shall abide under the shadow of the Almighty.*
> PSALM 91:1

SARONA
A Princess

> But ye are a chosen generation,
> a royal priesthood, . . . show
> forth the praises of him who
> hath called you.
> 1 PETER 2:9

SASCHA
Helper of Mankind

> Now the God of peace, . . . Make
> you perfect in every good work to
> do his will, working in you that
> which is well pleasing in his sight.
> HEBREWS 13:20–21

SATOA
Sweet Home

> To be discreet, chaste, keepers at
> home, good, obedient to their
> own husbands.
> TITUS 2:5

SAUDI
Noble Lineage

> But ye are a chosen generation,
> a royal priesthood, . . . show
> forth the praises of him who
> hath called you.
> 1 PETER 2:9

SAUL
Asked of God

> I have called upon thee, for thou
> wilt hear me, O God.
> PSALM 17:6

SAUNCEA
A Wise Scholar

> For the Lord giveth wisdom: out
> of his mouth cometh knowledge.
> PROVERBS 2:6

SAUNDIAGO
Following After the Lord

> Be ye therefore followers of God,
> . . . And walk in love, as Christ
> also hath loved us, and given
> himself for us.
> EPHESIANS 5:1–2

Spanish

SAUNTORE
Praise

> O magnify the Lord with me,
> and let us exalt his name
> together.
> PSALM 34:3

SAVANNAH
Peaceful Meadow

> The Lord is my shepherd; . . . He
> maketh me to lie down in green
> pastures.
> PSALM 23:1–2

SAVILLE
Peaceful and Quiet Spirit

> Let the words of my mouth and
> the meditation of my heart, be
> acceptable in thy sight, O Lord.
> PSALM 19:14

SAWYER
One Who Saws Timber

> He shall be like a tree . . . that
> bringeth forth his fruit in his
> season.
> PSALM 1:3

SAYOKO
Born of High Spirit

For the Spirit searcheth all things, yea, the deep things of God.
1 CORINTHIANS 2:10

SAYONADA
Of Royal Nobility

Ye have not chosen me, but I have chosen you, and ordained you, that ye should go and bring forth fruit.
JOHN 15:16

SCALF
Wise Counselor

I will bless the Lord, who hath given me counsel: . . . because he is at my right hand, I shall not be moved.
PSALM 16:7–8

SCARLETT
Rich Cloth

Strength and honour are her clothing; and she shall rejoice in time to come.
PROVERBS 31:25

SCHAFER
A Shepherd

He shall feed his flock like a shepherd: he shall gather the lambs with his arm.
ISAIAH 40:11

SCHELAU
Tranquillity

Let the words of my mouth, and the meditation of my heart, be acceptable in thy sight, O Lord.
PSALM 19:14

SCHILLER
A Tanner

And whatsoever ye do, do it heartily, as to the Lord, and not unto men.
COLOSSIANS 3:23

SCHNEIDER
A Tailor

And whatsoever ye do, do it heartily, as to the Lord, and not unto men.
COLOSSIANS 3:23

SCHOLASTICA
Scholarly and Learned

Study to show thyself approved unto God, . . . rightly dividing the word of truth.
2 TIMOTHY 2:15

SCHREE
Beloved and Cherished

Beloved, let us love one another: for love is of God; . . . every one that loveth is born of God.
1 JOHN 4:7

SCHRITA
One of Beauty and Fortune

I will praise thee; for I am fearfully and wonderfully made: marvellous are thy works.
PSALM 139:14

SCHRODER
Skillful One

> And whatsoever ye do, do it
> heartily, as to the Lord, and not
> unto men, for ye serve the Lord
> Christ.
> COLOSSIANS 3:23–24

SCHULZ
One in Authority

> He that ruleth over men must be
> just, ruling in the fear of God.
> 2 SAMUEL 23:3

SCHUSSLER
Maker of Wooden Dishes

> Whatsoever ye do, do it heartily,
> as to the Lord, . . . for ye serve
> the Lord Christ.
> COLOSSIANS 3:23–24
>
> German

SCHUYLER
A Shelter

> Lead me to the rock that is
> higher than I. For thou hast
> been a shelter for me, and a
> strong tower.
> PSALM 61:2, 3

SCOOTER
Beloved One

> Beloved, let us love one another:
> for love is of God; and every one
> that loveth is born of God, and
> knoweth God.
> 1 JOHN 4:7

SCOTSON
Noble Scottish Heritage

> Thy right hand hath holden me
> up, and thy gentleness hath
> made me great.
> PSALM 18:35

SCOTT
A Traveler

> Go ye into all the world, and
> preach the gospel to every
> creature.
> MARK 16:15

SEACOLE
Treasure and Great Value

> I press toward the mark for the
> prize of the high calling of God
> in Christ Jesus.
> PHILIPPIANS 3:14

SEALIA
Unseen Faith

> Faith is the substance of things
> hoped for, the evidence of things
> not seen.
> HEBREWS 11:1

SEAMUS
God Is Gracious

> But thou, O Lord, art a God full
> of compassion, and gracious.
> PSALM 86:15

SEAN
God Is Gracious

> The Lord God, merciful and
> gracious, longsuffering, . . .
> abundant in goodness and
> truth.
> EXODUS 34:6

SEASON
Salt of the Earth

> *Ye are the salt of the earth.*
> MATTHEW 5:13

SEBASTIAN
One of Reverence

> *Honour and majesty are before him: . . . give unto the Lord glory and strength.*
> PSALM 96:6–7

SECRET
One of Prayer

> *I will praise thee: for thou hast heard me, and art become my salvation.*
> PSALM 118:21

SEIKO
One of Radiant Light

> *Let your light so shine . . . that they may see your good works, and glorify your Father which is in heaven.*
> MATTHEW 5:16

SEIMA
A Sign from the Heavens

> *They that be wise shall shine as the brightness of the firmament; . . . as the stars for ever and ever.*
> DANIEL 12:3

SELAH
Quiet Pause

> *I will say of the Lord, He is my refuge and my fortress: . . . in him I will trust.*
> PSALM 91:2

SELENE
Radiant One

> *Let your light so shine . . . that they may see your good works, and glorify your Father which is in heaven.*
> MATTHEW 5:16

SELETA
A Shining Rock

> *The Lord is my rock, . . . my fortress . . . my strength, in whom I will trust.*
> PSALM 18:2

SELETER
A Shining Rock

> *The Lord is my rock, . . . my fortress, and my deliverer; my God, my strength, in whom I will trust.*
> PSALM 18:2

SELINA
Radiant One

> *Let your light so shine before men, that they may see your good works, and glorify your Father which is in heaven.*
> MATTHEW 5:16

SELLECK
Blessed, Happy One

> *Blessed are they that keep his testimonies, and that seek him with the whole heart.*
> PSALM 119:2

NAME *That* BABY!

SELMA
Divine Protection

> *The Lord is my rock, . . . my fortress, . . . my strength, in whom I will trust, . . . and my high tower.*
> PSALM 18:2

SELVA
Divine Protection

> *The Lord is my rock, . . . my fortress, . . . my strength, in whom I will trust.*
> PSALM 18:2

SENIR
Herdsman

> *He shall feed his flock like a shepherd: he shall gather the lambs with his arm.*
> ISAIAH 40:11

SENORA
One of High Esteem

> *Thou hast . . . given me the shield of thy salvation: . . . thy gentleness hath made me great.*
> PSALM 18:35

SEPTEMBER
Of the Lord

> *Ye have not chosen me, but I have chosen you that ye should go and bring forth fruit.*
> JOHN 15:16

SEQUOIA
Firm and Strong

> *The Lord is my rock, . . . my fortress, . . . my strength, in whom I will trust.*
> PSALM 18:2

SERAPHIM
The Ardent of God

> *I press toward the mark for the prize of the high calling of God in Christ Jesus.*
> PHILIPPIANS 3:14

SERAYA
Prince of Jehovah

> *Zadok . . . son of Ahitub, . . . Ahimelech the son of Abiathar, were the Priests; . . . Seraiah was the scribe.*
> 2 SAMUEL 8:17

SERENA
Calm and Tranquil

> *Thou wilt keep him in perfect peace, whose mind is stayed on thee.*
> ISAIAH 26:3

SERENDIPITY
Pleasant Surprise

> *I will praise thee; for I am fearfully and wonderfully made: marvellous are thy works.*
> PSALM 139:14

SERENITY
Peaceful and Serene

> *Thou wilt keep him in perfect peace, whose mind is stayed on thee: because he trusteth in thee.*
> ISAIAH 26:3

S

SERGE
To Serve
> Serve the Lord with gladness:
> come before his presence with
> singing.
> PSALM 100:2

SERGIO
To Serve
> Serve the Lord with gladness:
> come before his presence with
> singing.
> PSALM 100:2

SERILLA
Strong in the Faith
> Fight the good fight of faith, lay
> hold on eternal life, whereunto
> thou art also called.
> 1 TIMOTHY 6:12

SERJIO
To Serve
> I will praise thee, O Lord, with
> my whole heart; . . . I will sing
> praise.
> PSALM 9:1–2

SETH
The Appointed
> Thou hast . . . given me the
> shield of thy salvation: and . . .
> thy right hand hath holden me
> up.
> PSALM 18:35

SEUMAS
Following After the Lord
> Be ye therefore followers of God,
> as dear children; . . . And walk
> in love.
> EPHESIANS 5:1–2

SEVERA
Strong Determination
> I have set the Lord always
> before me: . . . because he is at
> my right hand, I shall not be
> moved.
> PSALM 16:8

SEVERINO
One of Strong Determination
> I have set the Lord always
> before me: . . . because he is at
> my right hand, I shall not be
> moved.
> PSALM 16:8

SEVILLE
Beloved One
> Beloved, let us love one another:
> for love is of God; and every one
> that loveth is born of God and
> knoweth God.
> 1 JOHN 4:7

SEVIM
Friend of Peace
> Thou wilt keep him in perfect
> peace, whose mind is stayed on
> thee: because he trusteth in
> thee.
> ISAIAH 26:3

SEVON
Victory and Protection
> Fight the good fight of faith, lay
> hold on eternal life, whereunto
> thou art also called.
> 2 TIMOTHY 6:12

SEYMOUR
Fame of the Land

> *Wait on the Lord, and keep his*
> *way and he shall exalt thee to*
> *inherit the land.*
> PSALM 37:34

SHABREA
God Is Gracious and Strong

> *They that be wise shall shine as*
> *the brightness of the firmament;*
> *... as the stars for ever and ever.*
> DANIEL 12:3

SHADLEE
Majestic and Learned

> *My mouth shall speak of*
> *wisdom; and the meditation of*
> *my heart shall be of*
> *understanding.*
> PSALM 49:3

SHADRACH
Majestic and Learned

> *My mouth shall speak of*
> *wisdom; and the meditation of*
> *my heart shall be of*
> *understanding.*
> PSALM 49:3

SHAELA
The Asked For

> *Now faith is the substance of*
> *things hoped for, the evidence of*
> *things not seen.*
> HEBREWS 11:1

SHAHAN
God Is Gracious

> *But thou, O Lord, art a God full*
> *of compassion, and gracious.*
> PSALM 86:15

SHAJAHAN
Everlasting Faith

> *Faith is the substance of things*
> *hoped for, the evidence of things*
> *not seen.*
> HEBREWS 11:1

SHAKIRA
Noble One of Radiance

> *They that be wise shall shine as*
> *the brightness of the firmament.*
> DANIEL 12:3

SHAKKINA
Praise and Radiance

> *For the Lord is great, and*
> *greatly to be praised: ...*
> *Honour and majesty are before*
> *him.*
> PSALM 96:4, 6

SHALAYNA
Strong in the Lord

> *For thou art my rock and my*
> *fortress; ... for thy name's sake*
> *lead me.*
> PSALM 31:3

SHALESE
Consecrated Princess

> *Strength and honour are her*
> *clothing; and she shall rejoice in*
> *time to come.*
> PROVERBS 31:25

SHALIFE
Royal Nobility

> *Thou hast also given me of the*
> *shield thy salvation: and thy*
> *gentleness hath made me great.*
> 2 SAMUEL 22:36

SHALIMAR
Complete Peace

> *The Lord will give strength unto his people; the Lord will bless his people with peace.*
> PSALM 29:11

SHALISTAR
Radiant One

> *They that be wise shall shine as the brightness of the firmament.*
> DANIEL 12:3

SHALITA
Beautiful One of Joy

> *Thou wilt show me the path of life: . . . in thy presence is fulness of joy.*
> PSALM 16:11

SHALOME
One of Peace

> *The Lord will give strength unto his people; the Lord will bless his people with peace.*
> PSALM 29:11

SHAMAH
He Hath Heard

> *I will praise thee: for thou hast heard me, and art become my salvation.*
> PSALM 118:21

SHAMAYA
Jehovah Hath Kept

> *Trust in the Lord with all thine heart; . . . In all thy ways acknowledge him.*
> PROVERBS 3:5–6

SHAMONDA
Beloved Counsel

> *I will bless the Lord, who hath given me counsel: . . . because he is at my right hand, I shall not be moved.*
> PSALM 16:7, 8

SHANANDOAH
Radiant Star

> *They that be wise shall shine . . . and they that turn many to righteousness as the stars for ever and ever.*
> DANIEL 12:3

SHANDALEIGH
Gracious and Contented

> *One thing . . . I desired of the Lord, . . . that I may dwell in the house of the Lord [and] . . . behold the beauty of the Lord.*
> PSALM 27:4

SHANDRA
One of Wisdom

> *The Lord giveth wisdom: out of his mouth cometh knowledge and understanding.*
> PROVERBS 2:6

SHANDY
A Strong Spirit

> *I have set the Lord . . . before me: . . . he is at my right hand, I shall not be moved.*
> PSALM 16:8

SHANE
God Is Gracious

> He . . . made his wonderful
> works to be remembered: the
> Lord is gracious and full of
> compassion.
> PSALM 111:4

SHANI
Marvelous

> I will praise thee, . . . I will
> show forth . . . thy marvellous
> works. . . . I will be glad and
> rejoice in thee.
> PSALM 9:1–2

SHANLEY
Hero

> The Lord is the strength of my
> life; of whom shall I be afraid?
> PSALM 27:1

SHANLON
One Who Is Wise

> For the Lord giveth wisdom: out
> of his mouth cometh knowledge
> and understanding.
> PROVERBS 2:6

SHANNON
A Refreshing Spirit

> The times of refreshing shall
> come from the presence of the
> Lord.
> ACTS 3:19

SHANTEL
God Is Gracious

> Thou, O Lord art a God full of
> compassion, and gracious,
> longsuffering, and plenteous in
> mercy.
> PSALM 86:15

SHANTHI
Ardent Spirit

> And whatsoever ye do, do it
> heartily, as to the Lord, and not
> unto men.
> COLOSSIANS 3:23

SHAPPELLE
Majestic and Learned One

> The Lord giveth wisdom: out of
> his mouth cometh knowledge
> and understanding.
> PROVERBS 2:6

SHAQUEL
Majestic and Learned One

> For the Lord giveth wisdom: out
> of his mouth cometh knowledge
> and understanding
> PROVERBS 2:6

SHARAI
A Princess

> I will praise thee; for I am
> fearfully and wonderfully
> made: marvellous are thy
> works.
> PSALM 139:14

SHARANNE
One of Strength and Grace

> The Lord will give grace and
> glory: no good thing will he
> withhold.
> PSALM 84:11

SHARI
Cherished One

> The Lord hath appeared of old
> unto me, saying, Yea I have loved
> thee with an everlasting love.
> JEREMIAH 31:3

SHARIF
Honest and True

> I will bless the Lord, who hath
> given me counsel: . . . I have set
> the Lord always before me.
> PSALM 16:7–8

SHARILYN
Refreshing Princess of God

> The times of refreshing shall
> come from the presence of the
> Lord.
> ACTS 3:19

SHARLA
Woman of the Lord

> Thou art my rock and my
> fortress; . . . for thy name's sake
> lead me, and guide me.
> PSALM 31:3

SHARLEEN
Woman of the Lord

> For thou art my rock and my
> fortress; . . . for thy name's sake
> lead me, and guide me.
> PSALM 31:3

SHARMAINE
One of Song

> I will praise thee, . . . I will be
> glad and rejoice in thee: I will
> sing praise to thy name.
> PSALM 9:1–2

SHARMARIE
Beloved and Living Fragrance

> Thy hands have made me and
> fashioned me: give me
> understanding.
> PSALM 119:73

SHARMIKA
Noble and Like unto the Lord

> I will trust, and not be afraid:
> for the Lord JEHOVAH is my
> strength and my song; he . . . is
> become my salvation.
> ISAIAH 12:2

SHAROLEE
Strong in the Lord

> In God is my salvation and my
> glory: the rock of my strength,
> . . . my refuge, is in God.
> PSALM 62:7

SHARON
Dearly Beloved

> Dearly beloved and longed for,
> my joy and crown, so stand fast
> in the Lord, my dearly beloved.
> PHILIPPIANS 4:1

SHARONROSE
Dearly Beloved

> Dearly beloved and longed for,
> my joy and crown, so stand fast
> in the Lord, my dearly beloved.
> PHILIPPIANS 4:1

SHARRI
A Princess

> *I will praise thee; for I am*
> *fearfully and wonderfully made:*
> *marvellous are thy works.*
> PSALM 139:14

SHARYN
Dearly Beloved

> *Dearly beloved and longed for,*
> *my joy and crown, so stand fast*
> *in the Lord, my dearly beloved.*
> PHILIPPIANS 4:1

SHAUGHNESSY
Peaceful Spirit

> *Thou wilt keep him in perfect*
> *peace, whose mind is stayed on*
> *thee: because he trusteth in thee.*
> ISAIAH 26:3

SHAUNTELLE
God Is Gracious

> *But thou, O Lord, art a God full*
> *of compassion, and gracious,*
> *longsuffering, and plenteous in*
> *mercy.*
> PSALM 86:15

SHAUWN
God's Gracious Gift

> *Every good gift and every*
> *perfect gift is from above,*
> *cometh down from the Father.*
> JAMES 1:17

SHAW
From the Shady Grove

> *The Lord is my shepherd; I shall*
> *not want. He maketh me to lie*
> *down in green pastures.*
> PSALM 23:1–2

SHAWN
God Is Gracious

> *I will trust, and not be afraid:*
> *for the Lord JEHOVAH is my*
> *strength and my song; he also is*
> *become my salvation.*
> ISAIAH 12:2

SHAWNEE
God Is Gracious

> *Thou, O Lord, art a God full of*
> *compassion, and gracious,*
> *longsuffering, and plenteous in*
> *mercy.*
> PSALM 86:15

SHAY
God's Gift

> *For by grace are ye saved*
> *through faith; and that not of*
> *yourselves: it is the gift of God.*
> EPHESIANS 2:8

SHAYE
One of Majesty and High Esteem

> *Thy right hand hath holden me*
> *up, and thy gentleness hath*
> *made me great.*
> PSALM 18:35

SHAYIL
Majesty and High Esteem

> *Thou hast . . . given me the*
> *shield of thy salvation: thy*
> *gentleness hath made me great.*
> PSALM 18:35

SHE'MAIYA
Heard of Jehovah

> I will praise thee: for thou hast
> heard me, and art become my
> salvation.
> PSALM 118:21

Hebrew

SHEARIN
Jehovah Hath Esteemed

> I will instruct thee and teach
> thee . . . I will guide thee with
> mine eye.
> PSALM 32:8

SHEFFEY
From the Sheepfield

> He shall feed his flock like a
> shepherd: he shall gather the
> lambs with his arm.
> ISAIAH 40:11

SHEILA
Unseen Faith

> Faith is the substance of things
> hoped for, the evidence of things
> not seen.
> HEBREWS 11:1

SHEKEITHA
Unseen Faith and Secure

> Faith is the substance of things
> hoped for, the evidence of things
> not seen.
> HEBREWS 11:1

SHEKINA
Likeness of Jehovah

> I will trust, and not be afraid:
> for the Lord JEHOVAH is my
> strength and my song; he also is
> become my salvation.
> ISAIAH 12:2

SHEKINAH
Likeness of Jehovah

> I will trust, and not be afraid:
> for the Lord JEHOVAH is my
> strength and my song; he also is
> become my salvation.
> ISAIAH 12:2

SHELBY
Little Rock

> The Lord is upright: he is my
> rock.
> PSALM 92:15

SHELDA
A Shield Bearer

> Thou hast also given me the
> shield of thy salvation: . . . thy
> gentleness hath made me great.
> 2 SAMUEL 22:36

SHELDEN
Beautiful Thoughts

> Whatsoever things are true: . . .
> honest, . . . just, . . . pure, . . .
> lovely, [and] of good report; . . .
> think on these things.
> PHILIPPIANS 4:8

SHELDON
Beautiful Thoughts

> *Whatsoever things are true, . . .*
> *honest, . . . just, . . . pure, . . .*
> *lovely, [and] of good report; . . .*
> *think on these things.*
> PHILIPPIANS 4:8

SHELISA
From the Peaceful Meadow

> *The Lord is my shepherd; . . . He*
> *maketh me to lie down in green*
> *pastures: . . . beside the still*
> *waters.*
> PSALM 23:1,2

SHELISE
Consecrated Princess

> *Strength and honour are her*
> *clothing; and she shall rejoice in*
> *time to come.*
> PROVERBS 31:25

SHELLYE
Gentle Lamb

> *He shall feed his flock like a*
> *shepherd: he shall gather the*
> *lambs with his arm.*
> ISAIAH 40:11

SHELVIE
Little Rock

> *In God is my salvation and my*
> *glory: the rock of my strength,*
> *and my refuge, is in God.*
> PSALM 62:7

SHEMA
Of Good Name and Fame

> *A good name is rather to be*
> *chosen than great riches, and*
> *loving favour . . . than silver or*
> *gold.*
> PROVERBS 22:1

SHEMARIAH
Guarded of Jehovah

> *He that dwelleth in the secret*
> *place of the most High shall*
> *abide under the shadow of the*
> *Almighty.*
> PSALM 91:1

SHEMONE
One of Grace

> *Wait on the Lord, and keep his*
> *way, and he shall exalt thee to*
> *inherit the land.*
> PSALM 37:34

SHEMUEL
His Name Is of God

> *The Lord is my strength and my*
> *shield; my heart trusted in him.*
> PSALM 28:7

SHENANDOAH
Radiant Star

> *And they that be wise shall*
> *shine as the brightness of the*
> *firmament . . . they that turn*
> *many to righteousness as the*
> *stars forever and ever.*
> DANIEL 12:3

SHEPHERD
One Who Tends Sheep
> *I am the good shepherd, and know my sheep, and am known of mine.*
> JOHN 10:14

SHER
Of Shining Courage
> *For thou, Lord, wilt bless the righteous; with favour wilt thou compass him as with a shield.*
> PSALM 5:12

SHERI
Cherished One
> *The Lord, thy God . . . will rejoice over thee with joy; he will rest in his love.*
> ZEPHANIAH 3:17

SHERIANNE
Purity and Grace
> *The Lord will give grace and glory: no good thing will he withhold from them that walk uprightly.*
> PSALM 84:11

SHERIE
Pure and Peaceful
> *The Lord will give strength unto his people; the Lord will bless his people with peace.*
> PSALM 29:11

SHERLENE
Woman of God
> *Strength and honour are her clothing; and she shall rejoice in time to come.*
> PROVERBS 31:25

SHERMAN
Shearer of Cloth
> *The Lord reigneth, he is clothed with majesty; [and] . . . strength, wherewith he hath girded himself.*
> PSALM 93:1

SHEROD
Of Shining Courage
> *I will sing of the mercies of the Lord forever.*
> PSALM 89:1

SHERRILL
Pure and Peaceful
> *The Lord will give strength unto his people, the Lord will bless his people with peace.*
> PSALM 29:11

SHERRONE
Royal Nobility
> *You have not chosen me; I have chosen you, and ordained you, that ye should go and bring forth fruit.*
> JOHN 15:16

SHERRY
One of Purity
> *Blessed are the pure in heart: for they shall see God.*
> MATTHEW 5:8

SHERRYLYNN
Pure and Refreshing
> *I press toward the mark for the prize of the high calling of God in Christ Jesus.*
> PHILIPPIANS 3:14

SHERWIN
A Shining Friend

> Ye are my friends, if ye do
> whatsoever I command you.
> JOHN 15:14

SHERWOOD
Industrious

> Let your light so shine before
> men, that they may see your
> good works, and glorify your
> Father, which is in heaven.
> MATTHEW 5:16

SHERYLANN
One of Purity and Grace

> The Lord will give grace and
> glory: no good thing will he
> withhold from them that walk
> uprightly.
> PSALM 84:11

SHIANN
One of Peace and Grace

> The Lord will give grace and
> glory: no good thing will he
> withhold from them that walk
> uprightly.
> PSALM 84:11

SHIELDS
Shield Bearer

> Take unto you the whole armour
> of God, . . . above all, taking the
> shield of faith, [and] . . . the
> helmet of salvation.
> EPHESIANS 6:13, 16

SHIGEKO
Abundant Life

> Then said Jesus . . . "I am come
> that they might have life, and
> that they might have it more
> abundantly."
> JOHN 10:7, 10

SHILO
Tranquil and Peaceful

> Thou wilt keep him in perfect
> peace, whose mind is stayed on
> thee: . . . he trusteth in thee.
> ISAIAH 26:3

SHILOH
Tranquil and Peaceful

> Thou wilt keep him in perfect
> peace, whose mind is stayed on
> thee.
> ISAIAH 26:3

SHIMAKO
The Name God Knows

> A good name is rather to be
> chosen than great riches, and
> loving favour rather than silver
> and gold.
> PROVERBS 22:1

SHIPPS
Dweller at the Sign of a Ship

> The isles shall wait for me, and
> the ships of Tarshish . . . to bring
> thy sons . . . unto the name of
> the Lord thy God.
> ISAIAH 60:9

S

SHIRAH
A Song

> I will praise thee, . . . I will be
> glad and rejoice in thee: I will
> sing praise to thy name.
> PSALM 9:1–2

SHIRLEY
Pure and Peaceful

> The Lord will give strength unto
> his people; the Lord will bless
> his people with peace.
> PSALM 29:11

SHOHREH
He Watcheth

> So will I watch over them, to
> build, and to plant, saith the
> Lord.
> JEREMIAH 31:28

SHORTY
Dear One

> Ye have not chosen me, but I
> have chosen you, and ordained
> you, that ye should go and
> bring forth fruit.
> JOHN 15:16

SHOSHANA
A Rose

> I will praise thee; for I am
> fearfully and wonderfully made:
> marvellous are thy works.
> PSALM 139:14

SHOSHANNAH
Rose

> I will praise thee; for I am
> fearfully and wonderfully made:
> marvellous are thy works.
> PSALM 139:14

SHRIKA
One of Beauty and Fortune

> I will praise thee; for I am
> fearfully and wonderfully made:
> marvellous are thy works.
> PSALM 139:14

SHUICHIRO
Song

> I will praise thee, O Lord, with
> my whole heart; . . . I will be
> glad and rejoice in thee.
> PSALM 9:1

SHUNG
Abundant Life

> Then said Jesus . . . I am come
> that they might have life, and
> that they might have it more
> abundantly.
> JOHN 10:7, 10

SHUNTAVIAS
Quiet and Peaceful

> The Lord will give strength unto
> his people; the Lord will bless
> his people with peace.
> PSALM 29:11

SHURLAN
From the Strong Fortress

> I will say of the Lord, He is my
> refuge and my fortress: my God;
> in him will I trust.
> PSALM 91:2

SHYRA
My Song

> I will praise thee, O Lord, with
> my whole heart; . . . I will sing
> praise to thy name.
> PSALM 9:1

SHYROCK
Modest One of Grace

> The Lord will give grace and
> glory: no good thing will he
> withhold from them that walk
> uprightly.
> PSALM 84:11

SIBYL
A Wise One

> For the Lord giveth wisdom: out
> of his mouth cometh knowledge
> and understanding.
> PROVERBS 2:6

SIDNEY
Noble One of Strength

> The Lord is my light and my
> salvation . . . the strength of my
> life; of whom shall I be afraid?
> PSALM 27:1

SIEGFRIED
Victorious Protection

> I will be with thee: I will not fail
> thee, nor forsake thee. Be strong
> and of good courage.
> JOSHUA 1:5–6

Teutonic

SIEGLINDE
Gentle Victory

> Thanks be to God, which giveth
> us the victory through our Lord
> Jesus Christ.
> 1 CORINTHIANS 15:57

SIERA
Royal Nobility

> Ye have not chosen me, but I
> have chosen you, and ordained
> you, that ye should go and bring
> forth fruit.
> JOHN 15:16

SIERRA
Royal Nobility

> Ye have not chosen me, but I
> have chosen you, and ordained
> you, that ye should go and bring
> forth fruit.
> JOHN 15:16

SIG
Conqueror

> But thanks be to God, which
> giveth us the victory through
> our Lord Jesus Christ.
> 1 CORINTHIANS 15:57

SIGNA
A Sign

> The Lord himself shall give you
> a sign; Behold, a virgin shall
> conceive, . . . and shall call his
> name Immanuel.
> ISAIAH 7:14

SIGNEY
Victorious Protection

> I will be with thee: I will not fail
> thee, nor forsake thee. Be strong
> and of good courage.
> JOSHUA 1:5–6

SIGRID
Conquering Counsel

> *I have set the Lord always before me: because he is at my right hand, I shall not be moved.*
> PSALM 16:8

SILAS
Secure One

> *And thou shalt be secure, because there is hope; . . . and thou shalt take thy rest in safety.*
> JOB 11:18

SILENCE
Quiet

> *I will meditate in thy precepts, . . . I will delight myself in thy statutes: I will not forget thy word.*
> PSALM 119:15–16

SILER
Guardian

> *He that dwelleth in the secret place of the most High shall abide under the shadow of the Almighty.*
> PSALM 91:1

SILVER
One of Precious Quality

> *I will praise thee; for I am fearfully and wonderfully made: marvellous are thy works.*
> PSALM 139:14

SILVERIO
One of Precious Quality

> *I will praise thee; for I am fearfully and wonderfully made: marvellous are thy works.*
> PSALM 139:14

SILVESTER
Forest Dweller

> *Make me to go in the path of thy commandments; for therein do I delight.*
> PSALM 119:35

SILVIA
A Girl of the Forest

> *I will praise thee; for I am fearfully and wonderfully made: marvellous are thy works.*
> PSALM 139:14

SIMBITI
Obedience and Devotion

> *I will bless the Lord at all times: his praise shall continually be in my mouth.*
> PSALM 34:1

SIMEON
Heard

> *I sought the Lord, and he heard me, and delivered me from all my fears.*
> PSALM 34:4

SIMMONS
Gracious Hearing

> *I will bless the Lord at all times:*
> *his praise shall continually be*
> *in my mouth. . . . I sought the*
> *Lord, and he heard me.*
> PSALM 34:1, 4

SIMON
The Lord Hath Heard

> *I will bless the Lord at all times:*
> *his praise shall continually be*
> *in my mouth. . . . I sought the*
> *Lord, and he heard me.*
> PSALM 34:1, 4

SINCERRIANNE
One of Grace

> *The Lord will give grace and*
> *glory: no good thing will he*
> *withhold from them that walk*
> *uprightly.*
> PSALM 84:11

SINCLAIR
The Sanctified and Shining

> *They that be wise shall shine as*
> *the brightness of the firmament;*
> *. . . as the stars for ever and ever.*
> DANIEL 12:3

SIOBHAN
One of Greatness and Merit

> *The Lord is my rock, . . . my*
> *fortress, and my deliverer; my*
> *strength, in whom I will trust.*
> PSALM 18:2

Arabic

SISSY
Unseen Faith

> *Faith is the substance of things*
> *hoped for, the evidence of things*
> *not seen.*
> HEBREWS 11:1

SIXTO
The Sixth

> *I would seek unto God, and*
> *commit my cause: . . . [He]*
> *doeth great things and . . .*
> *marvelous things without*
> *number.*
> JOB 5:8

SKEET
Beloved

> *Beloved, let us love one another:*
> *for love is of God; and every one*
> *that loveth is born of God, and*
> *knoweth God.*
> 1 JOHN 4:7

SKEETER
Beloved

> *Beloved, let us love one another:*
> *for love is of God; and every one*
> *that loveth is born of God, and*
> *knoweth God.*
> 1 JOHN 4:7

SKETCH
Creative Spirit

> *And let the beauty of the Lord*
> *our God be upon us: and*
> *establish thou the work of our*
> *hands.*
> PSALM 90:17

SKIP
One of Rejoicing

> This is the day which the Lord
> hath made; we will rejoice and
> be glad in it.
> PSALM 118:24

SKIPPER
Shipmaster

> I can do all things through
> Christ which strengtheneth me.
> PHILIPPIANS 4:13

SKY
Wise Protection

> I will instruct thee and teach
> thee in the way which thou shalt
> go: I will guide thee with mine
> eye.
> PSALM 32:8

SKYLER
Ambitious One

> I will praise the Lord according
> to his righteousness.
> PSALM 7:17

SLATE
Strong and Bold

> Be strong and of a good
> courage; . . . for the Lord thy
> God is with thee whithersoever
> thou goest.
> JOSHUA 1:9

SLAVENS
Glorious Position

> Thou hast . . . given me the
> shield of thy salvation: and . . .
> thy gentleness hath made me
> great.
> PSALM 18:35

SLAVICA
Glorious Position

> Thou hast . . . given me the
> shield of thy salvation: . . . thy
> gentleness hath made me great.
> PSALM 18:35

SLOAN
Warrior for the Faith

> Fight the good fight of faith, lay
> hold on eternal life, whereunto
> thou art also called.
> 1 TIMOTHY 6:12

SMITH
Skillful Worker

> I will instruct thee and teach
> thee in the way which thou shalt
> go: I will guide thee with mine
> eye.
> PSALM 32:8

SMITTY
Blacksmith

> Whatsoever ye do, do it heartily,
> as to the Lord . . . for ye serve
> the Lord Christ.
> COLOSSIANS 3:23–24

SMOKEY
An Ardent Spirit

> Whatsoever ye do, do it heartily,
> as to the Lord, . . . for ye serve
> the Lord Christ.
> COLOSSIANS 3:23–24

SMOKY
An Ardent Spirit

> Whatsoever ye do, do it heartily,
> as to the Lord, . . . for ye serve
> the Lord Christ.
> COLOSSIANS 3:23–24

SNOW
Pure One

> The statutes of the Lord are
> right, . . . the commandment of
> the Lord is pure, enlightening
> the eyes.
> PSALM 19:8

SOCORRO
Rock of Strength

> In God is my salvation and my
> glory: the rock of my strength,
> and my refuge, is in God.
> PSALM 62:7

SOCRATES
One of Virtue

> I press toward the mark for the
> prize of the high calling of God
> in Christ Jesus.
> PHILIPPIANS 3:14

SOFRONA
Of Understanding and Wisdom

> For the Lord giveth wisdom: out
> of his mouth cometh knowledge
> and understanding.
> PROVERBS 2:6

SOLANGE
Radiance of an Angel

> They that be wise shall shine as
> the brightness of the firmament;
> . . . as the stars for ever and ever.
> DANIEL 12:3

SOLEDAD
Unity and Consecration

> I will bless the Lord at all times:
> his praise shall continually be
> in my mouth.
> PSALM 34:1

SOLVEIG
Sunshine

> Then shall the righteous shine
> forth as the sun in the kingdom
> of their Father.
> MATTHEW 13:43

SOMMERLOVE
One of Love

> Beloved, let us love one another:
> for love is of God; and every one
> that loveth is born of God.
> 1 JOHN 4:7

SON
Son

> Wherefore thou art no more a
> servant, but a son; . . . then an
> heir of God through Christ
> GALATIANS 4:7

SONDRA   *also* SANDRA
Helper of Mankind

> The Lord is my helper, and I
> will not fear what man shall do
> unto me.
> HEBREWS 13:6

SONJA
One of Wisdom

> The Lord giveth wisdom: out of
> his mouth cometh knowledge
> and understanding.
> PROVERBS 2:6

SONNY
Son

> Thou art no more a servant, but
> a son; and if a son, then an heir
> of God through Christ.
> GALATIANS 4:7

S

SONYA
Loyal and Faithful

Thy mercy, O Lord, is in the heavens; and thy faithfulness reacheth unto the clouds.
PSALM 36:5

SOOTZIE
Beloved One

Beloved, let us love one another: for love is of God; every one that loveth is born of God.
1 JOHN 4:7

SOOZIN
One of Purity

Every word of God is pure: he is a shield unto them that put their trust in him.
PROVERBS 30:5

SOPHIA
Wisdom

Wisdom is the principal thing; therefore get wisdom: and with all thy getting get understanding.
PROVERBS 4:7

SORAYA
One of Nobility

Ye are a chosen generation, a royal priesthood, . . . show forth the praises of him who hath called you.
PETER 2:9

SPARKY
One of Joy and Happiness

Thou wilt show me the path of life: in thy presence is fulness of joy.
PSALM 16:11

SPARROW
Joyful One

Thou wilt show me the path of life: in thy presence is fulness of joy.
PSALM 16:11

SPECK
One of Inspiration

The Lord put forth his hand, and . . . said unto me, Behold, I have put my words in thy mouth.
JEREMIAH 1:9

SPENCER
Faithful Steward

Moreover it is required in stewards, that a man be found faithful.
1 CORINTHIANS 4:2

SPICE
Fragrant

Thy hands have made me and fashioned me: give me understanding, that I may learn thy commandments.
PSALM 119:73

SPIKE
Harvest of Grain

Jesus saith . . . "Lift up your eyes, and look on the fields; for they are white already to harvest."
JOHN 4:34–35

SPORT
Dedicated

> *I have longed for thy salvation, O Lord; and thy law is my delight.*
> PSALM 119:174

SPRING
Refreshing Spirit

> *The times of refreshing shall come from the presence of the Lord.*
> ACTS 3:19

SPURGEON
One with Pure Heart

> *Blessed are the pure in heart: for they shall see God.*
> MATTTHEW 5:8

SQUARE
Shield Bearer

> *Take unto you the whole armour of God, . . . above all, taking the shield of faith, . . . and the helmet of salvation, and the sword of the Spirit which is the word of God.*
> EPHESIANS 6:13, 16–17

SQUIRE
Shield Bearer

> *Take unto you the whole armour of God, . . . above all, taking the shield of faith, . . . and the helmet of salvation, and the sword of the Spirit which is the word of God.*
> EPHESIANS 6:13, 16–17

SQUIRELL
Prudent One

> *I have rejoiced in the way of thy testimonies, . . . I will meditate in thy precepts, and have respect unto thy ways.*
> PSALM 119:14–15

STACEY
One Who Shall Rise Again

> *Who seeth the Son, and believeth on him, may have everlasting life: and I will raise him up at the last day.*
> JOHN 6:40

STACY
One Who Shall Rise Again

> *Every one which seeth the Son, and believeth on him, may have everlasting life: and I will raise him up at the last day.*
> JOHN 6:40

STAFFORD
From the Rock of Strength

> *In God is my salvation and my glory: the rock of my strength, and my refuge, is in God.*
> PSALM 62:7

STALNECKER
Radiant One

> *Let your light so shine before men, that they may see your good works, and glorify your Father which is in heaven.*
> MATTHEW 5:16

STAMP
Genuine Quality

> Thy hands have made me and
> fashioned me: give me
> understanding, that I may learn
> thy commandments.
> PSALM 119:73

STANCIL
From the Rock of Strength

> In God is my salvation and my
> glory: the rock of my strength,
> and my refuge, is in God.
> PSALM 62:7

STANCLIFF
From the Strong Fortress

> The Lord is my rock, and my
> fortress, and my deliverer; my
> God, my strength, in whom I
> will trust.
> PSALM 18:2

STANCY
From the Strong Fortress

> The Lord is my rock, and my
> fortress, and my deliverer; . . .
> my strength, in whom I will
> trust.
> PSALM 18:2

STANLEY
One of Perseverance

> I have set the Lord . . . before
> me: . . . he is at my right hand, I
> shall not be moved.
> PSALM 16:8

STANTON
One of Stalwart Spirit

> Through God we shall do
> valiantly.
> PSALMS 108:13

STAR
Radiant One

> But the path of the just is as the
> shining light, that shineth more
> and more unto the perfect day.
> PROVERBS 4:18

STARLA
Radiant Star

> They that be wise shall shine as
> the brightness of the firmament;
> . . . as the stars for ever and ever.
> DANIEL 12:3

STARLEE
Radiant Star

> They that be wise shall shine as
> the brightness of the firmament;
> . . . as the stars for ever and ever.
> DANIEL 12:3

STARNES
Ardent and Zealous

> And whatsoever ye do, do it
> heartily, as to the Lord, and not
> unto men; . . . for ye serve the
> Lord Christ.
> COLOSSIANS 3:23–24

STAVRA
Crowned One

> When the chief Shepherd shall
> appear, ye shall receive a crown
> of glory that fadeth not away.
> 1 PETER 5:4

STEADMAN
Steadfast One

> For we are made partakers of
> Christ, if we hold the beginning
> of our confidence stedfast unto
> the end.
> HEBREWS 3:14

STEEL
Firm of Purpose

> I have set the Lord always
> before me: . . . he is at my right
> hand, I shall not be moved.
> PSALM 16:8

STEELMAN
Firm and Reliable

> I am thy servant; . . . Thy
> testimonies are wonderful;
> therefore doth my soul keep
> them.
> PSALM 119:125, 129

STEFANIE
Crowned One

> When the chief Shepherd shall
> appear, ye shall receive a crown
> of glory.
> 1 PETER 5:4

STELLA
A Star

> And they that be wise shall
> shine as the brightness of the
> firmament . . . as the stars
> forever and ever.
> DANIEL 12:3

STEPHANIE
Crowned One

> When the chief Shepherd shall
> appear, ye shall receive a crown
> of glory.
> 1 PETER 5:4

STEPHEN   *also* STEVEN
Crowned One

> When the chief Shepherd shall
> appear, ye shall receive a crown
> of glory.
> 1 PETER 5:4

STERLING
Genuine and True

> Whatsoever things are true, . . .
> honest, . . . just, . . . pure, . . .
> lovely, [and] of good report; . . .
> think on these things.
> PHILIPPIANS 4:8

STETSON
Son

> Thou art no more a servant, but
> a son; and . . . an heir of God
> through Christ.
> GALATIANS 4:7

STEVE
Crowned One

> When the chief Shepherd shall
> appear, ye shall receive a crown
> of glory.
> 1 PETER 5:4

STEVEN   *also* STEPHEN
Crowned One

> When the chief Shepherd shall
> appear, ye shall receive a crown
> of glory.
> 1 PETER 5:4

S

STEWART
Caretaker
> *[Cast] all your care upon him; for he careth for you.*
> 1 PETER 5:7

STILES
One of Gentleness
> *And the servant of the Lord must not strive; but be gentle unto all men, apt to teach, patient.*
> 2 TIMOTHY 2:24

STOCKTON
From the Estate
> *Thy word is a lamp unto my feet, and a light unto my path.*
> PSALM 119:105

STONE
Rock of Strength
> *In God is my salvation and my glory: the rock of my strength, and my refuge, is in God.*
> PSALM 62:7

STONEWALL
Rock of Strength
> *In God is my salvation and my glory: the rock of my strength, and my refuge, is in God.*
> PSALM 62:7

STONEY
Rock of Strength
> *In God is my salvation and my glory: the rock of my strength, and my refuge, is in God.*
> PSALM 62:7

STOREY
Strong and Powerful
> *Thou hast . . . given me the shield of thy salvation: . . . thy gentleness hath made me great.*
> PSALM 18:35

STORMY
Strong Spirit
> *I will meditate in thy precepts, . . . I will delight myself in thy statues: I will not forget thy word.*
> PSALM 119:15–16

STOWE
From the Holy Place
> *I will love thee, O Lord, my strength. I will call upon the Lord, who is worthy to be praised.*
> PSALM 18:1, 3

STRAULIE
Divine Counselor
> *For the Lord giveth wisdom: out of his mouth cometh knowledge and understanding.*
> PROVERBS 2:6

STRICKLIN
Peaceful Valley
> *The Lord is my shepherd; . . . He maketh me to lie down in green pastures: . . . beside the still waters.*
> PSALM 23:1–2

STROM
River of Life

> He shall be like a tree planted
> by the rivers of water, . . .
> whatsoever he doeth shall
> prosper.
> PSALM 1:3

STRYKER
Ardent Spirit

> I press toward the mark for the
> prize of the high calling of God
> in Christ Jesus.
> PHILIPPIANS 3:14

STUART
Keeper of Estate

> Thou art my rock and my
> fortress; . . . for thy name's sake
> lead me, and guide me.
> PSALM 31:3

SU
One of Purity and Grace

> The Lord will give grace and
> glory: no good thing will he
> withhold from them that walk
> uprightly.
> PSALM 84:11

SUDIE
Lily of Purity

> The statutes of the Lord are
> right, . . . the commandment of
> the Lord is pure, enlightening
> the eyes.
> PSALM 19:8

SUE
Beautiful One

> For the Lord taketh pleasure in
> his people; he will beautify the
> meek with salvation.
> PSALM 149:4

SUE ANN
Beauty and Grace

> The Lord will give grace and
> glory: no good thing will he
> withhold from them that walk
> uprightly.
> PSALM 84:11

SUEDE
Lily of Purity

> Blessed are the pure in heart:
> for they shall see God.
> MATTHEW 5:8

SUELLEN
One of Purity and Light

> Let your light so shine . . . that
> they may see your good works
> and glorify your Father which
> is in heaven.
> MATTHEW 5:16

SULLIVAN
Leader of Strength

> As for God, his way is perfect; . . .
> God is my strength and power:
> and he maketh my way perfect.
> 2 SAMUEL 22:31, 33

SUMMER
One of Warmth and Praise

> I will bless the Lord at all times:
> his praise shall continually be
> in my mouth.
> PSALM 34:1

SUNNY
Sunlike and Cheerful

> *I will bless the Lord at all times:*
> *his praise shall continually be*
> *in my mouth.*
> PSALM 34:1

SUNRISE
Dawn

> *This is the day which the Lord*
> *hath made; we will rejoice and*
> *be glad in it.*
> PSALM 118:24

SURENDER
Firm of Purpose

> *I have set the Lord always*
> *before me: . . . he is at my right*
> *hand, I shall not be moved.*
> PSALM 16:8

SUSAN
Lily of Purity

> *Blessed are the pure in heart:*
> *for they shall see God.*
> MATTHEW 5:8
>
> Hebrew

SUSANNAH
Beautiful One

> *For the Lord taketh pleasure in*
> *his people: he will beautify the*
> *meek with salvation.*
> PSALM 149:4
>
> Hebrew

SUTTON
From the Southern Village

> *Thy word is a lamp unto my*
> *feet, and a light unto my path.*
> PSALM 119:105

SUZANNE
Pure in Grace

> *The Lord will give grace and*
> *glory: no good thing will he*
> *withhold from them that walk*
> *uprightly.*
> PSALM 84:11
>
> French

SUZETTE
Pure in Grace

> *The Lord God is a sun and*
> *shield: the Lord will give grace*
> *and glory.*
> PSALM 84:11
>
> English

SUZIE
Beautiful One

> *The Lord taketh pleasure in his*
> *people: he will beautify the*
> *meek with salvation.*
> PSALM 149:4

SVENJA
Youthful One

> *For thou art my hope, O Lord*
> *God: thou art my trust from my*
> *youth.*
> PSALM 71:5

SYBIL
The Wise One

> *Whoso is wise, and will observe*
> *these things, . . . shall*
> *understand the lovingkindness*
> *of the Lord.*
> PSALM 107:43

NAME *That* BABY!

SYDNEY
Unselfish Spirit

> He that giveth unto the poor
> shall not lack.
> PROVERBS 28:27

SYLVESTER
Dweller by the Forest

> I will instruct thee and teach
> thee in the way which thou shalt
> go: I will guide thee with mine
> eye.
> PSALM 32:8

SYLVIA
Secure One

> And thou shalt be secure,
> because there is hope.
> JOB 11:18

SYMPHONY
Harmony of Sound

> Let the words of my mouth, and
> the meditation of my heart, be
> acceptable in thy sight, O Lord.
> PSALM 19:14

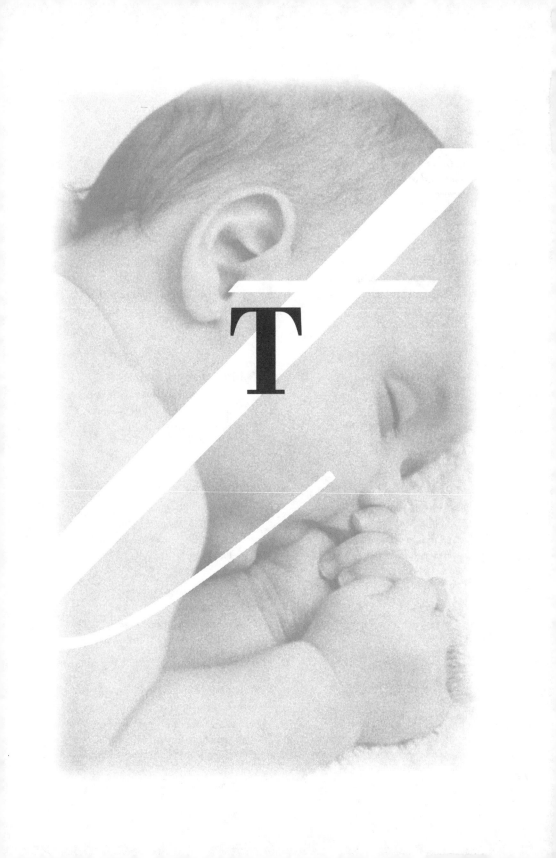

T

TABARI
Rejoice

> *In God we boast all the day long, and praise thy name forever.*
> PSALM 44:8

TABITHA
Symbol of Beauty

> *Strength and honour are her clothing, and she shall rejoice in time to come.*
> PROVERBS 31:25

TABOR
From the Strong Fortress

> *The Lord is my rock, . . . my fortress, and my deliverer; my God, my strength, in whom I will trust.*
> PSALM 18:2

TABRINA
Brilliant Among the People

> *My mouth shall speak of wisdom; and the meditation of my heart shall be of understanding.*
> PSALM 49:3

TACARA
Precious Treasure

> *Thy hands have made me and fashioned me: give me understanding, that I may learn thy commandments.*
> PSALM 119:73

TACHELLE
Strong in Purpose

> *I will bless the Lord, who hath given me counsel: . . . I have set the Lord always before me: because he is at my right hand.*
> PSALM 16:7–8

TACITA
A Quiet Spirit

> *My meditation of him shall be sweet: I will be glad in the Lord.*
> PSALM 104:34

TACO
Spirited One

> *Whatsoever ye do, do it heartily, as to the Lord, . . . for ye serve the Lord Christ.*
> COLOSSIANS 3:23–24

TAD
Praise of God

> *I will praise thee, O Lord, with my whole heart; I will show forth all thy marvellous works.*
> PSALM 9:1

TADAO
One of Praise

> *I will praise thee, O Lord, . . . I will sing praise to thy name.*
> PSALM 9:1–2

TADERAL
One of Praise

> *For the Lord is great, and greatly to be praised: . . . Honour and majesty are before him.*
> PSALM 96:4, 6

TAERA
My High Tower

> The Lord is my rock, and my
> fortress, and my deliverer; my
> God, my strength, in whom I
> will trust.
> PSALM 18:2

TAFFEY
Beloved

> The beloved of the Lord shall
> dwell in the safety by him; and
> the Lord shall cover him all the
> day long.
> DEUTERONOMY 33:12

TAFTON
One Who is Loved

> Whosoever believeth in him
> should not perish, but have
> everlasting life.
> JOHN 3:16

TAGGART
Son of the Priest

> I will praise thee; for I am
> fearfully and wonderfully
> made: marvellous are thy
> works.
> PSALM 139:14

TAHNEE
Beyond Praise

> For the Lord is great, and
> greatly to be praised: . . .
> Honour and majesty are before
> him.
> PSALM 96:4, 6

TAI
Noble One

> Thou hast also given me the
> shield of thy salvation: . . . thy
> gentleness hath made me great.
> PSALM 18:35

TAIKA
Of Divine Fame

> Wait on the Lord, and keep his
> way, and he shall exalt thee to
> inherit the land.
> PSALM 37:34

TAIYA
A Strong Leader

> The Lord is my strength and my
> shield; my heart trusted in him.
> PSALM 28:7

TAJAI
Crowned One

> And when the chief Shepherd
> shall appear, ye shal. ...... a
> crown of glory that fadeth not
> away.
> 1 PETER 5:4

TAJIA
A Crown

> And when the chief Shepherd
> shall appear, ye shall receive a
> crown of glory that fadeth not
> away.
> 1 PETER 5:4

TAKEISHA
One of Prayer and Peace

> The Lord will give strength unto
> his people; the Lord will bless
> his people with peace.
> PSALM 29:11

TAKIKO
Faithful

> O love the Lord, all ye his
> saints: for the Lord preserveth
> the faithful, and plentifully
> rewardeth the proud doer.
> PSALM 31:23

TALEITHA
Pretty One

> Favour is deceitful, and beauty
> is vain: but a woman that
> feareth the Lord, she shall be
> praised.
> PROVERBS 31:30

TALAYAH
Dew of Heaven

> The Lord by wisdom hath
> founded the earth; . . . By his
> knowledge the depths are
> broken up, and the clouds drop
> down the dew.
> PROVERBS 3:19–20

TALIA
Dew of Heaven

> The Lord by wisdom hath
> founded the earth; . . . By his
> knowledge the depths are
> broken up, and the clouds drop
> down the dew.
> PROVERBS 3:19–20

TALBERT
One of Great Strength

> In God is my salvation and my
> glory: the rock of my strength,
> and my refuge, is in God.
> PSALM 62:7

TALIAFERRO
Diligent Worker

> As a wise masterbuilder, I have
> laid the foundation, . . . which is
> Jesus Christ.
> 1 CORINTHIANS 3:10–11

TALCOTT
From the Peaceful Cottage

> The Lord is my shepherd; I shall
> not want. He maketh me to lie
> down in green pastures: he
> leadeth me beside still waters.
> PSALM 23:1–2

TALISA
Perfect

> As for God, his way is perfect:
> the word of the Lord is tried: he
> is a buckler to all those that
> trust him.
> PSALM 18:30

TALEAH
Understanding

> My mouth shall speak of
> wisdom; and the meditation of
> my heart shall be of
> understanding.
> PSALM 49:3

TALITHA
Damsel

> But a woman that feareth the
> Lord, she shall be praised.
> PROVERBS 31:30

T

TALLULAH
A Refreshing Spirit
> The times of refreshing shall
> come from the presence of the
> Lord.
> ACTS 3:19

TALMADGE
Of Spiritual Worth
> I will praise thee; for I am
> fearfully and wonderfully made:
> marvellous are thy works.
> PSALM 139:14

TALMER
Obedient Servant
> Let the words of my mouth, and
> the meditation of my heart, be
> acceptable in thy sight.
> PSALM 19:14

TAMARA
Flourishing Palm
> The righteous shall flourish like
> the palm tree: . . . he shall grow
> like a cedar in Lebanon.
> PSALM 92:12

TAMARAH
Upright and Graceful
> He that walketh uprightly, and
> worketh righteousness, and
> speaketh the truth in his heart.
> PSALM 15:2

TAMBERLY
One of Equality and Honor
> Strength and honour are her
> clothing; and she shall rejoice in
> time to come.
> PROVERBS 31:25

TAMBOURINE
One of Joy and Rejoicing
> I will praise thee, O Lord, with
> my whole heart; . . . I will sing
> praise to thy name.
> PSALM 9:1–2

TAMEKA
Devotion
> I will bless the Lord at all times:
> his praise shall continually be
> in my mouth.
> PSALM 34:1

TAMI   *also* TAMMY
One of Equality
> God is my salvation; . . . my
> strength and my song; he also is
> become my salvation.
> ISAIAH 12:2

TAMMI
One of Equality
> God so loved the world that he
> gave his only begotten Son, that
> whosoever believeth in him
> should not perish, but have
> everlasting life.
> JOHN 3:16

TAMMIANE
Perfect One of Grace
> The Lord will give grace and
> glory.
> PSALM 84:11

TAMMY
also TAMI

One of Equality

> God so loved the world that he
> gave his only begotten Son, that
> whosoever believeth in him
> should not perish, but have
> everlasting life.
> JOHN 3:16

TANA

Immortal

> I will make thy name to be
> remembered: . . . the people
> praise thee for ever and ever.
> PSALM 45:17

TANDRA

Helper of Mankind

> The God of peace . . . make you
> perfect in every good work to do
> his will, working in you that
> which is wellpleasing in his
> sight.
> HEBREWS 13:20–21

TANDY

Industrious Spirit

> And whatsoever ye do, do it
> heartily, as to the Lord, and not
> unto men.
> COLOSSIANS 3:23

TANEKA

Immortal

> I will make thy name to be
> remembered in all generations.
> PSALM 45:17

TANGY

Heavenly Messenger

> How beautiful are the feet of
> them that preach the gospel of
> peace, and bring glad tidings of
> good things!
> ROMANS 10:15

TANIELA

Peaceful Spirit

> Thou wilt keep him in perfect
> peace, whose mind is stayed on
> thee: because he trusteth in
> thee.
> ISAIAH 26:3

TANNER

Industrious and Skilled One

> And whatsoever ye do, do it
> heartily, as to the Lord, and not
> unto men; . . . for ye serve the
> Lord Christ.
> COLOSSIANS 3:23–24

TANYA

A Fairy Queen

> I will praise thee; for I am
> fearfully and wonderfully
> made: marvellous are thy
> works.
> PSALM 139:14

TANZI

The Immortal One

> As for me, I will behold thy face
> in righteousness: I shall be
> satisfied, when I awake, with
> thy likeness.
> PSALM 17:15

TAOTAFA
Faithful and Patient

> *Remembering without ceasing
> your work of faith, and labour
> of love, and patience of hope in
> our Lord Jesus Christ.*
> 1 THESSALONIANS 1:3
>
> Samoan

TAPPER
Rock of Strength

> *In God is my salvation and my
> glory: the rock of my strength,
> and my refuge, is in God.*
> PSALM 62:7

TARA
My High Tower

> *The Lord is my rock, . . . my
> fortress, and my deliverer; my
> God, my strength, in whom I
> will trust.*
> PSALM 18:2

TARCISIUS
Diligent Harvester

> *Jesus saith . . . "Lift up your
> eyes, and look on the fields; for
> they are white already to
> harvest."*
> JOHN 4:34–35

TARITHA
Diligent Harvester

> *Jesus saith . . . "Lift up your
> eyes, and look on the fields; for
> they are white already to
> harvest."*
> JOHN 4:34–35

TARLESTON
Strong in the Lord

> *In God is my salvation and my
> glory: the rock of my strength,
> and my refuge, is in God.*
> PSALM 62:7

TARSHA
Prosperous One

> *I will sing unto the Lord,
> because he hath dealt
> bountifully with me.*
> PSALM 13:6

TARVARIS
Leader with Strength

> *Thou hast . . . given me the
> shield of thy salvation: . . . thy
> gentleness hath made me great.*
> PSALM 18:35

TASHA
One of Prayer and Peace

> *Thou wilt keep him in perfect
> peace, whose mind is stayed on
> thee: because he trusteth in thee.*
> ISAIAH 26:3

TASHIANNA
Prayer, Peace, Grace

> *The Lord will give grace and
> glory: no good thing will he
> withhold from them that walk
> uprightly.*
> PSALM 84:11

TASHIMA
One of Prayer and Peace

> *Thou wilt keep him in perfect
> peace, whose mind is stayed on
> thee: becasue he trusted in thee.*
> ISAIAH 26:3

TASIA
Of the Resurrection

> This is the Father's will . . . that
> every one which seeth the Son,
> and believeth on him, may have
> everlasting life.
> JOHN 6:39–40

TATIANNA
Cheerful One of Grace

> The Lord will give grace and
> glory: no good thing will he
> withhold from them that walk
> uprightly.
> PSALM 84:11

TATTON
From the Peaceful Homestead

> The Lord will give strength unto
> his people; the Lord will bless
> his people with peace.
> PSALM 29:11

TATUM
From the Peaceful Homestead

> The Lord will give strength unto
> his people; the Lord will bless
> his people with peace.
> PSALM 29:11

TAUFA'AHAU
Ruler with Strength

> Thou hast also given me the
> shield of thy salvation: . . . thy
> right hand hath holden me up.
> PSALM 18:35
>
> Polynesian

TAURUS
Strength and Security

> He that dwelleth in the secret
> place of the most High shall
> abide under the shadow of the
> Almighty.
> PSALM 91:1

TAVISTOCK
Faithful and Loyal

> He hath inclined his ear unto
> me, therefore will I call upon
> him as long as I live.
> PSALM 116:2

TAWNYA
Beyond Praise

> The Lord is great, and greatly to
> be praised: . . . strength and
> beauty are in his sanctuary.
> PSALM 96:4, 6

TAYANA
Firm of Purpose

> I have set the Lord always
> before me: because he is at my
> right hand, I shall not be moved.
> PSALM 16:8

TAYLOR
Clothed with Salvation

> I will . . . rejoice in the Lord, . . .
> for he hath clothed me with the
> garments of salvation.
> ISAIAH 61:10

TAZMA
Angel Girl

> How beautiful are the feet of
> them that preach the gospel of
> peace.
> ROMANS 10:15

T

TEAGAN
Pure Heart

> The statutes of the Lord are
> right, rejoicing the heart: the
> commandment of the Lord is
> pure, enlightening the eyes.
> PSALM 19:8

TEAGUE
Praising God

> I will praise thee, O Lord, with
> my whole heart; I will show
> forth all thy marvellous works.
> PSALM 9:1

TEALA
Of Divine Fame

> Thou hast also given me the
> shield of thy salvation: . . . thy
> right hand hath holden me up.
> PSALM 18:35

TECLA
Of Divine Fame

> Let the words of my mouth, and
> the meditation of my heart, be
> acceptable in thy sight.
> PSALM 19:14

TECUMSEH
A Shooting Star

> He telleth the number of the
> stars; he calleth them all by
> their names.
> PSALM 147:4
>   North American Indian

TED
Blessed Protector

> In God is my salvation and my
> glory: the rock of my strength,
> and my refuge, is in God.
> PSALM 62:7

TEKORA
One of Fame

> Wait on the Lord, and keep his
> way, and he shall exalt thee to
> inherit the land.
> PSALM 37:34

TELISHA
Perfect

> It is God that girdeth me with
> strength, and maketh my way
> perfect.
> PSALM 18:32

TELITHA
Maiden

> Strength and honour are her
> clothing; and she shall rejoice in
> time to come.
> PROVERBS 31:25

TELSING
Little Cloud Over the Mountains

> They that trust in the Lord shall
> be as mount Zion, which cannot
> be removed, but abideth forever.
> PSALM 125:1

TEMPERANCE
Moderation

> Rejoice in the Lord always: . . .
> Let your moderation be known
> unto all men. The Lord is at
> hand.
> PHILIPPIANS 4:4–5

TEMPLE
Consecration

> *I desired of the Lord, that ... I seek after; that I may dwell in the house of the Lord all the days of my life.*
> PSALM 27:4

TEMPLE JOY
Consecration and Joy

> *I will bless the Lord at all times: his praise shall continually be in my mouth.*
> PSALM 34:1

TENLEY
Courageous Leader

> *Thou hast also given me the shield of thy salvation: ... thy gentleness hath made me great.*
> PSALM 18:35

TENOR
One of Endurance

> *I have set the Lord always before me: because he is at my right hand, I shall not be moved.*
> PSALM 16:8

TEOFILO
Divinely Loved

> *God so loved the world, that he gave his only ... Son, that whosoever believeth in him should not perish.*
> JOHN 3:16

TEQUILA
Happy Spirits

> *Thou wilt show me the path of life: in thy presence is fulness of joy.*
> PSALM 16:11

TERENCE
Tenderhearted

> *Be ye kind one to another, tenderhearted, forgiving one another, even as God for Christ's sake hath forgiven you.*
> EPHESIANS 4:32

TERESA
Diligent Harvester

> *Jesus saith ... "Lift up your eyes, and look on the fields; for they are white already to harvest."*
> JOHN 4:35

TERI   *also* TERRY
Tenderhearted

> *Be ye kind one to another, tenderhearted, forgiving one another, even as God for Christ's sake hath forgiven you.*
> EPHESIANS 4:32

TERINEY
Patient and Tender

> *Let us run with patience the race that is set before us.*
> HEBREWS 12:1

TERRALYNE
Refreshing Spirit of Tenderness
> *Be ye kind one to another,*
> *tenderhearted, forgiving one*
> *another, even as God for Christ's*
> *sake hath forgiven you.*
> EPHESIANS 4:32

TERRI
Tenderhearted
> *Be ye kind one to another,*
> *tenderhearted, forgiving one*
> *another, even as God for Christ's*
> *sake hath forgiven you.*
> EPHESIANS 4:32

TERRILL
Ruler with Strength
> *Thou hast also given me the*
> *shield of thy salvation: . . . thy*
> *gentleness hath made me great.*
> PSALM 18:35

TERRY　　　　　*also* TERI
Tenderhearted
> *Be ye kind one to another,*
> *tenderhearted, forgiving one*
> *another, even as God for Christ's*
> *sake hath forgiven you.*
> EPHESIANS 4:32

TESHUA
Christmas Born
> *For unto you is born this day in*
> *the city of David a Saviour,*
> *which is Christ the Lord.*
> LUKE 2:11

TEXAS
Bringer of Joy
> *Thou wilt show me the path of*
> *life: in thy presence is fulness of*
> *joy; at thy right hand there are*
> *pleasures for evermore.*
> PSALM 16:11

THACKSTON
Mender of Roofs
> *Whatsoever ye do in word or*
> *deed, do all in the name of the*
> *Lord Jesus, . . . for ye serve the*
> *Lord Christ.*
> COLOSSIANS 3:17, 24

THADDAEUS
Praising God
> *I will praise thee, O Lord, with*
> *my whole heart; I will show*
> *forth all thy marvellous works.*
> PSALM 9:1

THAINE
An Attendant
> *Thou hast given me the shield of*
> *thy salvation: . . . thy gentleness*
> *hath made me great.*
> PSALM 18:35

THAIS
Giving Joy
> *Thou wilt show me the path of*
> *life: in thy presence is fulness of*
> *joy; at thy right hand there are*
> *pleasures for evermore.*
> PSALM 16:11

THALIA
Refreshing Spirit

> *The times of refreshing shall come from the presence of the Lord.*
> ACTS 3:19
>
> Hebrew

THANA
Noble and Immortal One

> *That men may know that thou, whose name alone is JEHOVAH, art the most high over all the earth.*
> PSALM 83:18
>
> Greek

THANG
Victory

> *But thanks to be God, which giveth us the victory through our Lord Jesus Christ.*
> 1 CORINTHIANS 15:57

THARON
A Hunter

> *Thy word is a lamp unto my feet, and a light unto my path.*
> PSALM 119:105

THAWLEY
In the Service of God

> *I am thy servant; give me understanding, that I may know thy testimonies.*
> PSALM 119:125

THEA
Divine

> *Whereby are given unto us exceeding great and precious promises that ye might be partakers of the divine nature.*
> 2 PETER 1:4

THEADORA
God's Gift

> *For by grace are ye saved through faith; and that not of yourselves: it is the gift of God.*
> EPHESIANS 2:8

THEADORE
God's Gift

> *For by grace are ye saved through faith; and that not of yourselves: it is the gift of God.*
> EPHESIANS 2:8

THECLA
Of Divine Fame

> *Let the words of my mouth, and the meditation of my heart, be acceptable in thy sight, O Lord.*
> PSALM 19:14

THELMA
A Child of God

> *Suffer little children to come unto me, . . . for of such is the kingdom of God.*
> LUKE 18:16

THEMISTOCLES
One of Justice

> *Justice and judgment are the habitation of thy throne: mercy and truth shall go before thy face.*
> PSALM 89:14
>
> Greek

THEO
Gift of God
> *Every good gift and every perfect gift is from above, and cometh down from the Father.*
> JAMES 1:17

THEOBALD
Bold Over the People
> *Herein is our love made perfect, that we may have boldness in the day of judgment.*
> 1 JOHN 4:17

THEODORE
Divine Gift
> *Every good gift and every perfect gift is from above, and cometh down from the Father of lights.*
> JAMES 1:17

THEOLIA
of Divine Speech
> *I will be glad and rejoice in thee: I will sing praise to thy name, O thou most High.*
> PSALM 9:2

THEOPHILUS
Loved by God
> *Beloved, let us love one another: for love is of God.*
> 1 JOHN 4:7

THEORA
God Speaks
> *I will instruct thee and teach thee in the way which thou shalt go: I will guide thee with mine eye.*
> PSALM 32:8

THERA
One of Freedom
> *Stand fast . . . in the liberty wherewith Christ hath made us free.*
> GALATIANS 5:1

THERAN
A Hunter
> *Thy word is a lamp unto my feet, and a light unto my path.*
> PSALM 119:105

THEREN
A Hunter
> *Thy word is a lamp unto my feet, and a light unto my path.*
> PSALM 119:105

THERESA
Diligent Harvester
> *Jesus saith . . . "Lift up your eyes, and look on the fields; for they are white already to harvest."*
> JOHN 4:35

THESSALONIANS
Conqueroring Hero
> *But thanks be to God, which giveth us the victory through our Lord Jesus Christ.*
> 1 CORINTHIANS 15:57

THILATHEA
Healing and Wholesome
> *Heal me, O'Lord, and I shall be healed; save me, and I shall be saved: for thou art my praise.*
> JEREMIAH 17:14

Latin

THOLA
One of Peace

> The Lord will give strength unto his people; the Lord will bless his people with peace.
> PSALM 29:11

THOMAS
One of Equality

> God so loved the world that he gave his only begotten Son, that whosoever believeth in him should not perish, but have everlasting life.
> JOHN 3:16

THOR
The Deity

> Jesus saith . . . I am the way, the truth, and the life: no man cometh unto the Father, but by me.
> JOHN 14:6

THORNTON
Strong in Spirit

> Be of good courage, and he shall strengthen your heart, all ye that hope in the Lord.
> PSALM 31:24

THORRIS
Divine Nature

> Whereby are given unto us exceeding great and precious promises: that . . . ye might be partakers of the divine nature.
> 2 PETER 1:4

THORSTEN
God's Jewel

> Thy hands have made me and fashioned me: give me understanding, that I may learn thy commandments.
> PSALM 119:73

THOURAIYA
Of God's Power

> Thou hast also given me the shield of thy salvation: . . . thy gentleness hath made me great.
> PSALM 18:35

THURGOOD
God's Warrior

> Fight the good fight of faith, lay hold on eternal life, whereunto thou art also called.
> 1 TIMOTHY 6:12

THURMAN
Under God's Protection

> In God is my salvation and my glory: the rock of my strength, my refuge, is in God.
> PSALM 62:7

TIA
One of Joy and Gladness

> Thou hast put gladness in my heart, . . . let them also that love thy name be joyful in thee.
> PSALM 4:7; 5:11

TIARRA
Crowned One

> When the chief Shepherd shall appear, ye shall receive a crown of glory that fadeth not away.
> 1 PETER 5:4

T

TICO
Wise One

> *For the Lord giveth wisdom: out of his mouth cometh knowledge and understanding.*
> PROVERBS 2:6

TIEA
Royal Princess

> *Thy hands have made me and fashioned me: give me understanding, that I may learn thy commandments.*
> PSALM 119:73

TIEGAN
Excellent Countenance

> *Thou art my God, and I will praise thee: thou art my God, I will exalt thee.*
> PSALM 118:28

TIERNAN
Kingly Royalty

> *Ye have not chosen me, but I have chosen you, . . . that ye should go and bring forth fruit.*
> JOHN 15:16

TIFFANIE
Heavenly Example

> *Ye are bought with a price therefore glorify God in your body and spirit, which are God's.*
> 1 CORINTHIANS 6:20

TIFFANY
Heavenly Example

> *Ye are bought with a price therefore glorify God in your body and spirit, which are God's.*
> 1 CORINTHIANS 6:20

TIGER
Ardent Spirit

> *Whatsoever ye do, do it heartily, as to the Lord, . . . for ye serve the Lord Christ.*
> COLOSSIANS 3:23–24

TILBERT
Good and Illustrious

> *Thou hast given me the shield of thy salvation: . . . thy gentleness hath made me great.*
> PSALM 18:35

TILLIE
Mighty in Battle

> *For thou hast girded me with strength unto the battle: . . . Therefore will I will give thanks . . . and sing praises unto thy name.*
> PSALM 18:39, 49

TIM
Honoring God

> *Bless the Lord, . . . thou art very great; thou art clothed with honour and majesty.*
> PSALM 104:1

TIMBERLY
Honoring God

> *Thanks be to God, which giveth us the victory through our Lord Jesus Christ.*
> 1 CORINTHIANS 15:57

TIMMY
Honoring God

> Thou art my God, . . . I will
> praise thee: . . . I will exalt thee.
> O give thanks unto the Lord.
> PSALM 118:28–29

TIMOTHY
Honoring God

> Bless the Lord, . . . thou art . . .
> great; thou art clothed with
> honour and majesty.
> PSALM 104:1

TINA
A Christian

> Ye are washed, . . . sanctified,
> . . . [and] justified in the name
> of the Lord Jesus.
> 1 CORINTHIANS 6:11

TINEKE
One of Strength and Valor

> In God is my salvation and my
> glory: the rock of my strength,
> and my refuge, is in God.
> PSALM 62:7

TINSLEY
From the Hill

> They that trust in the Lord shall
> be as mount Zion, which cannot
> be removed, but abideth for ever.
> PSALM 125:1

TINY
Exalted One

> I will bless the Lord at all times:
> his praise shall continually be
> in my mouth.
> PSALM 34:1

TIPPIN
One of Courage

> Be strong and of a good courage;
> . . . for the Lord thy God is with
> thee whithersoever thou goest.
> JOSHUA 1:9

TIRZAH
The Pleasant One

> Let the words of my mouth, and
> the meditation of my heart, be
> acceptable in thy sight.
> PSALM 19:14

TISHA
One of Gladness

> I will be glad and rejoice in
> thee: I will sing praise to thy
> name.
> PSALM 9:2

TITUS
Safely Protected

> Nevertheless God, that
> comforteth those that are cast
> down, comforted us by the
> coming of Titus.
> 2 CORINTHIANS 7:6

TOBBY
Goodness of the Lord

> For the Lord is good; his mercy
> is everlasting; and his truth
> endureth to all generations.
> PSALM 100:5

TOBIAH
The Lord Is My Good

> *I will love thee, O Lord, my strength . . . I will call upon the Lord, who is worthy to be praised.*
> PSALM 18:1, 3

TOBILYNN
Jehovah Is Good

> *The Lord is good; his mercy is everlasting; and his truth endureth to all generations.*
> PSALM 100:5

TOBY
One of Goodness

> *The Lord God, merciful and gracious, longsuffering, . . . abundant in goodness and truth.*
> EXODUS 34:6

TODD
Watchful

> *Watch thou in all things, endure afflictions, do the work of an evangelist, make full proof of thy ministry.*
> 2 TIMOTHY 4:5

TOLA
The Treasurer

> *I will sing unto the Lord, because he hath dealt bountifully with me.*
> PSALM 13:6

TOLBERT
One Who Proclaims

> *How beautiful are the feet of them that preach the gospel of peace, and bring glad tidings of good things!*
> ROMANS 10:15

TOLEDO
Beyond Praise

> *For the Lord is great, and greatly to be praised: . . . Honour and majesty are before him.*
> PSALM 96:4, 6

TOM
One of Equality

> *God so loved the world, that he gave his . . . Son, that whosoever believeth in him should . . . have everlasting life.*
> JOHN 3:16

TOMMY
One of Equality

> *God so loved the world, that he gave his . . . Son, that whosoever believeth in him should . . . have everlasting life.*
> JOHN 3:16

TONDALOYO
Beyond Praise

> *For the Lord is great, and greatly to be praised: . . . Honour and majesty are before him.*
> PSALM 96:4, 6

TONI
Beyond Praise

> But I will hope continually, and will yet praise thee more and more.
> PSALM 71:14

TONJA
Beyond Praise

> The Lord is great, and greatly to be praised: . . . Honour and majesty are before him.
> PSALM 96:4, 6

TONY
Beyond Praise

> For the Lord is great, and greatly to be praised: he is to be feared above all gods.
> PSALM 96:4

TONYA
Beyond Praise

> "I am Alpha and Omega, the beginning and the ending," . . . saith the Lord.
> REVELATION 1:8

TOOTIE
Strong in the Lord

> For thou art my rock and my fortress; therefore for thy name's sake lead me, and guide me.
> PSALM 31:3

TOOTSIE
A Happy One

> I will praise thee with uprightness of heart.
> PSALM 119:7

TOPAZ
Precious Jewel

> I will praise thee; for I am fearfully and wonderfully made.
> PSALM 139:14

TOPHER
Quiet and Peaceful

> Thou wilt keep him in perfect peace, whose mind is stayed on thee: because he trusteth in thee.
> ISAIAH 26:3

TORBJORN
God's Strength

> In God is my salvation and my glory: the rock of my strength, and my refuge, is in God.
> PSALM 62:7

TOREY
One Who Is Majestic

> The voice of the Lord is powerful; the voice of the Lord is full of majesty.
> PSALM 29:4

TORI
Majestic

> The voice of the Lord is powerful; the voice of the Lord is full of majesty.
> PSALM 29:4

TORRIE
One Who Is Majestic

> The Lord is great, and greatly to be praised: . . . Honour and majesty are before him.
> PSALM 96:4, 6

TOSHIA
One of Prayer and Peace

> *The Lord will give strength unto his people; the Lord will bless his people with peace.*
> PSALM 29:11

TOSHIKO
Year of the Child

> *Be thou an example of the believers, in word, in conversation, in charity, in spirit, in faith, in purity.*
> 1 TIMOTHY 4:12

TOVAH
Good

> *For thou, Lord, art good, and ready to forgive; and plenteous in mercy unto all them that call upon thee.*
> PSALM 86:5

TOWNSEND
Suburban Dweller

> *Thy word is a lamp unto my feet, and a light unto my path.*
> PSALM 119:105

TOY
Beloved One

> *Beloved, let us love one another: for love is of God; and every one that loveth is born of God, and knoweth God.*
> 1 JOHN 4:7

TRACEY
Diligent Harvester

> *Jesus saith . . . "Lift up your eyes, and look on the fields; for they are white already to harvest."*
> JOHN 4:35

TRACIE
Diligent Harvester

> *Jesus saith . . . "Lift up your eyes, and look on the fields; for they are white already to harvest."*
> JOHN 4:35

TRACY
Diligent Harvester

> *Jesus saith . . . Lift up your eyes, and look on the fields; for they are white already to harvest.*
> JOHN 4:34–35

TRAFTON
Pressing Toward the Goal

> *I press toward the mark for the prize of the high calling of God in Christ Jesus.*
> PHILIPPIANS 3:14

TRAILER
Radiant Star

> *They that be wise shall shine as the brightness of the firmament; and they that turn many to righteousness as the stars for ever and ever.*
> DANIEL 12:3

NAME *That* BABY!

TRANQUILLITY
Peaceful One

> The Lord will give strength unto
> his people; the Lord will bless
> his people with peace.
> PSALM 29:11

TRANT
Productive

> The Lord thy God shall bless
> thee in all thine increase, and in
> all the works of thine hands.
> DEUTERONOMY 16:15

TRAVAREOUS
Walking with the Lord

> Thy word is a lamp unto my
> feet, and a light unto my path.
> PSALM 119:105

TRAVERS
At the Crossroads

> Thy word is a lamp unto my
> feet, and a light unto my path.
> PSALM 119:105

TRAVIS
One of Unity

> Behold, how good and how
> pleasant it is for brethren to
> dwell together in unity!
> PSALM 133:1

TRAY
One who Follows

> My soul followeth hard after
> thee: thy right hand upholdeth
> me.
> PSALM 63:8

TREASURE
Cherished and Beloved

> Ye have not chosen me, but I
> have chosen you, . . . that ye
> should go and bring forth fruit.
> JOHN 15:16

TREAVOR
Prudent One

> The wise in heart shall be called
> prudent: and the sweetness of
> the lips increaseth learning.
> PROVERBS 16:21

TREBLE
Joyful Sound

> I will praise thee, O Lord, with
> my whole heart; . . . I will sing
> praise to thy name.
> PSALM 9:1–2

TRELLA
Little Star

> They that be wise shall shine as
> the brightness of the firmament;
> . . . as the stars for ever and ever.
> DANIEL 12:3

TRENT
Productive

> The Lord thy God shall bless
> thee in all thine increase, and in
> the works of thine hands.
> DEUTERONOMY 16:15

TRENTON
Productive

> Let your light so shine before
> men that they may see your
> good works, and glorify your
> Father which is in heaven.
> MATTHEW 5:16

TRESHONDA
Diligent Harvester

> Jesus saith . . . "Lift up your eyes,
> and look on the fields; for they
> are white already to harvest."
> JOHN 4:34–35

TREVER
One Who Is Prudent and Kind

> Be ye kind one to another, . . .
> forgiving one another, even as
> God for Christ's sake hath
> forgiven you.
> EPHESIANS 4:32

TRILLA
A Star

> They that be wise shall shine as
> the brightness of the firmament;
> and they that turn many to
> righteousness as the stars for
> ever and ever.
> DANIEL 12:3

TRINA
Pure

> The words of the Lord are
> pure words: as silver tried
> in a furnace of earth,
> purified seven times.
> PSALM 12:6

TRINETTE
Pure Heart

> Blessed are the pure in heart:
> for they shall see God.
> MATTHEW 5:8

TRINH
Pure Heart

> Blessed are the pure in heart:
> for they shall see God.
> MATTHEW 5:8

TRINI
Pure Heart

> Blessed are the pure in heart:
> for they shall see God.
> MATTHEW 5:8

TRINIDAD
Power and Glory

> For the Lord is great, and
> greatly to be praised: . . .
> Honour and majesty are before
> him.
> PSALM 96:4, 6

TRINITY
The Deity

> Jesus saith . . . "I am the way,
> the truth, and the life: no man
> cometh unto the Father, but by
> me."
> JOHN 14:6

TRIP
A Traveler

> Thy word is a lamp unto my
> feet, and a light unto my path.
> PSALM 119:105

TRISH
Full of Honor

> Strength and honour are her
> clothing; and she shall rejoice in
> time to come.
> PROVERBS 31:25

TRISTA
Compassionate Spirit

> I will praise thee: for thou hast heard me, and art become my salvation.
> PSALM 118:21

TRISTAN
Compassionate Spirit

> I will praise thee: for thou hast heard me, and art become my salvation.
> PSALM 118:21

TROTTIER
Messenger

> How beautiful are the feet of them that preach the gospel of peace, and bring glad tidings of good things!
> ROMANS 10:15

TROY
Reliable

> What doth the Lord require of thee, but to do justly, and to love mercy, and to walk humbly with thy God?
> MICAH 6:8

TRUBY
True and Faithful

> I have set the Lord always before me: because he is at my right hand, I shall not be moved.
> PSALM 16:8

TRUCILLE
One of Truth and Light

> They that be wise shall shine as the brightness of the firmament; . . . as the stars for ever and ever.
> DANIEL 12:3

TRUDY
Maiden of Strength

> God is my salvation; I will trust, and not be afraid: for the Lord JEHOVAH is my strength and my song; . . . my salvation.
> ISAIAH 12:2

TRUITT
Faithful and Steadfast

> Therefore, my beloved brethren, be ye stedfast, unmovable, always abounding in the work of the Lord.
> 1 CORINTHIANS 15:58

TRUMAN
Faithful or Loyal

> Because he hath inclined his ear unto me, therefore will I call upon him as long as I live.
> PSALM 116:2

TRUTH
One of Truth

> Lead me in thy truth, and teach me: for thou art the God of my salvation; on thee do I wait all the day.
> PSALM 25:5

TRYPHENA
The Delicate and Luxurious One

I will praise thee; for I am fearfully and wonderfully made: marvellous are thy works.
PSALM 139:14

TUCKER
Master Weaver

And whatsoever ye do, do it heartily, as to the Lord, . . . for ye serve the Lord Christ.
COLOSSIANS 3:23–24

TUESDI
Born on Tuesday

Let the words of my mouth, and the meditation of my heart, be acceptable in thy sight, O Lord.
PSALM 19:14

TULLEY
Lives with the Peace of God

The Lord will give strength unto his people; the Lord will bless his people with peace.
PSALM 29:11

TURNER
Skilled Lathe Worker

God gave them knowledge and skill in all learning and wisdom.
DANIEL 1:17

TWAIN
A Twin, One of Equality

God so loved the world, that he gave his only . . . Son, that whosoever believeth in him should not perish.
JOHN 3:16

TWANNA
Walking with the Lord

Thy word is a lamp unto my feet, and a light unto my path. . . . Thou art my hiding place and my shield: I hope in thy word.
PSALM 119:105, 114

TWILA
Chosen of the Lord

Ye have not chosen me, but I have chosen you, and ordained you, . . . go and bring forth fruit.
JOHN 15:16

TWINKLE
One of Radiance

Let your light so shine before men, that they may see your good works, and glorify your Father . . . in heaven.
MATTHEW 5:16

TYANNE
Industrious One of Grace

The Lord will give grace and glory: no good thing will he withhold from them that walk uprightly.
PSALM 84:11

TYJUAN
Bold and Gracious One

A God full of compassion, and gracious, longsuffering, and plenteous in mercy and truth.
PSALM 86:15

TYLENE
One Who Shares

> Give, and it shall be given unto
> you.
> LUKE 6:38

TYLER
Industrious

> Whatsoever ye do, do it heartily,
> as to the Lord, . . . for ye serve
> the Lord Christ.
> COLOSSIANS 3:23–24

TYNYA
A Christian

> Ye are washed, . . . ye are
> sanctified, but ye are justified in
> the name of the Lord Jesus.
> 1 CORINTHIANS 6:11

TYRA
Rock of Strength

> In God is my salvation and my
> glory: the rock of my strength,
> and my refuge, is in God.
> PSALM 62:7

TYREL
Ruler with Strength

> The Lord is my light and my
> salvation; whom shall I fear?
> the Lord is the strength of my
> life; of whom shall I be afraid?
> PSALM 27:1

TYRONE
An Absolute Ruler

> He that ruleth over men must be
> just, ruling in the fear of God.
> 2 SAMUEL 23:3

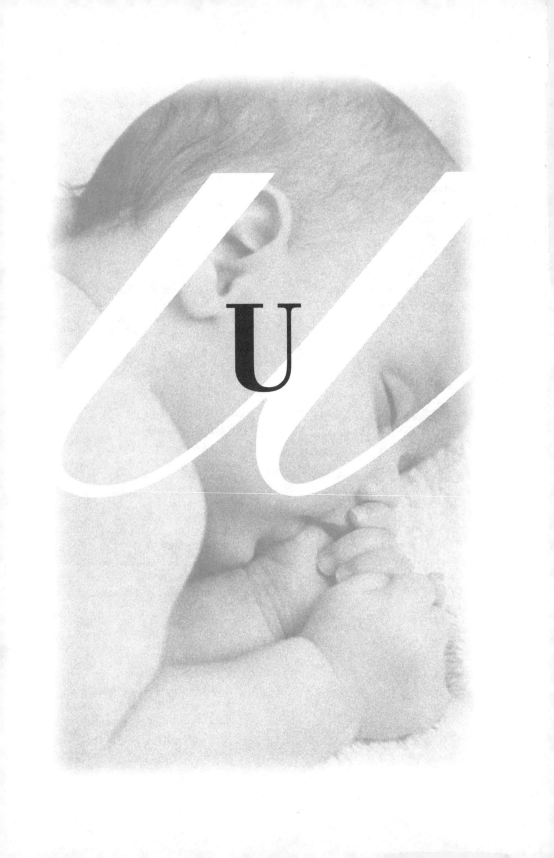

U

UBA
One of Wisdom

For the Lord giveth wisdom: out of his mouth cometh knowledge and understanding.
PROVERBS 2:6

UBALDO
Prince of Intellect

My mouth shall speak of wisdom; and the meditation of my heart shall be of understanding.
PSALM 49:3

Teutonic

UDAWNA
I Will Praise God

I will praise thee, O Lord, with my whole heart; . . . I will sing praise to thy name.
PSALM 9:1–2

African (Nigeria)

UDAY
Prosperous One

This book of the law . . . thou mayest observe to do according to all that is written . . . [to] make thy way prosperous, and . . . good.
JOSHUA 1:8

UEL
Heard by God

The Lord will hear when I call unto him.
PSALM 4:3

UERYL
Light of God

Let your light so shine before men, that they may see your good works, and glorify your Father in heaven.
MATTHEW 5:16

Hebrew

ULA
From The Land of the Noble

Ye are a chosen generation, a royal priesthood, . . . that ye should show forth the praises of him who hath called you.
1 PETER 2:9

Teutonic

ULDIS
Prosperous One

I will sing unto the Lord, because he hath dealt bountifully with me.
PSALM 13:6

ULI
Leader of Strength

The Lord is my rock, . . . my fortress, and my deliverer; my strength, in whom I will trust.
PSALM 18:2

German

ULKER
Noble Industrious One

And whatsoever ye do, do it heartily, as to the Lord, and not unto men; . . . for ye serve the Lord Christ.
COLOSSIANS 3:23–24

Teutonic

ULLA
My Yoke Is of God

> Take my yoke upon you, and
> learn of me; . . . For my yoke is
> easy, and my burden is light.
> MATTHEW 11:29–30
>
> Hebrew

ULRIAH
Ruler Over All

> He that ruleth over men must be
> just, ruling in the fear of God.
> 2 SAMUEL 23:3B

ULRICH
Noble and Powerful

> Ye are a chosen generation, a
> royal priesthood, . . . that ye
> should show forth the praises of
> him who hath called you.
> 1 PETER 2:9
>
> German

ULRIKE
Noble and Powerful

> Ye are a chosen generation, a
> royal priesthood, . . . that ye
> should show forth the praises of
> him who hath called you.
> 1 PETER 2:9

ULULANI
To Grow Spiritually

> Grow in grace, and in the
> knowledge of our Lord and
> Saviour Jesus Christ.
> 2 PETER 3:18
>
> Polynesian

ULYSSES
Strong Spirit

> I will say of the Lord, He is my
> refuge and my fortress: my God;
> in him will I trust.
> PSALM 91:2
>
> Greek

UMBERTO
Light of the Home

> Let your light so shine before
> men, that they may see your
> good works, and glorify your
> Father which is in heaven.
> MATTHEW 5:16

UNAZER
Perfect Unity

> Be ye therefore perfect, even as
> your Father which is in heaven
> is perfect.
> MATTHEW 5:48

UNDERHILL
Dweller at the Foot of the Hill

> They that trust in the Lord shall
> be as mount Zion, which cannot
> be removed, but abideth for
> ever.
> PSALM 125:1

UNDRA
Happy Victory

> Sing forth the honour of his
> name: make his praise glorious.
> PSALM 66:2

UNETA
The One of Perfection

> As for God, his way is perfect:
> the word of the Lord is tried: he
> is a buckler to all those that
> trust in him.
> PSALM 18:30

UNICE
Happy Victory

> Sing forth the honour of his
> name: make his praise glorious.
> PSALM 66:2

UPTON
From the High Estate

> As the mountains are round
> about Jerusalem, so the Lord is
> round about his people from
> henceforth even for ever.
> PSALM 125:2

URBAN
Courteous Spirit

> And be ye kind one to another,
> tenderhearted, forgiving one
> another, even as God for Christ's
> sake hath forgiven you.
> EPHESIANS 4:32

URENA
Heavenly One

> Ye are bought with a price:
> therefore glorify God in your
> body, and in your spirit, which
> are God's.
> 1 CORINTHIANS 6:20

URIAH
One of Light

> They that be wise shall shine as
> the brightness of the firmament;
> . . . as the stars for ever and ever.
> DANIEL 12:3

URIAN
From Heaven

> The heavens declare his
> righteousness, and all the people
> see his glory.
> PSALM 97:6

URIAS
My Light Is Jehovah

> I am the light of the world: he
> that followeth me . . . shall have
> the light of life.
> JOHN 8:12

URSULA
Great Protector

> I will say of the Lord, He is my
> refuge and my fortress: my God;
> in him will I trust.
> PSALM 91:2

USALANI
Heavenly Rain

> The times of refreshing shall
> come from the presence of the
> Lord.
> ACTS 3:19

USHER
One Who Guides

> I will instruct thee and teach
> thee in the way which thou shalt
> go: I will guide thee with mine
> eye.
> PSALM 32:8

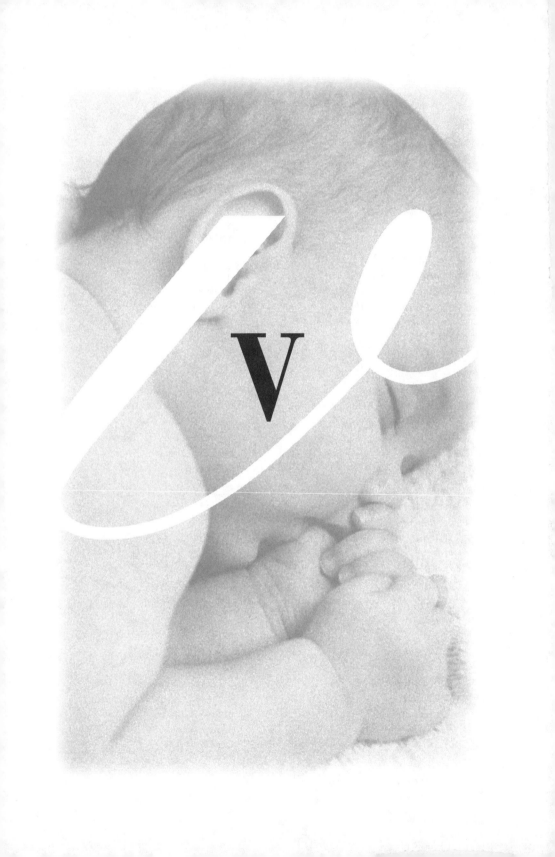

VADIA
Knowledge and Wisdom

> *For the Lord giveth wisdom: out of his mouth cometh knowledge and understanding.*
> PROVERBS 2:6

VAILE
Strong and Valorous One

> *The Lord is my light and my salvation; whom shall I fear? the Lord is the strength of my life; of whom shall I be afraid?*
> PSALM 27:1

VAL
One of Power and Strength

> *God is my strength and power: and he maketh my way perfect.*
> 2 SAMUEL 22:33

VALARIE
Determination

> *I have set the Lord always before me: because he is at my right hand, I shall not be moved.*
> PSALM 16:8

VALDOSTA
Strength and Power

> *The Lord is my light and my salvation; whom shall I fear? the Lord is the strength of my life; of whom shall I be afraid?*
> PSALM 27:1

VALEDA
One of Strength and Valor

> *Thou hast also given me the shield of thy salvation: and thy right hand hath holden me up, . . . thy gentleness hath made me great.*
> PSALM 18:35

VALENA
To Be Strong

> *In God is my salvation and my glory: the rock of my strength, and my refuge, is in God.*
> PSALM 62:7

VALENTINE
To Be Strong and Valiant

> *The Lord is my rock, . . . my fortress, . . . my deliverer; my God, my strength, in whom I will trust.*
> PSALM 18:2

VALERIE
Of Determined Purpose

> *The Lord is my rock, . . . my fortress, . . . my deliverer; my God, my strength, in whom I will trust.*
> PSALM 18:2

VALOMA
Strong Protector

> *He that dwelleth in the secret place of the most High shall abide under the shadow of the Almighty.*
> PSALM 91:1

VANCE
One from Afar
> *Blessed is the nation whose God is the Lord; and the people whom he hath chosen for his own inheritance.*
> PSALM 33:12

VANDE
Walking with the Lord
> *Thy word is a lamp unto my feet, and a light unto my path.*
> PSALM 119:105

VANDIVER
Noble and Strong Spirit
> *I press toward the mark for the prize of the high calling of God in Christ Jesus.*
> PHILIPPIANS 3:14

VANESSA
Butterfly
> *The Lord taketh pleasure in his people: he will beautify the meek with salvation.*
> PSALM 149:4

VANETTA
Devoted One
> *I will bless the Lord at all times: his praise shall continually be in my mouth.*
> PSALM 34:1

VANGIE
Bearer of Glad Tidings
> *How beautiful are the feet of them that preach the gospel of peace, and bring glad tidings of good things.*
> ROMANS 10:15

VANIA
Gracious Gift of God
> *Every good gift and every perfect gift is from above, and cometh down from the Father of lights.*
> JAMES 1:17

VANYA
Gracious Gift of Jehovah
> *Every good gift and every perfect gift is from above, and cometh down from the Father of lights.*
> JAMES 1:17

VARNELL
Bringer of Victory
> *Thanks be to God, which giveth us the victory through our Lord Jesus Christ.*
> 1 CORINTHIANS 15:57

VARRICK
Master of the Sea
> *O Lord, our Lord, how excellent is thy name in all the earth! who hast set thy glory above the heavens.*
> PSALM 8:1

VARY
A Stranger
> *Nevertheless the foundation of God standeth sure, . . . The Lord knoweth them that are his.*
> 2 TIMOTHY 2:19

VASHIA
Beautiful One

> I will praise thee; for I am
> fearfully and wonderfully
> made: . . . How precious also are
> thy thoughts unto me, O God!
> PSALM 139:14, 17

Slavic

VASILIKI
Magnificent and Kingly

> For the Lord is great, and
> greatly to be praised: . . .
> Honour and majesty are before
> him.
> PSALM 96:4, 6

Greek

VAUGHAN
The Little

> My grace is sufficient for thee:
> for my strength is made perfect
> in weakness.
> 2 CORINTHIANS 12:9

Celtic

VEARLENE
Faithful and True

> Therefore, my beloved brethren,
> be ye stedfast, unmovable,
> always abounding in the work
> of the Lord.
> 1 CORINTHIANS 15:58

VEDA
Sacred Understanding

> The entrance of thy works
> giveth light; it giveth
> understanding unto the simple.
> PSALM 119:130

Teutonic

VELA
Of Inspired Wisdom

> For the Lord giveth wisdom: out
> of his mouth cometh knowledge
> and understanding.
> PROVERBS 2:6

VELMAR
Chosen Protection

> Ye have not chosen me, but I
> have chosen you, and ordained
> you, that ye should go and bring
> forth fruit.
> JOHN 15:16

VELVA
One of Wisdom

> My mouth shall speak of
> wisdom; and the meditation of
> my heart shall be of
> understanding.
> PSALM 49:3

VELVET
A Fleece

> My soul, wait thou only upon
> God; for my expectation is from
> him.
> PSALM 62:5

VENCIE
Conquering One

> Whatsoever is born of God
> overcometh the world: and this
> is the victory that overcometh
> the world, even our faith.
> 1 JOHN 5:4

V

VENEDA
Blessed

> Blessed be the Lord God, the
> God of Israel, who only doth
> wondrous things.
> PSALM 72:18

VENETA
Blessed

> Blessed are they that keep his
> testimonies, and that seek him
> with the whole heart.
> PSALM 119:2

VENIDA
The Blessed

> Blessed are they that keep his
> testimonies, and that seek him
> with the whole heart.
> PSALM 119:2

VEOLA
Modest and of Quiet Strength

> Trust ye in the Lord for ever: for
> in the Lord JEHOVAH is
> everlasting strength.
> ISAIAH 26:4

VERA
Faithful Spirit

> Deal with thy servant according
> unto thy mercy, and teach me
> thy statues.
> PSALM 119:124

VERDINIA
One of Abundant Life

> I am come that they might have
> life, and . . . have it more
> abundantly.
> JOHN 10:10

VERLANE
Faithful and True

> Let the words of my mouth, and
> the meditation of my heart, be
> acceptable in thy sight, O Lord.
> PSALM 19:14

VERNANNE
Abundant One of Grace

> The Lord will give grace and
> glory: no good thing will he
> withhold from them that walk
> uprightly.
> PSALM 84:11

VERNETTE
Abundant Life

> I am come that they might have
> life, and that they might have it
> more abundantly.
> JOHN 10:10

VERNIA
Abundant Life

> I am come that they might have
> life, and that they might have it
> more abundantly.
> JOHN 10:10

VERNON
The Abundant One

> The grace of our Lord was
> exceeding abundant with faith
> and love which is in Christ
> Jesus.
> 1 TIMOTHY 1:14

VERNOR
Fighter for the Faith

> *Fight the good fight of faith, lay hold on eternal life, whereunto thou art also called.*
> 1 TIMOTHY 6:12

VERONICA
True Image of Christ

> *For as many of you as have been baptized into Christ have put on Christ.*
> GALATIANS 3:27

VESPER
The Evening Star

> *They that be wise shall shine as the brightness of the firmament; and they that turn many to righteousness as the stars for ever and ever.*
> DANIEL 12:3

VICENTE
The Conquering One

> *In all these things we are more than conquerors through him that loved us.*
> ROMANS 8:37

VICK
Victorious Life

> *But thanks be to God, which giveth us the victory through our Lord Jesus Christ.*
> 1 CORINTHIANS 15:57

VICKEY
Victorious One

> *But thanks be to God, which giveth us the victory through our Lord Jesus Christ.*
> 1 CORINTHIANS 15:57

VICKI
Victorious One

> *Thanks be to God, which giveth us the victory through our Lord Jesus Christ.*
> 1 CORINTHIANS 15:57

VICKIE
Victorious One

> *Thanks be to God, which giveth us the victory through our Lord Jesus Christ.*
> 1 CORINTHIANS 15:57

VICTOR
Victorious Life

> *Whatsoever is born of God overcometh the world: and this is the victory that overcometh the world, even our faith.*
> 1 JOHN 5:4

VICTOR GUADALUPE
Victorious Nobility

> *But thanks be to God, which giveth us the victory through our Lord Jesus Christ.*
> 1 CORINTHIANS 15:57

German

VICTORIA
Victorious One

> *Thanks be to God, which giveth us the victory through our Lord Jesus Christ.*
> 1 CORINTHIANS 15:57

VIKING
The Conquering One

> *In all these things we are more than conquerors through him that loved us.*
> ROMANS 8:37

VINCE
The Conquering One

> *In all these things we are more than conquerors through him that loved us.*
> ROMANS 8:37

VINCENT
Conquering One

> *In all these things we are more than conquerors through him that loved us.*
> ROMANS 8:37

Latin

VIOLA
Quiet Strength

> *In quietness and in confidence shall be your strength.*
> ISAIAH 30:15

VIOLET
One of Modest Grace

> *The God of peace, . . . Make you perfect in every good work to do his will, . . . that which is wellpleasing in his sight.*
> HEBREWS 13:20A–21

VIRGIL
Flourishing

> *Great is the Lord, and greatly to be praised in the city of our God, in the mountain of his holiness.*
> PSALM 48:1

VIRGINIA
Pure One

> *Blessed are the pure in heart: for they shall see God.*
> MATTHEW 5:8

VITALIA
Life

> *God so loved the world, that he gave his only . . . Son, that whosoever believeth in him should not perish, but have everlasting life.*
> JOHN 3:16

VITALIS
Life

> *The Lord is my light and my salvation; whom shall I fear? the Lord is the strength of my life; of whom shall I be afraid?*
> PSALM 27:1

VIVIAN
Lively

> *Whatsoever ye do, do it heartily, as to the Lord, . . . for ye serve the Lord Christ.*
> COLOSSIANS 3:23–24

VIVIANNE
One of Life and Grace

> *The Lord will give grace and glory: no good thing will he withhold from them that walk uprightly.*
> PSALM 84:11

VOLLMER
From the Famous Heritage

> *Thou, O God, hast heard my vows: thou hast given me the heritage of those who fear thy name.*
> PSALM 61:5

VON
Bringer of Victory

> *Whatsoever is born of God overcometh the world: and this is the victory that overcometh the world, even our faith.*
> 1 JOHN 5:4

WADDELL
One of Courage

> The Lord is my light and my
> salvation; whom shall I fear?
> the Lord is the strength of my
> life; of whom shall I be afraid?
> PSALM 27:1

WADE
Advancing with Humility

> I press toward the mark for the
> prize of the high calling of God
> in Christ Jesus.
> PHILIPPIANS 3:14

WAGES
A Wagon Maker

> Whatsoever ye do, do it heartily,
> as to the Lord, and not unto
> men; . . . for ye serve the Lord
> Christ.
> COLOSSIANS 3:23–24

WALESKA
Strong Ruler

> Thou hast . . . given me the
> shield of thy salvation: . . . thy
> gentleness hath made me great.
> PSALM 18:35
>
> German

WALKER
A Fuller of Cloth

> And whatsoever ye do in word
> or deed, do all in the name of
> Lord Jesus.
> COLOSSIANS 3:17

WALLACE
Industrious Spirit

> Whatsoever ye do, do it heartily,
> as to the Lord, and not unto
> men; . . . for ye serve the Lord
> Christ.
> COLOSSIANS 3:23–24

WALLIS
Industrious Spirit

> And whatsoever ye do, do it
> heartily, as to the Lord, and not
> unto men; . . . for ye serve the
> Lord Christ.
> COLOSSIANS 3:23–24

WALLY
A Traveler

> Go ye . . . teach all nations, . . .
> to observe all things whatsoever
> I have commanded you.
> MATTHEW 28:19–20

WALTEN
From the Fortified Town

> As the mountains are round
> about Jerusalem, so the Lord is
> round about his people.
> PSALM 125:2

WALTER
Mighty Ruler

> He that ruleth over men must be
> just, ruling in the fear of God.
> 2 SAMUEL 23:3

WANDA
Walking with the Lord

> Thy word is a lamp unto my
> feet, and a light unto my path.
> PSALM 119:105

WANITA
also JUANITA
Gracious Gift of God

> Every good gift and every
> perfect gift is from above, and
> cometh down from the Father of
> lights.
> JAMES 1:17

WARD
Watchful One

> Watch ye, stand fast in the faith,
> quit you like men, be strong.
> 1 CORINTHIANS 16:13

WARNER
Guardian of Strength

> Watch ye, stand fast in the faith,
> quit you like men, be strong.
> 1 CORINTHIANS 16:13

WARREN
A Protector

> The Lord is my rock, . . . my
> fortress, . . . my deliverer; my
> God, my strength, in whom I
> will trust.
> PSALM 18:2

WARRINGTON
Watchful

> Be ye therefore sober, and watch
> unto prayer.
> 1 PETER 4:7

WASHINGTON
The Wise One

> For the Lord giveth wisdom: out
> of his mouth cometh knowledge
> and understanding.
> PROVERBS 2:6

WATSON
A Mighty Ruler

> The Lord is my light and my
> salvation; whom shall I fear?
> the Lord is the strength of my
> life; of whom shall I be afraid.
> PSALM 27:1

WAVE
From the Peaceful Meadow

> The Lord is my Shepherd; I
> shall not want. He maketh me to
> lie down in green pastures.
> PSALM 23:1

WAYNE
Skilled One

> God gave them knowledge and
> skill in all learning and wisdom.
> DANIEL 1:17

WEAVER
A Weaver

> And whatsoever ye do, do it
> heartily, as to the Lord, and not
> unto men; . . . for ye serve the
> Lord Christ.
> COLOSSIANS 3:23–24

WEBSTER
A Weaver

> And whatsoever ye do, do it
> heartily, as to the Lord, and not
> unto men; . . . for ye serve the
> Lord Christ.
> COLOSSIANS 3:23–24

WELLS
From the Springs

> *The words of a man's mouth are*
> *as deep waters, and the*
> *wellspring of wisdom as a*
> *flowing brook.*
> PROVERBS 18:4

WENDELL
Walking with the Lord

> *Thy word is a lamp unto my*
> *feet, and a light unto my path.*
> PSALM 119:105

WENDY
Walking with the Lord

> *Thy word is a lamp unto my*
> *feet, and a light unto my path.*
> PSALM 119:105

WENOAH
Firstborn Daughter

> *Many daughters have done*
> *virtuously, but thou excellest*
> *them all.*
> PROVERBS 31:29

WENONA   also WINONA, WYNONA
Firstborn Daughter

> *I will praise thee; for I am*
> *fearfully and wonderfully*
> *made: marvellous are thy*
> *works.*
> PSALM 139:14

WERNER
Guardian Protector

> *The Lord is my rock, . . .*
> *fortress, . . . my deliverer, My*
> *God, my strength, in whom I*
> *will trust.*
> PSALM 18:2

WES
Prosperous Spirit

> *I will sing unto the Lord,*
> *because he hath dealt*
> *bountifully with me.*
> PSALM 13:6

WESLEY
Abiding in Him

> *If ye abide in me, and my words*
> *abide in you, ye shall ask what*
> *ye will, and it shall be done unto*
> *you.*
> JOHN 15:7

WESS
Prosperous Spirit

> *I will sing unto the Lord,*
> *because he hath dealt*
> *bountifully with me.*
> PSALM 13:6

WESTON
One of Quiet Peace

> *The Lord will give srength unto*
> *his people; the Lord will bless*
> *his people with peace.*
> PSALM 29:11

WHEELER
A Wheel Maker

> *Whatsoever ye do in word or deed, do all in the name of the Lord Jesus.*
> COLOSSIANS 3:17

WHITFIELD
From the White Field

> *Thy word is a lamp unto my feet, and a light unto my path.*
> PSALM 119:105

WHITNEY
Pure and Refreshing

> *The times of refreshing shall come from the presence of the Lord.*
> ACTS 3:19

WHITTY
The Wise One

> *For the Lord giveth wisdom: out of his mouth cometh knowledge and understanding.*
> PROVERBS 2:6

WICKE
Resolute Protector

> *As for God, his way is perfect: . . . It is God that girdeth me with strength, and maketh my way perfect.*
> PSALM 18:30, 32

WILBORN
From the Peaceful Brook

> *The Lord is my shepherd; I shall not want. He maketh me to lie down in green pastures.*
> PSALM 23:1–2

WILBUR
Pledge of Faith

> *If thou shalt confess . . . the Lord Jesus, and shalt believe . . . thou shalt be saved.*
> ROMANS 10:9

WILBURT
Bright of Will

> *My mouth shall speak of wisdom; and the meditation of my heart shall be of understanding.*
> PSALM 49:3

WILDA
Free Spirit

> *Stand fast therefore in the liberty wherewith Christ hath made us free.*
> GALATIANS 5:1

WILFRED
One of Peace

> *The Lord will give strength unto his people; the Lord will bless his people with peace.*
> PSALM 29:11

WILHELMENIA
Chosen Protection

> *Ye have not chosen me, but I have chosen you, and ordained you, that ye should go and bring forth fruit.*
> JOHN 15:16

WILKINSON
Resolute Protector

> *I will say of the Lord, He is my refuge and my fortress: my God; in him will I trust.*
> PSALM 91:2

WILLARD
Steadfast Determination

> *I can do all things through Christ, which strengtheneth me.*
> PHILIPPIANS 4:13

WILLIAM
Bold Protector

> *Be strong in the Lord, and in the power of his might. Put on the whole armour of God.*
> EPHESIANS 6:10–11

WILLIAMSON
Bold Protector

> *Be strong in the Lord, and in the power of his might.*
> EPHESIANS 6:10

WILLIE
Guardian Protector

> *He that dwelleth in the secret place of the most High shall abide under the shadow of the Almighty.*
> PSALM 91:1

WILLIEMAE
Resolute Protector

> *Be strong in the Lord, and in the power of his might. Put on the whole armour of God, that ye may be able to stand.*
> EPHESIANS 6:10–11

WILMA
Resolute Protectress

> *The Lord thy God is with thee whithersoever thou goest.*
> JOSHUA 1:9

WILTON
From the Farm by the Spring

> *The Lord is my shepherd; I shall not want. He maketh me to lie down in green pastures.*
> PSALM 23:1–2

WINFRED
Friend of Peace

> *Let us therefore follow after the things which make for peace, and things wherewith one may edify another.*
> ROMANS 14:19

WINNIE
Friend of Peace

> *Let us therefore follow after the things which make for peace, and things wherewith one may edify another.*
> ROMANS 14:19

WINONA   *also* WENONA, WYNONA
Firstborn Daughter

> *I will praise thee; for I am fearfully and wonderfully made.*
> PSALM 139:14

WINSTON
A Firm Friend

> *Ye are my friends, if ye do whatsoever I command you.*
> JOHN 15:14

WINTER
Child of the Winter

> *Thy testimonies also are my delight and my counselors.*
> PSALM 119:24

WLADYSLAW
Mighty Ruler

> *He that ruleth over men must be just, ruling in the fear of God.*
> 2 SAMUEL 23:3

Slavic-Polish

WOLFGANG
Guardian Protector

> *Have not I commanded thee? Be strong and of a good courage; . . . God is with thee.*
> JOSHUA 1:9

German

WOOD
From the Forest

> *Then shall the trees of the woods sing out at the presence of the Lord.*
> 1 CHRONICLES 16:33

WOODROW
Dweller by the Woods

> *Then shall the trees of the woods sing out at the presence of the Lord, . . . he cometh to judge the earth.*
> 1 CHRONICLES 16:33

WRAY
Call to Account

> *So then every one of us shall give account of himself to God.*
> ROMANS 14:12

WRIGHT
A Craftsman

> *Whatsoever ye do, do it heartily, as to the Lord, . . . for ye serve the Lord Christ.*
> COLOSSIANS 3:23–24

WYLENE
Chosen Protection

> *Ye have not chosen me, but I have chosen you, and ordained you, that ye should go and bring forth fruit.*
> JOHN 15:16

WYLEY
Brave

> *God hath not given us the spirit of fear; but of power, and of love, and of a sound mind.*
> 2 TIMOTHY 1:7

WYNONA   *also* WINONA, WENONA
Firstborn

> *A woman that feareth the Lord, she shall be praised.*
> PROVERBS 31:30

X

XANDRA *also* SANDRA
Helper of Mankind

> The God of peace, . . . Make you
> perfect in every good work to do
> his will, working in you that
> which is wellpleasing.
> HEBREWS 13:20–21

XANTHE
Golden Yellow

> I will praise thee; for I am
> fearfully and wonderfully
> made: marvellous are thy
> works.
> PSALM 139:14

Greek

XAVIER
One of Brilliant Splendor

> Thou shalt . . . be a crown of
> glory in the hand of the Lord,
> and a royal diadem in the hand
> of . . . God.
> ISAIAH 62:3

XELIA
Protected One

> He that dwelleth in the secret
> place of the most High shall
> abide under the shadow of the
> Almighty.
> PSALM 91:1

Greek

XENIA
Blessed One

> The Lord is my strength and my
> shield; my heart . . . rejoiceth;
> . . . with my song will I praise
> him.
> PSALM 28:7

XIAO
Break of Dawn

> This is the day which the Lord
> hath made; we will rejoice and
> be glad in it.
> PSALM 118:24

Arabic

XICA
Jehovah Hath Remembered

> I will praise thee: for thou hast
> heard me, and art become my
> salvation.
> PSALM 118:21

Hebrew

XIMENA
Gracious One

> But thou, O Lord, art a God full
> of compassion, and gracious,
> longsuffering, and plenteous in
> mercy and truth.
> PSALM 86:15

XIOMARA
Radiant One

> Let your light so shine before
> men, that they may see your
> good works, and glorify your
> Father . . . in heaven.
> MATTHEW 5:16

Greek

XOCHITL
Radiant and Noble One

> They that be wise shall shine as
> the brightness of the firmament;
> . . . as the stars for ever and ever.
> DANIEL 12:3

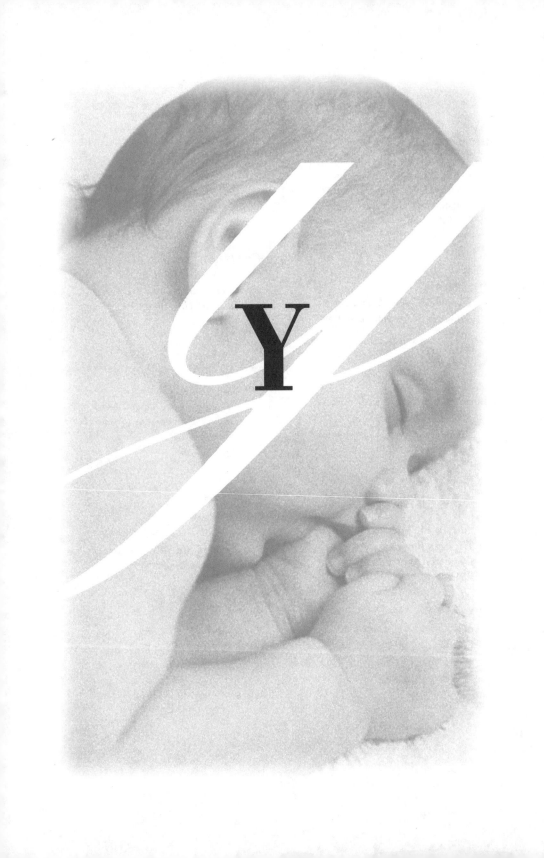

YAEL
Strength of God

> The Lord is my light and my
> salvation; whom shall I fear?
> the Lord is the strength of my
> life; of whom shall I be afraid?
> PSALM 27:1

Hebrew

YAHARAM
Jehovah Is High

> The Lord is high above all
> nations, and his glory above the
> heavens.
> PSALM 113:4

YAHWEH
Jehovah Is God

> The Lord JEHOVAH is my
> strength and my song; he also is
> become my salvation.
> ISAIAH 12:2

Hebrew

YALE
From the Fertile Upland

> Thy word is a lamp unto my
> feet, and a light unto my path.
> PSALM 119:105

YANCEY
An Englishman

> I praise thee; for I am fearfully
> and wonderfully made: . . . How
> precious . . . are thy thoughts
> unto me, O God!
> PSALM 139:14, 17

YANELIA
Victorious One

> Thanks be to God, which giveth
> us the victory through our Lord
> Jesus Christ.
> 1 CORINTHIANS 15:57

YANIGUE
God Is Gracious

> But thou, O Lord, art a God full
> of compassion, and gracious
> longsuffering, and plenteous in
> mercy and truth.
> PSALM 86:15

YAPHET
Beauty and Youth

> For thou art my hope, O Lord
> God: thou art my trust from my
> youth.
> PSALM 71:5

Hebrew

YASHA
Upright Heart

> Be glad in the Lord, . . . and
> shout for joy, all ye that are
> upright in heart.
> PSALM 32:11

YASMINE
The Yasmine

> I will praise thee; for I am
> fearfully and wonderfully
> made: . . . How precious . . . are
> thy thoughts unto me, O God!
> PSALM 139:14, 17

Y

YEHIEL
God Lives

> The Lord liveth; and blessed be
> my rock; and let the God of my
> salvation be exalted.
> PSALM 18:46

Hebrew

YESENDA
Gift

> For by grace are ye saved
> through faith; and that not of
> yourselves: it is the gift of God.
> EPHESIANS 2:8

YESENIA
Gift

> By grace are ye saved through
> faith; and that not of
> yourselves: it is the gift of God.
> EPHESIANS 2:8

YEVETTE
Courageous Heart

> My defence is of God, which
> saveth the upright in heart.
> PSALM 7:10

YIGAL
He Redeems

> God is my salvation; I will trust,
> and not be afraid: for the Lord
> JEHOVAH is my strength and
> my song; he . . . is . . . my
> salvation.
> ISAIAH 12:2

YOAV
God Is My Father

> The Lord liveth; and blessed be
> my rock; and let the God of my
> salvation be exalted.
> PSALM 18:46

Hebrew

YODER
One of Rejoicing

> I will praise thee, O Lord, with
> my whole heart; . . . I will sing
> praise to thy name.
> PSALM 9:1–2

YOKO
High Spirit

> For the Spirit searcheth all
> things, yea, the deep things of
> God.
> 1 CORINTHIANS 2:10

Japanese

YOLANDA
One of Manifest Grace

> The God of peace, . . . Make you
> perfect in every good work to do
> his will.
> HEBREWS 13:20–21

YONA
Dove of Peace

> The Lord will give strength unto
> his people; the Lord will bless
> his people with peace.
> PSALM 29:11

YORAM
God Is Exalted

> The Lord liveth; and blessed be
> my rock; and let the God of my
> salvation be exalted.
> PSALM 18:46

YOUNG
One of Youth

> For thou art my hope, O Lord
> God: thou art my trust from my
> youth.
> PSALM 71:5

YUL
Beyond the Horizon

> Blessed is the nation whose God
> is the Lord; and the people
> whom he hath chosen for his
> own inheritance.
> PSALM 33:12

YURI
Tiller of the Soil

> He that tilleth his land shall
> have plenty of bread: . . . A
> faithful man shall abound with
> blessings.
> PROVERBS 28:19–20

YUSEF
He Shall Increase

> The Lord thy God shall bless
> thee in all thine increase, . . .
> therefore thou shalt surely
> rejoice.
> DEUTERONOMY 16:15

Arabic

YVETTE
Courageous Heart

> My defence is of God, which
> saveth the upright in heart.
> PSALM 7:10

YVONNE   *also* EVONNE
Grace of the Lord

> By grace are ye saved through
> faith; and that not of
> yourselves: it is the gift of God.
> EPHESIANS 2:8

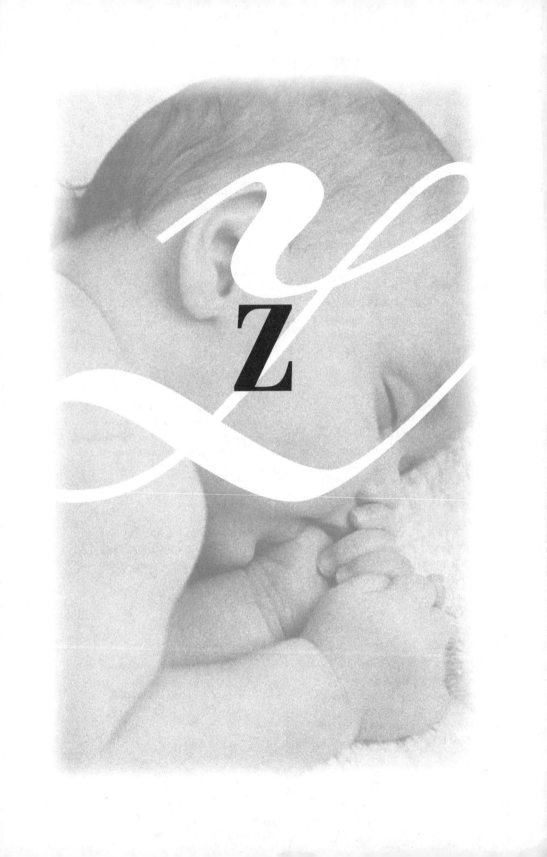

ZABIDA
Gift of the Lord

> Every good gift and every
> perfect gift is from above, and
> cometh down from the Father of
> lights.
> JAMES 1:17

Hebrew

ZABRE
Sword of the Spirit

> Be strong in the Lord, . . . And
> take the helmet of salvation,
> and the sword of the Spirit,
> which is the word of God.
> EPHESIANS 6:10, 17

ZACHARIAH
Jehovah Hath Remembered

> He is the Lord our God: his
> judgments are in all the earth.
> He hath remembered his
> covenant for ever.
> PSALM 105:7–8

ZACHARY
Remembered of God

> I will praise thee: for thou hast
> heard me, and art become my
> salvation.
> PSALM 118:21

ZAE
Life

> The Lord is my light and my
> salvation; whom shall I fear?
> the Lord is the strength of my
> life; of whom shall I be afraid?
> PSALM 27:1

ZAHID
Strong Will and Purpose

> I have set the Lord always
> before me: because he is at my
> right hand, I shall not be
> moved.
> PSALM 16:8

ZALINA
Devoted and Ardent Spirit

> And whatsoever ye do, do it
> heartily, as to the Lord, . . . for
> ye serve the Lord Christ.
> COLOSSIANS 3:23–24

ZAMIR
A Song

> I will praise thee, O Lord, with
> my whole heart; . . . I will be
> glad and rejoice in thee: I will
> sing praise to thy name.
> PSALM 9:1–2

Hebrew

ZARAH
Brightness of the Sunrise

> This is the day which the Lord
> hath made; we will rejoice and
> be glad in it.
> PSALM 118:24

ZARIEL
God Is My Rock

> In God is my salvation and my
> glory: the rock of my strength,
> and my refuge, is in God.
> PSALM 62:7

ZARIFA
One of Grace

> The Lord will give grace and glory: no good thing will he withhold from them that walk uprightly.
> PSALM 84:11

ZATAVIA
Beloved Son

> Beloved, let us love one another: for love is of God; and every one that loveth is born of God, and knoweth God.
> 1 JOHN 4:7

ZAYDA
God will Increase

> The Lord thy God shall bless thee in all thine increase, and in all the works of thine hands.
> DEUTERONOMY 16:15

ZEB
Jehovah Is Protector

> Be strong in the Lord, and in the power of his might. . . . And take the helmet of salvation, and the sword of the Spirit.
> EPHESIANS 6:10, 17

ZEBEDIAH
Holiness of Jehovah

> Rejoice in the Lord, ye righteous; and give thanks at the remembrance of his holiness.
> PSALM 97:12

ZEBIGNIEW
To Exalt and Honor

> For the Lord is great, and greatly to be praised: . . . Honour and majesty are before him.
> PSALM 96:4, 6

ZEBULON
Haven of Peace

> The Lord will give strength unto his people; the Lord will bless his people with peace.
> PSALM 29:11

ZEDEKIAH
Righteousness of Jehovah

> I will praise the Lord according to his righteousness: and will sing praise to the name of the Lord most high.
> PSALM 7:17

ZEDIE
Righteousness of Jehovah

> Righteous art thou, O Lord, . . . Thy testimonies . . . are righteous and very faithful.
> PSALM 119:137–138

ZELLIE
Zealous and Ardent One

> And whatsoever ye do, do it heartily, as to the Lord, and not unto men; . . . for ye serve the Lord Christ.
> COLOSSIANS 3:23–24

ZELLWOOD
Zealous and Ardent Spirit

> *Whatsoever ye do, do it heartily, as to the Lord, and not unto men; . . . for ye serve the Lord Christ.*
> COLOSSIANS 3:23–24

ZELMA
Divine Protectress

> *The Lord is my light and my salvation; . . . the Lord is the strength of my life; of whom shall I be afraid?*
> PSALM 27:1

ZENITH
The Way Upward

> *Jesus saith . . . I am the way, the truth, and the life: no man cometh unto the Father, but by me.*
> JOHN 14:6

ZEPHANIAH
The Lord Hath Treasured

> *Thou hast also given me the shield of thy salvation: . . . thy gentleness hath made me great.*
> PSALM 18:35

ZEPHIRAH
Dawn

> *This is the day which the Lord hath made; we will rejoice and be glad in it.*
> PSALM 118:24

ZEPHYR
Gentle Breeze

> *Thou hast also given me the shield of thy salvation: . . . thy gentleness hath made me great.*
> PSALM 18:35

ZIBIGNIEW
To Exalt and Honor

> *For the Lord is great, and greatly to be praised: . . . Honour and majesty are before him.*
> PSALM 96:4, 6

Old Slavic

ZION
A Strong Fortress

> *The Lord is my rock, . . . my fortress, . . . my deliverer; my God, my strength, in whom I will trust.*
> PSALM 18:2

ZITA
Refuge in Jehovah

> *I will say of the Lord, He is my refuge and my fortress: my God; in him will I trust.*
> PSALM 91:2

ZOE
Full of Life

> *God so loved the world that he gave his only begotten Son, that whosoever believeth in him should not perish, but have everlasting life.*
> JOHN 3:16